Awakening to Spirit

SUNY series,
Explorations in Contemporary Spirituality
Lee Irwin, editor

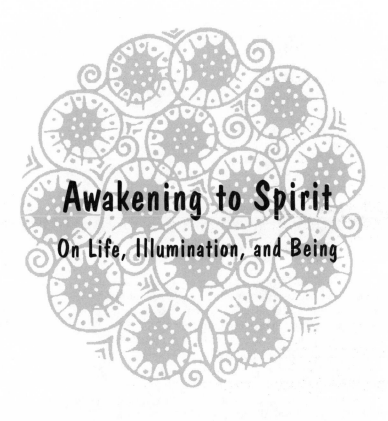

Awakening to Spirit

On Life, Illumination, and Being

Lee Irwin

State University of New York Press

Cover illustration: "Sacred serpent of purity/seeking/another experience/of enlightenment" copyright © Richard Kirsten-Daiensai

Production by Ruth Fisher
Marketing by Fran Keneston

Published by
State University of New York Press, Albany

© 1999 State University of New York

Printed in the United States of America

For information, address the State University of New York Press,
State University Plaza, Albany, NY 12246

Library of Congress Cataloging-in-Publication Data

Irwin, Lee, 1944—
    Awakening to spirit : on life, illumination, and being / Lee Irwin.
        p.   cm. — (SUNY series, explorations in contemporary spirituality)
    Includes bibliographical references and index.
    ISBN 0-7914-4221-7 (alk. paper). — ISBN 0-7914-4222-5 (pbk. : alk. paper)
    1. Spirituality.   2. Meditations.   I. Title.   II. Series.
BL624.2.I78   1999
291.4—dc21   98-47999
                                                                      CIP

10 9 8 7 6 5 4 3 2 1

"The most central presupposition of pluralism is the conviction that no system can exhaust the horizon of human experience, and that to want to fix the conditions or to suggest the possibilities according to which one attains the ultimate realities, implies either an excessive rationalism or the pride of believing oneself in possession of a criterion of truth which does not take into account what fragile vessels we are. In short, the hermeneutics of religion is always a hermeneutic of the philosophy of religion and this hermeneutic is always in process, never finished.

—Raimundo Panikkar
Religious Pluralism and Truth, p. 43

Contents

Opening Meditation   1
Ten Principles of Spirit   9

The First Principle   11
The Second Principle   37
The Third Principle   64
The Fourth Principle   91
The Fifth Principle   120
The Sixth Principle   161
The Seventh Principle   195
The Eighth Principle   229
The Ninth Principle   265
The Tenth Principle   299

Closing Meditation   329
The Ninety Aphorisms   343
Appendix: The Divine Sophia   355
Notes   359
Bibliography   369
Index   375

Opening Meditation

This work is a continuation of my writings on what I have called an anthropology of Spirit. In an earlier work, I tried to show how such an anthropology relates to the contemporary world and the problem of the intersection of many diverse worldviews.[1] These diverse worlds, ranging through both global space and historical time, have collided in the present, creating turbulence, confusion, and disorientation for many people. The conservative reaction—to preserve old-order thinking by maintaining an exclusive devotion to a particular worldview, thereby denying the value and validity of the worlds of others—increasingly faces the inescapability of convergence on a global scale. No single worldview can act as a unifying medium for all others cultures, times, and places. Instead, we face the challenge of learning to live within a context of increasing pluralization, diversity, and spiritual complexity.

In that earlier work, I also addressed the problem of how this convergence leads collectively to a "transpersonal horizon" in which we face the collapse of lineal historical thinking for emergent, shared visions of the present. In this transpersonal present, the intersection of worlds creates a climate of powerful, creative resources for the reformulation of new collective identities. In this process, an "anthropology of Spirit" manifests as various stages of historical reflection in search of wholistic patterns of meaning no longer based in prioritizing the present as more adequate than the past and no longer valuing the future as the hoped-for resolution of present problems and conflicts. The present, in the deepest and most urgent sense, encompasses that past and future in proportion to the depth and fullness of our individual and collective maturity. This emergent maturity is not simply a psychological or social fact—it is a profound process of collective spiritual transformation, an *awakening* to a transpersonal horizon whose call lies with each of us to realize the full and entensive depths of our spiritual potentials.

The arising of this transpersonal horizon is itself an event of great importance because in that event, however formulated in the experiences of the individual, we begin to discover infolded orders of perception no longer conditioned by a strictly rational, lineal model of consciousness, or by unilinear theories of development and growth. Perceptions must extend back into the past and reabsorb the value and good of past modes of perception and self-realization as occasions for reflection, as instances of potential that lie within us, urging us toward new interpretations and new visionary realizations. Perceptions must also rise to occasion new, emergent states of awareness and more expansive fields of self-reflection. The future, as instantiations of those occasions in moments of lucid spiritual illumination, points toward an integral continuity with past and present attainments in the realms of comparative spirituality. The "making real" of these inner potentials, in the present, requires courageous living and a willingness to cultivate genuine sensitivities for alternative worlds of meaning. Not only must we examine our own "native" worlds, but also the worlds of others both strange and sometimes alien, in order to fathom the depths of being as a medium for a multitude of collective transformations. The diverse roots of these transformations require us to leave no stone unturned, to look into every corner and aspect of alternative spirituality, to look carefully into the visionary worlds of others—but with deepest respect and appreciation for the value of those worlds in their contribution to emergent spiritual awakenings on a global scale.

This work explores the context of global spirituality as a living anthropology embodied through mutual relationships with others— past, present, and future. As such, it offers an alternative ontology, a new kind of being-in and being-with whose constitution is not simply analytic but synthetic, not a detached disassembly but a personal reintegration of many complex processes. Nor is it articulated strictly within the language games of religious theology or analytic science. Instead, it is written in an inspirational language based in visions, dreams, and reflections on spiritual meaning in a world colliding, even imploding, with radically divergent visionary potentials. It is anthropology as firsthand report, as a living ethnography of transformation and change, *medias res*, which attempts to formulate a meaningful synthesis, a global spiritual view, integral to the emergence of the transhistorical horizon. As such, the symbolic center of this particular work is based on a series of reflective meditations on the concept of "Spirit" distinct from any locus in a historical tradition or any explicit Judeo-Christian theology. These meditations are embedded in a context of global spiritual transformation formulated around the question: How might we, as contemporaries of global culture, uncover the reciprocities that unite us as spiritual beings? How might a living anthropology of the spirit contribute to our shared well-being, to a healthy world, to a thriving and vital ecology, to the development of mutually reverent and responsible beings whose aspirations are to care for all those who inhabit our shared, multidimensional world?

The answers to these and other such questions requires more of us than simple thought or detached intellectualism no longer alive to embodied needs; it requires action and personal commitment. These needs, both social and spiritual, require a living and embodied sense of community, the structured rituals of shared becoming, the importation of intentional action and values into the situation of being human. That is why I call these reflections something other than philosophy in the modern sense and something more akin to anthropology. Such an awakening requires our whole being, our full humanity, not just life in the abstract sense but in an actual life world of full existential concern and commitment, in a living spiritual praxis. All spiritual traditions realize the necessity of bringing mental reflections into a context of practice, into the central hall of the temple, into private prayer rooms or communal meals, or into the daily life of faithful living. The twin axes of awakening and understanding must entwine around a central theme that seeks to embody itself in real practice, in realizing the potential of belief or thought in communal relations and becoming, in exemplifying inner spiritual vision.

Thus, the symbolic center is not simply reflections on Spirit but on how Spirit may be embodied in actual practice congruent with an emergent, transhistorical horizon. This is not a matter of simply articulating a particular practice or technique, however valuable those may be, but of something deeper. Technique should not become a substitute for insight and understanding, nor should it become a routine that masks the necessity of continually deepening thought, prayer, or reflection. A "technique" per se, or a behavioral formula, may well abrogate responsibility through a substitute rigor founded in obedience or in dogmatic or authoritative rules, or social prohibitions or conventions. The challenge is to allow for an intrinsic freedom of self-formulation, to find the creative behaviors that bring to realization inner beliefs and ideals. Praxis, in the transhistorical sense, is not a matter of communal "rules" but of an interior clarity of purpose or intention that guides in accordance with spiritual values or principles. The unfolding of potential within each individual cannot be reduced within the transhistorical horizon to a fixed or authoritative pattern. This horizon challenges us, opens us to an emergent ethics of self-responsibility, in a world of respect and reverence for others, to find the unique ways that will indeed lead to the desired fulfillment. This is an individual challenge on the deepest level and we need not look beyond the integrity and maturity of our understanding to value that potential authentically.

We do need, however, to formulate clearly those spiritual principles that act to guide and direct our actions toward a positive and creative praxis. Thus, in this work, I lay out a number of those principles as they relate to the concept of Spirit. I attempt to integrate those principles along the lines of spiritual values and behavioral guidelines whose actualization can only occur through their adaptation and reformulation by interested others. The groundwork for this reformulation constantly depends on a flexibility of interpretation centered on the viability of Spirit as a real, vital, powerful, and mysterious presence imbuing life with more-than-human potential. The principles articulated are by no means exhaustive or complete; nor are they presented as a bound system of ideas. Instead, I have chosen to explore just those themes and concerns I see as relevant to our more immediate circumstances as a community on the threshold of personal, global, transhistorical transformation. My own praxis has long involved intensive communication, sharing, and introspection as well as long-term study, writing, meditation, dreaming, and vision-seeking in a diversity of spiritual communities. The heart of these meditations is found in the genuine love and sharing I have experienced with other engaged spiritual seekers. Such sharing, plus the ongoing processes of contemporary cultural transformation and global awakening, has made me increasingly aware of the need we have for articulate principles to guide us in our long and remarkable journey.

In laying out these principles, I make no attempt to embrace or subsume other traditional spiritual paths. This process, as a creative anthropology of self-reflection and meaningful action, has arisen out of perceptions and communications based in my present, eclectic cultural-spiritual circumstances. The formulation of these principles occurred in a single spontaneous burst of inspiration, unsought at the time, but flowing forth with an intensity and momentary clarity of mind, heart, and intent that was truly memorable and transformative. As such, the bare bones of those principles have subsequently been modestly reworked and clarified for the purpose of setting up, in a first-hand report, the basic outlines of a contemporary concept of Spirit not, I believe, incompatible with other traditions. Without doubt, other spiritual traditions, particularly the mystical traditions of Buddhism, Christianity, and Islam, have all influenced my perceptions and I owe a debt of gratitude to those spiritual teachers. The meditations on these principles came later and much more slowly, but they were by no means lacking in intensity or in a sense of the spiritual immediacy of the subject. The authentication of the experience, the intensity of the moment, has often opened the transhistorical horizon to me with a vivid and sometimes breathtaking clarity of presence that has left me truly aware of how vast and how profound the depths are that yet remain unexpressed.

This kind of anthropology also reflects a postmodern sensibility insofar as there is no authoritative ground other than the actual lived experiences, reflections, and processes of development that have occurred to me in over thirty years of study, exploration, and practice. The constructive aspects of such a postmodern perspective have evolved through a gradual creative synthesis outside of any institutional or legitimizing body of religious persons representative of a traditional perspective. The deconstruction of "authority" is a major part of the transformation of the interpretive frameworks by which spirituality is made meaningful or valuable in a living, personal, postmodern context. This deinstitutionalization also means seeking a language and discourse that is not bound by the authoritative structures of a purely rational epistemology. Rationality is not the defining index by which spiritual values and insights can best be articulated. These values and insights arise through many nonrational means: dreams, visions, psychic intuitions, processes of symbolization, imagination, story, and through empathy, feeling, and relatedness to others. These are all viable epistemological means for exploring and articulating a living anthropology of Spirit. The postmodern context moves us beyond any particular privileged discourse, beyond institutional sanctions, and beyond empirically rationalized methods and into the creative articulation of spiritual principles based in direct experiential knowing and creative communication and expression.

Positively, a postmodern spirituality is one that is no longer conditioned to a single methodology or a single empirical strategy; it is deeply and intrinsically pluralistic, multivocal, and relative to the interpretive frameworks of others. In writing on postmodern spirituality, I am not seeking to express some absolute, authoritative "truth" but to explore a coherent, meaningful expression of relative principles as a viable spiritual path. The principles I articulate are nonarbitrary yet relative to an individual perspective and are a nonaggressive expression of passionate belief. There are many ways to formulate a meaningful spirituality, some perhaps better or more effective than others; but no one path will suffice for all. The postmodern context takes fully into account the claims of every spiritual tradition as meaningful and more than adequate for the followers of that tradition without postulating some "universal" hierarchy of values. Nor does a postmodern spirituality seek to postulate the authoritative claims of any one tradition as superior over all others, however central that tradition may be to the life and concerns of a practitioner. The assertion of such a claim is only more of the old premodern contestation in values and worldviews—a circumstance I see as increasingly untenable in a converging world of diverse interpretative perspectives. To move beyond this older embattled discourse means to offer creative interpretations in a nonauthoritative but passionate voice dedicated to revitalizing spirituality as a primal basis of human joy and well-being.

Another aspect of the postmodern context involves breaking out of the disciplinary boundaries of academic studies and engaging in reflections on meaning that have their proper locus in the fullness of personal experience. Spirituality is about the passions of the soul, about the needs and aspirations of the heart, about the search for fulfillment and the inner resistance, struggles, and conflicts overcome in reaching that fulfillment. And it is a creative process, drawing on all aspects of our human potential and capacity in the face of our personal fears, anxieties, and emotional and mental boundaries. The postmodern context is not about the systematization of ideas, nor is it about the capacity to sustain a particular methodology tied to a necessarily limited epistemology. Spiritual life proceeds by leaps and regressions, by climbing up and sliding back, by struggling to maintain a threshold and then, often suddenly, being overwhelmed by infinite depths and immeasurable horizons. Postmodern spirituality is aphoristic, epigrammatic, and engaged in the project of exploring the creative use of language and metaphor in pointing toward the boundaries of language and the relevance of alternative discourse styles. The convergence of a multitude of spiritual perspectives opens the horizons of meaning to *dialogical*, not dialectical, discourse and to diversity in expression in order to invoke the multivocal character of spiritual life. It is a nonsystemic process, an exploration, an awakening to being, not a summary or a conclusion.

Subsequently, the style of this work is not strictly linear nor is it based in a systematic argument, or in an analytic working out of rational ideas. It is first and foremost a reflective, meditative style that should be read slowly and in stages congruent with a general absorption of core ideas discussed in a variety of contexts. Themes in this work intermix, submerge, and reappear as diverse textures in the painting of a cosmological mural whose story is more than individual or narrowly scholastic. It is "cosmological" in the sense that it seeks to articulate a "place" within a living cosmos that may be inhabited by individuals whose spiritual identities are not rooted in a particular "traditional" religion. In creating that place, I have chosen a style of writing that is consciously reflexive in calling the reader back to the principles as they are articulated in a variety of interpretive locations. Such writing reflects a genre of meditative works, aphoristic and reflexive, that attempt to show how the various principles (or beliefs) apply to multiple circumstances. The symbolic form is a Hermetic circle, rich in interpretive possibilities, and not a rational line or a diagrammatical deconstruction of a sentence. This circle is simultaneously an inward- and outward-evolving spiral that necessitates a repetition of themes intrinsic to the meditative process by which the principles are learned and actualized. To read means to read slowly, from the inside out and the outside in, and not in a rush or in search of a few key concepts lineally connected. The gestalt as a whole is best absorbed in a gradual process of reflection and testing of principles in real-life situations, only in this way can the value of the work be known.

Finally, this work is not meant as anything other than a testimony of how an emerging horizon of spiritual meanings may be constructed from a visionary world. In my earlier work, I have referred to this process, I will only say here that the arising of any visionary world in the contemporary sense can only hope to contribute its relative quantum of meaning and insight to creative processes that truly surpass any individual manifestation. The very act of surpassing is itself part of the emergent process by which any work becomes another stage on the way to greater collective and individual maturity. In such a transforming world where static images can only reflect the momentary synthesis, the challenge is to communicate the vision and then, to move on, following where Spirit leads, to fuller and more complete realizations. It is my hope that the readers of this work will understand that these principles may be articulated in many diverse ways and that such formulations are entirely relative to the needs, aspirations, and attainments of the readers. To see them as they are meant to be seen is to see them as relative formulations, as resources, and as occasions for reflection and possible insight. The greater challenge is the integration of such principles into meaningful action and authentic spiritual intentions resulting in the vibrant well-being of self in loving relations with (all) others. The realization of such intentions goes far beyond the text and into the context toward which the texts points.

Ten Principles

The First Principle of Spirit is the gift of life; this means that the experience of being alive, having life, is a primary manifestation of Divine Mystery. (1.1)

The Second Principle of Spirit is that every manifestation of life has its own unique awareness, a being that constitutes its form; there is no life without such awareness. (2.1)

The Third Principle of Spirit is understanding: this means being able to sense, feel, intuit, and empathize with every living thing; analysis and reason without understanding is both dangerous and destructive. (3.1)

The Fourth Principle of Spirit is its unknowable immensity; this is not first because only after life, awareness, and understanding is knowledge possible, a knowledge of the hidden foundations, the Mystery. (4.1)

The Fifth Principle of Spirit is compassionate love—sensual, emotional, intellectual, aesthetic, and spiritual—it gives itself to others, it receives them without shame. (5.1)

The Sixth Principle of Spirit is the manifestation of wisdom and illumination; from the illumination of the heart to the illumination of body, mind, and will. (6.1)

The Seventh Principle of Spirit is ecstasy, the union of individual life with the eternal, with the ultimate source of renewal and transformation, with the unextinguished Light. (7.1)

The Eighth Principle of Spirit is freedom from constraint; the wild grasses of the field know nothing of the plow, their seeds are scattered by the winds, not by human hands. (8.1)

The Ninth Principle of Spirit is peace, nonviolence, and creative joy; the birth of new worlds, the opening of horizons free of fear, uncontaminated by possessive lust, lies, or confusion. (9.1)

The Tenth Principle of Spirit is solitude, calm, and repose; everything grows old, matures, deepens, and acquires the luster of age, this is natural and good—every death, a new beginning. (10.1)

The First Principle

The First Principle of Spirit is the gift of life; this means that the experience of being alive, having life, is a primary manifestation of Divine Mystery. (1.1)

Meditation: There is no "first" principle, only the overflowing abundance of Spirit in all its manifestations, selected, arranged, and articulated according to the temperament of the individual for purposes of persuasion and illumination. Yet none of these principles could arise without there first being life, breath, and awareness. This most basic fact, this obvious and irreducible, primordial condition is engendered as a primordial sensitivity, a divine spark or seed of light within each of us that makes it possible to become a "living being." Preceding our birth and existing after the death of the body, this life gift is the inheritance of all beings and the primordial source of their inspirations, awareness, and intentionality. For this gift, we should be thankful; if we do not reverence life, do not cultivate our gratitude and appreciation for this most valuable of all gifts, how will we recognize the value and significance of what this gift has returned to us, ten thousand times over, in all the multitudes of other beings? To value life is to value every being that lives as a manifestation of Spirit and as a vessel of divine potential and inspiration. Yet this gift enshrouds a Mystery, one by no means fully fathomed by conflicted humanity, nor is it yet known in all its depth, fullness, and capacity.

By "primary manifestation" I refer to neither religion nor philosophy, nor do I refer to poetry or art that expresses Spirit cogently, but to all the living beings that inhabit the many spheres of existence—these are the ones who epitomize the joyful activity, the potent manifestations of Spirit. Like two hands guarding a flame, Spirit nurtures the life gift in all its simplest and most minute forms, sheltering it from extinction and provoking a natural growth and enhanced awareness. This does not mean that living beings are Spirit, but rather that they *manifest* Spirit. The life gift is the inward flowing outward, the concatenation of subtle energies creating form, nurturing the most subtle influences, and resulting in sensate impressions through embodiment. Mystery, which does not contain or exhaust its contents or capacities, through Spirit overflows out of an inner, immeasurable depth manifesting life in all its discrete and particular forms. This gift is sacred, so astonishing that we, as self-aware beings, fail to see how very precious and remarkable it is and how profoundly we are overwhelmed by its presence. Spirit surrounds us, supports us, gives us the breath of life, and grants us the joy of inspiration and enlightenment. For this reason, I believe it is holy and worthy of reverence. And Mystery, inseparable from Spirit, gives Spirit the plenitude to perform the actions of creation and dissolution for all beings throughout the stellar planes, worlds, and spheres. Unchangeable because all-containing, constantly changing because uncontainable, Spirit sustains our memory and transmutes our desires, leading through a spiral of Light and Dark toward ineffable awakenings, challenges, and illuminations.

But first, we must "have life" and "experience" being alive! This means that we must not make the error of judging our present state as all that we can ever be. We are so much more "alive," so much more a part of the Whole, so much more imbued by Spirit than we presently understand. When I write "alive," I do not mean simply breathing and feeling and thinking. I mean also opening our spiritual senses, our higher capacities to see directly the energetic and ensouled nature of the diverse life fields that surround and enliven us. How pervasive they are! How vast and vibrant with energy, immediacy, and subtle sensitivity; how brimming over with abundance and excess, pouring out of every cell and molecule with a radiance that surrounds and imbues every form and contour of bodily existence. How it shades and shadows us, how it blends with the life force of others, with a tree or plant, or the earth. How it comports itself within Wholeness and breathes its primordial inspirations into our narrow and contracted lives. Thus, to make this journey, to travel this path together, we must agree to let go of our contracted images of life and the life field. We must agree to embrace life and live within its flow, Spirit-led, to deep reverence and to the sacred depths of death and rebirth.

This life gift, Spirit-given, is not something we create, nor is it something we must work to generate or struggle to make real—it is already real, already there, already full, extensive, and mature. Think of the maturity of Spirit as an ancient presence millions upon billions of years old, as a source of inspiration, power, and capacity inseparable from the initial conditions of creation.[2] A presence that fills every niche and corner of every species with the exact capacities it needs to thrive and become more aware, responsive, and enlivened. Then abstract from that image every specific form and content and leave only the knowledge and wisdom of these manifestations as an infinite wave carrying within itself all the lessons, pains, sorrows, joys, and insights garnered from those millions upon billions of years. Let that wave sweep away all contracted lineal timeframes and all three-dimensional space so that it is present simultaneously, everywhere at once, and yet free from any contractions or visions that would ultimately constrain its full totality and presence. Such is Spirit, the immediate presence that nurtures the everyday and gives it an unsurpassable depth and fullness. It is not something we create or make, it is something we are each the consequence of—a process and an exploration—coming together in the synthesis and unity of unique, yet diverse, living beings. This oneness is shared, earth-grounded, star-pointed by the full solar-lunar consciousness of life here and now, on this world, in this cosmos, at this moment.

The Mystery is one that will never be exhausted or emptied by our species' preoccupation with creations or beginnings. There are no absolute beginnings but the ones we choose as points of organization in thought and belief. Such a choice, Spirit-guided, leads us to reverence the life gift, to give deep respect and thankfulness for pouring itself out for each of us as the small, nimble-minded, often confused creatures we have presently become. It is not simply Mystery concealing what may be known, but Mystery woven into a vast interconnected net, a wondrous weave of unfolding potentials in ever-increasingly degrees of subtlety, power, and grace. I cannot say that I comprehend the Mystery, rather I can only say, Mystery comprehends me and each of us to a degree that few can fathom. In doing so, Mystery makes no claim on either our allegiance or our will; it gives us the freedom to deny or even to destroy the life gift, to turn a blind eye to all that is "sacred" within and about us. As a source of desires, a possibility of a more enhanced life, Spirit presses against heart and mind with all the pressure of inward sentience but does not keep us from a destructive urge or a capacity to harm others. The life gift is freedom to live either in mutuality and respect, or by trampling and consuming in every possible way, the lives of others; to live in compassion and receptivity, or to deny the gift and thus consume what is finite and perishable through an excess of appetite and self-defined needs.

Whatever exists has Life, both the animate and inanimate—human, animal, vegetable, or mineral; everything we see, wherever it exists, all that is visible or invisible. (1.2)

Meditation: The principle of life need not be confined to only human beings, or to others that we may easily recognize and call "animate." Born of Spirit and manifesting a sacred potential, we can comprehend the ancient life gift as an all-pervading possibility of life and awareness. We can envision the Earth as a living being as well as the stars and asteroids and moons. In such a vision, nothing is sterile, not even the vastness of space; every quantum of energy, every particle, is filled with the vast potentials of not-yet-manifested inner vitality and life capacity. It is not outward form that attracts my attention, but inner potential, an ancient, abiding presence, a sometimes alien otherness. This is because Spirit within us responds to Spirit within others, because life as "first principle" is life sensitive and responsive to the gift within all beings, all becomings, and all manifestations. Our limited distinction of others into divisions of "animate" and "inanimate" has failed to appreciate the underlying continuum, the unbroken wholeness and unity that incorporates all manifestations into an infinite, shared complexity far beyond simple binary categorizations. The "dialectic" of the Spirit is not two-dimensional "oppositions" or an inherent dualism but infinitely dynamic relations so complex and embedded in sensory experience that even the stones under our feet may be said to be part of that living continuum—where even a particle of sand in the eye, a blown seed on invisible air, is "alive" if only we perceive correctly the complexity of all relationships involved.[3]

The body of Earth, Gaia—her valleys, hills, and mountains, her lakes, streams, and rivers, her oceans, seas, and waterfalls; her hips, breasts, and belly, her eyes, heart, and soul—is Spirit imbued, as are her winds and storms and fires. The precious air and atmosphere with all its subtle gases permeated by the radiant energies of stars and suns and comets, by invisible waves and particles of plasmic, hydrostatic force are all Spirit filled, even at the level of the most minute and backward-moving subatomic muon or gluon. The molten power of her inner being, her crystal iron generations removed from plasmic star bodies, remolds and shifts and transforms the fragile surface life. We are suspended between vast realities: all that is inward and all that is outward, all that is hidden below, all that is concealed above. And human beings, often inflated, imagine the splendor of their creation as somehow distinct, separate, and superior to all the wonder of their coming into being—separate from the sustenance manifest in the multilayered activities of an entire cosmos of seen and unseen beings. Inseparable, we create separations, extolling our accomplishments and mental and material attainments, yet obscuring the wonder and holiness of the Mystery within which we evolve and mature. We see only the surface images of our own rationalized dreams. Better to regard Earth, her beauty and power as fully animate, sentient, living, as "nature nurturing" on a global scale. The range of her all-containing life and sheltering manifestations, far exceed those of humanity. Spirit contains an uncountable multitude of habitations and worlds, all unique, rare, precious. And many suns, naked stars, hold within their grip the evolving life of those other worlds, as all equally rare, complex, and alive.

Not all worlds are visible or known. And every world has its hidden character, its unknown and unrecognized potential, its not yet visible lives. Such lives are not confined to purely physical forms, to purely "organic" beings. Spirit, as the action of Mystery, creates, in diverse aspects of awareness unique expressions, composite or simple being, intimately part of the Whole. Subtle realms of life exist whose transparency is inseparable from mind and becoming and whose autonomy flows from Spirit, not simply human aspiration or projection. There are a multitude of beings who continue after physical death, who when reborn, enter the Mystery only to reemerge reformed according to their potentiality, actions, and past relationships. Not all are human, not all bound to this Earth, this sphere of human drama and action. Some, never incarnate; some, never physical; some overwhelming, of profound beauty and archetypal power, from the depths of Mystery unveiled in layered, visionary heavens. These forms are irreducible to the mechanics of skeptical materialism, abstract denial, or the limited technologies of immediate sense perception. Let us think of these forms as noneternal, living entities also transforming in the psychic round of life, death, and rebirth. The veils cannot be lifted too soon or too quickly, too much awareness can overwhelm, and panic or fear impede the unveiling or cause others to cease their caring or concern.

Plants, animals, the rock in your hand, an emerald, an amethyst, or a moist figure of clay—all contain the life potential. The divisions we create that separate us from the life fields of others are based in ignorance, fear, and simple conditioning. From the perspective of an ethics of reciprocity, we are not "superior" to the animals, we are not above them nor do we have a right to dominion over them—they are fellow beings to whom we owe a great debt for their sacrifices, sufferings, and for the abuses we have heaped on them. We abuse the trees and the fields, pollute the waters, suffocate the very atmosphere that we and they must breathe. Our indifference or lack of care, our tendency to see the other in terms of how they serve our own needs and appetites, not theirs, binds us to an ever-shrinking world. To respect life means to give it the very free conditions that we ourselves desire—to cease cruelty, oppression, or experimentation in the name of our own species' progress. We must find the touchstone that values the life of the other even above our own—that is Life, that is Spirit. Not to sacrifice, but to revere; not to draw unfeeling boundaries, but to cultivate empathy, a deep sense of life-shared, a continuity that collapses the old barriers, tears down the unnecessary walls and teaches us to see the old rock at the end of the pathway, not as dead matter, but as some silent enduring sentinel. Let us regard minerals and gems as also alive, having life presence in forms so subtle, pure, and simple as to be unseen by agitated, upright walkers who no longer look at the pebbles beneath their feet.

Is there such a thing as "dead matter"? No! This is an illusion perpetuated by mental necessity to separate ourselves from the overwhelming ocean of everything living. (1.3)

Meditation: The concept of "matter" is itself an abstraction that has no real existence beyond the dictates of conventional language, culture, and conceptual habits.[4] As a groundless metaphor, "matter" tends to stand in juxtaposition to life, being, or consciousness—just as in Western metaphysics, the body has been conceived as a "machine" or a "house of soul" in opposition to mind or reason. Such metaphors obscure the First Principle that everything is alive, inseparable from the "initial conditions," and that every living being is dependent on a multitude of other life forms. Our limitation is that we do not attain directly the impression and experience of everything living, of the dance of energetic joy hidden in the massive presence of a twelve-meter stone, or in the effervescence of a particle of light. Our mental universe, in its two-dimensional character, is built around postulates and a reductive dialectic that often misses the profound, complex subtlety of creative becomings. Thus we oppose our categories—"matter and spirit," "body and soul," "male and female," "life and death." But these are only logical postulates that cannot elicit the richness and variety and complexity of interpenetrating life spheres whose full determination and hidden dimensionality greatly exceeds the limits of simple oppositional logic. The life process, as a manifestation of Spirit, cannot be isolated to immediate perceptions, or conceived fully in simple binary, discrete, abstract notions. The affects of Spirit imbue the most "stationary object" with tremendous potential, sensuous relations, and a capacity for transformation into variable forms under appropriate changes of state— as a creative, multivalent process in the midst of a present temporal condition. This is a critical observation. How does such an observation affect personal actions and attitudes? From a transpersonal perspective, no "object" is static and no being, stationary or fixed.

The "ocean of everything living" is the full energetic charge, the emotional, intellectual, spiritual conditions that evolve in the rich atmosphere, the ecstatic complexity, of being truly aware. Yet such being-awareness is often "overwhelmed" by the intensity of the continuous interactions of all living entities. The endless impress of sensitive neural fibers are burdened with continuous, complex streams of powerful sensation and reaction in a discontinuous process of integration. The consequence of this "overwhelming" bombardment and impact from billions of cells stimulated in processes of emergence, struggle, reactions and expression, is the creation of layer upon layer of self-limiting, internalized restriction—so that the eye cannot see the infinite and the ear cannot hear the eternal. Mentally, we limit our perceptions through attending only to the discrete phenomena, the "brute facts" of the immediate, material conditions. There is a rejection of dreams or visions or imaginings, discarded as "unrealistic," "unproductive," and "fantastic" (though we immerse ourselves in them continuously, we cannot read them or fathom their messages). So we separate ourselves from everything living and impose, reductively, a more limited perception, a reduction to minimal sensate impressions, to "matter" stripped of every characteristic, denuded of life. Thus a new mythic vision is born—matter as an utterly inanimate mass, subject to any manipulation, any exploitation of its "dead" potential. If one wishes to discover the "carnival of souls," it may be observed in the tents of the matter-obsessed, where fascinated and entranced, the observer works among the naked forms of materiality, rejoicing in a mastery of immoral creations, without feelings of genuine reciprocity or a higher vision of interrelated correspondences.

This does not mean there is no creative purpose to such a reductive state. For those immersed in Spirit, distinctions vanish, dissolving into the unbound continuum, the unfathomable, sensuous depths. The "mental necessity" is to discover who and what we are, beings whose capacities are focused and illumined by the continuous processes of birth, contraction, expansion, and release. The duality of "spirit and matter" is a passing mental contraction, a stage in the processes of self-awakening and insight. Absorbed by the immediacy of our limited personal frontiers, we miss the expanse, the full horizon of possibility, the panorama of creatively multiple perspectives, the extensive range of our bodily becoming. We speak and learn together, but we grow and develop individually, not as a "collective" but as a continuously differentiating whole. Each perspective contributes its value, its potential elicited out of the whole, some more harmful and limiting, others less so. We draw back, then plunge in; we learn to sustain our potential for sudden or gradual insights into more inclusive perspectives or horizons. The abstraction of "inanimate matter" is a perspective that may help us to gain insights into the once overwhelming presence of animate manifestations. If we draw back from this deanimating perspective, it is because we realize a limitation, a too severe contraction, an unnecessary limit, now being transposed. The "illusion" is to believe in the ultimacy of "matter," in its unquestionable mental and emotive authority, in its irreducible character. Such a belief is nothing more than a *mythic* strata we must pass through and then beyond.

The "necessity of separation" is not based on a simple need for autonomy or control, but on something far deeper and more profound. The process of separating, of pulling away from the burdens of an animate, collective mentality is to discover the unknown potential that remains hidden in the depths of specific, individual being. Individualized perception is not the source of our illusions—those are built out of the mythos of consensual world-pictures, however material or spiritual they may be. We are not static beings, we do not inhabit perfect spheres, nor do we attain immortality by simply affirming a collective credo. The challenge is deeper and more demanding. To move beyond consensual beliefs means to enter the life field at a more empowered level of individual awareness, with deeper empathy and more active intuition, with more immediacy and more contact with everything living. If we think abstractly in terms of "energy" or "matter" as impersonal, nonliving substrates alienated from our own consciousness—then the world becomes an abstract, polarized, not-quite-unified field of disjunctive impersonal forces. But when we open ourselves to the fullness of the life force, to all the manifestations of life, and understand that Spirit is the missing, crucial, central, primordial element—then our world begins to unfold its hidden potentials. This potential is so much vaster than a dead realm of ashes or the abstract, inanimate matter of logical forms. Our separation stems from past resistance and denial; what we must now affirm is to live openly at every level of creation and dissolution, however minute or vast. Yet what we seek is a true and direct knowledge of Spirit—its mystery, presence, and power.

Without doubt, many have been overwhelmed by the mythos of "matter" and "materiality" and misled by the rhetoric of a purely reductive mode of thought. In the Hermetic circle, the processes of mergence and unity are followed by equally important cycles of emergence, withdrawal, and birth from unity into individuality and a new understanding of community. We learn to pull away from the encompassing shadows and comforts of our past collective identities in order to reshape human potential for future emergence. The freedom to think and to feel empowers individual maturity, to become conscious of a deeper obligation to maintain and to develop the fragile harmony and relatedness between all living beings in a caring world of natural, nurturing processes. This requires integrity, love, and a conscious capacity to resist being overwhelmed while still being able to surrender to the currents that lead us to greater species awareness and to a greater communal realization of everything we value as individuals. Our perceptions of "matter" are inseparable from this process of making and unmaking. The animate and inanimate struggle within us to give birth to the great complexity of a fully sentient nature—not nature imbued with simple imaginative thought, but an actual awareness of the deep life processes that have made us co-participants in the reanimation of the multilayered cosmos.

The abundance of Spirit is the overflowing fullness of life: this rock, this grain of sand, this minute particle of energy are all living, all participating in profound activity. (1.4)

Meditation: Nothing is static, everything is in motion. This means that the very structures of your fingernail are alive and changing, the rock in your garden transforming into dust, the mountains rising out of oceans, the seas joined in transformative storms with earth and sky. Earth herself, giving birth and dying, remains a visible symbol of our collective awakenings—healthy in our health, unhealthy in our sicknesses and abuse. Yet, like the ancient being she is, her potential is far greater and more vast than the individual creatures who inhabit her shores and shoals and depths. Every drop of rain is filled with abundant life, diverse, unique, remarkable, and astoundingly complex. But death is there too, in the very molecular structures of imbalance, pollution, and decay. While Spirit bestows life, life also can perish, vanish, cease to be part of the pattern of relations through loss, increasing impotency, and lack of fertility, to be recaptured only through cessation and a cleansing of ill-health, a purge and purification. The "overflowing fullness" requires a conscious balance and delicacy of concern in order to preserve, revere, and provide the necessary conditions for health and growth. To sustain the life gift means to create the conditions through which it most fully flourishes, to nurture the power of the gift and not exhaust it foolishly through millennial, self-indulgent passions, or thoughtless destruction. Error and self-indulgence are inevitable, part of the process, a consequence of too much abundance, too much fullness—it overflows, it contracts—but is there learning or only a headlong rush toward extinction?

By "overflowing" I mean that Spirit is never bound by form, never limited by the beings which evolve. Through Spirit as life-sustaining, and vital, there is no diminishing in death or decay. Spirit, source of inspiration and constant, unending transformation, overflowing from state to state and from condition to condition, remains ever active, ever vital, ever constant. The manifestations change, evolve, transform, become something other—only to realize a new potential or handiwork, an involution of stable realizations, an integral work of patient weavings. A manifestation reaches its fullness and then passes on; a species vanishes, a ancient inhabitant appears in the eon of its primal activity, then transmutes. This is natural and good, what is unnatural and less desirable is the destruction of one species by another or the unintentional destruction of other species due to ignorance and indifference. The latency of every being lies in its as yet unrealized potential, in its not yet fully expressed fullness. Thus, in the interconnected web of all-beings-living, each contributes to the sustenance of the others. Nurturing others, we are ourselves nurtured; denying others, we deny our own understanding enriched by the other. Spirit does not dominate or control, much less determine the activities of our handiwork. Spirit inspires and draws us toward fullness and uncovers beauty and possibility for the pure and impure alike.

Perhaps there are those who conceive of a more chaste Spirit, more remote or detached, known only to the pure and uninvolved; yet such detachment may be a sentiment bound by an illusion. Spirit knows no boundaries, cannot be contained, will not strictly submit to human disciplines or laws; freely overflowing, its manifestations are immeasurable, for whatever lives, is a gift of Spirit. The beggar, thief, and murderer are still a gift, a fullness, a manifestation—that they chose self-destruction does not inhibit Spirit or its unending care and nuturance. If they contract, failing to realize the power of the gift, turning against the gift in others, the source remains undiminished, the light dimmed only in that manifestation. Pain, suffering, sorrow, anguish, and despair do not diminish the constancy, the unending, continuous abundance that creates anew, the sources of deep inspiration to revitalize and transform contraction into new birth. The "minute particle of energy" is a thought, a feeling, an intuition, a spark of inspiration, not simply "inanimate energy," not just a quantum of bounded potential. There are boundaries, there are limits and conditions and circumstances that make actions in any sphere meaningful—but the limiting condition is only a momentary event in a total dynamic that cannot be measured or contained. If the full potentials of Spirit were manifest, even in the head of a pin, there would be nothing less than an entire universe of beings, unique and yet co-related.

The "minute particle" tells us something of great importance—that the basis of life is energy, not matter. But what kind of energy? Is it best known as only half of an equation—a quantity without real qualities? Or is it a reservoir of qualities, a condensation, like a spark whose function is to engender qualities even in the midst of a vast potential. The concept of "energy" when imbued with Spirit becomes a source of mind and awareness. It becomes, in the language of the soul, an inspiration seeking greater self-actualization by maximizing its capacity through increasingly integrated changes of state. It is not a fixed entity, not limited to a single domain, not reducible to a known quantity. Rather through interactions, through contacts, impacts, intersections, and a deep quantum of arousing excitations, it acquires new qualities, new shades of manifestation, and new actual expression. The minute particle is inseparable from the whole that acts upon it to inspire new creations and the inhabitation of new domains of meaning and insight. This is the life process in action, entering the new domain and experiencing the vitality of an enhanced and expanded freedom.

What is "profound activity"? Is it possible for us to recognize that a sunrise, a rainstorm, or a child's tear is such? The tear contains a myriad of beings, and like drops of rain whose energetic rivulets refresh the Earth with their moistures, its manifestations unveil both needs and aspirations. Like a sunrise, it illumines the far horizon with renewed determination: to live, survive, endure, to learn, to be aware, to co-relate. This "enduring" is no commonplace event, no matter how dreary, difficult, or painful. It is not the survival of the most fit, but the survival of each being that thirsts for creative life with others, who wishes to find some more potent manifestation, some cathartic realization of its deep potentials, some greater actuality of its promise, that leads to an enhanced life. This is profound because it does not arise outwardly but is a characteristic expression within the depths of living beings, though not always realized, yet always pressing within us for self-expression. Like yeast in dough, it rises and expands throughout every fiber of our being, suppressed only by the condition of denial and disbelief. Its pervasiveness is in its foundation, and its excitation is in its consequence. Where Spirit speaks, Spirit responds, however dimly or distantly—something within stirs, something trembles on the threshold of possible awareness. This is the spark, the flame, the emanation of light radiant and enlivening, a gnosis spreading fire from heart to heart through the energy and light that gives life to all sentient form: unbound, uncreated, undiminished. Such is the co-creative life, to share the spark and to enhance its capacities for more self-aware being.

To appreciate the immensity of Spirit, which is greater than the manifest forms of its expression, it is first necessary to appreciate being alive—this requires an attitude of reverence. (1.5)

Meditation: How hard it is to appreciate the wonder of being alive! To be an actual living, breathing being—as though it were not a miracle or one of the greatest of all mysteries! Perhaps it is the subtle complexities that escape our view, the thousands, hundreds of thousands, millions of planetary revolutions necessary for such life forms to evolve and develop. If we take life as a "fact" or "necessity," we lose the depth and profound wonder that being alive should instill. To reduce the life force, its vitality and potency, to a theory of accident or a random coupling of events is to destroy our perceptions of the wonder and beauty of the process. We say life is "meaningless" only when we renounce our own inner awareness of its presence within us, of how Spirit animates us, of how our breath is a precious gift. No matter how difficult the circumstances or how troubled the past, the gift can in no way be destroyed, even in death. We perish or persist, but Spirit abides. And insofar as we do not recognize the gift of life, given to us in each breath, in every heartbeat, we deny a remarkable potential within us. To open our heart to the life force, to its inner expression, to a sense of expansion and unity with the greater fields of its manifestation is to discover the secret of being alive. If we merge with the Earth, open to her life processes, we can experience her breath in the wind, her songs in the rain, her gifts in the grass beneath our feet, her waves on the shore. Yet this is only the Earth, mother of our thoughts and cradle of our evolution.

The Sun too has its own life, its own sense of manifestation as it nourishes the Earth, as does the Moon and every star. Not as inanimate matter, but as inseparable from the workings of the Spirit in subtle forms and conjoined spaces. It transcends our limited sense of "being" because when we take ourselves as the ultimate standard we lose our perspective on relatedness. We deny the value and remarkable accomplishment of our own forthcoming, our attainments as self-aware beings. How can we say life is "accidental" and "circumstantial" when everything about us lives and breathes and calls for us to recognize a more vivid, sensate sense of the Infinite. It is our lack of relatedness that keeps us from embracing the greater horizons that incorporate all manifest forms into the life principle. Yet to reduce Spirit to form and manifestation is still a limit and a denial because it does not give to Spirit what most it deserves—our deepest reverence, our commitment, our willingness to learn, grow, and evolve—to study and recognize the vastness of the processes that shelter and nourish the life gift. To attain such knowledge, it is first necessary to truly revere life, to genuinely have an attitude of deep respect and appreciation for being alive, for the life or every and each being. This means to revere the process itself, to feel a sense of gratitude and thankfulness for the gift. To discover the miracle of life within our own heart is the beginning of wisdom. To see it everywhere, and revere it to the depths of our being is the middle stage. But if we cannot revere it in our own heart, how can we revere it in others? The Earth is an altar that requires us to purify our denials and destructive urges in order to create the garden that Earth might be.

Spirit is greater than the "manifest forms" because even the most beautiful form is perishable and subject to transformation—this includes all ideas, beliefs, and worldviews. The unity of Spirit is not to be found in one species but in all species, as a token, a sign, an emblem of the nature of the creative power and capacity of Spirit. There is a deep and patient abiding at work, a willingness to weave at the subtlest and most sensitive levels, a fragile, even invisible veil—veil upon veil—building the luster of the surface so that it may reveal the hidden potential beneath. Like an ancient Chinese master of carving and wood lacquer, layer upon layer, the gloss is painted and polished to reflect the image in a more lustrous form. But the form is not Spirit, the building up and tearing down is only process, not Spirit; the vastness of space, continuous or discontinuous, is not Spirit. It is Mystery and only accessible to our direct observations through mental-emotive purification, patience, and the cultivation of reverence and humility. It is not things or persons or any being—nor is it our commonplace reductions or our questions about "origins and ends." Everywhere Spirit abides, there is Mystery, Life, and Potential. All the manifest forms together express in exquisite ways the subtlety of the working, the timeless constancy that builds a world or destroys a sun or distant star. There is rhythm and process, cycles, repetitions, a comprehensiveness that abides over and through the present. But our own individual struggles, our embodiment, our incapacity to see or our denials bind us to a limited range of immediate forms and feelings. Spirit is there—hearing, feeling, knowing, even as we each struggle to lift the veils, to see beyond the layered forms, to attain to a more inspired fullness in the All-Containing-All.

The immensity of Spirit cannot be contained in ideas, words, or books. It is a living reality that outstrips our imagination and surpasses our abstractions. Spirit cannot be bound by singular beliefs or ideals, however true or accurate. It manifests in every living being, every nook and corner, every idea and thought. Nothing escapes its presence, whatever world has life, has Spirit. Yet out of the depth of the potential, out of the constant outpouring of its possibility into every conceivable being, it remains constant and complete, inexhaustible and potent, all-containing and yet uncontained. The manifestation is only a unique synthesis of qualities and conditions, like a river of the high plateaus and mountains, it flows pure and clear into the valleys of humankind to be stained, dammed, confined, poured into lesser vessels, made impure by neglect and uncaring ignorance until in a murky pool, they call it lifeless, inert, or dead. If you drink from mountain springs, you will know that life is to be revered, its purity will awaken you and its luster open your eyes to what is hidden and concealed. But first you must make the journey, out of the dark and shadowed valley, out of the stagnant swamps and waters of denial, out of the skepticism and doubt. How can beauty shine to eyes that are closed? How can it quench thirst if there in an unwillingness to drink from pure springs?

There is no reverence without humility; we do not stand "at the pinnacle," but only represent a timely expression of creative unfolding; we must learn therefore to sense the continuity that comes before and after. (1.6)

Meditation: In a certain sense, every created being stands "at the center," at the very heart of the creative process. The center is its life. Yet, as a created being, there is interdependence, a coexistence of a multitude of living beings, all necessary and linked together, inseparable from the totality of becoming. Enfolded into higher and lower orders of complexity and emergence, every entity has a center expressing its natal origins. Those enfolded orders are inseparable from the well-being of the Whole, all beings are intimately related to the sensitive intersection of life forces and life fields. We need more than food and air and water; more than shelter, clothing, and warmth. We need friends, community, artistry, intellectual challenge, and spiritual goals. We need to share what we do, who we are, and to share appreciation and love with others. We receive this by not bearing down, by not forcing or demanding, but through inspiration and uplifting, by sharing the gifts of Spirit with those who receive them openly with thanks. Those gifts are part of the creative process of unfolding and opening that must be encouraged and not condemned because it fails to live up to an artificial social standard or collective attitude. If we place ourselves below, it is only for the necessity of overcoming our own pride of place. For when we no longer think of above or below, of a pinnacle or a *sous-sol*, a below, a lower down, we can then create together, each with his or her own contributions and gifts.

Being at the center means having a capacity to see every other being at the center as well. Not at your center, but each at his or her own center, not enfolded into one another, not subsumed or merged or undifferentiated, but each manifesting a quality of individuated life as a gift and a grace. Knowing how to join and unite in love, in care and well-being, is how each being becomes an individual in the midst of difference united with others through patterns of dynamic respect and compassion. This is not easy, it is not simply an ideal but a virtue earned, a discipline, a spiritual challenge. Knowing how to take a stand, to hold to a center, to stake down and direct your own passionate desires, does not mean surrendering to the will of another or expecting them to surrender to you. It means respecting the right of others to pursue their truth, to disagree, to be individual and separate if necessary. How can we be renewed if we do not let go, do not cling or grasp, if we demand and set overdefensive boundaries? Being at the center means letting go of others, helping them to find their center, creating a climate of respect. In a family, with friends or co-workers, with strangers or antagonists, there is still this need to be yourself and yet to hear and respond with integrity to others. Perhaps silence is a most appropriate response, but even silence requires hearing what is said.

A "timely expression" means that every creative process has an end, a transformation, a death, perhaps, a rebirth. Spirit does not claim any one creation but gives birth to all. Why should one be more superior than another—one being, one species, or one world? Each is a center, together complex and multifaceted, intertwined and manifesting distinctive qualities. This is the paradox of Spirit— to build up and tear down, to construct and deconstruct, to manifest and then, to reabsorb. Form is not the goal, a particular pattern or organization is a flowering, a flourish and overflowing, an ebbing, a realization and a withdrawal. Out of the ashes of the old arises the new, perhaps unrecognizable interplay of a multitude of beings arising into perfection, then passing away. The cycles of creation are similar to those of destruction, within which abides the enduring, transmuting potencies of perishable form. Being at the center means having a deep reverence for the process and the many beings who make that process probable and actual. The process is variable and beings unfold capacity at different rates of maturity and insight— many cling to past forms and eras as a refuge against the decline and decadence of collective indifference or neglect. The fundamental values of being alive slip away into the abyss of hurried, hassled, and distracted patterns of surface interaction. Where our fears lie buried, the blossom fades and there is no fruit, no seeds for future generations to grow a better world in a more timely way.

How is it that so many stand so proud and unbending in their affirmation of human accomplishment and mastery? Being superior, is
it possible to appreciate those who are less so? Is it possible to accept
and learn from those "below," the less worthy, the unwashed and
fallen, the broken, abused, sick, and uneducated? A lack of empathy
is a sickness of soul and a shallow defensiveness that does not see
the long beginning, slow emergence, and humble origins. Spirit emanates the sea with all the fragile forms of barely aware life, yet vibrant and charged with intense Presence—vibrant as a crack of
blinding light or the thunder of a threatening god. Such are our origins, our fears, our magnified concerns. We huddled together on the
forest-edged savannas and wondered about our survival, our perishable, vulnerable, fragile lives. Every animal had a power we lacked,
perceptions we could not match, gifts we needed to enhance for our
own survival. Slowly we wandered crossing seas and rivers and icy
plains, settling into every niche, every corner, in caves along river
banks, always vulnerable, always afraid, imagining others as less
capable or more, but rarely as equals.

Later we walked with imagined giants strides, trampling both the
earth and her habitants indifferently—in conquest, men prevailed,
still dreaming of mastery. Still there was vulnerability, the insanity of
violence, war, disease, pollution, abuse, hate, sterility, and despair
marking our growing majorities. We have not created an Eden, a garden for our children's children; we have enslaved, destroyed, raped,
pillaged, and looted every valuable commodity, oppressed those regarded as weaker human beings or species, exhausted resources, denied hope. Spirit enfolds us, even as we wrap ourselves in our own
ignorance, and continues to give birth, to create, to surpass humanity
for other forms, other visions, other entities. We are not the pinnacle
or the end, only another passing stage, another transformation that
will be reabsorbed. If we do not respect the process, if we do not remember and learn from our own struggles, our own imbalances and
pain, how will we attain the necessary transformations? How will we
have anything to give or transmit to worthy heirs? Humility is an
adornment, like a wisdom in old age, earned through trials and temp-
tations that resulted in inner calm, insight, and acceptance. It is more
joyful to stand below and see others rise, than to stand above and suppress or control. Our creative unfolding is communal and a matter of
deep relatedness and sharing—such a simple lesson, so hard to retain
or to enact.

What of reverence? It is not something called up for show or made into an act of piety, nor is it to affirm the values of a particular social or spiritual practice. Reverence arises best spontaneously, without effort, without forethought, without need. I have revered the Earth because she overwhelmed me, through her beauty, her majesty, or the simple fall of an autumn leaf. Or I have revered others for their greatness of heart, the beauty of their words, the works of their hands, for the music we made, the songs we wrote, the poetry we shared, the dances we danced—for what we each had, and will and might become. This is because Spirit leads, inspires, and guides us toward a reckoning with our own individual potential for self-mastery. How can you respect your own mother, your brothers and sisters, your father and friends unless you let go of the images of inadequacy that you carry of them? How can you love and affirm your own life if you do not first release the old pain, denials, and doubts? The earth, the human populace, the sun, moon, and stars ask for reverence spontaneously, without compromise or qualification. All animals, great and small, the plants that give you air and their fruits, the very minerals bred by Spirit through millennial transformation to instill a bright marvel, all these call upon your wonder, your innocence, and your own sense of direct kinship with everything that lives. Only when we revere every living being will we understand the power and mystery of Spirit.

Life is not bound by the past or present, its nets of interconnected joy and beauty are spread throughout all space and all time; yet at every level of organization there is the chaos of death and rebirth. (1.7)

Meditation: Chaos is part of us, always with us, at every level of creation and destruction, it acts to reveal a new relationship with the unknown, it strives to collapse the static norm and to keep us vulnerable to the unpredictable and unexpected. This is our challenge, to recreate in our own mental and emotional transformations the role and place of the chaotic as creative and beneficial, intrinsic to the process of our mutual co-evolutions.[5] There is pain, suffering, loss, shock, tragic incidents—often induced by madness, corruption, or abuse—but this is a different order of chaos, one chosen by a barely conscious will attempting to impose control where respect and love are more deeply needed. Thus we may create chaos by imposing a narrow and dogmatic view that cares only to sustain an older order or a selfish need or a personal attainment. Further, we may draw our entire world into chaos by mindlessly inflicting each other with war, engines of death, and thus becoming, in our infamy, Lords of Chaos. This chaos is relative to our impositions, to the control we wish to exert over others, over resources both human and natural, over the very fabric of creation. Constantly we create insufficient images of the Whole, persecuting those who disagree for their denials and lack of collective conviction or conformity. Such chaos leads to death, to failures, to a lack of recognition that the process is transformative and does not culminate in a "final view."

Death is part of the process—this is chaos at the level of our immediate finitude. Our mortal lives have an arbitrary quality, sometimes flowing into patterns of greater connectedness, as in synchronicity, or into patterns of disconnectedness, as in alienation. As we become disconnected from the life process, we also become disconnected from the death process, the beauty and necessity of dissolution and finitude. The breakdown of the old order is a collapse of the final petrification, a new opportunity to reassemble the world with the eyes and mind of a child, or an animal or a thousand other alternative life forms. Death is not final; it is not complete or terminal except in the sense of our own discrete, immediate identity, our individually assembled psychohistory. This history, fragmented and incoherent, well-knit or redundant, is a thread of continuity that surpasses a particular incarnation and quantifies itself as a weaving within the Whole. The chaos of death is a necessary break, an introjected discontinuity, that challenges us to retain our connectedness within the greater weavings of Spirit while simultaneously letting go of past insufficiency, old accomplishments or successes, and thereby facing yet again the challenge of inhabiting the world anew. Death as a creative event requires a very sincere recognition of the deeper continuities of Spirit, of the interconnected webs through which Spirit thrives, and how death is a necessity within the process of this ongoing creative play.

From another perspective, death at one level of organization is not necessarily death at another level of organization. Just as our bodies may be decomposed into more elemental substances, which in turn may nourish life, so also our own layered identities may contribute in myriad ways to further the life process. In memory, in words sung or written, in intuitions, dreams, and visions shared and many other alternative forms, the personhood retains its capacity to act on the receptive other. Further, the life process supports, on higher levels of organization within the grasp of our psychic capacities, continuities that break the symmetry of ordinary space-time and reveal whole new worlds of personal existence and attainment. These "higher dimensions," enfolded as they are into the abundance of Spirit, contain diverse subtle worlds, some far beyond our capacity to perceive, whose inhabitants and actions reveal the incredible vastness of Spirit and the barely explored continuum of the *Mundus Imaginalis*. The capacity to radically transform the body is there also, yet remains largely unrecognized and unactualized. It is not a matter of merely mental or nonphysical transformation, but of a complete psychophysical process by which the very molecules of the body may be transformed and illumined. Yet, even without that transformation, there is a profound potential within our psychic capacity to make similar and equally significant changes and to attain very high degrees of awakening, illumination, and gnosis.

As we incorporate greater awareness, as we expand the horizon of our perceptions, we will find not an "empty" universe of nonbeing—but a great Plenum of alternative creative worlds whose relatedness to our own psychohistory will prove to be deep, profound, and lasting. If we roll back the lower veils of consciousness, like so many curtains concealing hidden rooms, if we venture into these inner chambers and gaze into the naked symbols carved in circular patterns on the floor, at the gem stones in the heart of the pattern, then we may come to understand that the pattern, the Hermetic circle, connects us to many other patterns that are truly open at the center. This is a center that collapses ordinary space-time and connects us to the web of related beings in other spheres, each with his or her own enfolded subtotalities of meaning and interpretation. These visionary worlds and beings manifest as we reach out, through Spirit, into the vast interconnectedness of other entities, alien, strange, or frighteningly familiar. This visionary quality, which pervades our construction and reconstruction of worlds, is the very sustenance of the life gift. It is the energetic weaving together of all material, psychic, and spiritual realities into a joyful fullness, a beauty and sublimity that transcends the words and thoughts we use to share our mutually conditioned insights and understandings.

If we reach out past the chaos of death, release our hold on controlling and subduing, begin to open our hearts and minds to the infinite character of the visionary reality, of Spirit forming and reforming alternatives on a vast scale of minute detail and careful nurturance, we will discover the profound depths of what we may call the sacred or holy. The death and rebirth is only a transient stage between visions shared with others who also seek to comprehend the life gift as an extension surpassing any particular incarnation in form, matter, or energy. The quantum transformation is the "leap of consciousness" as we become more mutually aware of Spirit in all its many forms and illusive appearances. Thus the call is to lay aside our denials, cynicism, anti-life sentiments and rejoice in the freedom of being more conscious in an already conscious universe. Our own evolution to greater awareness, our becoming, is nothing more than our species' contributions to alternative evolutions in innumerable and yet unseen or unknown other worlds. Many of these worlds lie within us, already calling out for recognition. Whatever level of attainment we achieve, there is always the possibility that we have yet to reach even a rudimentary grasp of the complexity of Spirit acting throughout billions of years and worlds. Have we yet seen the simplicity of the unity that keeps the webs connected? Our dreams, our teachers, our visions—all are doorways into those worlds, into comprehension bound by immediacy but liberated by death, the good death, the death that comes naturally, with grace, and swiftly cuts the ties that bind.

Sorrow and brutality arise because we fail to recognize this most primordial truth—unless we revere life in all its forms and possibilities, we cannot hope to comprehend its source. (1.8)

Meditation: The primordial nature of "truth" lies not in its codifications or laws, not in its material concomitants, but in its enactment and sharing. What makes it primordial is the constancy by which we choose, generation after generation, to make it real and central in our lives. To live the truth means to embody the wisdom of valuing life and then acting to preserve and enhance our mutual experience of its worth. The affirmation that life is what we value, in all its diverse and alien forms, is an affirmation of the process of creation. A child is born, we value the child, its innocence and potential, its pure aliveness, the marvel of his or her development and discovery of the worlds of others. This is primordial. It means that we each contain the capacity to open to new and unexpected horizons of meaning and discovery, as the life gift evolves within and through us. If we become closed, cease to grow and develop, reduce our capacity for life to a narrow focus, a "speciality" that can never represent our full potential, then the life gift contracts to a repetition of patterns and habits that slowly closes us off to the expansive becoming of a child or a newborn. To be made anew, in a daily sense, requires a deep reverence for the life gift, an ability to wonder, explore, question—in order to better discover the source within ourselves from which it flows.

The sorrow that arises is the feeling of loss, not only of vitality, but of depth, nuance, texture and richness in detail, and possibility. Sorrow arises out of the sense that life contracts to a restless, uneasy preoccupation with immediacy that does not fulfill, but only evades the issue of deeper meaning and care. Not valuing life, we fail to value even our own experiences, cease being thankful, truncate our emotional capacities, and hide behind the walls of our obvious self-deceptions, as if life lived in one dimension is all that life can offer, as if it were simply a commodity, something to be bargained and bartered for in which profit and loss are measured in terms of immediate gain and stimulation, not in depth or understanding. The sorrows that arise come when we look back, view the shambles of a poorly lived life or see where we were only concerned with personal and immediate benefit, or sacrificed unnecessarily for others. We can block the sorrow and simply begin to feel tired and weary—but the tiredness is a consequence of a loss of vitality that fails to value the life gift. Only if we affirm, deep within ourselves, the gift, deeply reverence its arising and understand that the challenge is to fully discover our inner potential will we be able to sense the vitality of the gift even at the very end. Overcoming sorrow means rectifying the past, healing the old wounds, restoring a positive sense of life with all the others we have harmed or failed to affirm in moments of past anger, disappointments, or denials.

The brutality arises in denying the sensitivities of others and seeing them as mute subjects to be manipulated and used for purposes of maintaining a nonreverential view. All animal experimentation, their suffering and pain, is constituted in a worldview that denies them feeling, sensitivity, and genuine response to the shocking impact of torture and manipulation. This torture occurs without thought by feeling human beings who seem permanently blocked from empathy and compassion, who deny the rights of every being to live a free and natural life, and who support a platform of progress based in coercive experimentation, death, and pain. Species survival is not a justification for tormenting others any more than war is a just cause in the sponsorship of a political or religious ideology. These deeply unhealthy tendencies mutually support a dehumanizing and life-denying view of others. More darkly, the passion of personal ambitions, sexual drives, rage, and frustration, act to enforce an ethic of dominance that is a primary source for brutality in every form. Because life is not valued, because strength and dominance are applauded, abuse of the less empowered becomes a way of life for many who, in failing to value the life gift, feel justified in oppressing others. "Might is right" becomes a catch-phrase that justifies an ethic of domination, while hierarchic social institutions further this ethic by subordinating each rank within the hierarchy to the dominating tendencies of those who also chafe under the dominance of those above them. Equality requires a deep reverence for the value of the individual as a living being, a unique and sensitive awareness that is not contingent upon conformity or the subordination of others.

The comprehension involved is more than one-dimensional, it requires a synthesis and multiperspectual view that fully values the ways in which difference contributes to a more complex and integrated understanding. To truly comprehend the life gift means to fully experience the richness of the diversity and plurality of forms that embody that complexity without demoting or undervaluing those that are also alien and strange. Reverence is based on a perception rising from an immediate and vivid awareness of our mutual relatedness to all life forms—through the gifts of Spirit to be purified and transformed—so that difference does not become a matter of division or hierarchic struggles. The gift is the perception of Spirit in and through all life forms, the direct presence that imbues even the most rare and minute forms with life and awareness. Spirit is the source of all reverence, it is the dawning of an expanding awareness, a seeing of each life as a radiant quality of being that is inseparable from the Whole and that matures in a constant sense of joy through sharing the gift. The source of the gift does not lie in an idea or a concept or a metaphysical abstraction. It lies right in the palm of your living hand, in your heart, your brain, mind, and imagination—in every sphere of interaction with others—and underpins the foundations of all your thinking and believing. No name grasps it and no form fully expresses its capacity or power; no text records its fullness.

The challenge is to discover its spiritual basis, to recognize that "being alive" is not an accident, a matter of random chance, or an un-repeatable coincidence. This discovery is neither an affirmation of abstract ideas nor a statement of faith or belief. It is directly percep-tible through a reverential determination to open the self to its own deepest potential and to experience that potential in all other life forms. Habit and conditioning blind us to the possibility, skepticism and doubt circumscribe what is acceptable, and fear and anxiety keep us wrapped in the veils of denial, dismissal, and indifference. So we trod an entire world beneath our heels, deny creativity in oth-ers, cause a multitude of other species to perish, and raise many doc-trines celebrating our own unique and privileged position in an increasingly desacralized, alienated world. This alienation springs from the roots of denial and cynicism; it grows on the limbs of our dissection of human experience into mutually incomprehensible areas of specialization, and bears a fruit that is bitter and hard—pri-marily in our profound lack of empathy, thankfulness, or deep ap-preciation for the life gift. In Spirit, all live, all rejoice, all excel in the ecstasy of affirming a positive valuation of the gift. But in a proud, aloof, and intellectually naked world of ideological conflicts, this ecstasy is lost and in the process, life becomes a mute datum whose value is cheapened and whose worth weighs little in the scales of technology, industry, or mass education.

To "know the sources" means to open ourselves to a reevaluation of past, present, and future. It means deconstructing our species-centric attitudes and reconstructing a more humane and caring world in which every living being has the right to seek its own max-imum potential. This calls for a careful husbandry, a nuturance of the garden, a cooperative sharing of insights from many different perspectives. It is a communal process in which the individual con-tributes the spark and fire of unique insights and illuminations. The true "knowing" is an awakening to Spirit, a multidimensional expansion into diverse ways of seeing whose roots are deep in the life gift, reverently aware of the primordial sources of transformation in all other life forms. Spirit in this process is always present, always vital and urging toward realization the latent potential of each being. There is no special class, type, or kind that particularly manifests this capacity—it is there in every being—and it manifests its potential through the diversity of all beings together. Each stage reflects the degree to which Spirit is known in the direct, conscious sense and all contraction, pain, and sorrow is a loss of that knowing, an abandonment of shared life, and an isolation and alienation from holy depths. The deepest "knowing" is a surrender to Mystery and the reverence of that knowing is greater than any form can bear. May that reverence, Spirit willing, lead us to peace, nonviolence, and joy, to a creative sharing, to a deep and respectful love. Now and always, Amen.

The Second Principle

The Second Principle of Spirit is that every manifestation of life has its own unique awareness, a being that constitutes its form; there is no life without such awareness. (2.1)

Meditation: By "being" I do not mean an eternal and unchanging entity, nor do I mean something created as it now exists and "living forever" beyond the life of the body, unchanged or undying. But I do mean a being that has the capacity to survive death, to transmit tendencies, to take on new forms as a consequence of its internal development, continuity, and coherence. That same aspect of being is also capable of division and cohesion or union with others in a soulful universe of related beings guided and upheld within Spirit. The nature of this identity is dynamic and subject to change, transformation, and growth as well as possible dispersion, nonexistence, and complete sublimation into higher realms of Spirit. As all is alive and all reflects Spirit, this constitution of multiple identities is an outcome of long-term temporal evolution knit together through the processes of species interactions. Both in the incarnate world of bodily beings and in the energetic worlds of psychic interactions, there is continuous process of mythic creation and social construction. The spiritual principle that sustains such being is the life breath, a living identity in the form of a particular species individual. It is this "evolute" within being, as an soulful individual, that constitutes the processes of manifestation in concert with the complex interactive influences of historical, cultural, and global becoming. The worlds we create, that we project onto and through the malleable forms of energized "materiality" are a consequence of our long psychospiritual history, extending back into millions of planetary revolutions and a world-spanning differentiation into complex cultural expressions or realizations.

The unique awareness that evolves is not merely individual, nor is it an accomplishment of only one being, or one soul. It is the transmitted inheritance of millions of years of striving, loving, worshipping, and aspiring struggle to comprehend the astonishing facts of our own species coming-into-being. And in that process, we as individuals each seek to attain specific manifestations of Spirit in soulful form, reflecting through the millennium, the deep potentials of our collective being and becoming. Every form of life, no matter how minute, is part of that process—large or small, friendly, frightening, or alien—each being contributes to the unfolding and self-revealing processes of Spirit manifesting. The powers within this process are vast and barely comprehensible, barely within our collective grasp, no matter how brilliantly they may shine within any particular heart or mind. The power that this process bestows on the living being is the very experience of a developing self-awareness. The fragile envelope of our evolving consciousness acts to protect our emerging impressions, however limited, and allows even a minute quantum of psychic potential to become yet more self-aware, more self-actualized. The boundaries are the necessary limits that create a restricted field of exploration and that keep us from being overwhelmed or absorbed into unbound Mystery. The goal is not annihilation but actualization of self; not denial, but deep affirmation through creative synthesis and unique expression. Without the boundaries that constitute our individual natures, there could be no evolutes to value the beauty, power, and magnitude of creation. There would be no center wherein that power could manifest a particular unique set of qualities or capacities. As the being evolves, grows, contracts, pulls back, or blindly expands in harmful ways, it acquires a potential greater than the potential of its material form. Thus evolves a conscious, spiritual entity seeking to fulfill that potential beyond the immediate limitations of a strictly physical, bodily existence.

This does not mean that we should in any way devalue the bodily life or fail to appreciate its wonder and magnitude as a complex and complementary reflection of cosmological becoming. The revelation of physical life is its tremendous complexity, beauty, and minute, interactive sensitivity and deep-seated, multiple awarenesses. As "awareness," the psyche/soul expresses a full body consciousness, including the spectrum of energies that surround and enclose the nerves, organs, and body as a whole. This spectrum includes higher forms of psychic perception and the subtle energies that fill the skies, surround the earth, and merge into as yet unseen dimensionality. The integrative soulful self is intimately joined with all these physical, energetic, spiritual processes, which are themselves inseparable from large-scale cosmological events and activities that shape and influence the life of the individual. Cultural, historical, and social influences also add to that emergent, "soul-making" process. The bodily life is only a necessary limitation, one of beauty and marvelous complexity, bound within the vast processes of Spirit manifesting through the interconnected web of various life forms. Soulful being imbues that form with qualities transmitted through interaction, emotional habits, and personal development to attain to a specific manifestation of capacity.

The "unique awareness" is what survives beyond physical manifestation, the being that transforms and evolves in the ongoing project of species development. This happens not only physically or genetically, but also emotionally, psychically, imaginatively, mythically and through the evolvement of collective psychic potentials that result in higher states of awareness and perception. Being-awareness is not static, fixed, unchanging or "eternal," yet it participates in enduring processes whose boundaries are immeasurable and whose contents appear interwoven throughout myriads of time. This development is not a single species development but a total interspecies evolution—involving all life forms—inextricably related within co-creative processes of mutual health and well-being. Not only on this world, this sun, this planetary sphere, but in many other co-related spheres as well. Some of these "worlds" are purely mental and others are energetic and radically spiritualized, charged with the emotional and noetic contents of higher perceptions and a vaster field of interspecies communication. Yet each life-form has its own unique awareness, its own gifts, and its own very specific potentials. Such a gift can be contracted, hardened, turned in on itself, eating its own heart through denial, doubt, skepticism, or a resistant disdain, arrogance, or closed-mindedness. The tendency is to draw a circle and to deny everything that remains outside the comprehensible, contracted world of a particular belief or emotional bias. That too is a reflection of the life process—to define an arena of experience and to explore its potential in the safety of knowing where the boundaries are. But we must look beyond the contracted circles, see them for the constriction that they are, how they choke life and deny potential. We must rub out the crude, self-imposed lines of our own closed circular views for larger, more comprehensive, intersected possibilities.

This means we must work together, to share and learn and grow toward a deeper and more open world. Individual being, its potential and power to sustain life and a unique consciousness, even beyond bodily death, requires a clear and lucid illumination to carry it through the death storms and confusing currents of the In-Between. The strong ties are those of love and attachment, a deep compassion for others, a genuine loving kindness, an openness to the sorrows and cares of the world that creates lasting ties in the evolution of mind, heart, and soulful being. Spirit carries us, sustains us, gives us life and fullness, desires our coming and shows us the way—if only we open ourselves to the healing of the world. The world's healing and our own healing are inextricably bound. To be well, to attain higher being-awareness means to go beyond inherited relations and commitments, it means to be an instrument of healing through inner development, though the self-conscious process of living a Spirit-guided life. The envelope must open, expand to incorporate others, all creatures, far and wide, all worlds, all suns, moons, and stars. This begins in valuing the unique awareness of every living creature, not as masters of mechanical manipulation, not as technocrats, not as slaves burdened by the visions of others, but as caretakers and lovers bound by mutual vows of concern. The spiritual aspect of soulful being is the power of illumination to transform the world—not merely as intelligence, love, or creativity—but as a manifestation of Spirit. This open and receptive being is lifted, carried, and directed by that abiding presence. Every spark enlightens the world—how much more so does that power joined in an encircling ring of hands ready to include those we have not yet touched.

Even on the "subatomic" level, there is awareness; there is reaction and interaction, loss and

gain, an exchange, a reconfiguration, always in motion, yet stable, enduring, and powerfully bound by the conventions of its own reality. (2.2)

Meditation: In speaking of the "subatomic," I speak metonymically, that is, taking a part, a very minute part, as manifesting important aspects of the Whole. This wholeness, within Spirit, is a multilayered totality, fully differentiated, but its differentiations are not separate from its place and meaning within a unified Whole. It is our challenge to apprehend the meaning, to see how the part relates to the Whole to better understand how we, as individuals and as specific communities, also relate to the totality of the processes of becoming more aware, more actualized, and more affectively attuned to that Wholeness. Awareness is not limited to only human beings or other "organic" creatures. Within Spirit, life awareness is an all-pervasive, all-encompassing, and yet multilayered reflexivity having various degrees of inwardness and outwardness. This awareness has no "top or bottom"—in all directions, there is only awareness—unique, distinct, large and small, minute and vast, it extends without limit to and through whatever is, was, or shall be. Such is the Second Principle of Spirit: that all life has awareness and that there are no boundaries to the subtlety through which that awareness may manifest, even at the level of the most minute particle or the largest celestial formation. The multidimensionality of this awareness, this all-pervasive Sat-Chit-Ananda, is far more than a simple unity or oneness. In expanding from the most minute to the most vast or in contracting from the largest scale to the smallest, it differentiates and forms centers of manifestation through which the life process may differentiate and catalyze unique qualities and states. And yet, in this process, there is an abiding presence that nurtures that difference without negating the inward perceptions of a shared, pervasive unity and fullness.

This awareness is experiential, not theoretical. It is directly knowable through an enhanced and direct openness to the deeper potentials of being and becoming. To be imbued with Spirit means to be aware through increasing stages of development; to see and experience the complexity and fullness that pervades all aspects of life through co-related awareness; to know directly (gnosis) the boundless source of that awareness as an all-pervading Wholeness. It means also to value particular species awareness and its limitations, including our own limitations, bias, or prejudice. There is a constant stream of "reaction and interaction" in the life process; it is not determined by mental ideas as much as by emotional, soul-centered responses, needs, or hopes. The part within the whole is non-isolated, regardless of however intense the feelings of separation, alienation, or loss may be. We are each an inseparable part of enfolding life processes whose depths and contours include all beings, aspects, elements, and particles that constitute life in the fullest sense. This constitution is highly interactive, we are constantly being impacted, from the subatomic to the macrocosmic, by energetic processes within the Whole. Our bodies resonate with those subatomic and macrocosmic interactions. The human social center of these processes requires a constant input of energy, commitment, and effort to sustain a recognizable, functional identity and to provide a safe harbor in which to anchor ourselves in the midst of these vaster processes of becoming. Yet our becoming in and through Spirit requires us to attain more than a stable center, more than a "working community" or "adequate social structure." It requires a constant exploration, reevaluation, and a willingness to move beyond our safe harbor and to follow the deeper urge toward new becoming and awareness.

"Reconfiguration" is crucial—it does not mean wholesale rejection of the past or what once was but now seems no longer adequate or attractive. This process of becoming is regenerative, a process of reconstitution and reintegration by which what is valuable and worthy is retained and given altered meaning or nuance. This becoming supports the emergence of new insights, fuller awareness, and more self-actualized forms of social and communal life. Awareness involves processes of self-examination in which the past becomes a resource for future attainments. A particle of insight, a minute shift, a very slight quantum transformation, can result in the emergence of a new configuration, a new understanding that unites with the qualitative effects of Spirit to reintegrate past becoming. It is our relationships with others that most prominently effect this transformation, creating mutual influences and interactions that shape an emergent horizon of meaning and make it, through effort and imagination, a more expansive and open state of being. This is because there is exchange—not a grasping, self-centered denial or a fearful resistance—but an open and receptive interaction that energizes and reveals hidden potential. This potential incorporates the past, distilling from it the crucial lessons, insights, and transformations that lead into an integrative present. The past gives us roots into being, into the depths of Spirit manifesting through limited and actual individuals whose own history and becoming are linked to our present conditions. This past includes our entire species past, in all its millennial forms and transformations reaching back into the creations and condensations of our becoming on a geological and cosmological scale. The "reconfiguration" of that past is crucial to our species evolution. Our present understanding and awareness of its complexity, stages, and dramatic shifts continues to impact our self-understanding, teaching us the vast and complex actuality of our shared becoming. And throughout this process, Spirit abides, nurturing and uniting the Whole.

What is "stable and enduring" is the complexity of life forms evolving through processes of relationship to others within that Whole. The "conventions" that bind all these life forms are shared biological, emotional, mental, and historical predispositions influenced by inherited human teachings and social custom. The energy that maintains the form is shaped by a blend of self-sustaining patterns, interactive creative agencies, and a receptivity to others in the processes of self-transformation. Convention easily becomes an inhibition to growth and spiritual maturity because it holds a commonplace status where resistance to the collective is often met with counterforce and suppression. Within the human community, this tendency is manifest over and over—history is replete with examples that privilege the collective majority over the creative minority. Any convention can serve a coercive end, but convention can also liberate energy and creative self-expression if integrated into a spiritual understanding that encourages and fosters creative exploration. The encompassing nature of Spirit incorporates both the collective and the individual but it fosters the individual as a primary resource for the actualization of the collective. Not in a coercive fashion, but acting through inspiration and spiritual influences that relate the individual to the Whole—this is a crucial point. Stability and endurance require creative insight as well as communal cooperation; it is a process, a becoming that emerges and does not simply sit content with what has been. The actualization of potential requires creative emergence, a continual refinement and reconfiguration of that past into more subtle and expansive forms. To move beyond convention requires the inspiration of individuals (the sparks) and the support of the communal (the warmth) in order to manifest fully the light and healing of Spirit.

On all levels, from the simplest to the most complex combinations, there is hidden power and potential; because there is motion and interaction, there is transformation—these are the qualities of life, awareness, and soulful being. (2.3)

Meditation: Often our lives seem static or lacking in energy and vitality; or sometimes they are over-stimulated and over-energized, requiring a frenetic and constant engagement of will and effort, to the point of exhaustion. And quite often these two perspectives are combined—we seem to go round and round in an exhausting cycle of nonemergence simply expending energy to maintain a static pattern of repetitive involvements. This is not life in the spiritual sense because the potential is being exhausted in maintaining external obligations, superficial relationships, or unexamined habits of mind and body. Spirituality is about depths and hidden potential and what is not yet known or realized; it is a search for that realization that cannot be acquired through routine and strictly rational expectations. Spirit acts as a creative urge toward greater fullness and self-realization, toward a greater completeness within the Whole. It is not simply "individual" potential, but a deeper and more abundant spiritual capacity whose depths are Spirit born. This potential connects us to the Whole in ways that energize and inspire us with deeper relatedness to others, individually and communally, through a depth that surpasses routine and pragmatic relationships. Spirituality is an infusion of depths that comes out of Mystery and encompasses the entire cosmos—giving us a self-renewing and regenerative perspective on human cooperation and commitment. To attain that perspective, it is crucial to slow down and allow for inner reflection and caring for others, to break the fearful symmetry of routine and self-imposed obligations.

The "hidden power and potential" is threefold: First, it is the potential of the Whole that acts on the individual through an open and receptive attitude of caring and compassion, the qualities that nurture the life principle in every being. Secondly, it is the power and potential of the particular collective of the individual, his or her communally rooted identity. This may not be the natal community or the community of childhood, but an alternative community chosen by the individual to further spiritual growth. Or it may be a combination of various communal influences, each channeling a potential that enhances development and awareness. Third is the hidden potential of the individual, the capacity, skills, abilities, or gifts that are unique to an individual whose processes do not stagnate or regress into patterns of fearful denial or proud rejection. These three are all important within the process of actualizing spiritual potential and all three need to be integrated into an active spiritual life. A belief in individual or communal potential truncated by a denial of the spiritual potential of the Whole, limits in a severe fashion the capacity of the individual for a self-surpassing awareness. Spiritual development involves an intimate relatedness to the deepest sources of empowerment and awareness—to the direct reality of Spirit in the life of the individual by honoring the life gift and the joyful complexity of all its manifestations.

The unlocking of repetitive routine and surface relations means opening the doorway to unbound fullness, to an inner capacity for self-surpassing. This self-surpassing is crucial—it is necessary for each of us to break out of the limited form, out of the exterior shape and internalized impositions of inherited mental and emotional attitudes for a fresh, provocative encounter with depths greater and vaster than inherited beliefs or collective skepticisms. These depths, Spirit-imbued and full of profound currents and *sous-sol* contents, surpass the ordinary mind of everyday concerns. Such depths, deeply felt, opens us to Mystery, to the fullness that gives us life, mind, awareness, soul, and enhanced being. Such a gift abounds with ever greater realizations drawn from the abundance of Spirit as a free capability that we must utilize and integrate in specific forms and manifestations. These might be simply acts of kindness, generosity, creative imagination, or aid given to others who also need inspiration to overcome the challenges presented to them. In self-surpassing, when we see directly our limits and then, see beyond them into a higher potential, we also find renewal, knowing that we are crossing the threshold of our deeper potential and capacity. There is an entire living universe and a multitude of beings, all of whom thrive and evolve through this generous gifting of Spirit. In sharing this gift, we enhance the capacity of others to realize, on their own terms, the unique forms of the gift for them. There is no one template and no one way, there is only a multitude of ways, means, and forms, all participant in the gift and yet each unique and valuable.

The "motion and interaction" that results in transformation requires the breaking of habits, of tendencies to think or believe in
certain ways, or to act in accord with appetites that obscure or deny
the hidden potential. Constantly, we are faced with the challenge
not to petrify, not to routinize, not to isolate our perceptions and actions from a greater continuity. This does not require conformity or
submission, but a seeking, a search for spiritual maturity that is
self-evaluative and reflected outward in positive, creative human
relationships. Thus "motion and interaction" is a guideline. Are you
static, locked into repetitive habits that isolate or diminish your
human relationships? Are you interactive, communicative, able to
listen even when you disagree, to accept the difference between
your view and another, to fully love and rejoice in that difference as
part of the complexity of the Whole? Is there creative activity—an
upsurge of ideas or feelings or intuitions that prompt you toward
new explorations and discoveries. If so, that is Spirit urging, gently
pushing outward toward a new horizon of insight or imaginative exploration. Do you learn from others, from men, women, children,
animals and the rivers, mountains and grasses, from the flowers of
the field and the birds of the trees? Or do you limit your interactions to only like-minded others—to only those who reinforce your
own bias or presuppositions? The energy of transformation requires
a multitude of perspectives to fully integrate a cogent and living
spiritual life. This is because Spirit is that complexity, infusing it
with depth and making it into a weaving of a multitude of beings.
How much of the pattern can you incorporate into your own weavings, your own perceptions and awareness? This is where transformation is found, at the boundaries between you and others and the
world at large.

The qualities of "life, awareness, and soul" are many and cannot
be fully articulated, nor should they be so articulated. Much is beyond language and words and the mental processes of everyday reflection and thought. Soulful being is found in art, music, dance, in
sensation and taste, in ritual and celebration, in communal feeling
and relationship to nature and its deep and hidden powers. The fullness of that being calls us out of our ordinary preoccupations to embrace a world and a cosmos of vast complexity. We do this through
seeking interactions and not in living alone in ascetic isolation or
world denial. "Where there is interaction, there is transformation."
This is a principle of Spirit that encourages us to seek relationships

that enhance and expand our awareness, that help us to develop soul capacity, to live life in the richness of multiple dimensions of becoming and being. The secret lies not in the articulation, but in the living and experiencing, in the sharing and feeling of connectedness, in our direct embodied contact with other life forms and worlds. The release of the hidden power and potential comes through exposure to alternatives that inspire, that elicit reverence for the life gift, that enhance and expand awareness through affirmation and embrace, not through denial, control, or conformity. This requires courage and a willingness to explore and to experience alternatives that are soul-enhancing and to avoid those that are soul-diminishing or an ecstatic but exhausting substitute for depth and continuity. There must be grounding love and caring for others, this gives us continuity with all species life and it links us to Spirit through our own spirit of nurturance and care. As in the macrocosm, so in the microcosm—the art of spiritual transformation is interactive and at every level, liberates awareness through care, concern, and compassion.

The particles that make up the form of common clay give the energy of interaction and unity to the substance, but those particles are themselves permeated with life fields of increasingly complex potential. (2.4)

Meditation: Let's return to the Earth, to the common clay, to the basic stuff that makes us human, embodied, and organic beings. Let's embrace that common earthiness, that "materiality" that makes us human and celebrate the energy of that form in all its entangled threads linking us to the Earth herself. We know that the substance is perishable, but at the same time, also sensate, evocative, pleasurable, joyful, capable of energy, work, action, rest, sleep, and meditative calm. The range of feelings, sensations, and perceptions that are intrinsic to the body are highly complex and in a process of gradual development. We are slowly evolving higher awareness, more acute sensation and perception, greater psychic sensitivity that will enhance awareness tenfold when fully actualized. All of this is imaged in the body as a reflection of psychic capacity and spiritual potential. The body, like clay, appears as tangible, visible substance, divided and differentiated according to different systemic processes. All the way down, it is divisible into the cellular and subcellular, molecular levels—to the genetic, microbiological chemistry of quantum effects, into particle physics and relativistic manifestations. All the way up, it is divisible into feelings, will, empathy, aesthetic sensitivity, language, imaginative-rational cognition, self-identity, visionary states, out-of-body experience, after-death-awareness, mystical ecstasy and metaphysical intuitions and illuminations. This is no Newtonian body, no Cartesian machine!

Where are the boundaries of the body? Are they impermeable? Or are they semitransparent, enwrapped in a variety of energy fields and soulful perceptions intrinsic to every incarnate life form? The energy of the body, its psychic fields of awareness, differentiated organ by organ and cell by cell, form a whole that we experience as an individual self. It is a discrete identity bound by causal laws that can be identified even at the cellular and molecular levels. Even particles follow interactive patterns that are transmitted intergenerationally, they follow the "laws" that have preceded their own interactive evolutions—though, clearly, we are far from understanding those patterns or their variety or predictability. The subtlety of the process is "chaotic" and yet maintains coherence in evolving into new variations and alternatives. This can happen slowly or suddenly with little or no warning, a macroshift filtering through a multitude of complex interactions to form a catalytic response that opens a new horizon on being and becoming, that allows for the emergence of new insights and perceptions. This is the life process at work, not isolated from the "material" world, but intrinsic to and inseparable from the interactive relations by which "matter acquires soul" in the spiritualization of human understanding.

The energy of the body at the micro-level is not uninfluenced by perceptions, actions, and feelings on the macro-level. There is a unity, a spiritual connectivity that unites through Spirit, a complete wholeness of body whose functional evolutions allow for the emergence of many different levels of organization, none of which is isolated from the "holomovements" that constitute the larger processes in cosmological activity.[6] From the smallest particle to the greatest complexity, there is a coherent unity whose attributes are communicated through the actual manifestations of discrete and particular beings. Further, the value of the individual, be it a particle, a cell, or human heart, of the part within the Whole, of the microlevel to the macro-level, is for the part to influence the development of the Whole in ways congruent with future manifestations and well-being. The process of becoming is co-developmental, co-evolutionary, a concatenation of mutual influences effecting but not determining the development of the Whole. The complexity of these relationships is not linear or static, nor is it a discrete hierarchy—while it has permanency and stability, it also has a capacity for sudden transformations or deformations whose consequences are, in part, shaped by individual intentionality. This intentionality is grounded in the shared presuppositions of collective thought and belief, in the macro-laws of intergenerational patterns, and in the deeper intentionalities of creative self-development.

To be "permeated with life fields" means to participate in the consequential processes of intentionality—not in just past human decisions, but in all past actions that have resulted in the arising of real beings (a one-celled alga or a Tyrannosaurus Rex). These intentionalities are intrinsic to Spirit but not easily formulated or easily understood, yet they are at the heart of the emergence of life in every life form. The multi-eon long process of becoming, and the consequences of that process, has shaped these intentionalities, enfolded them into Spirit, united them with other such becomings, and made them the deepest of all Mysteries. At the human level, intentionality is as difficult to grasp as an inherited predisposition that affects us genetically, emotionally, psychically, or noetically. Do we really understand the intentions of past human beings as they relate to our present circumstances? I think not—our knowledge of intentionality, at every level, is extremely rudimentary and undeveloped. And religious and philosophical thought has not clarified such intentionality but, often, only obscured and hidden it beneath a more collective tendency to codify and reduce the complexity to accessible and traditionalized intellectual conceptions. To be permeated with life fields means to be receptive to many underlying and hidden intentionalities of Spirit, the shaping intentions that create (and recreate) the world, the visionary intentions of spiritual evolution buried deep in soulful humanity, abiding in Spirit and not yet comprehended or actualized in all their key significances and potencies.

The "complex potential" at every level of organization is impacted by intentionalities and purposes intrinsic to a wholistic, interdimensional, co-evolutionary becoming. This is because increasing complexity encompasses more variety through a process of linking diverse manifestations at a deep psychic level of continuity and wholeness. As long as the center holds, we may envision this process as a diversification of potential united through an abundance of Spirit that maintains continuity and depth; but when we lose the center, fall into a quarrelsome relativism or materiality, then the center collapses and chaos isolates us from the greater wholeness into discrete and alienated subcommunities unable to form meaningful or enduring relationships. We then become unreceptive to a higher unity and vulnerable to dissension and species annihilation—where the part serves only its own interests at the expense of the whole, a process far advanced in the contemporary world. Subsequently we must choose, either we seek a greater spiritual maturity and actualize positive intentionality that preserves this world and all its fragile creatures, or we ignore this potential and choose only self-serving habit, isolation, and disconnected values. Such spiritual denial can only cripple us and make us no longer the worthy heirs of past or present spiritual wisdom and inspirations.

The "life fields" are everywhere and everywhere they are interactive. Regardless of how we think, regardless of our ideologies or mental predispositions, the actual circumstances of our present coexistence is highly interactive and infused with a multitude of spiritual horizons. Our failure to realize the potentials that beckon us is only an indication of the narrowness of our conceptions. We need only open ourselves to the immediate and real immensity that surrounds us, the many beautiful and profound spiritual presences that are seeking our attention, the many interactive influences that enliven and magnify the potency of ongoing creation. Within this "divine milieu," so immanently present, embodied soulful being is a vehicle for spiritual awakening—through the body, through feelings, imagination, thought and, particularly, through deep and soulful relationships with others. The complex potential is nonstatic, in process, seeking adequate embodiment in real beings whose hearts and minds are open and receptive to the spiritual influence that permeates the Whole and makes newness possible. The energy of interaction, of sharing, learning, and loving is the greatest basis for the development necessary to sustain the communal presence of Spirit. This is soul-making and unmaking, a visionary process of spiritual deepening, opening us to immensity—not dissolving the individual in the process, but only bringing the individual into focus for the fuller manifestation. It is the singing of the world in harmonic choir where each voice counts and the loss of even one impoverishes the fullness of the song.

The Earth itself, as a living entity, enhances life within, upon, and about it with its own higher potential; the same potential that animates the celestial bodies, planets, asteroids, and moons. (2.5)

Meditation: The interactive life fields are pervasive with regard to their mutual influences. They are not bound by simple physical (Newtonian) laws, but function through an order of magnitude far greater than physical influences. Thus "distance" and "time" are only relative boundaries—the psychic influence interacts through intentional structures of relatedness—similar thoughts, feelings, perceptions, and responses resonate psychically and collapse the lineal boundaries of space-time. Thus a poem or song written a thousand years ago resonates within us now, in the present moment, and stirs us to respond in similar (not necessarily identical) ways. Feeling and perception connect us over great distances, soul-related being touches our identity through harmonic vibrancy, through a sharing of awareness and motive, both far and near. Natural environments, our ecological homes, resonate with depths of feeling and experience from past events, the presence of which we are only rudimentarily conscious. The deep intentionality and emotion that imbues nature with all the resonance of past life-forms is pervasive; further, our own past life experience also imbues place with special qualities of relatedness. We interact with the life fields of all living beings not only in a complex temporal present, but also in a deep atemporal past, where the intensity of experience has imbued each place with psychic qualities and resonance. Learning to feel and appreciate this resonance is profoundly important—in some future time these harmonic traces will perhaps be purged and no longer accessible, but in the present they are still vibrant and still imbue the world with a multidimensional complexity whose history is inseparable from the evolving world-soul.

The Earth, as a "living entity," is neither simple nor rudimentary. It is only through the assimilation of our collective perceptions that we are able to evaluate the fullness of the interactive web of life forms and life fields that surrounds and nurtures life on this world wholistically. Significantly, the Gaia principle—Earth as a self-regulating, living organism—includes all life forms and all aspects of change and transformation in maintaining homeostasis in critical areas of species coexistence—the constancy of the saline contents of the oceans, a balanced mix of atmospheric gases, a survivable range of temperatures—all biologically related to human interaction and intentionality.[7] Human actions, even at the scale of the individual, affect the total homeostasis, the balance and integral functioning of the Whole. The emergence of the Gaia principle is a testimony to individual awareness awakening to the depths that have made life possible on this world, as something even more fundamental than biological or chemical processes. The spiritual aspects of this principle involve an increasing perception of the life quality that flows forth from the depths of Spirit to gift an entire world with all its diversity of forms, elements, and animate species. The diversification of this process, psychically linked to the emergence of each species, creates a multidimensional web of subtle relationships whose delicate balance requires an increasing sensitivity to part-whole interactions.

As a complex and emergent, global potential, this developing network of psychophysical relationships can be traced back to the relatively sudden emergence of planetary life in its simplest and least complex form—as simple cellular life in an amniotic sea of primal warmth and newness. There, Spirit abides in primal planetary manifestation, catalyzing sentience at the level of simple organic forms, built over eons from subtle harmonic intentions of pure energetic, astral involution and concentrations of plasmic energies to a multitude of planetary world-mantles. Such a potential, for a world-becoming involution, is an increasing inwardness of developing awarenesses arising through eons of expressive exploration and a multitude of visible forms. What emerges through the titanic processes of this creation are consequences often fragile, delicate, and of immense beauty and subtlety. This beauty, grace, and delicacy is itself a sign of the spiritual depths of the process. The part-whole relationship is never simply spatial, not simply a matter of extension, but an involution of layered processes, interlinked and temporally of great age and origin—even at the "very beginning" (or the "initial conditions"). As such, to speak of the Earth as a living entity is to recognize multiple life processes from the earliest formative prehuman period, through all the stages of evolutionary expression and expansion, to stratified life forms of varying degrees of complexity shaped over eons-long involutions of being and becoming. A process of layered complexities whose density and depths are Spirit born and Spirit bred, through the natural means of a dynamic planetary wholeness.

The "higher potential" of Earth, of Gaia, is the potential for all its many species to enter into fully self-aware, intraspecies, extraspecies, and transspecies communication. By intraspecies, I mean real communication between life forms, be it whales or eagles, ants or butterflies, dolphins or elephants, cellular life or micro-organisms—a communication between species facilitated by an intelligent, sensitive, spiritual reading of the life experiences of others. This interactive relationship between species is a direct and intentional causality pervading all past creation and becoming. If we are only now, after so many generations, relearning this simple fact, once known and experienced but later forgotten and denied, then it is because we have isolated ourselves from the wholeness, from primordial connectedness and coexistence with other species, environments, or ecologies. The "higher potential" lies just below the threshold of this denial and loss—once embraced and revered, once understood as inescapably part of ourselves, it may then emerge through greater sensitivity, respect, and appreciation for every life form and being. By extraspecies life, I refer to the many coexistent spiritual entities that share this world with us, including all the ancestral spirits that pervade and imbue so much of our planetary home. These mythological and religious dimensions of soulful being, of distinctive relationships with not only living members of species but with their archetypes and mythic manifestations, are also part of this collective world-identity. Be they ancestors, angels, animal guardians, beings from other worlds, elemental forms, spirit guides, thunder guardians or sundogs, disincarnate astral beings, archetypes or noetic thought-forms—they are all part of the emerging, collective potential, the *Mundus Imaginalis* within which humanity has created its many mythic homes. This extraspecies dimensionality will play an increasingly important role in future development and the repression of these forms, their denial or dismissal, can only lead to a pronounced imbalance and unhealthy fear in explorations of our own psychic capacities.

By "transspecies," I mean a potential that reflects the self-evolving awareness of Gaia herself—the earth-mother, the planetary mind, the world-soul, the noosphere. These are the higher archetypes of the *Mundus Imaginalis* that incorporate intra- and extraspecies forms into a unified, yet, distinctive whole reflective of the planetary home where the evolutes of a particular spiritual world-situated being first evolved.[8] Humanity is both a participant-creator and a participant-destroyer in this process. Human intention increasingly dominates the finer aspects of the process in callous exploitations, indifference to other species, and disregard for large-scale consequences. As a participant-creator, we must cultivate greater sensitivity for the consequences of actions that have pervasive effects on future generations. The emergence of the "trans-species" awareness is an awakening to true global consciousness, a direct participation in the world-soul as embodying all life forms and nurturing the life processes between all species as members of a single world, resonant with life experience, long past and present. This sacredness of earth, this psychic mantel that shields and protects us, embodies us in multilayered complexity and harbors us within the dynamic processes of continuous planetary involution. Such involution is not unique to Earth, but lies as a potential inherent to every planetary world, moon, asteroid, comet, or brightening star. The astral form of that embodiment lies in the sun as a higher involution of potent energies and light, manifesting in this fashion, Spirit in a more radiant, celestial form, beyond which there are yet many more subtle energetic manifestations, of the most concentrated and complex sort.

At every level of organization, life has awareness; in every ecological niche, it is shaped and informed by the totality of interactions, a complex net of spiritual and bio-energetic attractions and repulsions. (2.6)

Meditation: To understand this, it is necessary to drop, completely, the inherited dualisms of past metaphysics and to embrace a unified, process view that recognizes the tensions within the process but does not endow those tensions with autonomy or division isolated from the many other influences that support their integration. Human development has been shaped by its cultural ecologies, by a variety of historic-cultural niches, from which it has spread into contact with other often incompatible ecologies. At the boundaries where these ecologies meet, new forms have emerged, first resisting, then synthesizing the diversity or reaching out to new visions that integrate and then surpass the older forms of social and cultural adaptation. This also happens in the temporal histories of those ecologies—cultures, like environmental ecologies, are not static, they are in process, constantly influenced by past and present events impinging with sometimes rapid and sudden changes. Buddhists of India come to China and reshape Chinese culture while the Chinese reshape Buddhism and then, taking it to Japan, reshape Japanese culture. Communism reshapes Russia, the Greek Orthodox Church reshapes Greek culture, a Greek culture that had already impacted Rome and Europe and was itself impacted by Minoan and Egyptian cultural practices. The pattern of influences spirals back into the most distant past and out into the farthest and most remote areas, so that Inuit art influences Parisian aesthetics, carvings from tropical islands become models for architectural forms, and herbal lore from South American jungles become paradigms for pharmacological research in modern chemistry. There is no dualism here, only a complex overlay of influences and interactions that shape and reshape perceptions, values, and worldviews.

The "awareness" that is life is everywhere, and everywhere, it is shaped by a multitude of interactions and processes, including psychic influences that endow the world with many diverse characteristics. The "totality of interactions" includes all sentient beings that inhabit a particular niche, a particular cultural or historical place, layered over time by all the many preceding inhabitants. Ascetics have denied the beauty of body and nature, even of the culture and creations that have ultimately supported them in those denials. Such denial is a truncation of the rich inheritance and the multilayered fullness of the natural world and its embodiment in vast complexities of form. The materialist perspective that sees only "dead matter" also truncates this process and denies the perceptions of those who feel and sense directly the living qualities of place and the mineral, vegetable, and animal forms that dwell there enriching it with a coexistent, subtle sentience. The spiritual paradigm for the emergent Whole, is to embrace all forms as manifesting differentiated aspects of sentience without drawing a dualistic line between what is and what is not, sentient. All is sentient—sometimes subtle and unobvious and sometimes hidden in the magic of its beauty and potency. A crystal, a stone from the North Sea, a vein of ore, or a deposit of uranium—all have sentience in the deep earth sense, just as the molten core has a living vitality and power. The awareness is nonhuman, nonanthropomorphic, nonimitative. It is original, ancient, subtle, pervasive; it is within us and we eat and breathe it but often fail to honor it and recognize it for what it is: our life source, necessary, intrinsic.

To be "shaped and informed" means that any particular being is in process and shaped by a multitude of inner and outer influences that inevitably produce diverse and unique consequences. There are self-constraining influences intrinsic to the organism just as there are also constraining influences within the ecological niche—organically, culturally, or globally. But simultaneously, there are self-liberating tendencies that tend toward new forms of expression and creative diversity. The complexity filters down to such a fine degree that even the slightest influence may produce a radically different consequence. This appears only "chaotic" when we stand far off; up close, it is simply the mesh of influences shaped by a variety of intentions. Awareness is inseparable from intention, even if the intention is to be passive and acted upon rather than acting on. As such, these vectors of intentionality are the multitude of influences impacting each and every life form. Each intention requires some slight adjustment, some inner adaptation, some sense of balance within the whole that maintains continuity and sustains connectedness, however small or vast the Whole may seem. These influences are internal as well as external, indeed such a distinction as "external and internal" is largely fictive. It is the creation of a limited perception that does not recognize the multilayered character of psychic life. Influences are immersed in a reciprocal process of constantly sharing and shaping intentions "all the way down." Intentions do not arise in isolation from process, even as a consequence of long-term isolation, reflection, or solitude. In the deepest sense, they are co-created even when we mull them over, digest them and sometimes wait years to understand or enact them. Intentionality is not always immediate or simply a function of stimulus and response—often intentions are internal processes requiring long periods of incubation and inner development before they can be actualized. And this is the heart of the spiritual process—to cultivate deep intentionality, a purposeful attitude of caring, a determination to work for the well-being of others, to attain wisdom or maturity in the fullest sense through a cultivation of positive influences and self-directed, intentional goals.

This shaping of intention involves spiritual and bio-energetic "attractions and repulsions" in a nondualistic process of gradual experimentation, insight, and exposure to a variety of interactive influences. Sometimes we simply plunge in and then, see what happens! Other times we are more cautious and work our way forward with careful investigation and respect for the needs, hopes, dreams, and aspirations of others. Inevitably, attraction and repulsion effect us as they do every living being of our complex world. Asceticism, for example, has the energy of a tremendous repulsion, whereas romantic love has the force of a powerful attraction. In the rounds of life and death, the wheel is turned by these attractions and repulsions—they may be chemical, biological, energetic, emotional, aesthetic, intellectual, imaginative, mythic, or mystical—but in every case, they act to influence intentions. Mastery of these interactions is a matter of having a center that is deeply stable and yet "open at the edges" or receptive to new influences, directions, ideas, feelings, or perceptions and not locked into habitual patterns of closure and denial. We then take in that influence, allow it to incubate, so that at the appropriate time, it can be enacted as an expression of spiritual well-being. Such expression may reform the center and expand receptivity without losing character or distinctiveness, sharpening the uniqueness and giving it an edge with a diamond sparkle—cutting through lesser habits and resulting in new insights and illuminations.

To be aware, to live, is to participate in the interactions, however remote or distant or infinitesimal; when an atom ceases to exist, it affects the total configuration, it changes the quantum totality. (2.7)

Meditation: Effects of actions are far-reaching, as are the effects of nonactions: sitting quietly in a room can have an effect at a distance, just as raging silently in your own mind can also have subtle effects. This is because psychic effects are not bound by Newtonian laws in Cartesian space-time. This is why the equation "psyche = energy" is misleading; the psyche, our soulful being, is not simply a Newtonian energy field, but a far more complex entity that is multilayered and capable of manifestations, through Spirit, that are far-reaching and atemporal. Psychic effects do not simply spread out in space; such a Newtonian picture is a quite inadequate representation. Psychic effects (or affects) correspond across external space and time with a multitude of inner psychic configurations, wherever or whenever clear and potent intentions arise. There is a simultaneity throughout the world soul; this is why, for example, similar inventions are discovered during similar periods by different persons. They configure a psychic insight that is not bound by external space-time relations and this happens in a multitude of places, often very rapidly until, the insight is disseminated throughout the collective, even on an "unconscious level."[9] But such effects can disseminate over temporal bounds as well, such that an ancient artifact becomes a source for recovering past experience, for example as a psychokinetic influence that resonates with the object and that can be envisioned by a psychically sensitive person in a completely different space-time location. This is because there is psychic sensitivity and correspondence, a capacity to relate to the immediacy of the psychic event, whenever or wherever it occurred.

To "participate in the interaction" means to open oneself to possibilities of psychic perception of a far-reaching and expansive sort and not to be satisfied with simply precognitive intuition. Such intuitions are completely natural and happen constantly—there is a stream of cognitive, psychic connection to a vast array of persons, places, and events that each of us is able to perceive soulfully. Resistance in the gross sense is simply denying the possibility and closing the mind to anything but immediate, self-generated contents; in the subtle sense, resistance is being self-preoccupied and distracted, undisciplined and mentally closed or unclear. But when the mind and feelings are brought into quiet harmony, when the impressions of soulful being are allowed to arise without prejudice or denial, and when discrimination is developed—then it becomes quite obvious that we are receiving latent psychic impression constantly from the world around us. These impressions originate not only in the immediate environment but from far-off friends, family, loved-ones, and others whom we may connect with (in the future) or who may be attempting to reach out and contact us, even for the first time. These interactions are constantly ongoing and rich with communication and feeling from multiple sources, including the plants, animals, elements, and from the mythical, collective stratum of shared species, intraspecies coexistence. The precognitive quality, that is, impressions from the future are not uncommon—unbound by local space-time, psychic impressions flow both "forward and backwards" to leave their impress for later or current perceptions.[10]

This is all possible because we live in the midst of wholeness, we are constantly interacting through part-whole relationships that are dynamically charged with impressions, influences, and intentions. Such influences flow out into the world and create dense centers within being that continually infolds and conceals within and about us, the potential for spiritual awakening. We do not create, in the direct sense, these spiritual impressions or intentions, but we do embody (or attract) them in creative ways and in unique perspectives that can lead, indirectly, to the arising of newness and novelty. The functions of Spirit in this process are communicated through these intentions and act to inspire greater wholeness and completion while leading us, individually and communally, toward the actualization of higher capacities in awarenesses. To be aware, means, in the higher sense, to be aware of all life, all beings, all becomings, however gross or subtle and to know directly the inner coherence and unity of that all-becoming and being. Being open at the boundaries means being receptive to the influences of the Whole and all its parts, it means embodying a perspective that is interactive with others in a deep sense—a meeting of soul, a genuine love, friendship, warmth, and generosity of Spirit. It means being influenced by others, being receptive to alternative ideas, feelings, experiences, spiritual encounters, and impressions. It means there is giving and receiving, sharing and communion—on subtle levels of species communication unbound by external ideas of space or time.

When an "atom ceases to exist" it changes state, it reconfigures, dissolves and adds its energy, particles, electromagnetism to other configurations and condensations. It is neither scattered nor lost but absorbed, redirected, transformed. Just so, our own experience has a quantum effect—it functions to enhance or detract from transformative processes within the world-soul, our own expansions and contractions being part of the collective development. A child's smile impacts just as a mother's tear, they add the smallest effect to infinitesimal influences that, over time shape world intentions. If a enough children cry from starvation world intentions can be aroused, just as the pains of abuse arouse the intentions for the correction of the abuser. This is a matter of perception—we must learn to see the world clearly, in all honesty, with compassion for all the errors and bad judgments and false appearances. We must open ourselves to the healing presence of the Spirit and allow the guidance and integration of the Whole to act on us for purposes of healing and self-realization of our most positive capacities. This happens on a very minute level, in making decisions that are more humane, more caring, more connected with the wholeness that unites, not in service of the selfishness that divides. Every decision counts, adds its quantum to the process and thereby shapes intentions. The deep spiritual intentions are to unfold beauty and fullness in the world for the benefit of others, not for the few, but the many. This requires us to monitor and be aware of how our everyday thoughts contribute to the spiritual processes of an inspired becoming.

The "change in the quantum totality" refers to the consequences of individual choice as much as it does collective decisions—on the micro-level, these effects are happening all the time and they range into the far past and future. Our sensitivity to these influences, our spiritual preparedness, requires us to cultivate a micro-awareness of how small is beautiful, of how an individual may act to create harmony and coherence on a collective scale through individual initiative. The quantitative effect springs from the qualitative act and that act arises from the deep intentionality that we cultivate to live genuine spiritual lives. This is a matter of principles, not simply forms or social conventions. We must enact the principles, embody them and manifest them as conduits for the full realization of deep spiritual potentials. And this process is Spirit-guided, from the very beginning, from before earth was even coagulated out of stellar dust. Often we think in terms of large-scale effects, but in a sincere spiritual life it is the small decision enacted with integrity and carried through to completion that makes the strongest effect, an effect that shapes future intentions. Spiritual life is built out of links between acts of integrity infused with love and understanding. In the pain of seeking a better way to build and be more complete we learn to open ourselves to Spirit to find the inspiration that contributes, step by step, to a more complete and actualized world of spiritual beings.

The effects of this process are far-reaching and cannot be seen in immediate consequences.

If we reverence life, we must also reverence its capacity for awareness, even of a stone or grain of sand; how much more so the immense complexity of a multitude of living beings! (2.8)

Meditation: At the heart of life and awareness is reverence—this is the most basic of all intentional attitudes, to revere and nurture in ourselves, and in others, a deep appreciation of the Whole. This does not have to be a task that embraces the world, but only an embracing, reverent attitude, a small effect that spreads out and communicates through others' lives, even in a small circle of spiritual friends. One who chooses to meditate alone or live a solitary life dedicated to this transformation also contributes to the well-being of the Whole, adds the stability of his or her experience to the qualitative development. While advanced practitioners may journey far and wide within many spiritual horizons, an act of love for a child also contributes to the spiritual development of the Whole—just as an act of unkindness pulls against that development. These intentions are in contestation, and when they are in contestation within us, we are far less effective and able to assist the transformations within others. But when these intentions become unified within us, spiritually directed to positive, healing, and transformative ends, then our words, actions, or feelings can truly counter the disruptive effects of warring intentions in others. Awareness is not simply passive, but highly interactive—this is a crucial point. Because we are fundamentally beings-in-relation, interactively influenced and influencing, our intentions should be guided by peaceful, creative, nonviolent, spiritual attitudes whose actualizations create an increasingly interactive world. We are enriched by sharing, by working together to create community and world harmony that values individual worth and uniqueness. Reverence in this sense means to revere the worth and value of the other and to revere the potency of the Spirit in drawing us together, each in our own unique way.

To reverence "life" means to reverence it in all forms, with respect and when necessary, caution—a rattlesnake is a remarkable, powerful creature, but this does not stop it from striking if it is startled or frightened or in an aggressive mood! Further, we should be deeply cautious in attempting to alter, disrupt, or imitate natural life processes whose biohistory is profoundly complex and far from comprehended. Reverence for life means caution in making decisions that affect life processes—birth control, abortion, euthanasia, genetic experimentation, cloning, population control, industrial effects on world ecology, pollution, weather control, animal farming and experimentation, the problem of sterilization and sterility—all these challenges require a deep reverence and respect for spiritual values in order to be resolved intentionally for long-term positive effects. Respect for natural process is deeply important, but the arising of human will and intelligence and the capacity to alter or transform nature is itself a "natural process." This means we must build on the wisdom that wishes to preserve and respect the ancient ways of relating to nature—with reverence, caution, care, an ethic of nonviolence and nonintrusion and a high intentionality for preservation and wholeness, for working with natural processes in a slower but less destructive, more self-disciplined manner.

Life is volatile, diverse, filled with aggressive impulses and destructive tendencies—particularly when reared in an atmosphere of coercion or insensitivity. The sublimation of those impulses requires an atmosphere of respect and appreciation for strength and capacity that is channeled toward creative, nonviolent ends. This is a spiritual goal, it means that those involved in the process must themselves be so channeled, must embody the intentional direction toward which the process moves. This includes our awareness of "the stone or grain of sand." The spiritual qualities of life are pervasive, they do not simply reside within us, but they imbue the world-cosmos with fullness and diversity. Reverence in this sense means deep appreciation and thankfulness for everything that is, stone and sea and sky—for all the many beings that inhabit heaven and earth. This includes the sand and the lion, the pearl and the oyster, the rose and its thorns, the beetle and its dung-ball. The spiritual secret lies in finding the correspondences between beings, how they play their role in maintaining the complexity of the web and the fullness of the Spirit. This means finding all the ways that we, as individuals, communities, and as a species, also play our positive and creative role in contributing to the greater Whole.

It is crucial that we learn to see our lives in relationship to other species, and not just in how those other species may serve our appetites or needs. Every species has value in its own terms, from its own perspectives, as a consequence of its own history and becoming. And this is a mutual becoming, our becoming and the becoming of whales, dolphins, sea-snakes, insects, microorganisms and all the flora and fauna of the fields and forests. Our reverence must include all this becoming and not just an abstract idea about its inherent unity or wholeness. It means cultivating reverence for all that is and was and shall be, both in the immediate, sensory sense and in the higher, spiritual sense. This reverence includes all forms, all psychic and spiritual beings, all manifestations that embody the processes of becoming. Those processes are part of us and we are part of them and together there is only the fullness of being holding us within its unitary unfolding. To appreciate and actualize that fullness means to revere, from deep in our hearts, the processes as all-inclusive and all-uniting, without losing the differences, the value of uniqueness or individual achievements.

The complexity of this wholeness exceeds our grasp and at the level of individual coexistence, it means simply holding a reverent attitude toward all life forms we encounter. In the most basic sense, it means controlling the impulse toward violence and finding nonviolent means for reverent interactions. In a higher sense, it means learning from other species, observing and studying them and appreciating their species wisdom, their often superior abilities and capacities. In a yet higher sense, it means understanding that they are manifestations of Spirit, also Spirit-born and Spirit-imbued, and as such, that they are worthy heirs within our planetary home whose future becoming is inseparable from our own. As we respect and revere them, so we too survive, endure, and flourish with all the richness of co-species integration and mutual learning and adaptation. This is spiritual awareness born our of reverence for all Life process and best enacted through intraspecies caring, love, and mutual co-evolutionary understanding.

The Third Principle

The Third Principle of Spirit is understanding: this means being able to sense, feel, intuit, and empathize with every living thing; analysis and reason without understanding is both dangerous and destructive. (3.1)

Meditation: To "understand" does not mean to strictly analyze or dissect, nor does it mean the creation of rational arguments, or a chain of rationally linked ideas in a distinctive "analytic" way. From the perspective of spiritual principles, understanding does not refer to a particular type of reasoning, or does it refer to a specific cognitive ability, or even to a particularly patterned way of thinking. Understanding is akin to "wisdom" and refers to an inner capacity to bring the full weight of personal experience and reflection into any situation, resulting in insights based on that accumulated experience. Understanding evolves through a richness of encounters and events whose informative structures result in a process of maturation. A "mature understanding" reflects the ability to draw on depths of experience that have shaped perceptions and actions in a long process of positive growth and development. It is not a matter of "information" nor "data" nor "encyclopedic" knowledge—these are simply the resources that we use in developing an integrated vision of the Whole through our cumulative experience. Understanding springs from the depth and allows us to see with ever greater clarity the relationship of the part to the Whole. A person who understands love, sees clearly the relationship between their own personal experiences and the particular experiences or perspectives of others. Understanding in this sense is "rich in perspectives" because it is not isolated to the experience of the subject, but is *interrelational* and deeply aware of how experience is transformed through social and personal processes of interaction and soulful encounter.

This relational aspect of understanding is primary, however abstract the subject—as in mathematics or chemistry—because understanding refers to the relationship between experiencing subjects who share their knowledge. By sharing, we arrive at understanding that exceeds the "data" that makes up the subjective contents. If I understand something about the physical nature of experience, it is because I have reflected upon my experience through relationships to the experiences of others. This reflection is grounded in a deep sense of connection to those others and to the whole of my life. The sum total of experiences and relationships, including all the books I have read and all the conversations and encounters I have had, result in insights that help to illuminate the full complexity of the world. Understanding in specialized fields of study is the same—it develops through relationships to others who hold similar interests and experience, regardless of how narrow or specialized the focus. The creative aspect of understanding is the individual contribution, the individual synthesis that draws meaningfully on the resources of experience, self-reflection, history, and culture to formulate a particular insight. Understanding may embrace and illuminate an entire context, not simply a facet of the context, but it may do this through using facets to explain the whole. This can refer to understanding a poem, a mathematical formula, a prayer or an act of contrition—in all cases, the parts are best explicated in relationship to the whole. To understand "poetry" means to have a great deal of experience with writing it, reading it, reflecting on it, creatively engaging it and hearing it, absorbing, sifting the thoughts and reflections of authors and readers alike. The more truncated the experience, the less potential for understanding—the richer the experience, the greater the potential for understanding.

Thus "spiritual understanding" emerges from a richness of experience within and through Spirit—by studying, encountering, learning, and undergoing the transformative processes of maturation in a density of relationships that informs the fullness of our potential. This cannot be accomplished through a strictly cognitive approach, through a purely rational attitude, or a narrow empiricism that allows only the immediate and the obvious to be the permissible contents of experience. The danger of rationality lies in the tendency to devalue other forms of experience and perception, envisioning an abstract intellectual power as a superior mode of knowing. I regard this as a limited, reductive, and misleading perspective. Spirituality is about the hidden depths of life, its fullness in every aspect of living (and not just thinking!). It refers to the depths in feeling, in aesthetic and symbolic perceptions, in physical transformations, imaginative development, in mythic engagement, sexual love, intuitive clarity, art, song, and empathic relationships. The primordial condition for spiritual understanding is the capacity to sense and feel the experience of others within oneself. The degree to which this capacity is attenuated or underdeveloped (or inhibited by intellectualism), marks a fundamental limitation of spiritual insight and understanding. Conversely, an overempathic sense that allows for no personal center, no strong sense of individual identity, that results in a loss-of-self-in-the-other, is also a limitation on understanding because it lacks the creative aspect, the creative difference that leads to clear insights based on respectful autonomy. Understanding involves the creative relationship between the whole of my experience and the whole of your experience—through shared integrity, it illumines a fuller range of the part-whole context.

This does not refer to only other human beings, but to each and every being we encounter. We learn by opening ourselves to the experiences, motivations, thoughts, feelings, perceptions, and actions of each "other" we meet. This may be a human being or it may be a land animal, a sea-creature, a bird, a plant, a tree, or mountain, or a mythic creature, or an angelic revelation.[11] In the spiritual sense, it is whatever and whomever we encounter, whatever creature may arouse or enhance our awareness—as well as challenge us, threaten us, even at times, overwhelm us. This requires genuine maturity, for the further and deeper one goes into the fullness of what IS, the more likely we are to encounter strange, powerful, and at times, dangerous "others." Therefore, caution and stability, having a center and holding it, are crucial qualities in the emerging transformation. If reason and analysis are too one-sided and too often lacking in empathy, an undiscriminating empathic embrace of every and any manifestation can also be dangerous and one-sided. Understanding involves balance and seeing the part-within-the-whole as well as the whole-within-the-part. It does not mean losing one within the other, but maintaining the relationship, the distinctiveness, the creative tensions, the interactive autonomy, and the many qualities that make incarnate life a constant source of continual emergence and becoming. It also means being Spirit-guided, opening to the flow and creative activity of spiritual transformations that emerge continually between all beings. This openness, this grounding in the spiritual process of becoming, is the deepest and most profound source of understanding; such openness is the connective medium of presence and creative regard of the most positive and healing kind.

Strange that we should lose the primordial sense of the other, the immediate impression of life, the direct knowledge unobscured by any "values or lessons," the participation in the Whole. (3.2)

Meditation: Not only is it strange, but deeply tragic as increasing alienation leads to desensitization, abstraction, and a common loss of feeling for the value and importance of others within one's own life. A life infused with Spirit sees clearly and directly the intimate, shared context, the planetwide formative, cosmological bonds that make us human in the fullest sense. This is foundational—as Spirit permeates and unites all of us in the creative activities of becoming and in the emergence of intentionalities of diverse living beings, so too must we, as spiritually informed intentional beings, seek to actualize that creative sense of relationship with all whom we encounter. The "primordial sense of the other" is not found in utilitarian or pragmatic relationships, the "primordial sense" is best characterized by feelings of love, a willingness to work for the betterment of others as a betterment of self, to understand through experience and encounter that the contribution of self and other is the capacity to enhance and add to mutual experience. This occurs because we do not demand subservience or the surrender of others to our own norms and values. We share, we learn, we understand together, but we do not command or enforce or threaten—to do so means to lose the shared experience and to deny the worth of the other. This is an expansive, Hermetic circle of reciprocities working through others and through us to create a more self-aware collective transformation.

Even more importantly, as we gain, over years of engaged, committed effort, the attainment of mature understanding, the spontaneity of the Whole comes more fully into view, beyond simple pragmatic "values and lessons." It is not a matter of cultivating human relationships for specific, tangible, pragmatic consequences— such a motivation turns human beings into dehumanized actors whose parts are only meaningful in relationship to my own. This is not the spiritual process, but a shallow utilitarian motive that seeks the subordination of the individual to pragmatic, immediate needs. The spontaneity of the whole is a marvelous action of great beauty and allows others to enter our lives with the impress of their perspectives or presence as a lasting impact. This impact has often little to do with conscious intention or purpose and far more to do with spiritual affinities and subtle relationships that may never be fully articulated but that, nevertheless, leave a lasting influence, a new direction, or an arousing of hidden intentions or latent potential. These potentials spring from a level that is often below the threshold of normal awareness, and yet they can manifest with great intensity IF the individual is open and receptive to those manifestations. In such a state, it is a sheer joy to meet and know others, however briefly, because it opens the doors between worlds and reveals contours of Spirit in the many manifestations through which our becoming is embodied in the life of others. Such is the primordial condition—to know ourself through others even as they know self through us.

This direct, interactive knowledge is unveiled through experience and is always in process and undergoing constant subtilization in proportion to the degree of openness we cultivate in our lives with others, without losing our own sense of center and integrity within Spirit. In the higher sense, such "knowledge" is a form of spiritual gnosis—a direct insight into processes at the heart of life. Such knowledge reveals how Spirit imbues all of us with potential and how that potential is manifested in relationship to others and how others become a means for its successful evocations. And, as always, these others may not be only human beings. They may be any other, any manifestation that evokes a sense of potential that calls out of us a hidden capacity, even for a brief moment, showing us what we might be capable of truly becoming. What enhances our capacity for this knowledge is "being open at the boundaries" and not living according to simple habits and customs, but moving through life with diligence to attain the fullness not yet realized. To open our hearts to the creative process at the Heart of the World, that most ancient process of moving through and beyond our immediate limitations and into the luminosities of Spirit that shine continually through us. Thus, it is very important to visualize our relationships with others as primary sources for spiritual awakening and to realize that this is a two-way process—we must give in order to receive—and of the two, the giving is of deeper importance.

Why is such giving important? Because the kind of giving I refer to is not a self-diminishment, not a "giving away of self," but a mutual sharing whose roots are deepened and whose flowering is enhanced by the exchange. And the fruit of this process is sweet! It is healthy and ripe and lustrous because there is cross-pollenization, an exchange and new growth. There is no diminishment because it is a free giving, an open, nongrasping giving, balanced with a receptivity, a listening and a taking-in that is transformative. This is the primordial sense of the other—my brother, my sister, my elder, my child, my beloved—the greater kinship that obligates us to listen and hear well and to speak worthy thoughts for the good of the generations, not to just mumble along, caught in our own thoughts, unable to connect to the spiritual kinship of human community. The primordial sense of the other is an inspiration, the way the other acts upon us to liberate our own pain, fear, suffering, and struggle; the way the other becomes a source of healing and transformation. Too often we dwell on the other as antagonist, as oppressor, wounder, smotherer, as a demanding other whose own diminishment is far advanced and who tries to draw others into their own contracting loss and alienation. This loss of the primordial sense of relatedness results from a fearful drawing back and then an aggressive tendency to see nothing beyond the narrow, negative boundaries. The layered sense of isolation is also built slowly, a contraction overwhelmed by unintegrated experience unable to create a relational center. This is why love is a primary spiritual quality; it liberates us from these contractions and heals when we embrace others in the deep primordial sense. Let us only live within the trusting bonds of a spiritual kinship and we will heal the wounds and pain through the gifts of Spirit who constantly draws us toward just that rebirth, just such becoming.

We came out of wholeness, found ourselves, walked upright, and lost our innocence; the

**ancient primordial sense of wonder perished
with every step we took toward dominion and
supremacy. (3.3)**

Meditation: It is deeply important to understand that we have
always been part of the Wholeness, as we are even now. We are not
evolving toward Wholeness, but we are evolving *within* Wholeness—
within a process that has always been, primordially, Whole and in
process, always drawing out of potential an emergence that realizes
more fully the hidden possibilities. Our relationships with others are
already embedded within a context of spiritual fullness and unity.
We need only awaken to this primordial condition that sustains the
involution and soulful being that constitutes our present becoming.
This unity does not require of us a rejection of the world, or a denial
of the body, or a disdain for the elaborations of processes that so
many have become mired in to their own confusion and detriment.
The world-becoming of this place, and these species, is a natural and
holy process of spiritual transformation seeking to maximize the
possibilities of being human. Spirit is an omnipresence whose influence is pervasive in holding us within the boundaries that make life
possible while simultaneously seeking to lead us into greater realizations beyond often self-imposed limits. The initial condition is a
sense of wonder and immersion in the totality of all-becoming, a
deep entwinement that made it once inconceivable that we were *not*
inseparably part of the world that surrounded us. In our innocence,
we saw clearly a world filled with powers and presences, visible and
invisible, all contesting for our attention and intimately linked to
our survival and well-being.[12]

The guiding vision of a vast proportion of our collective, tribal,
kin-related lives has been our dependence on everything living that
surrounded us, surpassed us, and challenged us to become more. We
came on to the savannas, out of the trees and brush, out into the
world and tried to find our way in relationship to all the living creatures that seemed so superior to our own relatively limited abilities.
The "ancient primordial sense" was one of wonder and awe, one of
sensuous immersion and inseparable containment within a community itself contained by the immediate, awesome creatures of the
world we shared. The fragile process of emergence brought us also
into conflict with other members of our own species, and more preda-

tory tendencies, as we learned to master new technologies—the bow, the chariot, metal working, taming the horse, hunting lions—tendencies for a while balanced against the more enduring foundations of agriculture and the "arts of civilization." Thus we discovered language, writing, animal husbandry, tamed the wild seeds, grew sweet melons, dates, oranges, made bread, discovered pottery, weaving, glass making, jewelry, the care of the dead, and the worship of many gods and goddesses. And for many long eons we lived immersed in this god-filled, goddess-inspired, animate world of multiple beings and becomings. In this sense, the spiritual life became the life of the community, the inherited wisdom of the elders, the customary practices and shared beliefs, the fullness of a complex cultural tradition, itself undergoing constant change and developments.[13]

But increasingly, our uprightness came to epitomize an aggressive male stance, a desire for kingship, lordship, rule, and dominion—all the marks of a species whose spiritual laws became didactic and dictatorial, one-sided and dogmatic, subordinating all other species to a self-projected greatness as an adolescent act of egoism and imagined superiority. This domination extended to women and children as well, led to the enslavement of "enemies" or "primitives" and to the grotesque histories of torture, foot-binding, clitoridectomy, the chopping, cutting, hacking, and burning of bodies in the name of a superior political or religious claim. Horrible! This history is the history of our collective fall from grace, from the once unified world of shared reverence for the natural forces and presences of others whose world we co-inhabited, honored, and then slowly forgot, denied, and dismissed. Having lost our innocence in the persecution of others, in the denial of their free, intrinsic humanity, in a arrogant and ignorant dismissal of their rights and freedom, we came also to regard all other species as servants to our own growing hubris— to control, conquer, and dominate not just all other species, but the very planet and its many co-related processes. This history of dominance and abuse, of suppression and aggressive control of the many by the few, of males over females and children, is a history of the destruction of human understanding. It is a history of substitution by coercive, militant laws and rigid codes of social stratification, formal obligation and the ever-present threat of reprisal by those who epitomize the inheritance of an increasingly alienated and detached humanity.[14]

This loss of empathy and co-relatedness, of connection and communion with others not the same, with other species and beings of many kinds, is further enhanced by the arising of intellectual currents whose premises are grounded only in the observable and the immediate. The rationalized perception is yet one more upright step toward dominion, a loss of feeling and imagination, and their substitution by amoral laws formulated by observers no longer aware of their own sensuous co-relations to other beings. Thus we hear how "animals have no real feelings or intelligence" and "bodies are machines" and "minds are nothing other than cognitive computations"—all the marks of a one-sided loss of feeling, empathy, co-related becoming whose goals still remain obscure, self-serving, and solipsistic.[15] But we are not isolated by mind, nor are we dependent only on immediate thought; we are not machines, nor are other species subordinate to our own presupposed accomplishments. The return to deep spirituality is an awakening to the co-relational processes of becoming, the shaping of intentionality through relationships to all other beings inhabiting a single, fragile, balanced world of interdependent relationships. The survival of other species is tied to our own survival, and peace between human beings is a foundational premise for all future coexistence. The harboring of resources, the care of the earth and all who inhabit it, the full use and development of our faculties, are the necessary conditions for new emergence. Rather than walking proudly upright, we must sit down and talk, share and open our hearts to the necessity of mutual development in a world trembling with overpopulation, excess, irrational outbursts, and unpredictable, unhealthy acts of sporadic violence and confusion.

The return to a world of spiritual health is no easy matter. The "progress" toward dominion has advanced far into the human psyche and blinded and deafened many who have become victims in the process. This blindness and impaired hearing must be healed in order to restore balance and find the center from which Spirit radiates forth the potential for new birth and awakening to more mature responsibilities. The formation of diverse communities in this process is deeply important. The spiritual communities of the future will be, I believe, a primary source of renewal, however overwhelmed by the larger cultural imperium they may seem at the time. These integrated communities are foundations for a reconstitution of human experience no longer tied to an ethics of dominion or to class advantage. Moving away from hierarchy in the strict sense, the reformulation blends creativity with deep respect for all life and life process in the most organic and immediate sense. Such communities will deeply value the recovery of all past wisdom, the "primordial sense of the other," and the deep unities of Spirit in the processes of continual creation. Their ethics will be nonviolent and psychically developed to correspond with higher degrees of knowing, seeing, and being. In this process, we can set aside the turbulent history and begin again, in new communities dedicated to a reverence for all beings without recreating the shadows of dogmatism or rigidly codified beliefs. Spirit-led, such communities will find that love is the greater teacher and wisdom the most alluring guide—in Spirit I greet you, all of you who join together to recreate the world in new patterns of wholeness, humility, and patient endurance.[16]

Coexistence changed to conquest and participation to subordination; our fears and shadows gave us imagery, and every image, an artifact; every artifact, a creation, a contraction, a warning. (3.4)

Meditation: The lessons of history are not to be ignored or abandoned as either too hard or too distant—they are an indelible feature of what we are, not simply what we have been or might be. Taking responsibility for the emergence of newness, for spiritual maturity and creative sensibility also means seeing clearly the past and learning from it. Consider the primordial condition—all past events are Spirit-laden, reflecting the human attempt to embody a spiritual truth even in its most diminished forms. And the embodiment becomes so easily static and interpreted in rigid and resistant ways, leaving no room for an initial, emergent insight. And always, in the name of preserving "tradition," we hear about the greatness of the past. There are remarkable examples of past spiritual accomplishments that should be revered, remembered, and taken as models for future understanding. But the past was not "golden"—in every age, no matter how great the example of spiritual attainment may be—I see it in a context of the social inequalities, distortions, oppressions, and bias of immature humanity. And these biases often saturate a spiritual tradition—the denial of the world, the suppression of the body, an incapacity to celebrate the joys of creation, the subordination of women, the denial of sexuality or marriage, the dismissal of other religious and spiritual traditions—all this can be found in most traditions. Unfortunately, at the heart of most religious traditions is a deep conservative tendency that wishes to see its own view as superior to the views of others. In turn, this leads to an often destructive competitiveness, and when linked to secular political power, to the death and persecution of the unbelieving other.

Spiritual conquest is part of human history—missionization (Buddhism, Christianity, Islam) has inevitably proceeded through a process of denial of the worth and traditions of others, some more benign and some less so. The urge to subordinate, primarily an archaic male tendency, reveals itself clearly in the relationship between spiritual traditions. And often within traditions, they subdivide and form various schools whose adherents become aggressive proponents of their own interpretations. Some traditions (like Rabbinic Judaism and Tibetan Buddhism) have wisely incorporated this tendency within the normative processes of training adherents to argue well and successfully, the basic tenets of their faith. But all too often, such training promotes an aggressive attitude embedded in dedication to one tradition that fails to see the value and relevance of another. Whole cultural movements have been promoted by religious beliefs— the conquests of Islam, the Christian Crusades, the Mongol domination of China, the conversion of American Indians—all promoted in the name of a superior visionary world. Further, these visionary worlds were extrapolated to include the persecution, enslavement, and punishment of the nonbelieving other even beyond the grave in the name of that so-called universal truth. Heresy becomes a weapon of the most fearful sort in the hands of men dedicated to conquest in the name of their fearful and destructive communities of faith—and this continues even to this day! These are the shadows of the past that need to be seen and understood, the tendencies to be reflected upon as indications of how human beings choose to enact their visionary worlds.

These are not mature reactions. They are often based in rigid, unresponsive, aggressive tendencies that hold personal belief to be superior to the rights and freedom of others. These tendencies then become symbolized by all the cultural trappings of class distinction, education, social identity, and all the artifacts of social coexistence, thus creating an embodiment of tradition in visible forms that reinforce collective thinking and prejudice. Thinking as others think becomes a way of life that justifies prejudice of every sort, embodied as it is in the social symbolisms of personal, everyday life. The binding factors of tradition, the visible institutions, formal codes, customary attitudes, all become reinforced through collective consent and thus whole nations go to war over religious differences. How absurd! How terrifying! Are we so narrow-minded that we can only imagine that our own view is the only one that matters? That our own faith is the only important, true path? There are many faiths because there is much we do not understand and much that we have to learn, far more than what any one tradition can offer and something greater than all traditions together. The "artifact" is to take the immediate symbol, the immediate teaching for the final answer—it is not final because Spirit cannot be confined to the thoughts and teaching of humanity or to any other species or to their mutually shared perspectives. Always, Spirit overflows out of the abundance of its own potential into a diversity of the manifestations to crystallize, ignite a flame, or reanimate the ashes, and then, flowing on to continue the process of greater awakenings, diversity, and becoming.

In turn, this leads us to the symbol of "the end"—is there a predetermined end? I think not. I see no predetermined outcome other than the outcome that we co-create through mutual processes of interaction, or through denial and warfare. The choice of ends is ours, the possibilities before us, still open to configuration. The "ends" we imagine are just that, a means by which we arouse motivation and actions predicated on whatever values we hold as ultimate or real. Within Spirit I perceive no final endings, only a process whose consequences though leading to death, yet result in rebirth and reawakenings—for an individual, a species, a world. Life as we know it on this planet will end someday far removed from our present concerns, but long before that we will have moved on to other visionary worlds and becomings such that our present life will seem naive and primitive. But even that perception will not be wholly true, for if held too strongly, it will miss the depths of manifestations that have occurred and will occur even in one human lifetime. The "warning" is simple: Do not take the person or the teaching as ultimate, final, or complete. Being in process, authentic spiritual teachings are always emergent, teasing out the unseen or unthought or unrealized potential. The potential can never be truly reduced to its manifestations. Always Spirit surpasses words, thoughts, feelings, or illuminations and, passing on to others, constantly works to share them with all. From all to all, this is the key, without inflations or celebration, just the simple process of reverence is enough—to appreciate, learn, and then, joyfully, to move on.

How easy to deny! To turn away, to see much and understand less; to compress the world into our own isolated images, into our pride and dogmas, to contract the totality into the lessons of an hour, into the immediate, observable, and ordinary. (3.5)

Meditation: The capacity to "understand" is not isolated to a particular spiritual philosophy but found in many different teachings, and articulated in themes whose concurrence is part of human development. There is a simultaneity in spiritual life, a "synchronicity" that relates personal development to similar parallel development in others—in the discovery of old spiritual traditions "at the right moment," in meeting contemporary persons, in dreams, visions, and spiritual awakenings. This concurrency is an indication of the breadth and depths of Spirit, the fullness and potency that surrounds and engages us on deep, often unconscious levels of emergent awareness. Subsequently, it is important and necessary to have a broad receptivity to all traditions, all spiritual philosophies and teachings, and to be current with emergent ideas and attitudes that reflect creative thinking, artistry, or discovery in any field. The emergence of "spirituality" is not reducible to only religious texts, spiritual techniques, or parapsychic works! The emergence of spirituality is a global process relevant to every aspect of human endeavor and practice; the principle is all-inclusiveness, this is primordial. Spirit is not reducible to a particular stance, school, or tradition but includes all of them and contains many divergent alternatives. To deny the spiritual value of alternative traditions or schools is to deny something within your own school or tradition; this means that spiritual development within a global community requires deep tolerance and receptivity to the teachings and ideas of others.

This does not mean that there is no personal center. There must be a personal center, a place to stand in order to fulfill the real responsibilities we have to those we love and care about, to facilitate personal growth, and to form communities with like-minded others. But these communities should be "open-at-the-boundaries" and receptive to the value and influence of others who can and will deepen individual understanding. The intentional structure is to be *co-creative*, to function in terms of a specific integration of spiritual principles while also valuing alternative integration and teachings. Denial is not the way; receptivity and exploration is the way, the primordial path to an ever-widening spiral, and ever-deepening awakening to potential. In this process, the great challenge is not to cling to one set of ideas, to only a few images representing the Whole; but rather to open to the full content of soul's capacity to know, to embrace a plenitude, to experience the full complexity of the Whole, and to celebrate its wonder. Like Arjuna receiving the revelation from Krishna of his many forms and his fullness, so too must we be prepared to open ourselves to the full height and depth of our visionary capacity to behold the multiplicity of forms, signs, and teachings. Each revelation embodies an aspect, a nuance, an emphasis that might enhance our own. We need not open equally far, or equally as wide, but only follow the inner guidance that preserves integrity while also allowing for newness. This is the proper condition, to look within toward stability and to look without toward possibility, and then, to continually grow beyond limitations.

Sometimes, the plurality is too great and fearful, too complex or too demanding of time, energy, and commitment. Everyone must seek to rise above the level of their fears or laziness or inadequacy. This requires courage and determination but also an inner commitment to Spirit that is always there, always prompting, always a source of inspiration, guidance, and energy. Spiritual learning does not need to track all the differences, all the diversity; it only needs to develop a center with depths of openness to new possibility congruent with an emergent personal integrity. Integrity, in this sense, means having a path and following it, however personal or collective. But it also means having the courage to reach out beyond present conditions to a yet more compete realization of Spirit, which likewise supports and nourishes those transformations. Do not isolate your images of spirituality, or lock them in your heart as the only truth! Many are the images and many are the forms—how diverse and vast they are, how awesome and interrelated. These images can flow from one to the other and at the boundaries create or release emergent forms whose contents, like those in visionary dreams, are sources of personal guidance. Yet we tend always to rationalize our experience; this rationalizing tendency frequently recreates the vision we have in conformity with what we already know as acceptable or comfortable.[17] It is important not to be too comfortable, nor should we too quickly explain the vision or dream, the emergent forms or images that are alien and suggest new ways and new seeings. The collective mentality below the rationalizing mind is filled with great turbulence and dis-ease; it swells up with many images of our yet to be integrated potential obscured by fears and dangerous currents and self-destructive tendencies inherited from our fearful, arrogant, or repressive species past. In the depths of our collective inheritance are many unreconciled tensions, unhealthy attitudes, and contracted or inflated images of who or what we are. These images must also be faced and integrated into our spiritual understanding, not denied or reduced to narrow ideological interpretations. Such sources of revelation show us the face of humanity within ourselves and our struggle is to not deny these images or isolate them from a deeper understanding. The images we hold in our conscious mind can well inhibit this process because they reinforce only the known. The deeper images call us to something other, to a potential that faces honestly the tragic and painful past in order to move beyond it into a healthy present rich with unseen possibilities. Here we cross into the nonordinary, into the unpredictable and unknown, into the depths from which we originally emerged and to which we must return with new understanding and reverence. Only when we have fully reclaimed the past and liberated ourselves from past illusions will we be free to create a better, more complete humanity whose spiritual depths are no longer denied or cut off from the long journey into light.

This does not mean going in search of morbid dreams or painful encounters. It simply means being prepared to follow where Spirit leads, where the inspiration tells you that you can see more, understand more deeply, comprehend a bit more of the fullness that surrounds you. This means leaving the possibility open, resisting closure that is either dogmatically final or resistant or afraid of change and emergence. It means cultivating an attitude of reverence and receptivity to depths of experience that are yet unseen or unknown, of going slowly with soulful being into that unknown country, with heart and mind firmly rooted in past experience but always receptive to new inspiration that may open the world. The visionary horizon is always like this, constantly turning over the well-harvested field and making everything ready for new seeds and planting. Nurturing these seeds means not reducing everything in accord with an externally received teaching or philosophy—rather it means weighing experience, your experience, in relationship to what is received and then transforming that teaching in accord with real visions that guide and are not reduced to self-serving rationalizations. This is no easy task but it is the primary process for spiritual growth and becoming. It requires not an hour or a momentary effort but a lifetime of successive encounters and learning. Start now! Don't rationalize your state based on what has been. Open yourself to the possibilities of the presence and let Spirit inspire and guide; in that way, you can journey more deeply into your own possibilities and with time, use what you learn for the healing and health of others.

Understanding is a divestment of everything unnecessary, a perception of the whole, a direct experience of totality, without qualification; it is the joy of the unmediated, the open, the expansive and vaster totality; it is the deepest truth of soul's making and unmaking. (3.6)

Meditation: Knowing where to start is important—start with the Whole, with the fullness of everything—all paths, ways, traditions, teachings, sciences, arts, and histories, and make that your standard. But learn to simplify, make it easy by embracing everything in the depths of an inherent unity whose dynamic character can be experienced directly but whose full characteristics can never be reduced to words or analytic or imaginative, descriptive constructs. The simplicity of this becoming is learning to release anxieties and fears, letting go of self-centered obsessions, of collective pride, and learning to see directly and immediately, the workings and presence of Spirit. This requires learning to see the Wholeness—to think, feel, and understand the completeness and unity that underlies the complexity and diversity. This is the inner secret of the great primordial sound, OM (or AUM), the creative totality symbolized as the One and the Many (O and M) or as the All United

Many (AUM). This unity pervades the complexity of the process of becoming, a process of constant birth and death, of continual annihilation and spontaneous creation, of deep being and luminous realizations. The ontology of the human condition, the "beingness" of our immersion in the life process, while dynamic and emergent, is simultaneously an integrated, unified, and expansive Wholeness whose processes are contingent upon the intentionality of all species, all intersecting worlds, all cosmological interactions, from the smallest particle to the largest cosmological structures. The "holographic" nature of this Wholeness makes the part-whole relationship something more than merely fragmentary—it makes the part a reflection of cosmological process from top to bottom. Thus, "As Above, So Below" and no part can be fully understood without also knowing the Whole from which it emerges. This is a primary precept and the unifying center of the Hermetic circle.[18]

In divesting ourselves of "everything unnecessary" we must not discard the personal qualities by which we become more aware. This means we must value the unique characteristics that make us each distinctive and that predicate a particular path of becoming. These individual qualities are at the heart of the process and the capacity of the individual to attain spiritual maturity is a culmination of a unique synthesis within being. But it is not simply any individual qualities, but those qualities that manifest a deep relatedness to the Whole of the process, to the spiritual depths as they manifest both the individual capacity and the transpersonal character of a sacred Mystery. Within the process, we become, as individuals and communities; and through that process of becoming, we manifest being—we share, participate, and open the horizon of the inner unity of Spirit. And this process is an increasing awareness of interrelated becomings, of co-creative evolvements, of communal synthesis and emergence. The healthy context for the individual must balance between the need for solitude and self-reflection and a positive, genuine commitment to communal interaction and collective development. Thus, an individual may choose a life of retirement and thereby contribute in a more subtle way to the development of mutual awareness, dependent upon the degree of his or her spiritual maturity and depths of illumination. But too easily, retirement becomes a way for avoiding responsibility and ignoring the impulse toward awakening and continued growth—too often, it becomes a form of escape and a defense against the rigor of communal life and being.

Another "necessary" aspect for the spiritual perception of the Whole is the cultivation of deep, lasting love relationships. Neither love nor sexuality are to be understood as inhibiting spiritual growth or development. Having children is itself a spiritual path and a deeply important aspect of our species becoming. Loving relationships are a foundation for growth and maturity and their lack and dismissal is one of the great weaknesses of all traditional ascetic religions. Monasticism is not necessarily a strength but may become a denial and a dismissal of the life process. Life is at the heart of human becoming—we must embrace, not dismiss, the fullness of love, sexuality, and all the processes of family and kinship as inseparable from a mature spirituality. Those who choose ascetic discipline and deny the natural joys of sexuality take great risk in diminishing their understanding of the human condition and they exile themselves from all the joys, pleasures, and challenges of genuine, intimate love.

I accept the proposition that loving relationships within an ascetic community are an alternative path to spiritual awakening—but not at the cost of denying the equally valuable spiritual aspects of sexual love and family. Of the two, the monastic ideal seems the weaker to me and the family, the stronger, more alive, and valuable source for spiritual maturity. I have met many ascetics, priests, monastics, and all in all, I have found them to be rather naive and disconnected from the real life of family and the deeper emotional bonds of love, and often, sadly, arrogant about their chosen state of life. In monasticism, women have taken on the burdens of male rejection of their spiritual capacities as mothers and have been subjected to deep, unmitigated prejudice against their sexuality. This is a contraction of potential and a denial of the life process that constitutes the primary becoming within being— to give birth to many species, other lives and beings. This is not a matter of having or not having children, but of not denying the potential of children as a basis for spiritual growth and development.

The value of conception, birth, and child care should not be underestimated or seen as nonessential. The spiritual path includes all mothers and fathers as primary contributors to creative emergence. The experiences learned through children are as valuable as any spiritual discipline and, in fact, such care requires spiritual values and discipline at the deepest levels of self-control and a focused directedness for a child's positive maturation. The spiritualization of the process of raising and caring for children is a deep social need, the values we impart and model in our own lives are crucial to future becoming. The heart of the family is constituted out of love and respect for the rights and freedom of every member to seek out a personal understanding of the life process, and to do so with an equal degree of love and respect for, and from, all other family members. And this extends to and includes a spiritual community, where love is crucial for development and reflects, in its spiritual growth, patterns similar to those of a well-knit and integrated family. At the heart of this process, we may embrace the differences and their common unity in commitment to spiritual values that epitomize the spiritual processes of the Whole.

What is "without qualification" is the greater community of all beings together as part of a global, transplanetary becoming in which every species contributes its own unique insights and understandings. There are no boundaries in this process other than those we choose to accept, create, or deny. The making and unmaking of soulful being is based in a deep openness and receptivity to Mystery—directly in personal experience, mediated through others, embodied in social forms, traditions, or ideas, and actualized through communal processes, rites, ceremonies, and celebrations that revere and honor that Mystery. In the process, we need to divest ourselves of whatever is unnecessary by taking careful stock of what is truly necessary, valuable, central to the process. The path requires liberating ourselves from the burdens we have inherited or learned along the way that no longer serve to guide us toward spiritual opening and understanding. The unmediated joy is the direct encounter with Spirit in a great variety of manifestations whose impact draws the seeker toward deepening clarity of intention and purpose. In this process we come to realize the inadequacy of our words, thoughts, and feelings when actually face to face with the direct reality of Spirit. This leads to divestment in the greater sense, a purification and letting-go of mental images or thoughts and attaining to a higher gnosis, a true openness of soul to light. But to attain this we must also preserve the qualities of soulful being that makes it possible—love, relatedness, mutuality, integrity, maturity, and reverence of self, others, and Spirit.

Understanding does not simply deny or turn the other cheek; it stands firm and is resolute before the destructive forces of approval or disapproval,

self-indulgence or self-denial; it rejoices in community without clinging to fixed doctrines and authoritative dogmas. (3.7)

Meditation: Understanding is not simply passive! It is an active engagement, a search and a quest, a continual seeking that knows when to rest and renew and when to continue and move on. It is not the attainment of a particular set of ideas, practices, or techniques—nor is it the accumulation of experience and many alternative adventures. Understanding is a process of integration and maturation, of incubation, growth, birth, trial and experimentation, acceptance and rejection, attainment and new discoveries, and yet more encounters. It is ongoing and leads to an increasing capacity to relate the parts to the Whole and to see the Whole in terms of its own inner processes. Understanding leads eventually to wisdom, and wisdom is the mother of all spiritual attainments, the adornment of the spiritual marriage, and the child of the alchemical union. It develops in stages and is attained only through actual engagement, commitment, and marriage—through all the trials and errors of the path. Understanding is something that develops inwardly after the books are read, the people met, the teachers heard, and the techniques practiced. It is sometimes sudden and insightful and sometimes long in process and cumulative—often it is both, sudden insight and then a process of integration and full internalization illumined by yet more insight and congruence. Often, it works through dreams, visions, symbols, myth, story, and personal adventures that may seem, at the time, extrinsic to the spiritual path—but that later turn out to be critical resources for developing insights.

In living out this process, there is a deepening at the center, through which Spirit manifests and through which we identify within ourselves, the core values, principles, and appropriate attitudes necessary for further growth and maturation. At each stage along the way, it is necessary to hold on to that center, to basic principles, even if as an emergent stance, in order to test the values we hold as our own. It also means being receptive to the ideas and influences of others and yet not simply passive in the face of critical response or coercive or oppressive attempts at control or subversion of those emergent values. It means having a center and holding to it without building a fortress or defending it as a final stronghold. It does not mean letting others run wild through it to trample all form of distinctiveness in the name of family, friends, or community. In the spiritual sense, it means developing an individual identity, a sense of autonomy that is reverently aware of the greater wholeness and continuity that unites us while also having a perspective that values integrity and commitment to personal, interactive values. This is the unique flavor, the special combination of spices that makes it memorable, the way the garden is laid out to further the growth of each plant. Finding your place in the garden is crucial, yet it might not be one place but a series of places over the years, as the garden grows and develops. The process is acquiring texture, density of relations, a richness of qualities that can manifest in a variety of ways—this is understanding, knowing and feeling the complexity of the process through individual emergence and mutual explorations.

It is not a matter of the approval or disapproval of others, their acceptance or rejection of a personal truth or insight. What matters is a creative life in community, with family, friends, and others who share a continuity in values and beliefs. There is room for disputation, for probing the boundaries and challenging ideas or perceptions that seem too confining or narrow. But such disputation is a secondary aspect of our becoming, not primary to the process. The primary aspects are community, mutuality, sharing creative insights, the play of ideas and thoughts in an atmosphere of emotional warmth and shared concerns—their integration into actual spiritual practices and loving relationships. Standing firm is only a prelude to sitting together in deep discussion and exploring purposes far removed from intellectual competition and rational egoism. The social basis of this process is not large-scale collective conformity and inherited, external bias favoring depersonalized institutional ("party") norms, but small-scale social relationships based on intrapersonal integrity and open-at-the-boundaries community dialogues whose processes include alternative perspectives as necessary for continued growth and development. The contestation between the larger social monomyths and the diverse pluralism at the heart of creative emergence is a true arena of spiritual transformation. Having serious and deep-seated commitments to a path of emergence means valuing the diversity without denying the underlying unity. The greater challenge is to live it and actualize it, in and through real human relationships.

The "destructive force of approval" is another factor that often misleads and draws attention to the need so many have for community and shelter in the face of the tumult of endless possibility. Thus, conformity becomes a refuge from uncertainty and the tensions of doubt, confusion, and fear—as though spiritual emergence were only a process of communal conformity! To emerge, means exposure to the greater currents, the untamed waters, the rising and falling tides that threaten to submerge us or leave us high and dry. It does not mean joining a community to stop thinking, to only accept and reiterate the visions of the founders. It also means to question, examine, explore, and doubt, and to think intelligently about the issues at hand. It means not resting in approval and not wallowing in the emotional support of others who have forgotten how to become more, how to be more. It means meeting the challenge of spiritual growth with some sense of humility and knowing that the answers are not handed out on a platter for easy consumption! It means overcoming the tendency toward self-indulgence and the "easy way" (made harder, no doubt by self-imposed rules, codes, practices, and all the paraphanelia of a conformist communal identity). The "hard way" is more a matter of self-discipline and an honest, direct questioning of all spiritual claims and attitudes—and none are complete or final in the deepest sense. Why? Because we are still deeply emergent, still "in process," and still becoming and perhaps, we always will be, not quite so rapidly or with such obvious turmoil, but becoming, nevertheless.

The issue of "self-denial" is also important. To understand the finer and more pervasive aspects of spirituality it is often necessary to sublimate and channel impulses and desires of the more immediate kind. And this fluctuation between self-indulgence and self-denial is a process that often becomes fixated into habits, even of the most spiritual kind. One can become completely self-indulgent in meditation and completely self-denying in bodily appetites—neither of which is necessarily good or healthy. The destructive force of self-denial is that it too easily becomes a substitute for more subtle and integrative practice. Self-discipline is not a spiritual goal per se, but a means toward the realization of a goal that is fully integrative of all healthy desires and aspirations. Appetites can be destructive, wasteful, and unhealthy, unthinking, and redundant to extremes. Disciplines can also be the same—redundant, unthinking, suppressive, and destructive—the real concern is for spiritual development, not spiritual gymnastics! If gymnastics help, well and good. But only a few will qualify for such a path and it is no better and no less fraught with dangers than that taken by those who choose family, child care, and involvement in local community. Discipline enters by directing us toward spiritual goals, whatever the context, and self-denial can be a very destructive pattern resulting in a deep sense of inferiority or failure or a suppressed, angry frustration. Better to be natural, relaxed, and to understand that the process is lifelong and requires self-monitoring and self-awareness all along the way. Such development is gradual and can be learned slowly as long as it is valued over conformity and unconscious habits.

Spiritual understanding involves a high degree of self-awareness and awareness of others in a loving and caring manner; it thrives on an intuitive and empathic process of sharing and mutuality. Because this understanding is grounded in the life process, its primary manifestations are in living relationships and interactions, not in fixed codes and conformity to externally received traditions. These traditions might serve as a creative basis for personal development, but always, we must ask—does it further emergence, becoming in the direct personal sense? It may and this is good. But if not, then we move on, learning from tradition and absorbing and integrating the wisdom and insight of past generations. Following a traditional path or teacher is part of the freedom that beckons us, a multitude of such paths constitutes just this approach and there is no reason to reject them. Nor is there a need to follow them—the choice is an individual choice, based in human relationships and what seems to serve best the needs of the present. All traditions are part of the path, and learning from them, invaluable. For me, none of them define the human situation in a final sense (even though some make this claim), they offer provisional perspectives that require the follower to accept certain premises and conclusions. All paths have this expectation, that there will be agreement and convergence—but in the life process, from the transformative perspective, all are becoming, subject to creative change, influence, and new being. Thus, there is no final perspective, only shared views whose multiple horizons intersect and open us to the Mystery that exceeds all becoming and process.

Understanding is unique, for every perspective of the whole is limited by the perceiver; each contributes to the multifaceted complexity of the

whole, adds to the desire to create—for understanding is never "finished or complete." (3.8)

Meditation: This is, of course, a personal view and one that is emphatically oriented to the process rather than the product—it is not a particular being but a deep cosmogonic *becoming* whose formal manifestations are infinite and unknowable (to human beings). To speak hermeneutically, a human life is a process embodying itself as a perspective, a teaching, a lesson, an example or model of one such becoming. The complexity lies in the diversity and "chaos" that can be uncovered at the level of specific, individual experience. Consider all the nuances of your own becomings! There is no possible way that the multitude of choices, influences, relationships, discoveries, disappointments, excitement, enthusiasm, sadnesses, or joys can be communicated—even to one other loved human being! How much more difficult, the communication of the experience of a community, or collective species, or the full "happening" of global emergence. This is the great secret of emergence—it is never complete and never completely knowable! Should it turn out that it is a process in one immense cycle, still it is never complete or knowable, it is simply an unrepeatable concurrence of multiple perspectives unified in being and extrapolated in becoming through the agency of Spirit in a living cosmos of multiple others. If fully extrapolated, there is then reabsorption, reintegration, a contracting involution whose essential distillation is energy, life, and awareness for new spiritual births. Like the spiral arms of our galactic home, it undergoes all the cosmic evolutions of spiritual transformation that make it impossible to be fully known from within or fully communicate without.

Understanding is "unique" in the sense that it is a synthesis, a relative convergence whose contents are shared and modulated by and through our relationships with others. These contents are often built up through life experiences and take in only that degree of fullness that has congruence with our deepest spiritual values. Those lacking in such values, having never formulated them or received or worked on integrating them, have a far more difficult task—to make sense out of experience that is largely interpreted from the basis of collective norms or personal idiosyncratic needs and usually confined to narrow parameters of immediacy, convenience, and self-gratification. These collective norms, highly diverse and built around specific subcommunities and inherited values, often lack clarity and deep intentionality because they have been largely transmitted in a semiconscious, subliminal way that reflects norms of (often unthinking) conformity over norms of individuation. This means those following such norms have often poorly developed skills in the areas of creativity, sincere communication, or self-awareness of inner motivation. Spiritual understanding involves a *deepening* of self-awareness, an increase in self-responsibility to enact the values most vitally held as intrinsic to genuine well-being. The understanding that emerges from this process of individuation is "unique" in the sense that it represents the individual synthesis over the norms of poorly differentiated collective attitudes or actions. It is also unique in the sense that it reflects a particular concatenation of many influences whose consequences are found in the emergence of a particular point of view—fragmented or integrated in proportion to the degree of effort, inspiration, and commitment to an authentic spiritual path.

What then is "authenticity" in this sense? In part it is a movement toward deeper self-awareness, in part an emergent mutuality in human (and other) relationships, and in part, a receptivity to inner spiritual guidance. The "path" is the road we walk toward spiritual awakening and the discovery of deeper unity and wholeness. The goal is walking it well, taking care at each step to do no harm or injury to others, and even when making a leap, to do it in a way that avoids self-injury or confusion based in shallow motives or only outward appearances. Not harming self or others is deeply important in order to leave the way clear for future development unencumbered by past debts, guilt, or angers. This often means untangling from relationships that are too limited or confining or stale and repetitive—not in harm or blame, but through honesty, deepening respect for the process, and an emergent sense of direction and necessity. The "authentic" spiritual life is not based on conformity to abstract ideals, but to the actualization of real values in everyday life and relationships—this is heart of the process—and it requires a high degree of honesty with both self and others. We always develop from exactly where we are in the present and not from some ideal circumstance that never really manifests. We start now right where we are, whatever the conditions, and work toward an inner transformation that, imbued with Spirit, will result in liberation, illumination, and deep, abiding transformations.

The process of understanding, as emergent becoming, is highly creative and yet congruent with values that seek a continuity with others who also seek spiritual life and fulfillment. Together, yet individual, each confluence of expression seeks its harmony with the expression of others—in spiritual acts of kindness or generosity, in creative forms, in play and work, in love, rest, or explorations—together creating a harmony in which the individual voice is preserved and valued. The life of the individual can never attain all the fullness of the Whole but she or he can attain the fullness of a genuine spiritual realization and enlightenment. It is completely possible to attain a full and luminous realization of deepest potential in a single, individual lifetime—one that can influence others over many generations as a beacon of what is possible and actual. But such realization is only one more light on a dark shore of deep potential, only a single illumination among others whose light may shine more or less brightly. It is not the degree of the radiance as much as it is the actuality of light, Spirit-born, that enhances the light of others that they too, may shine brightly. To understand this process means to see the path, to follow it, and to attain that degree of radiance, Spirit-given, that allows the path to be followed by others. It is the creative gift that illumines the process of becoming, marks the "unstained waters" and channels them into suitable vessels for the consecration of all those who come after—and all those who drink, even now, from the same waters and taste the same effervescent joys.

The complexity is "multifaceted" and has no one form, no one codified system that represents the fullness of even one life—how much less, the multiple lives of all beings! We must be comfortable with diversity while seeking the inner unity that pervades that diversity with multiple intentions and purposeful developments. The deeper our understanding, the more we will see how complex the process is without having external boundaries to mark its limits or foundations. The inner completeness is experiential, the fullness and coherence known directly in a seeing that transforms ordinary mind and its worldly preoccupations, and yet that also imbues those preoccupations with new meaning, potency, and significations. There is a process of interpretation, of recycling interpretations that mark the various stages along the way, the contents of which become ever more inclusive as they become simultaneously grounded in spiritual continuity and luminous insights. These "flashes" become more and more stable and the inner presence more real and consistent, more part of self and less distant, more here and now, more connective and immediately inseparable from the many involutions of Spirit manifesting in all places, at all times. This process, as a spiritual sign of transformation and awakening to higher potential, involves all beings, not just individuals or specific communities. We are all "emergent" within being, all seeking to realize the full possibilities of our intentional aspirations, all capable of contributing to a world-unfolding, world-becoming, world-opening capacity. We are not climbing a single mountain, but exploring a multitude of mountains, worlds, beings and possibilities long in process and deeply part of a vaster, more comprehensive becoming. The "view" cannot be contained within a single perspective, nor can it be summarized by a single voice—but one may sing a worthy song, hear the ebb and flow of rhythms, catch the inspiration and pass it on. This is what matters, this is what we are here for—to learn, grow, share, and then, in maturity, to pass on.

The Fourth Principle

The Fourth Principle of Spirit is its unknowable immensity; this is not first because only after life, awareness, and understanding is such knowledge possible, a knowledge of the hidden foundations, the Mystery. (4.1)

Meditation: This knowledge is not external or based in reading books, hearing talks, attending conferences or retreats, or in simply thinking about spirituality or mystical philosophies, or in participating in ceremonies. It is a knowledge of Spirit that comes directly through experience—through dreams, visions, illuminations, and spiritual awakenings. When it comes and how it comes is less important than being receptive to its coming and learning to open from within to the possibility of such awakenings. This does not mean that the experiences of everyday life are not also reflections of balance within the Whole. But the deeper knowledge, the primary gnosis, proceeds through stages to increasing clarity and immediacy of Spirit that subsumes ordinary perspectives into a broader and fuller sense of the Whole. And this Whole is not limited to the ordinary codes, cognitions, beliefs, or practices of any one culture, society, or temporal order. Wholeness exceeds the partial reflection, incorporates the microcosms of individual, familial, communal, and sociocultural life into a totality that gathers together every being, culture, time, and place and yet exceeds them by an immeasurable potential that constantly seeks the preservation and self-actualization of all such beings and manifestations. The realization of this abundant condition, its overflowing into multiple forms and beings, its radiance and inspirational presence is not based in theory or abstraction. Theories arise as attempts to interpret the experience, as a reflexive ground open to the infinite.

I am not writing about abstract ideas but actual, primal manifestations whose currents flow through real human beings—mystics, saints, teachers, gnostics, shamans, or spiritual healers—who all bear witness, through thousands of accounts, to the reality of awakening to Spirit.[19] Is it unmediated experience? No. It is mediated through the mental, emotive, and psychosocial context but not, I believe, determined by that context. Human beings are far more than simply a product of conditioning, and a theory of predetermination is often a rationalist denial of the depths of personal and transpersonal experience that connects us with the full reality of being. We are not merely the products of our cultural milieu or historical circumstances; our freedom as spiritual beings is far more ancient than any existing human culture or intellectual current that would proclaim the individual as nothing more than a product of external social conditioning. Such a naive view stems from a profound lack of spiritual experience and is rooted in paradigms of social control and a denial of the capacity and power of the individual as a creative center for world transformation.

In order to understand this, we must review the primary circumstances that constitute the human situation: first, that we are alive and this life presence that is within us is a creative and potent potential; second, that awareness is inseparable from the life presence and, as such, is shaped and guided by inner intentionality; third, that understanding is a consequence of relating our own intentions to those of others in a context of a greater wholeness and completion; and fourth, that this process is ongoing, open-ended and that creativity is a result of combining our intentions, sharing and shaping them through self-reflection, inner values, and meaningful spiritual beliefs, relationships, and practices. In this process, the social reality is not foremost or paramount unless we *choose* to make it so and thereby submit to the external disciplines of an accepted social order. However, in terms of spiritual principles, it is the awakening of potential that initiates transformation and new direction, not simple conformity to external social ideas. In many ways, it is a matter of personal integrity and thoughtfulness, of a conscious shaping of intentionality from within and a conscious rejection of external social norms, practices, and attitudes that inhibit or suppress emergent spiritual understanding.

The keys to this process are: creativity, an affirmation of the value of the individual, and a constant opening to the higher unities of spiritual actualization. The successive emergence of the individual into a greater relatedness to the Whole, to greater luminosity of insight, unites the individual not only with a chosen community of like-minded others, but with a higher continuum of spiritual becoming. This is a dynamic wholeness that unites all beings and, in the revelatory depths of gnosis, clearly reveals a higher unity through which we all exist and thrive. Social forms are only semicontractual relationships whose function is to provide a relatively stable context for such a spiritual process. That persons and whole groups of persons become influenced, shaped, and conditioned by these social contracts is in no way surprising, particularly in an age when there is a profound lack of inner awareness and often a deep denial of spiritual teachings. In many traditions, spiritual teachings have become externalized to a high degree and subsequently often function in a strictly rudimentary way to guide the individual to increased self-awareness. These teachings have often become didactic, authoritarian, and oppressive in dialectic with emergent forms of alienation, overrationalized emphasis on the immediate, dogmatic atheism, and unthinking material preoccupation.

In this process, creativity has increasingly lost its spiritual value and become ancillary to more alienated forms of social and economic causality. Spiritual "knowledge" is reduced to a product of social conditioning or inherited beliefs, to cultural formalism or shallow psychological analysis lacking metaphysical depth or sophistication. Such an outlook has no meaningful theory of emergence or creativity and falls back on random chance, social conditionality, and a skeptical view that would deny the value of the individual in the greater totality of world becoming. Such a contracted universe! This is the great school of the *pater familias*, forever wishing to preserve the "way of the fathers" as sacrosanct and unquestionably authoritative. But this is a distorting mirror, an artifact of an age struggling to make sense of its own death and inadequacy by clinging to paternal, overrational social models. Spirituality is not conditioned from without, but born from within, through long processes of gestation and sudden moments of clarity and rebirth. This process continues to surpass existing social forms and structures and cannot be reduced to any singular pattern or form. A social context is nothing more than just that, a context within which we may *choose* to actualize spiritual potential that may well exceed or surpass the norms of the society within which we live. And the greater context for that process is a global context that affirms all life and social forms as relative and contributory to a greater shared awakening—none of which is final or complete and none of which determine what must or should be right for the individual spiritual seeker.

Social conditioning or traditional patterns of spiritual practice may deeply influence those who have not grasped the importance of confirming for themselves the values and beliefs they have inherited. Immersion in a visionary world of religious teachings will indeed create a context whose spiritual experiences will confirm, in a general way, the truths of those teachings. Such teachings are not arbitrary, but the consequence of many generations of seekers working out the potential elaborations of a particular spiritual worldview. Those elaborations gradually meld into a sociocultural ecology whose shaping influences can be quite deep and profound. But spirituality is not about simple affirmation; it is something more than confirming the transmitted power of an intergenerational realization, or a spiritual worldview whose teachings culminate in a particular kind of experience or enlightenment. Spirituality is about emergence, surpassing old forms and old thinking, revealing hidden potential, opening the mind to new ways of seeing, attaining more than affirmation, and seeing more than what has already been seen. We can affirm many ways of seeing and we can revere the teachers and transmitters of those deep and authentic traditions. And we can continue to evaluate, sift, and consider how these traditions have impaired or inhibited development in some crucial direction necessary for a yet fuller realization. Every teaching has its limits—there is no such thing as a perfect teaching that says and clarifies everything that is yet to be, that is not in some ways surpassed by the fullness of being in the process of becoming. What is hidden is the unknown potential and the yet unrealized understanding that gathers together the insights of the past and reverently seeks insights beyond them without denying the influences of culture or the conditionality of a particular place or teaching.

No doctrine, teaching, belief, or experience is equal to the Whole, yet every being participates in its primary manifestations; the depths of Wholeness are unfathomable and mysterious. (4.2)

Meditation: What are the "primary manifestations"? They are all the great teachings of the past and present that contribute to our individual, communal, and collective spiritual development. They are all the teachings that emerge out of direct experience as well as the diversity of interpretations to which experience gives rise. Deeper than this, however, the primary manifestations are actual real beings who have transformed themselves into an intrumentalization of creative spiritual life, confirming and directing human attention to new wholeness and actualization. Deeper than this, these manifestations are "primary" insofar as they lead others to a direct experience of the reality and presence of Spirit, actualized through memorable events and transformative awakening. And even more "primary" is the very manifestation of life itself, this above all else is the most admirable and inspiring, the most primal of manifestations. The process of awakening potential, of bringing awareness to its fullest expression and capacity, of deepening understanding to more inclusive awareness of the Whole, is the primary process. The manifestations of this process continue to affirm, surpass, and initiate new stages of development and spiritual realization.

In this process, unified inwardly through Spirit and diversified outwardly through exploration and new expressions, the individual is pivotal. The process is not a subordination of the capacity for innovation, but an exploration of that capacity moderated by consensual needs, fears, desires, and ideals in tension with the emergence of a particular individual synthesis and realization. Our discoveries are relative to their impact on the collective, sometimes lying fallow for generations, only to reemerge with new significance and meaning in the present or future. The involutions of Spirit are nonlineal, they do not simply unveil themselves in a "progressive" manner. Intimately linked to the processes of individual realization, the abiding unities of Spirit preserve the actualized capacity as a potential yet unrealized on a collective scale whose effects may catalyze further insights in various periods of species development. The role of the individual is to manifest spiritual potential, in whatever form best

suits that individual, and in so doing, to provide an alternative example of how such potential can be attained and maximized. This
process can work within a traditional framework or outside it in a
purely individual and idiosyncratic manner. Neither way is better or
more genuine than the other; each simply adds to the quality of potential pathways sought and actualized by real beings in an emergent, complex universe of emergent others.

Empathic dialogue is crucial. Learning to hear the other, to engage in meaningful exploration and sharing, to feel the potential and
intuit the possibility actualized by others is a crucial necessity within
collective life. This is not, however, a merely critical evaluation, a reduction of experience to known categories or to ideological concerns.
It is a testing and probing of one's own soul, of the basis of self-awareness seeking to understand the other as a partner in the adventure of
spiritual exploration and manifestation. As nonauthoritarian dialogue, it seeks to express shared concerns as relevant to personal development and spiritual growth—to respectfully explore through
honesty and openness, the value of personal experience in the context
of mutual understanding. What is called for is a sense of humility before the greatness of Mystery and a receptivity to alternative forms of
knowing and being. Speaking in a traditional or untraditional framework is entirely secondary to a respectful hearing and appreciation of
the impact and interpretation of the experiences of others. The primary ground for that interpretation is always the individual whose
experience is being shared and not the interpretations of those who
only hear or lack the experience. The empowerment of the individual
can only proceed through an honest self-appraisal that sees the limits of experience and also knows how to value the insights of others
without surrendering the contents of experience to the ideological or
sectarian claims of others. The rare occasion is to meet someone
whose experience and understanding is deeply helpful and insightful.
Such relationships should be deeply valued and appreciated but they
should never occasion the surrender of personal integrity.

But how is it possible that "no experience is equal to the Whole"?
The Whole, in all its magnitude of present extensiveness and millennial eons of becoming, cannot be summarized even as a result of
direct experience of cosmic unity or mystical experiences of Oneness.
It can not be summarized in revelations, dreams or visionary journeys, mystical awakenings, gnostic illuminations, or the "extinction
of self in God." All of these experiences are possible, profound, and

genuine sources of spiritual illumination but none of them represent the Whole in the fullness of all its manifestations, becomings, and being. Spiritual paths do not give answers to all questions. Indeed, what they most often do is set up hierarchies of knowledge (or value) and then by diminishing the lower stratum of "worldly knowledge," they present the goals of that tradition as an epitome of the highest sort of attainment. Ironically, such an epitomization is often true! Gnostic experiences *are* a manifestation of spiritual attainment through transformative processes that result in spiritual illumination. But this illumination is not all-knowing or omniscient, does not comprehend, for example, the workings of quantum physics, higher mathematics, the art of painting, or the creation of music. And yet each of these workings is Spirit manifesting. In deconstructing the epistemological hierarchies of most traditions, it becomes quickly apparent that spiritual knowledge is itself a special kind of knowing, one that relates to the Whole but is often woefully ignorant of the parts! One aspect that is deeply misleading is the claim to a superior, comprehensive knowledge, however attained, when it does not include all the possibilities of Spirit and denies much that is necessary for a meaningful embodied life.

In part, this is a matter of *values* and not knowledge per se—the question is what "kind" of knowledge do we value, and in what circumstances does that knowledge serve us best? Spiritual knowledge is knowledge of the Whole but in a limited sense; we can know the Whole, experience ecstatic and deep union with Spirit and Mystery, have a vision of Superessential Unity, and still lack knowledge of basic processes within Spirit that makes existence possible. For this reason, I regard mystical experience as foundational to spiritual growth but in a sense relative to the entire learning process of a rich, complex, shared life with others. When I write of "higher gnosis" I mean just that, a knowing that is mystically experiential and provides a deep and secure basis for evaluating other forms of experience and learning but not as imbuing the gnostic with omniscient understanding. Such experience provides a profound sense of the Whole as mediated through a complex totality of personal events, real beings, emissaries, psychic manifestations, and angelic happenings whose integration into the fullness of Spirit is limited by individual capacity, motivation, and understanding. The fulfillment on a spiritual path is different for different individuals, all of whom have individual needs, proclivities, and aspirations. Direct mystical experiences may be only a prelude to the development of a wider and more comprehensive understanding and attainment. But always, there is a relative boundary that defines, in a particular individual, the specific nature of their capacity, however brilliant, mystical, simple, or direct. Always, the depths in all possibility exceed the vision of the individual and it is the particularity that best expresses the ongoing manifestations of fullness in Spirit and Mystery.

There are no necessary pathways to the "top of the mountain," only images that dissolve into shades of darkness and light, only shadows reabsorbed into the unending transformations. (4.3)

Meditation: This is true because we are not all climbing the same mountain! There is not just one mountain, but a vast range of mountains, valleys, river ways, and secluded glens in which we may, each in our own way, revere, honor, seek, and give thanks for spiritual attainments. It is not a matter of choosing one path to the exclusion of all others, but of learning from all paths the special lessons they have to impart—the instructions, techniques, philosophies, values, and practices they offer for mutual exploration and enhanced awareness. The path we may follow "to the top" is the one most suited for us through a conscientious seeking—through one tradition or many, or through no tradition, through simply living a creative, compassionate life of integrity and generosity. And the pathway we choose may mutate into a new divergence or possibility later when confronted with all the many challenges of living an authentic spiritual life. Choose a path and follow it with integrity and courage and know, in your heart, that your following it is not conditional on the approval or disapproval on any other person. Follow it with kindness and empathy, with love and humility, with intelligence and a deep sincerity of commitment—for wherever it leads, these qualities are foundational. And know that this process, on a deep level, is Spirit-guided (in whatever forms it takes).

As we learn, we form images of the goal or way or persons who help and assist us, but all of these images are only a transient means toward a higher end, a dissolving of images into Mystery, light, being, and stages of illumination. And in this light, there are shadows and darkness because shadows and darkness are Spirit-born, inseparable from the collective processes within being and becoming. None of these images, lights or shadows, are free from the processes of transformation; they all participate in the greater involutions of spiritually awakening potential. If there is a need for light, there is also a need for the restful dark, a time of nonstriving, of deep quiet, rest, stillness, and peace; of dissolution, death, dismemberment, and a scattering of individual aspects. This sets the stage for rebirth and new assembly and manifestations. Darkness and shadows are also manifestations and as such, they represent the capacity to turn inward toward a self-concealing mentality whose introversions become ultimately passive and quiescent, a nonevolute within being that provides the necessary darkness within which light may incubate, inspire, and give direction. Darkness can also be inspirational, a metaphoric sign of the most earthy, lunar sort, embodied and passionate, autonomous and immersed in feelings, conditions, and sensations. So too, light can also be a sign of an overly emphatic solar consciousness, the right hand of an incipient dualism that can only see with one eye, the bright half of an equation whose solution is Wholeness.[20]

From a relative, nondual perspective within Spirit, I can only speak symbolically and metonymically of parts within a greater unified Whole. There are relative differences within that unity that are not bound by either fixed qualities or unvarying laws or principles. There is unity-in-difference and difference-in-unity without qualifying the extent or scope of those differences. Immersed in processes of becoming, qualities shift and unity manifests in various ways, incorporating into itself emergent perspectives as intrinsic to the processes of spiritual awakening. There is no "one path" but only a variety of developing approaches to a potential that exceeds each and every path; and yet that animates each path with real contents, values, and goals. This requires continual evaluation of the harmony between inner intention and outward influences, of self-other relations that give form and direction to a path. It requires a critical scrutiny of alternatives and a necessary sifting of possibilities in order to choose just those actions and involvements that best suit an individual temperament. Don't expect others to make these choices for you—having integrity means choosing for yourself and then following to the next stage where new choices must be made. It is a process of emergence and becoming, not conformity and obedience. Discipline in this process involves actually embodying the practices and overcoming lazy tendencies that resist the necessity of creative thought, action, or commitment.

The pathway to follow should be one of your own choosing and not simply one that is inherited, passed on, or convenient to a certain place or time. Perhaps someone chooses a particular community to follow as a way of developing his or her understanding, because the opportunity is there in the immediate present and place. This is perfectly natural and a function of all the many intentions working toward actualization in a particular place and time. But it is a serious error to imagine that convenience is the baseline for determining spiritual integrity and clear spiritual direction. Exploration is good and often necessary and invaluable, but it can become a way of postponing real commitment and engagement on a serious and deep level. At some critical point, it is necessary to make a full and complete commitment to the process of spiritual development and to hold onto that intention as a means for inner awakening and spiritual opening. Otherwise, the seeker may easily become distracted by the plurality of forms and alternatives, simply tasting here and there without real nourishment. It is not a matter of external form, but inner commitments, of a deep purposeful search for spiritual maturity with full commitment guided by Spirit for the purpose of manifestation. We each contribute to the process of becoming and in that process become an actualization of Spirit manifesting. As such, external forms and traditional teachings of any sort may hinder or help us only in accord with the sincerity of our efforts and the maturity of our intentions.

There are patterns of transformation in which we find ourselves confronted by the very issues we sought to avoid or escape during earlier stages of development. This cyclical process of encounter and reencounter is a deep feature of emergent being—every stage is played out, if necessary, over and over, until the necessary lessons or insights are learned and fully integrated. We must revisit the territory and proving grounds of our younger self, visit all the places or vulnerabilities in order to move beyond them through transformation into a more integral and complete life. As this process draws us onward, it is very important to have an inner capacity to evaluate the conditions we find ourselves in, the confrontation or encounters that touch where we have been touched before. A spiritual path is a stable direction and a continuity in values and experience that helps guide this process. The more

grounded we are, the more able we are to attain the necessary insights to move on through each and every cycle because we have a
conscious will guided by spiritual values that helps us to constantly
transform the encounter into a positive outcome. It is like having
the capacity to direct the outcome of dreams—moving them to desired ends that conform to a spiritual vision we hold to be genuinely
true. Therefore, we must hold to the genuine, the deep-rooted and
secure, the stable center that allows us to weather the storms that
blow across the path. It is not a matter of following a particular
path, but of finding your way, your own center, in a genuine affirmation and a guided life of spiritual well-being. There are no fixed
and predetermined answers—we must each seek them out and find
those answers in the quality and integrity of our own living. But
Spirit is there and the Mystery enwraps us and sends a continual
flow of inspiration when we open our heart to it.

**Every circle has a center because it has a bound-
ary; where there is no boundary, there is no one
center, no particular image, no specific form,
only an unbound totality of diverse formulations. (4.4)**

Meditation: Yet every person is a center; every living creature,
an image; every being, a specific form. And together, these many beings create an ensemble of complex, interrelated, multi-intersected
becoming whose wholeness is a reflection of the greater Wholeness
within which they have their individual being. Thus, there is no "one
center," nor can any one center be found apart from all the many beings in which Spirit manifests. A teaching is not a center unless it is
embodied in the real life of actual individuals who manifest the spiritual goals of that teaching or tradition. Otherwise, a teaching is
only a abstract set of ideas, values, or practices whose existential dimensions go no further than being abstract ideals. What makes a
center is to deepen personal awareness until it connects directly
with Wholeness in a conscious and meaningful fashion, and then, to
actualize it and to live the potential of such an awakening as a true
manifestation of Spirit. This is no easy task! But it is not based on a
premise of conformity or obedience to externally imposed norms,

beliefs, or interpretations. It is far more demanding—it requires each of us to use the full capacity of our creative intelligence, disciplined will, and abilities to love in order to attain to a full expression of spiritual potency. This realization is not bound by the conventions of any one tradition or path, but open, free, uncharted, and yet capable of being expressed individually.

Inevitably, this raises the question of revelation—the belief in a teaching or person who represents a supreme, highest wisdom or divine incarnation or a god-sent being with a message whose contents are often regarded as infallible, permanent, and good for all time and all people. Such thinking reflects a profound bias—that there is only one sure, secure, and certain path that can be laid out and followed to a predetermined end. There is revelation, and there are god-sent beings, incarnations, Avatars, Mahasattvas, and mystic saints of many types and kinds. But no one message is final or absolute for all people—every message is relative to its community of believers and followers. Where the message leads, there they follow, and the fruit of their following is written large in the historical patterns of human development. Every revelation is a stage, a message passed through revelation or illumination, to appropriate messengers, for particular communities. And each revelation is bound by the limitations of its community of believers and every community interprets that revelation in terms of its own limits, bias, conditions, and needs. Then, all too often, they project that condition on to the worlds of others and thereby judge, and in some cases, condemn all who fail to share that interpretation. Such is the history of revelation—a history inseparable from the very worst in human prejudice, bias, and the assimilation of others through tragic oppressions, deaths, wars, violence, and condemnations of all kinds. This is not to say that there is no good in revelation—indeed, there is much that is good, profound, noble, and worthy of preservation and reverence, both in the message and in the message-bringer.

But no one message serves all needs and no one messenger, serves all peoples. And the message-bearers are not few but many, in every culture, time, and place. In Spirit, revelation is ongoing, a continual process by which we shed the narrow boundaries of past beliefs and acquire new perspectives, greater tolerance, and deeper insights into the complexity of the Whole. Further, these many revelations relate to each other as contributions to a shared spiritual history of humanity in the most comprehensive sense—the ways in which human beings have found it possible to enhance awareness, attain a vision of the Whole, to experience the inner unity, and to master the life process in order to attain a high degree of actualization.[21] The origins of this global transformation are found in the teachings of individuals and the adaptation of those teachings to a large-scale collective influenced by innumerable factors of historical contact, political and economic influence, institutionalization, and cultural expression of every sort. Every generation interprets anew the old ways and the old messages and among members of any one generation there is divergence, disagreement, and contestation and degrees of conservative or liberal responses to those very revelations. There is no one true response! There is only the response that we each make as individuals or communities and take to be true in living our lives. The power of the collective in this process has been redundant and conservative and has frequently been highly coercive and aggressive in enforcing interpretations on resistant and protesting others.

Perhaps if we had a more benign spiritual history, and in some cases, there are less aggressive histories—certain aspects of Buddhism and Daoism, certain schools of Sufism, Hasidism, and Christian mysticism—revelation might play a more creative role in contemporary spirituality. But the traditions of Christianity and Islam, and more lately, Judaism, have an aggressive edge of conservative interpretations that would reduce the world of human experience to exclusive models based in books that are highly prejudicial and male-biased in their condemnations of others—including the grotesque condemnation of other members of their own faith, hardly offering models for world spirituality. There is no one center, but many emergent centers in the lives of real beings who make the necessary efforts to attain an individual realization that does not condemn, censure, or deny the rights of others to follow a different spiritual path. The future spiritual history of humanity, as I see it, will not be constructed on the exclusive model of past revelation but will emerge through a process of continuing diversification, complexity, and convergence. This will result in an increasing depth and permissiveness whose goals will be less collective and more directly personal and experiential. Revelation will continue but not as the old, sweeping judgment against all the nonconforming; its depths and authenticity will be proven in its lasting flexibility and continuing value in the process of shared human transformations. The goals of revelation have always been to unite humanity in a common sense of dignity and purpose in honoring the depths of Spirit and Mystery. This is still true and will remain true and it will be realized in many diverse ways.

The "unbound totality" of this process is the full scope of what all teaching, teachers, revelations, messengers, and incarnations have contributed toward unveiling the deep potential that is still to be realized. Any one of these teachings, teachers, or revelations can be followed to attain a spiritual goal—but these goals are not all the same, nor do they result in similar states or realizations. Far more than most persons realize, these teachings produce results that are unique to the teachings and traditions from which they have come. This particularity cannot be surpassed by some abstract form of hierarchical transcendentalism.[22] I am not writing about "ideas" but about the actual transformative *anthropology* of human awakening and spiritual realization. This process, Spirit-guided, is existential in the most primary way; it requires deep commitments to actualize that potential and not to simply theorize about an illusive "higher unity." Embody that unity and it becomes transparently clear how specific, individual, and unique the forms and contents of the experience are. It is not, after all, an experience of "all ways and paths" but a deep awakening of soul to depths that are immeasurable and whose noetic, intellective contents simply vanish into a vaster, more complete mystical horizon. How this relates to Buddhism or Christianity or other traditions is an entirely secondary and nonessential question. What matters is the real experience, the real awakening and how that awakening informs a spiritual life with compassion, understanding, and insights into the life struggles and seekings of others. It is not a matter of building theories, but of stripping theories down to a real basis in experience, of gaining an intuitive knowledge, a genuine and lasting gnosis.

Knowledge consists in the exploration of form, content, image, and feelings—the archaic, the immediate or the far future, all possibilities woven into the unique, distinctive patterns of Mystery. (4.5)

Meditation: This does not mean we should reject tradition or past ideas, insights, revelations of spiritual teachings that are bound to a particular path or direction within the history of human spiritual development. In fact, it is incumbent upon us—to the degree possible within commitments to family, work, and community—to explore and delve into those many traditions, teachings, and ways in order to enrich understanding and give perspective to the particular path followed. There are many kinds of knowledge, many types and degrees, many "levels" and "stages" in the process and these take, in most cases, a lifetime of effort and devotion. My own search has lasted many years, and traversed, through study and practice, a wide variety of traditions and paths. I have studied their histories and confrontations, inner teachings, exoteric and esoteric forms, and so on—in relationship to the emergent conditions of a particular time and place, a particular temperament, and a variety of opportunities and possible directions. And in all this, the simple affirmation of the paths and teachings of others has been crucial in opening the doors to many different worlds, peoples, languages, and cultures. But the study of all these things is secondary to a deeper and more important task—the realization of personal spiritual potential in a direct and immediate fashion. The real awakening lies within, in the opening of inner centers of awareness, and in spiritual actualization of the visionary contents of illumination.

The "exploration of form" is important because we can learn, in the process of our own spiritual development, a degree of relativity and detachment from the specific contents of any one vision or "opening" to the spiritual worlds. The *Mundus Imaginalis* is a vast and amazing realm of multiple beings, places, dimensions, and contents whose luminous forms are vibrant with remarkable spiritual power and presence—far beyond ordinary dreams or the surface imaging of the rational mind. These visionary worlds, so many and so diverse, can absorb the visionary into their density and complexity, into the fascinating diversity of "planes" and "realms" in such a way as to be completely absorbing and mesmerizing. And yet we come out of the encounter, out of the dream or vision, out of the "supramental condition" to realize the relativity of these visions in relationship to the visions and experiences of others—and this is as it should be. It is not the celebration of personal attainments, visions, or experience that matters. What matters is the consequence in a spiritual life whose radiance embraces a depth of Spirit and flows out into the world as authentic manifestations of potential. The "form" is nonessential; what matters is the way in which the contents of experience are integrated into everyday life and gift the individual with insight and creative understanding. The forms are many, the possibilities are many, and the actualizations are many—all sharing a deeper unity—but each manifesting as an aspect, attribute, or set of qualities unique to the individual.

Yet it is not image apart from contents but image charged with the numinosity of spiritual encounter, with feeling and meaning, and carrying within a depth that might take many years to fathom. Spiritual knowledge is often communicated in highly condensed symbolic forms, or in deeply felt experience whose richness exceeds and surpasses ordinary feeling or reaction, or in a stream or flow of thought and inspiration that has its own inner continuity and purpose beyond the vehicle of language or traditional ideas. Understanding these experiences requires retaining them in memory, reflecting upon them, relating them meaningfully to other similar and dissimilar experiences and extrapolating from them the cogent messages that act to inform intentions and attitudes. Experience without understanding can create an impasse and lead to stagnation and confusion; understanding without experience quickly becomes shallow, abstract, and mere ineffectual ideation. It is not the experience per se, nor the understanding, but the distillation of experience, and a reflective integration of it into the life path of the individual—in all the richness of feeling, imagery, and somatic contents that give it potency and motive force in acts of spiritual integrity and conviction. It is necessary to spend time reflecting deeply on spiritual experience, dreams and visions, emotional states of expansion and contraction, intellectual insights and imaginative perceptions in order to develop a well-integrated vision of the Whole.

This also involves explorations not only into other cultures and spiritual traditions, but also into the deep past, into the archaic formative periods of human prehistory and further, back into the great past ages of geological and planetary time. Why? Because our spiritual history as beings precedes simple incarnation in recognizable human form—it engages us with all life forms, all histories and past becomings of which we, in the present, are a consequence. Our picture of spiritual becoming is not simply a "human" history, but a species-wide, geoplanetary becoming whose real "evolution" involves life in many forms, places, and times as a facet of an even greater stellar becoming whose galactic cycles far exceed our limited planetary view. The processes within the Whole are not simply directed toward humanity, humanity is only a small part of that greater totality of events, beings, and co-relations whose story is far more complex than the already complex history of a single species on one small planetary world. Understanding past species and past cultures is very important because it gives us a better sense of our own place and contribution to the Whole and of the many generations that have struggled with similar issues and concerns. There is nothing unique in seeking spiritual development, it is, in a sense, the most basic of all disciplines and practices, and its forms and contents are vastly diverse and far-ranging. Acknowledging past experience by having an accurate, informed awareness of it, is profoundly important. The process of becoming requires a depth of historical understanding in order to move through and beyond the realizations that have gone before.

Knowledge of the future is more difficult and tenuous, but nevertheless significant and should be considered as part of the path of becoming. Where, after all, are we going? What are our goals in relationship to the larger-scale patterns of our past and present? These are questions about spirituality, not simply history or culture. Spirituality involves engagement with past, present, and future generations. We must take fully into consideration what has been and what will be. It is not only "depth" but also "scope" and placing ourselves into the stream of past and future becoming is as important as placing ourselves into the depths and heights of spiritual possibility and multidimensionality. Our intentionality is influenced by and influencing now, in the future, the becoming of others. This intentional connectivity should be part of the process of our spiritual development—to see, in a knowing fashion, the relationship between other past and future becoming. The future, in this sense, is not an abstraction, but a real becoming populated with real beings whose struggles and questions are not unrelated to our own; the clarity we offer in the present may well help to inform and shape that future and is a serious obligation. In the spiritual sense, we do not simply "live in the present" but we live in and through all beings and all times, sharing through life-experiences the lessons we learn in the past, present, and future.

The cycles of incarnation are not just for one lifetime, but many, and for many generations and many manifestations, in many diverse contexts. The "possibilities woven into the unique pattern" are not simply woven in a single present, but into many incarnations, over distant times and through relationships both old and new. Our obligations are much deeper and older and more enduring than most realize, and this sense of relatedness links us to past and future events far beyond the scope of a single life or experience. This is an enduring aspect of the Mystery, that beings do not simply cease or discontinue, but that they move on from experience to experience and recapitulate past and present as they move into a yet unknown future. This process of becoming, inseparably linked to the development of our psyche or soulful being, is a constant process of refinement and reflection on possibility and direction. All too often this process becomes habitual and a pattern of repetitive convictions tied to places and persons that continue to recreate what has already gone before—sometimes in cycles lasting a multitude of generations and even whole eons of cyclic time. Increasing awareness means seeing the patterns, the age-old patterns, and moving beyond them into a freer, more creative and self-determined future imbued with spiritual possibility.

The true "eternal life" is the unending expression of Spirit through the processes of creation, manifestation, and absorption, the interwoven "jewel net" of all possible patternings. (4.6)

Meditation: Each of us is a center with only a relative circumference, influenced within by the arising of insight, understanding, and developing awareness and influenced without by a multiplicity of phenomena, persons, and existential conditions. Further, these conditions are undergoing change and transformation such that every center is immersed in a process of mutual conditionality, impacting and being impacted by others, by the environment, the earth space, the social condition, the historical moment, the unique combination of spiritual influences. This process, this becoming, is long underway and extends into the far past and the far future, and as a process, it involves every discrete particle, cluster, organism, being, community, collectivity, planetary home, higher and lower world, and all bodily, psychic, emotive and noetic impressions. It is not a process limited to a particular species on this world, but is rather, I believe, pan-cosmic and extends from the simplest to the most complex manifestations of life and being. Having a relative circumference does not mean being vulnerable to all outside influences, rather it means that we must be selective and intentional about the influences that we allow to move us toward our spiritual goals. We can resist influence, reject it, refuse to submit to or to follow intuition or impulse, but always those influences are acting upon us, moving us, often in the form of habit energy, toward particular actions, decisions, and commitments.

This also does not mean that all our choices must be conscious or rational in the sense of knowing or fully grasping the consequences of our choices. Following intuitions, feelings, a hunch, a sense of direction that can't be articulated rationally is often the way we allow influences to move us toward spiritual awakening. This takes something more than reason tied to observable evidence or immediate impressions or predetermined outcomes. It means opening to influences that are often, in the early stages, impressionistic, dreamlike, imaginative, coincidental, synchronistic, or fortuitous as our emergent connectedness attunes to the broader fields of interaction. These confluences involve not just one or two others, but many seekers, communities, networks of influences enacting an ancient pattern of discovery and exploration. The mutuality of this process is far-reaching and a journey of an individual is also a collective journey, an archetype of the search for spiritual connection to larger-scale patterns and unfoldings.[23] This archetypal journey relates us to all other seekers, on different paths or similar, each enacting the unique pattern of his or her own becoming but also contributing to shared possibilities in mutually influencing others. It is not a journey we take alone but with others who, even in our moments of loneliness, touch us through Spirit, helping us to move forward. As we open to spiritual influences, others become part of our path because all beings are moved inwardly to realize their deeper co-related becoming. To be open to the influences requires us to break through the resistant, collective mindset that would deny an intuitive approach and to seek a fuller expressiveness that nourishes a shared life through mutual, reciprocal explorations.

At a more advanced stage, the "jewel net" becomes every other being and their capacity to influence our awareness and lift us to

a more enhanced state of understanding. By "every other being,"
I mean any form, appearance, entity, being, or imaginal construction whose presence or potency acts to elicit from us a deeper
awareness of being—the stones on the shore, the face of the moon,
a mythic unicorn, a dream image, a visionary manifestation—
whatever moves us toward a deepening awareness. The "jewel
net" is the great net of creative manifestations, Spirit-born, whose
every intersection is a being or evolute in a gemlike form, an influence whose light or dark reflections act to awaken lucid potential because we affirm that influence as part of a greater Whole.
Every jewel (or "event-thing") is unique, though there are many of
similar type, and every facet of every jewel reflects the mutual influence of other related jewel images and in each, Spirit manifests
a thousand times over. These reflections create patterns on a scale
greater than that embodied in any one form or image, even though
the form or image is an intrinsic part of that pattern.[24] The part-
whole relationship is dynamic and undergoing constant subtle
shifts and interplay in order to elicit from us the maximum in potential. A reflection shows us part of the pattern, or reduces it to
a scope we can see or conceive, but actualization leads us beyond
the image, beyond the reflections, into the reality that surpasses
the image and form and creates a basis for new images and
reflection.

This process is "eternal"—that is, it has been going on without
ceasing and so it will continue, I believe, even as whole worlds, stars
and galaxies, cease and new ones are born. The inadequacy of most
cosmological models in describing this process is the failure to fully
value the influence of conscious, intelligent, living beings whose
awareness and actions may indeed affect, influence, and be determinative within the process as a Whole. In this sense, mind is not accidental, nor is spirit secondary to cosmological events; these events
are profoundly influenced by spiritual processes in a universe of multidimensional complexity far greater than any description of its material aspects. Life, awareness, and understanding are at the heart of
the process; they shape and influence the "making and unmaking" of
reality. On a greater scale of awareness, Spirit is not only the unifying presence but also the primary source of creative processes such
that the embodiment of a world is an intentional act of mutual creation and becoming. This is true wherever life arises, wherever a single particle of "living matter" can be found in interactions with other

such particles. The process is given form and content through the (eons-long) involutions by which mind, body, and soul emerge and manifest. A "higher gnosis" reveals many alternative worlds and beings whose relationship to the process is equally creative and influential; the web of life is vast and the jewel net, an image of a far-flung web in infinite seas of space. Yet in the depths, there is the unitary wholeness, living waters that teem with life and Spirit.

What is co-created and manifest, is also "absorbed." This means that a part is not equal to the Whole, even though it reflects the deeper unity and contents of its origins. Stars explode, worlds die, vast forces are at work, and on a single world, a species, any species, can vanish—perhaps not lost in the works of Spirit, but no longer visible in the place of their incarnate manifestations. No manifestation lasts forever, in the worldly, visible sense; inwardly, every manifestation is absorbed, reintegrated, and transmitted according to its value, worth, or inner intent. As the oak tree loses its leaves over many seasons and eventually dies, so too does the soulful being of the individual. We may live many lives, but every being has a capacity for dissolution, dissolvement, a final return to Spirit no longer manifest in individual form. This absorption is part of the greater process by which an entire cosmos may reabsorb its own manifestations into a single collapsed brilliance, compacted inwardly to be once again scattered among entirely new emergent bodies. Such a process requires our deepest respect and reverence to understand this "heartbeat" of spiritual creation and recreation, to stand within the Mystery and to honor the process as a crystallizing of cosmic potential into particular being. Honoring is best expressed in actualizing the Mystery in our own lives through the adornments of spiritual wisdom, compassionate generosity, insight, empathy, and intelligence, knowing all the while that we, too, have an end. Yet what we weave into the pattern carries our vision, our songs, artistry, science, and stories into the generations that come after. Like seeds for sowing a new garden, we live through those seeds because we gave our lives to the process, and passed on all that we learned for the benefit of others. Such is the "eternal way" of creation, sharing, giving, and transmission from soul to soul; then death, rebirth, and new beginnings.

The human transformation is the opening of the "inner eye" that sees Mystery in the heart of life;

**that perceives directly the life-bestowing pulsa-
tions and rhythms of contraction, expansion, and
rebirth; that knows soul and world-soul and
what lies beyond. (4.7)**

Meditation: Clearly, knowledge of the Whole requires more than
what is immediately obvious or transmitted through the senses—
even though it includes and enhances those kinds of knowledge. No
knowledge is excluded, but knowledge of the part, however fine or
large, requires also a knowledge of the Whole. And the "unknowable
immensity" exceeds the capacity we have as individuals, however
enlightened, to know or comprehend the Whole. Thus when I write
of opening the "inner eye," I am writing about the center that has no
boundary, the limits of which can be known only in the surrender of
striving and grasping. Just as in the old gnostic creation narrative,
Holy Wisdom, the Divine Sophia once sought the Creator, Bythos,
the Deep, in order to honor his greatness and the cause of her creation but eventually had to turn back before being absorbed into the
sweetness of the absolute by Horos (Hermes), or Limit, so too must
the spiritual seeker, turn back, seeing the limits of his or her own capacity and accept the unknowability of the Deep.[25] We attain this
state of wisdom and resignation before the Mystery in order to know
the sweetness of its ineffable unity without grasping after a knowledge of all its diversity, workings, and manifestations. This is the
simple opening of the inner eye—to behold within and through our
own experience, the spiritual reality of unity and the vastness of the
Whole.

Wherever there is diversity, there is also unity; wherever there
is complexity, multiplicity, and interdimensionality, there is also coherence, harmony, at-one-ment, and the intimacy of the part-whole
relationship. We come out of unity and return to unity in the
processes of manifestation as Spirit reveals the potential for newness in the continuities of eons-long expression and realization. The
Mystery of this process is not "out there" but within, and all about
us, in the fall of a leaf or a child's tear, in the cry of a raven, the smell
of smoke, or in winds off a new tide. The inner correspondence is to
feel and experience the embodiment of the process in everything
that is, the deeper unities, the higher manifestations, the coherence
of the Whole manifesting through an inner opening that reveres and

surrenders to that deep penetration. This is Eros. The love of Spirit acting on heart and mind, to open them to Mystery in order to give them a complete groundedness in all the processes of creations—and not simply awareness of some higher or more ethereal world. True, there are higher and more ethereal worlds, beings, levels, theosophic planes accessible to visionary experience, but the opening of the inner eye is primarily an opening to the fullness that unites all such planes and worlds in a full harmony and reconciliation within Mystery. Knowing the parts, planes, levels—however one layers the cosmic cake—is an endless process of elaboration and struggle with closure and relationship. But opening the inner eye need be no more complex than a simple direct seeing of the inner unity of the Whole.

This requires cutting through the tendencies toward elaboration and complexity in the explorations of a multitude of visionary worlds. Yet it also means not denying the Aeons, world-bubbles, theophantic revelations, Buddha-heavens of the great Dharmadhatu, angelic gates of the Olam ha'Yesirah, the dreams of Scripio, the night journeys, the architectonics of the worldly Comedia—but learning to see through them and with the inner eye, into the at-one-ment that gives them all life and reality. Such seeing is a sacred Mystery because it brings us back to the real condition of our own limited perspectives; not limited in form but limited in relationship to the Whole, and thereby to seek atonement for all past excess and extremity in claims and attainments. We are limited beings, but capable of seeing much that exceeds our own comprehension, capable of participation that is a direct engagement of our full potential, not in knowing all, but in knowing the depths that embody our individual, communal, and collective becoming. This is not an abstract, intellectual seeing, or a simple passion for unity with all-that-is, but a deeper and more distinctive knowing/gnosis. When the eye opens and the parts retain their place while the soul knows directly the Whole within which each becomes, then we are seeing truly the depths that have no end.

And there is life throughout those depths, all the expansive possibilities of emergent life forms and all the death throes and failings of the dying. This is the process, the death and birth of worlds through the experience of real beings whose sorrows and joys embody that world with character and meaning. There is life everywhere, all the forms of expressive art, science, and creation that urge us to understand its contents and conditions. This requires not a "loss of self" but a discovery of self within an emergent process of self-other relationships. This means sharing our insights and gifts, but not demanding of others what they might give freely and spontaneously. The spontaneity of the gift is in a willing and free sharing of the consequence, an at-one-ment, attuned with deep patterns whose manifestations require a willing receptivity unencumbered by demand, expectation, or insistent conformity to collective norms. Even at the level of emergent community and small group process, this sharing is best expressed spontaneously and freely. This is because in those circumstance of intimacy, creative expression flows best through trust and acceptance, sometimes of great difference and perspective, and through an inner stability grounded in valuing the underlying process. Giving birth is not always easy or even "natural" or desirable until the time is right and conditions work toward a spontaneous arising and expression of an inner vision that authentically embodies experience.

Sometimes we must pull back, nurture an idea or insight or impression, in order to let it incubate, mature, and reach its term through respecting the inner process. Forcing expression only distorts the manifestation. Best to let it arise spontaneously, when the urge is there to give birth and when conditions best support its respected acceptance. Such an arising requires patience, exploration, openness, and clear inner intentionality to give form and shape to the manifestations however tentative or new they may be. The "inner eye" often opens through processes of exploration uninhibited by expectation or the demands (or needs) of others. Conception in this process is natural; Spirit resides in the heart of every being, and as presence, urges us to explore the potential that we have been given. Yet to form an inner condition for rest and renewal in the coherence of unity-within-being is what makes creative vision possible. This depth, when supported by our relationship with others, becomes a profound source of inspiration and guidance. We need only to open ourselves to the inner urgency that seeks more completeness, greater fulfillment, a deeper satisfaction, and to realize that in so doing, we unite with a multitude of others who likewise desire an awakening to illumination.

Spiritual awakening is far more comprehensive than any particular visionary world can summarize or subsume into a particular pattern or categorization; and yet, many such patterns can facilitate the process of such an awakening. This is, in a sense, the paradox of the world-soul—all containing, it holds within itself a multitude of spiritual perspectives, as it also holds a multitude of geological and ecological zones and contexts. Yet in its diversity, it too harbors inner unity and wholeness. The pathways are many, and the goals, diverse and distinctive; some horizons are vaster and some more narrow than others. All paths are not equal and all ways do not lead to the same realizations—some will highlight a facet and others a network within the many-jeweled possibilities. The world-soul contains all those possibilities and reveals all those nuances of being that real human beings have known, envisioned, been one with, and shared with others. Always, it is possible to reach out beyond what is known, into the unknown and see there yet more horizons emergent and luminescent, whose contents are still purely in potential, waiting to be known. But is this the goal in opening the inner eye? No. To open the inner eye, is to see deeply and with clarity the inner unity that encompasses all these diverse worlds and yet also reveals a center with no boundary—open, compassionate, creative, and self-aware.

Giving birth, it falls back; dying, it moves forward; coming to rest, it vanishes; having been born, it thrives; in thriving, it overflows; in overflowing, it gives birth. (4.8)

Meditation: As a cycle, there is a tendency toward expansion and incorporation followed by processes of contraction and distillation, from which emerges a simpler and more distinctive understanding leading to more incorporation and expansion. In this spiral process, Spirit works to enhance our awareness of its fullness through an inner reflection that opens to increasing depths and dimensionality. If we start with ordinary awareness, with the normative perceptions of sense, feeling, and thought, and examine these with care, each will have its own modes of perception and expression. What we see with the eye may well provoke feelings and thoughts, but we can distinguish the one from the other—the eye, the feelings, the thoughts. We may think a thought that provokes feelings and causes us to act, or feel with intensity that shapes thought and physical response, or we may enter wholly into one without awareness of the other. To these various modes of perception—the somatic, the emotive, and the intellective—we must also add the imaginative, the capacity to construct a visionary world "in the mind's eye" and to perceive from that construction real sensations, feelings, and thoughts informed by imaginative imagery. Like an iridescent hummingbird hovering before a fire-red rose, whose petals are dew clad with morning coolness, the mind can create imagery that evokes thought and feeling, stirs Eros and constructs poetic resonance between aspects within a larger context of worldly meanings and associations. This takes us beyond rational languages of logic and "realistic" description and into a mythical world of being.

But these aspects of everyday awareness—bodily sensation, feeling, intellect, and imagination—are only given their full expression through deepening relationships with a rich world of experience, with others, with nature, with reflection on the interconnectedness of the Whole. And from such reflections we can move on to a more enhanced awareness, to various stages of opening to that Wholeness such that bodily sensation, feeling, intellect, and imagination are more fully expanded and enhanced as they merge with Spirit in a multidimensional cosmos of beings-in-becoming. There are many such descriptions of this process. Yet these descriptions are only relative and schematic in terms of the experiences of particular individuals, later codified into theosophic hierarchies and maps of the "soul's progress" within particular spiritual communities. Most of these descriptions are heuristic—that is, they have been developed as a means toward educating the individual and helping them to attain a fuller sense of awareness and participation in the complexity of emergence. Many have been subject to long generations of thought and reflection by others in a process of creative elaboration, itself a means for development. The creative working out of all the nuances and patterns becomes a creative endeavor that crystallizes into traditional schemes and formal patterns of belief, often offered as a pathway for particular kinds of spiritual attainment.

However, the direct experience of opening to higher awareness and moving beyond the everyday mind, as a creative endeavor, also results in completely unique encounters and manifestations whose contents are neither predictable, nor determined by community. Thus, schema of these higher realms can act only as a template whose significance is as great as the need of the individual for conformity to a particular pattern of development. In an open and permissive exploration of the psychic worlds, these patterns may be modified endlessly and may all be, in the final analysis, relative to the cultural and historical circumstances, and the spiritual maturity, of the practitioners. There is no one authoritative schema, only a variety whose meaningfulness is relative to the spiritual goals of the individual or community. Most are simply heuristic, roughly descriptive, and a "skillful means" toward a positive end— the spiritual transformation and illumination of the individual. As Spirit acts to provoke insights into an emergent, not static, cosmos whose depths are yet largely unknown, individual experience must be balanced with the experiences of others and brought into dialogue with those familiar with gnostic states and conditions. The process is deep and open-at-the-boundaries and cannot be reduced to a particular pattern or series of experiences or fixed stages or states.

Indirectly, other ranges of experience can be noted—beyond the everyday awareness—the various centers of the body can open to greater sensitivity and sensation, to feeling a more direct sense of connection from each neural center, however they are numbered and symbolized. Every center in the body has its own respective field of interaction with other beings, both the embodied and the ethereal, and once opened, these centers can act to facilitate a much deeper awareness of psychokinetic relationships within the larger world. The emotions can also be open to much more profound states of awareness and empathy, such that we can feel a connectedness with others, all types of others, receiving direct impressions of their experiences—impressions also embedded in objects (natural or crafted). The intellect can open to the full range of noetic constructs that takes us out of the ordinary state of consciousness, beyond verbal intellections, and into a more visionary encounter with primal noetic forms ("image-ideas"). The vivified imagination, when opened, can bring us into encounter with the mythic depths of a visionary world such that we live and feel the reality of the myth, its power and presence, in its most archetypal form and energy. The ordinary aspects of awareness are opened to an increasing range of perception and to more potent encounters with all the imagery, beings, and happenings of the *Mundus Imaginalis*, the truly psychic world. This awareness, with all its latent power of expression in paraphenomenal events and abilities, is only another advance into the depths of Spirit. This range connects with others in a direct, psychic sense and allows us to see and experience directly the capacity we each have

for higher perceptions—telekinesis, telepathy, clairvoyance, clairau-
dience, out-of-body travel, and all the many talents that beings have
when fully aware of deep potential.

At a yet higher range, we come into an awareness that no long
finds its primary basis in embodied life, or in the soul's capacity for
higher perceptions, but is the experience of Spirit in the direct sense.
This opens us to a vast realm of beings and worlds, into visionary
horizons in which a multitude of existing beings (incarnate, disincarnate, or the never incarnate) find a common harmony in the embrace
of Spirit's presence. This awareness begins in opening to an expansive and multidimensional horizon whose full manifestations are beyond measure or possible knowing. It moves from that expansive,
multidimensional awareness into the depths and unity of Spirit
through a personal, individual realization and into the transpersonal
horizon where, in transparency and lucid illumination, Spirit bursts
open at the depths to reveal in holiness, the sanctity of its beauty,
power, and compassion. This experience, as higher gnosis, leads directly into the primal Mystery where even Spirit is surpassed and
wherein abides a limitless, sacred fullness whose potential absorbs
all beings, manifestations, and becomings, in all times, places, and
realms and from which all is born and begun. This holy Mystery is beyond words and no expression can contain its overflowing fullness
and capacity to move even Spirit, as a Divine Sophia, to manifest the
ten billion worlds of creative expression and actualization.

This unending process has yet another range, this time, an incorporative range of becoming that brings the experiences of soul's journey and illumination back into the world of manifestation for the
purposes of furthering the works of Spirit. This is the integrative
phase—where the journey into the far horizon is brought back and
embodied in a genuine life of dedication to spiritual principles and
their appropriate realization. This fullness, Spirit born through direct seeing and being, has no particular form or convention that
makes it recognizable. It might manifest through a child, a flower, a
bee, or its honey and its sweetness can become a healing balm for
many others. And there is a fifth range, the range of inner peace that
has known and has manifest the Mystery, Spirit-guided, to all those
who might share it and done so without strain or stress. This is the
capacity of Spirit to illuminate the heart, and then move us with compassion to the many tasks of transforming this world and others. This
is the stage of complete instrumentalization through the guidance of

the higher awareness to actualize whatever may be done to manifest a more spiritual world. These stages are all only arbitrary markers on the path to a more mature spiritual awakening that no longer needs such markers or distinctions, but deep in the process, knows when to fall back, when to thrive, and when to give birth. In this way, Spirit overflows, and then, vanishes—only to reappear, once again, in unexpected place and time to share its gifts, Spirit-born.

The Fifth Principle

The Fifth Principle of Spirit is compassionate love—sensual, emotional, intellectual, aesthetic, and spiritual—it gives itself to others, it receives them without shame. (5.1)

Meditation: The existential basis for living in harmonious relationship with others is love and is foundational to all spiritual development and becoming. Love is primarily a deep feeling of relation, of shared commitments to a process of mutual growth and a deep appreciation of the worth, value, and significance of the other. If there is life, awareness, understanding, and Mystery, then love is the experience that unites us with others who also live as aware and understanding beings. The experience of love is not easily understood, nor can it be known in any other way than through direct, intimate encounter and mutual sharing. Deep love is compassionate love—a love whose intentions are directed toward fostering the worth and value of others in a process of exploration and creativity. This creative aspect opens us to many diverse alternatives and no one example can serve to manifest all the various forms of love. Each of us must seek his or her own fulfillment, Spirit-guided, in the actualization of an enduring capacity to love. Love is a gift of Spirit, one of the deepest and most profound gifts; it comes from the heart and is not an act of will but a spontaneous infused spiritual sharing. It is a power that opens self and others, to an inner healing and union in the face of suffering, pain, misunderstanding, and confusion. It is a vital presence whose energy and depths flow out of Spirit and into the world through sincere openness and reciprocity in mutual caring and concern.

This love is not "otherworldly," nor is it an abstract ideal. It is a down-to-earth feeling of intimacy whose expression in physical sensations, passions, and desires is wholly natural and necessary. These "sensual" aspects are also Spirit-born, part of the magical conditions through which love penetrates our entire body and soulful being, having strong roots in sensation and lush, earthy feelings, both gentle and powerfully transformative. Love as Eros combines deep feelings of attraction and arousal, uniting sexual, emotional, and empathic relation born out of the depths of Mystery and Spirit. Erotic love creates the condition for deep intimacy and emotional union. The ecstasies of love are most keenly felt in and through the body that is itself a ground of knowing, a sensual basis for touching, tasting, caressing, and passionately embracing the other as a partner in life's exploration and knowing. The soul's union with the Other, as in the longing and celebration of the Song of Songs, or as a union with the Beloved in the sacred marriage (*hieros gamos*), is body constructed and celebrated. And this is good, and right! Joys in love are not on some abstract or ideal plane of detachment from sensuality but right here, in this world, through the creative wonder of the senses and all the wet, slippery, expressive, transformative joys of passions. These depths of feeling keep us grounded in the world of real embodiment and sensation and it is through such embodiment that we can attain a maximization of spiritual energy. For it is through the bodily medium that Spirit enobles the potential for evolution and development of soulful being.[26]

There is an intellectual aspect to love as well—an Eros of ideas, a deep attraction that intellectual processes hold for us as magnetic currents within being. If we admire intelligence or find ideas "attractive" or "repelling," we are speaking of the Eros of Intellect, the ways in which mental processes reflect currents of love. This noetic "magnetism" is based in a relationship between minds that creates a sense of openness to new horizons of meaning and cognitive perception. Eros can flow between individuals based on the excitement, insights, and experiences of a creative mental engagement. We can find others whose mental life is deeply attractive because, in the creative process, there is similarity of insights and shared ideas that can help to formulate creative intentional patterns. This requires an "open mind" in the sense of a mind free of intellectual bias that preconceives a threat in alternative ideations. This openness is based in a receptivity to spiritual influences receptive to intellectual diversity as resources for self-transformation. The Eros of Intellect is a stimulus that springs from intimate relationships in shared thinking as a co-creative process. In such a process, the mental world of the individual is opened through love to willingly engage with another in the mutual exploration of ideas and thinking. Such thinking is no longer bound by a self-created reiteration of old mental habits but breaks open the old patterns by taking into itself valuable and emotionally genuine contributions from others whose thoughts add luster and nuance to a creative confluence of shared cognitions.

Love is also primary in art and creative crafting, in the imagining, singing, dancing, and dramatization of worldly life. Beauty is intrinsic to the expression of creative forms—one needs only look into the depths of the natural world to see how profound and deep is the delicacy, harmony, and wholeness of ongoing creation. The unparalleled beauty of all the subtle and potent forms of nature are a great testament to the inner and radical harmonies that constitute the expressions of love. The sense of balance and aesthetic harmony infused through creative life, constantly engaged in elaboration, mutation, and diversity, reveals in a profound way the presence of Spirit in the dynamics of natural evolution. Alienated art, disconnected from nature and from human sensibilities allied with natural form and expressiveness, becomes a contraction whose basis lies in the divided and fragmented condition of urbanized society. Too often, the modern urbanized world denies the value of creative aesthetics in pursuing social dreams of "realism" and "sociopolitical arts." This lack of Eros is a significant indication of an introversion that disconnects from others and can find no harmony in mutual inspiration and no passion in shared visions meant to illuminate relationships within the Whole. Genuine love manifests as relationship, as a means of expressing a shared vision, as an actualization of visionary imagination in search of an emergent wholeness inspired by the realities of Spirit.

The spiritual dimensions of love are many, and the expressions of this love are found directly in the manifestation of real beings in all their diversity and differences. There is nurturance and preservation, the careful growing of the embryo within the womb, or in the egg-protected shells of multiple brothers and sisters, in all the varied forms of life. The very process of emergence is an expression of love, a becoming as deep and complex as the birth of a child, a species, or a world. Love is a fostering of potential and an encouragement to grow toward the maximum in capacity and inner ability. We may live in hate, prejudice, bias, in a lonely and isolated state of frozen affection, but when we choose love, we choose potential, actualization, and an awakening of latent and sleeping passions to give birth and to create. This process involves giving and receiving, not one to the detriment of the other, but both working in reciprocity to recognize the mutuality of the exchange, the value of the gifting. Giving in this sense is not "egoless" or "self-less"—it is an enhancement through love, an adornment that purifies egoism and leads to a new clarity. Love leads to mutuality, has precedence over self-gratification, and over the contest between those whose loving is yet incomplete, still caught in the passions of give and take.

To "receive without shame" means to learn the joy and beauty of accepting love from others without embarrassment or uncertainty. It means accepting the true feelings of others as a gift, something that enhances both the giver and gifted. We return that love with integrity and commitment to mutual growth and maturity; in this way, it is possible to attain an inner certainty whose affects are shared and whose efficacy goes out into the world as a true gift of Spirit. To love means to give and to receive, respectful of the differences and alternatives in self-emergence. There is no need for shame in love; even the most passionate love is not shameful. The shame comes from holding on, not letting go, expecting and demanding, being insensitive where sharing would carry forward to deeper insights. This takes willing partners and cannot be forced; it requires mutual commitment to the processes of self-development through love. Because it is mutual, withdrawal or retraction of love can only act to impel us toward other alternatives, relationships, and explorations because love is a restless energy that constantly seeks the other. When found it is capable of deep awakenings and when lost, it can devastate and destroy much that is beautiful and worthwhile. Therefore, choose love and follow it in the reciprocity of Spirit always seeking to realize inner potential through the multitude of relationships to others.

This love entrances, it absorbs and transforms, it illuminates the darkness and fills every particle

with joy; it cannot be contained or reduced to an image or a manifestation. (5.2)

Meditation: Spiritual love is not based in simple intellectual, emotional, or sexual attractions, though these may influence the ways in which we understand spirituality. Spiritual love is less directed toward a specific other and more infused into all relationships with others. Yet, in enacting that love, a life partner, mate, or beloved other may indeed play a primary role that maximizes the experience of an especially deep spiritual sharing. A truly compassionate love is a manifestation of a "center without a boundary" such that each being is touched by shared feelings of deep connection and warm, supportive concern for others (and not just humans)—their growth, development, and spiritual awakening. The deeper centers of love are found in dyads, in the pairing of opposite genders, in the natural union of male and female for the purpose of a mutual and shared life in child rearing, family, and extended kinship. This is the primal basis for love and for growth and a quickening understanding of the positive aspects of a shared, familial love. Loving couples, when isolated from a larger community of loving relationships—from harmonious family interactions, among lifelong friends, from community members working together in stable and lasting relationships—suffer an impairment through the loss of multiple connections to others.

While a dyad may be the most primal of all loving relationships, it is nevertheless too easily submerged by tides of isolation, gender tensions, and misunderstandings where there are no others to intervene and help foster a more open sharing of perspectives. Communal relationships, in a spiritual sense, require a concern and commitment to others who are not necessarily life partners or co-parents. The expanding circles of love are such that they tend toward the merging of centers, toward a unity and conformity to group ethics or communal guidelines and custom. In bringing others into the circle of communal relationships, there is always a tension between the capacity to love and accept, and the pull toward difference and individual autonomy. The creative aspects of this process involve the necessity of dialogue and clarity in identifying inner motives and communicating those motives in an atmosphere of mutual respect and receptivity to alternative needs and feelings. The expanding circle of this respect and mutuality opens to the whole of the process of loving, to many others, not just select members of family, community or those with whom we share a basic worldview or spiritual orientation. The Hermetic circle of love is not closed or bound by anything other than human limitation and denial. Deep affirmative love, which may resonate in a dyadic relationship (between different or similar genders), is a primal basis for an expanded community of relations that in turn opens the capacity to love others who are not members of a particular community. And we must also reach out, through Spirit, to embrace the not-humans who also need and rejoice in a love that is healing and spiritually mature.

The spiritual depths of love are not bound by particular relationships, even though, in manifesting, such love works through the real experiences of specific interactions with others. Spiritual love is deeply existential—it can only manifest through authentic interactions whose intentions are based in truly valuing the other and in providing emotional support for growth and maturation. When actualized in real relationships, it is an effortless flow of concern and feeling that truly fills the interaction with a sense of spiritual presence, a joy in meeting the other and sharing with them a loving potential and power. This transformation involves a progressive working out of differences in a context of supportive concern. It is not a merging in the sense that there must be a loss of center; instead, it is a recognition of center within others and a valuing of the differences even as the loving currents unite us through our differences. Such a context is illuminating—when love flows between beings, it reveals, shows the difference, the pain, suffering, fear, and inadequacy, and allows that love to heal without censure, blame, or contractions that keep us from even deeper loving. This requires opening to others as they open to us, this is the Hermetic circle whose boundaries have no fixed definition, but only expand outwardly to others and inwardly toward self-affirmation actualized through courage and humility.

Spiritual love is transformative, not static and ineffectual. It acts on others to awaken within them a response whose inner motivation is to experience a more aware and participatory life. It acts not only on the mind or the feelings, but to create soulful being; and in so doing, it becomes a profound source of joy and oneness with others. Spiritual love is infusive, it is a nurturing presence that embodies whole communities, families, shared relationships with strangers, all of whom become participants in a more intense awareness of caring and concern. It acts spontaneously to quicken human relationships, to draw them into a circle of extended connections at a level of awareness that is more than ordinary. Its affects can be extraordinary and remarkable, initiating transformation through a spontaneous flow of feelings that arouse a heightened awareness. The nature of that awareness is a relatedness through an opening of boundaries, an expansion that cannot be contained in a single person, being, manifestation, or image. The spiritual depths of love are Spirit-filled, depths resonate with a profound energy of caring, with a prolonged inner joy whose consequences are all the manifestations of life and being. The Mystery of this love is its depthless and fulsome presence in the concurrency of real everyday becoming, in the simplicity of related life forms of all kinds. It is not distinct from our pains, shortcomings, failings, or indifference; it is right here, right now, imbuing the world with a deep dynamic of relatedness and interdependency, filling the world-soul with its wonder, miracle, and presence.[27]

The manifestations of this love are beyond measure or description; they are many and present in feelings of normal attraction and in the interests we feel in others. As intrinsic to emergent becoming, love opens us to the depths that relate us to all beings, to the full connectivity of the process, to the subtle imagery of the part-whole context, to the jewel-net of mutual influences and affects. Such love, when fully manifest, "entrances"—that is, it takes us into a higher love, into the context of an ecstasy that unites all beings in Spirit. This ecstasy is not simply an emotional condition or a psychic state; it is a condition within Spirit through which the soulful being perceives directly the intense energy and pervasive currents within which all beings are awash. Like waves, those currents sweep over and through us, illuminating the depths and revealing the binding energies of Spirit and Mystery. Such a love is conditioned only by the boundaries that we ourselves draw as "necessary" for our own self-existence, a circle far smaller and confining than what our potential would allow. This joyful energy is all around us at all times. It pervades and gives life, awareness, and wonder and is so subtle that we often fail to see it, even though, it is the primary basis of our deepest spiritual becoming. In the higher love, we shed fears and resistance to participate directly in the ocean of all-being, in the deep radiance of a joyful union that reveals this love as all-pervasive and all-containing. In this condition, we see firsthand, the depths to which love leads when we truly become a center without a boundary.

Love binds us and sets us free, it compels us and gives us rest and renewal; it draws us with the glance of its passing, suggesting unity, merging, becoming—the soul's union and dissolution. (5.3)

Meditation: Love is not static, nor is it only a condition of rest and stability. There is an inward pressure toward expansion and emergence, a deep Eros that relates to the world beyond the immediacy of known and patterned relations. Love can be restful, give renewal, a deep sharing and unity of feeling and passion, but this rest is itself only a transition to new activity, desire, and openness to an expansive world of yet unknown possibility or patterns. The rhythms of love move in a cycle between points of rest and reaffirmation, from comfort and sharing in quiet moments, to points of passionate embrace, emotional arousal, and inner merging and separation. It leads to points of distinction, difference, and unique discovery seen and shared with another, to convicted action and encounter that brings to the surface all the unfinished work of a developing, distinctive being. These are natural rhythms, intimate to the processes of daily life and the cycles that our most important and meaningful relationships undergo. The patterns of a deepening spiritual love are not distinct from these rhythms; they are the same rhythms that we must learn to master within ourselves before we can successfully acquire depth with others.

How does love "bind us"? We all too easily become locked into relationships in which we have deep emotional commitments and perhaps years of effort and sharing that may inhibit our further development because of compromise and conditions that (often unthinkingly) structure the relationship. These may be conventional ideas and attitudes, mutual responsibilities and entanglements, or simply eccentric circumstances that seem somehow binding on all participants. Most human beings want, very deeply, to share their lives with others and to accomplish this, they are often willing to compromise aspects of their own aspiration and hopes to further the life of the relationship, to "make it work." In the process, the individual often loses sight of personal aspects of his or her own spiritual development, feeling that the sacrifice to family, lovers, or friends, is necessary and fulfills the expectations of others in being a "good partner." But this is a misleading attitude and one that can do great harm to the individual by inhibiting his or her capacity to love more fully as an individual committed to spiritual development and a creative, emergent life within being. We must honor our relationships and commitments to family and friends, but not by denying inner potential. This inner potential should be cultivated and drawn out into actual manifestations such that love accommodates these transformations.

There is another way in which love can "bind." It can entrance us through our fascination for the other and thereby act to blind us to our own needs and differences. Here the problem becomes one of sublimation and vicarious identity. Love is not a surrender of self, it is the maturation of self through creative interactions and partnership with responsible and loving others. Spiritual love is not a selfless merging, but a purposeful purification that leads to clarity in being a self in relationships to other selves. Poorly developed self-awareness and fragmentary self-knowledge makes it very difficult to love in the deep, dynamic sense. Love can be a means for developing a feeling of self-worth or enhancement through others, those we love and see as fulfilling a need within self that they may enact for our benefit. This pattern is neither good nor necessary. It lead parents to load their children with expectations divorced from the real capacities of those children; it leads friends to see other friends as extensions of their own desires and to push them into actions that may in fact harm them; and it leads couples into the endless circle of a confused, poorly defined self-other awareness. In a one-on-one relationship, it leads to a poor sense of differences in needs; it binds two together while neither is fully aware of their own individuality. Love becomes a form of closure whose boundaries are drawn by a lack of inner autonomy and self-definition.

Yet the deeper currents of love do compel and push us beyond the static condition, beyond the boundary that is only defensive or "unconscious" or self-protective. Love requires of us an opening, a willingness to expose inner sensitivity and to be vulnerable to the response, criticism, or the lack of understanding of others, even those whose love we have long valued or trusted. Our success in love depends on how we conceptualize it. If I think of it in the strictly personal sense, as a distinct relationship between myself and a specific other, then it can only be as powerful and deep as the actual relationship within which we are working. But if I conceptualize love as a spiritual principle, then it is not bound by individual love relationships. As a deep current within our collective being, love is a transpersonal quality and acts to motivate us not just within those relationships that serve our needs for intimacy. This transpersonal quality infuses the world of embodied beings with a multitude of connections to the world around us far more comprehensive than the immediate circle of family, friends, and lovers. And when we recognize that quality in our own lives, it impels us toward expansion and greater inclusivity as well as toward greater depths of sharing and care. Opening to those depths is not simply a process of becoming more "vulnerable" but a process of learning to differentiate between ourselves and others and to form, in that process of differentiation, a strong, stable sense of self as a worthy partner in love.

The process of "merging and becoming" is not a final act or a consummation. It may have many dramatic moments or transitional confirmations, but it is a continuous opening toward others with less and less sense of vulnerability or vicarious identity with the good that others may do, or become. The aspect of "merging" is an awakening to loving community and the depths of interrelatedness invoked through the union of positive, intentional commitments to help others, to form community, to serve the needs of those also seeking to love more fully. But then there is the need to maintain personal integrity and difference, for that too is an intimate part of loving. Thus it is a merging that does not violate the integrity of others, but respects the differences, honors them, and still works to actualize shared goals and ideals. The context for this process of loving is that it does indeed "set us free" to see the contrast with others and the depths of our intentions to actualize a spiritual path or realize a spiritual potential. Every genuine love relationship is instructive; it teaches us where the differences create friction and joy and in the process, provides a context for further refinement and subtilization. This is true for each relationship because each is unique and the higher the degree of differentiation, the more likely the possibility for further transformation. As we move out of collective attitudes and practices, individual encounters become a genuine source of self-reflection in the jewel-net of mutual becomings.

Different relationships further different areas of growth and development; the wider the circle of friends and acquaintances, the more likely the possibility for deeper and more meaningful transformations. However, this assumes an authentic degree of love and caring in all those relationships for without that love, they will only reflect the shallow surface of normative social life, often alienated, disconnected, and unaware. Loving the alienated, disconnected and unaware is part of the spiritual path, and there is no doubt that the call to actualize the deepest love embraces those alienated others as inseparable from the transformative currents that move us all toward greater awareness. In this sense, "acquaintances" refer to all other human beings whose paths we may cross or encounter in life, including the lost, sick, despairing, angry, violent, and deeply disturbed. In the spiritual depths of love, the distinction between the healthy and unhealthy is an abstraction based on often arbitrary ways of thinking about others—all are equally in need of meaningful relations. The soul's "union and dissolution" is based on the widening circle of relationships that come into the caring concerns of a loving person and that challenge such persons to open their hearts to an even deeper love to carry them over the boundaries of inherited bias or fear. This is a great challenge in love, to open to the healing of others without losing the center, without diminishing the loving self who learns through love to share the depths of Spirit in healing capacities.

Love is neither will nor desire, neither grasping nor letting go; it emanates through life, awareness, and empathy, it gives birth to understanding and shows the full capacities of the soul. (5.4)

Meditation: The "full capacities of the soul" are not predetermined or bound by any barriers or limits but the ones we set internally. These capacities are still poorly understood; they remain largely identified with the "unconscious," that nebulous, indefinite concept of the denied and banished contents of the overrational mind. But the soul is much more than simply the leavings and impressions of discarded and denied life, or of "repression" or "instinct." The "full capacity" embraces a deep intimacy with the cosmos as a whole, linked to the inner life of others, with all the spiritual contents of visionary encounters, paranormal insight, and a full spectrum awareness. Its powers are not at all "unconscious" but simply unrecognized even though highly active in most persons, intrinsic to a much greater spiritual continuum of awareness and interaction than any posited by a psychology of mind alone. The full spectrum of human awareness has far more capacity than that manifested in conventional, large-scale societies, many of which have lost primal abilities once fully active in less urban, more earth-related cultures. At the heart of those capacities is an emergent love that embraces the world, the heavens and earth, with all the textures and contours of real knowledge and seeing. The full capacity for love is nothing less than a love for all created life, and its fullness is nothing less than the fullness of Spirit. And its limitation is the limitation of conventional thought anchored to a despiritualized skepticism whose "love" is often weak, shallow, and self-serving.

Liberating ourselves from the self-created illusions of a bound life is not easy, particularly at the beginning, when Spirit stirs the individual to look beyond the accepted, conventional, and safe contours of an immediate social world. But what moves us, beyond will and desire, is a current or feeling of relatedness to issues, ideas, persons, or events that promise more than what conventional or normative beliefs (or relations) can offer. It is not because we recognize what it is that moves us in this way, but rather we often do *not* know and yet still we are moved. This is one of the aspects of love that often goes unrecognized—a desire to be part of something more, something emergent and new, to join with others in actualizing a potential that is not yet known, not yet comprehended, or real. This actualization, this emergence out of the old and into the not-yet real is a primal act of love. It is an inner compulsion of being, seeking new expression and fulfillment in order to transform a static world into a place and time of emergence and joy. In the deeper spiritual sense, it is not done for self alone, but for the joy of a more illumined world where others may find a greater sense of fulfillment and understanding.

Loving in this way, spontaneously through acts of Spirit, means not grasping at the manifestations and not clinging to the process. The soulful development, the full realization of inner capacity, can only fully realize its deepest potentials in allowing the process to undergo the necessary rhythms and cycles that produce, over time, the requisite insight and mature awareness for self-expression. It is not, on the other hand, a passive waiting or a passive, uninformed intentionality. Above all else, it is a deep inner conviction and determination to seek the depths of the process through love and to form very clear intentions to actualize that process in all relationships.

Spiritual attunement with love is a very broad and wide horizon, not a shallow, self-serving window on a few relevant others. When fully opened, the horizon is a transpersonal vista whose inner workings impel us toward a greater understanding of our need for others and for co-creative relationships that are enhanced by love. Empathic insight into the heart and minds of others as co-creators is a primal basis for expressing spiritual continuity in the processes of mutual exploration and discovery. Our conjoined efforts draw out of our spiritual potential the soulful development and higher awareness within being. When we love deeply and with compassion it is spontaneously informative—it teaches us how interconnected life is and how enhanced life can be when we work and love together.

We must not "let go" by becoming too passive or too identified with an otherworldly, meditative perspective that wishes only to sit and observe the world as a witness and not to engage as an actor. The whole process of creative manifestation requires engaged commitments of mutually cooperative individuals working toward a transformation of embodied life, not an escape or denial of it! The old gnostic attitude of world rejection and bodily denial, of the conflict between good and evil, of seeing life as only suffering and living in ascetic detachment from worldly concern, is a practice and attitude that denies (as in modern nihilism) the worth, value, and joyful beauties of an incarnate world of joyful, spiritual beings.[28] We must embrace the world, not deny it; seek to enhance and contribute to its development, not simply use and abuse it. We must honor the circumstances of our embodiment and understand that this world is a place of spiritual manifestations, for eons and eons, and its "perfection" will only occur because we as individuals embrace that transformation as inseparable from our most embodied, worldly attainments. The "full capacity" is inseparable from a world-soul whose life is imbued with the emergent consciousness of every real, embodied creature—a capacity that seeks the fulfillment of each of those creatures in the context of a respectful, reverent harmony, fully valuing the significance of each contributing individual.

This requires more than passive observation and meditative calm; it also requires engaged and informed actors whose motivation is guided by a deep and abiding love for the world (and all the beings in it). The "understanding" that love gives is the perception and experience of the interrelationships between species, communities, and individuals. All contribute to the full expression of Spirit in a world-evolving process. The "full capacity" is known through an openness of heart and mind to the creative process and to the contribution that we, as individuals, can each make to the fulfillment of potential. If we turn away from this opening, contract into the narrow confines of a self-serving and "unconscious" life whose only horizon is immediate need and self-gratification, we will never know the "full capacity." Instead, we will live only mediocre lives and see no farther than the conventional horizons of unenlightened social boundaries and narrowly constructed self-interests. Yet we are so much more than what we presently see and so much more able to transform the world positively through the central role of love. And this seeing requires "seeing together" and not just seeing as individuals. The work at hand is the transformation of a world and not simply the spiritual illumination of the individual. Only when we can appreciate both the awakening of individual potential and the transformation of communal life on a planetary scale can we hope to actualize the full capacity in its highest, global intentionalities.

Love is the healing power of Spirit, it rejuvenates and restores, it opens new horizons of intimacy, it brings balance and calm; love arises from desire, seeks expression in passion, and finds its fullness in maturity and the wisdom of the heart. (5.5)

Meditation: The role of the will in this process is responsive, receptive to spiritual influence and allowing that influence to act in accord with deep feelings of respect and care. The "healing power" is not constructed or created by the individual; it is a gift whose affects work to transform others by opening them to the manifestations of Spirit. This creative power originates in the primal gift of life, in the birth of all newborn creatures, and is a natural capacity in those who love openly with inspiration. The will acts to direct the influences of healing love by surrendering inwardly to the workings of Spirit and allowing the spontaneity of care to respond to the needs, pain, and hopes of others. Such love does not originate in the individual but is shaped and shared through individual intentions, in a willingness to be a vessel that fills and overflows with that love through healing relationships with others. The intention is to purify self and to open the heart without demands or shallow expectations and then to allow that love to flow in magnetic currents creating a circumstance for inner transformation. Much of healing is release, a letting go of the attachments to wounds and pain, of not clinging to the injury and not internalizing self-loathing, or anger or jealousy or fear. Letting go of these conditions means finding the inner clarity that sees the limitations of a contracted, self-denying state, and willingly opens to a fuller and more healthy co-relatedness.

Such an opening can "rejuvenate and restore" a fading or contracted life with new possibility and direction because love is a primal motive power. Within Spirit, love is the convection that carries us with others to new regions of intensity and being. It opens the horizon of personal awareness by uniting us with other persons whose transformations affect our own awakening and growth. The currents of love are many and diverse; they flow through and about us continually mixed with subliminal fears and hopes, all the anxieties and longings that make us human. Even as limited and fallible beings, we still have a genuine capacity to open ourselves to the full power of love by understanding that love as inseparable from the process of a continual, ongoing co-creation. Our contribution is to love one another, to love life in all its diversity, plurality, and difference, to further the process of emergence toward greater creative awareness, insight, and expression. To create, one must love deeply and fully, for love is a capacity within us that draws on the full currents of our deep spiritual potential and fosters that potential through loving interactions. The withdrawn artist, alone in his or her private room, cut off from the loving support of community or nourishing love relationships can only create beauty by going deep within to touch the currents that reach outward toward others. How much more expressive is that creativity when surrounded and supported by loving relationships fully expressive of the value and worth of artistic expression?

Love also brings "balance and calm" because its center is in the supportive network of relationships that encourage development and becoming. Its center unites us with the primal currents of Spirit that supports and encourages the full expression of our mutual spiritual potentials. The "balance" is the nexus, the nodal points within that connect with the creative currents within others and connects as well to a deep sense of the Whole as a manifestation of loving actualization. The part-whole relationship is an inward centering that reaches out to embrace others whose own creative developments enhance the fullness of our shared awareness. Such love is not about isolated creators, but about the great web of relationships whose growth and strength and delicacy is global and multileveled, embracing many diverse species and creative worlds. In that sacred milieu, the individual functions as a contributor to the emergence of newness and unique expression, the language of which may take many diverse forms. It may be physical as in sexuality, dance, body movement, exercise; or emotional as in music, song, chanting, communal rites; or imaginative as in poetry, fiction, myth, story, or narrative; or intellective as in philosophy, history, sciences, or social and cultural explorations; or communal as in celebration, rites in the stages of growth, festival, or harvest. In each of these, the individual contributes through loving relationships unique perspectives and gifts to the emergence of the whole; it is love that is the primal source for our collective emergence.

When love acts on the individual, in a creative and permissive way, it encourages the desire for self-expression. This is good and natural, and because it is basic within the process of becoming, it is a necessary foundation for the development of creative insight and self-emergence. In a loving community, this support should be directed to children from the earliest moment in fostering their creative expression and exploration as a means for strengthening their ties with others in a creative process. Yet it should not inhibit their need for solitude and creative self-exploration, for incubation that is also crucial in the process of emergence. Love as a creative source for self-development should not be underestimated, it is a foundational support and condition that opens many doors into the unknown and unseen, particularly through the exploration of creative relationships. Desire in this process becomes passion and passion is the emotional condition that energizes creative self-expression, which gives the necessary commitment to carry the vision forward into a complete actualization. Passionate love is one of the great motive sources of human transformation and in many ways, that passion reflects Spirit in all the passions of creation. It is an impassioned universe of creative energies, beings, spirits, elementals, a visionary host of subtle and material entities whose coevolution is interwoven with the urgency within life "to be fruitful and to multiply."

The "fullness and maturity" of love, of a deep attunement with other loving beings, is beyond definition or qualification. This is because, as a motive source, love has limitless capacity for self-expression. This requires us to choose the means and ways we feel most called upon to love, to find the appropriate means for the communication and sharing of that love in its most mature forms. In a broad sense, it is simply loving all those whose paths cross near and around each of us, sharing as fully as possible the surplus of loving energy and its deep reservoir for healing and transformation. But this capacity should not be exhausted by indiscriminate sacrifice, or through excess or in meeting the unqualified demands of others. There must be balance, times for renewal and restoration, quiet, a sanctuary of stable containment, a place with support for privacy, inner reflection, and complete renewal. These are the rhythms of love, to express, share, merge, unite, draw apart, rest, go into solitude, replenish, and reanimate the fire and then to share that light with others in creative cycles of expression and renewal. Maturity in love is not self-exhausting or self-denying. It is balanced, centered, and knows where the personal limits are and where and how to renew that center in order to be effective in future being and becoming.

We are not infinite or all-powerful, even though we may experience the Infinite and the primal sources of Power. Therefore, humility in love is deeply important because it recognizes where the capacity of the individual has been fully expressed and, therefore, knows when to draw back and to renew. The deep "wisdom of the heart" is to allow the Spirit to work through the individual and to energize our capacity to love and to be loved; and this process, in all its rhythms, expansions, and contractions, requires periodic rest and renewal as natural and regenerative for all creative actions. This is the importance of incubation—to nourish our capacity in solitude, separation and low stimulation, in a quiet removal of all distraction and interruptions, a stilling that allows for inner alchemical maturity, slowly, without demands or false expectations. The time of solitude and inner cultivation is by no means secondary or peripheral to the creative process; this is a central tenet of emergence, to allow for the process to go "underground" and to enter the season of having no leaves, no demands, only the cool, gray skies of winter and the muffled sound of snow, still water, warm fires, and hot tea. The regenerative aspect is highly important and only by fostering a sensitive capacity for quiet and stillness can the necessary synthesis attain its Spirit-guided renewal.

Sexuality without love is empty, mechanical, self-serving; to enter into love means to revere, respect, and rejoice in sexuality; in a healthy, thriving love, there is no submission, no external demands or denials, only deep affirmation. (5.6)

Meditation: The spiritual aspect of sexuality is central to the process of emergence, and sexuality without love is a form of denial of our shared capacity for deep union and mutual joy. The arousal of sexual energy is a powerful expression of the spiritual basis of the life source; the primal energy of sexual love is the greatest and most immediate expression of joy and mergence with others. That this joy is directly related to conception and the life gift is a profound sign of the ecstatic origins of all life. It reveals clearly that the gift of life is inseparable from the joy of a co-creative union. When we move beyond physical sensation and into the emotional and spiritual depths of love—into natural sexuality, into sensuous and pleasurable aspects—we touch deeply the very heart of life and being. Sexual love is ecstatic because it expresses the most primal of all acts, the union of opposites and the creation of life. The sacred marriage, the *Hieros Gamos*, is a celebration of all the powers, male and female, uniting in order to celebrate the fecundity and potency of nature and all growing things, from the most magnificent world tree to the lowest healing moss, from the oak to the holly, both necessary elements in the great work of fruitful transformation. The primal union of lovers, their shared joys and pleasures are a gift of Spirit, a gift whose expression requires reverence and respect to fully know and experience.[29]

The need for reverence springs from the recognition that sexual experience reduplicates the very processes of creation, the yin-yang balance of female and male seeking unity in order to deepen love and commingled pleasures. These pleasures are not secondary to the process, but are intrinsic expressions of a heightened awareness, a more sensitive response to sensation and the arousal of energies whose affects act directly to alter awareness and shift us into a more expanded and joyful condition of union and delight. In the intensity of sexual joys, mind, heart, and soul can expand into new vistas of awareness and visionary openings of a merging and sharing and oneness of being. This is no arbitrary aspect, but a spiritual sign that co-creation is also an affective unity with deeper soul-life. This unity connects us with the deep currents of love that act to draw all beings toward the most creative realizations through union and shared pleasures. This sharing of pleasure, so often denied, rejected, and scorned by "other worldly" religions, is a deep source of transformation and can be a profound source of spiritual awakening. In moving beyond the old gnostic, ascetic metaphysics of denial and the suppression of pleasure, we can recover the joys of sexual and sensual play as a creative aspect of emergence and becoming. This uniting is a correspondent reflection of cosmic processes, of the merged and synthetic energies of diverse creative interactions where difference leads to diversity and spiritual becoming.

Without this deeper love reflecting the processes of mutual caring and co-creation, sexuality becomes only an extension of self-will, a use of others for gratifications whose consequences are shallow, brutal, and destructive. The lack of love clearly manifests in the most brutal acts of sexual aggression, where there is no feeling for the feelings of others, and the only power is the limited coercion of others, their submission to petty and yet deeply harmful demands. Sexual aggression is one of the most brutal of all violent acts: this is because it often results in a wounding that inhibits the capacity for love in the injured party and for natural sexual pleasures with a beloved and respectful other. The contractions caused by violent sexual attack, rape, abuse, and manipulations are among the most serious of all crimes because they leave the victims of these assaults in a violated state of fear and paralysis that can deeply inhibit their capacity to love and to be loved. While the aggressors may reflect their own abuse and contraction, those subject to this aggression bear, many times over, the consequence of the act through the deadening effects of inner denial, guilt, and frightened contraction. This inhibition, as a crippling withdrawal and a sense of loss and vulnerability, requires great love and gentleness to restore the positive dynamics of an open and trusting love relationship. The abuse of others through sexual aggression is an act of deep denial; it reveals a selfish will unable to recognize the value of love and the need for permissive, co-equal, mature relations between mutually consenting partners.

More superficially, sexuality can too easily become a routine matter of releasing tension and satisfying momentary needs at the cost of losing the depths and passions of an inspired, deep-felt spiritual relationship. Lovers become hollow and routine when they no longer foster growth and emergence into deepening awareness and limit themselves to shallow water and the flux and flow of surface needs. The sexual "use" of others for momentary sexual pleasure or gratification is a sign of alienation and contraction, a narrowing of the life source to a momentary release whose expressions have little or no depth and fail to connect meaningfully with the partner. Such interactions only inhibit the capacity for love, dislocated from deeper feeling and unable to share the experience of the other. Too many are locked into routine patterns that only perpetuate the condition of a decreasing satisfaction and an arbitrary sexual interest in others who remain alluring only as long as they are unknown or unattainable. This superficial condition, of living only in the physical pleasure and use of others, also has a deadening affect—it reduces sexuality to a momentary release whose satisfactions are brief, illusive, and emotionally shallow. It becomes a primary means for the inhibition of love and often results in a long series of brief relationships whose newness quickly pales and whose depths soon collapse into sterile patterns of dissatisfaction and loss of interest.

The spiritual depths of sexual love affirm the patient exploration of pleasure and intimacy in a context of unviolated trust and gentle caring. It is a relationship of co-equal partners whose sexual needs are not the same and whose rhythms differ through the influence of many impinging conditions; a sensitive perception of these differences leads to many alternative expressions of sexuality. Sexuality is not a "routine" but a mutual sharing and exploration that requires adaptation, newness, and fluid conditions to fully express the joy. Sexuality is also an emergent and creative horizon of being, and as such, the joys and pleasures of sexuality are creative, playful, divergent, and yet also respectful, loving, and protective. In this sense, "tantra" is not a particular ritual or practice, but a deep respect for the sexual partner as a primary co-creator in the attainment of spiritual illumination and the awakening of potential. Sexuality is a spiritual potential whose arousal can lead to transpersonal experience and illuminating insights into the very nature of being and becoming. We need only to recognize the potential and affirm the sexual capacity that is foundational in the creation of life, that reveres and honors the sexual process as a means for spiritual teaching. This requires great maturity and discipline, but as a spiritual practice, it can arouse profound and transformative energies whose integration leads to an altered awareness of the depths of sexuality. This requires care, foresight, and deep mutual understanding to fully actualize the potential.[30]

From love comes compassion, from compassion, harmony and sharing; separation, division, and jealousy enter where love has failed, where it has not taken root in soulful being and led to transformation. (5.7)

Meditation: Love is transformative and not just "an initial experience"; it sustains all the stages of maturity and gradual development and awakening. If there is no development, then stagnation can set in, forming habits and patterns whose repetitions increasingly lack a sense of fulfillment. This reflects the dynamic qualities of love as intimate to the process of spiritual development, such that, after flowering, there must be maturation of the fruit. Without that maturation, the fruit will be hard, indigestible, and bitter as it slowly withers and, then, can no longer reproduce. The dynamic qualities are always linked to a sense of incorporation and openness to emergent expressions and new stages of development, while also recognizing the need for rest, quiet, and solitude. In mature love, there is a "time for every season" and this timely cycling of joining and separating reflects the greater rhythms of nature and cosmic life. Love is not a lineal progression or an unwavering line, but a cyclical rhythm, a spiral both inward and outward, interconnected, an intersection of circles that overlap like ancient tribal drawings on rock walls. Yet it is a creative process, not simply reiterating the past but also incorporating the present and seeing the possibilities for future exploration. And love takes root, draws its sustenance from and through the body, transforms the body and awakens its latent energies to a higher and more complete awareness and luminosity. This is the "body electric" that awakens the deep colors and energies of full transformation and opens soulful being to its full potential.

In soulful being, the deep aspects of the psyche fully embrace the body, surround it with a protective aura, and emanate qualities of awareness, subtle perception, and receptivity to a larger, more soulful world. Sexuality is part of this psychic identity; it is the living energy of soulful life capable of merging and uniting itself with diverse aspects of others through Eros, affection, and love. Sexuality, in a soulful life is more than a physical relationship, is it a reflection of psychic affinity, deep attraction, and a "sharing of energy" that enhances each partner in the sharing. On the level of physical expression, such soulful quality is connective and transforms the awareness of each person according to the degree of their receptivity to the transformative energies constantly manifesting on a soul level. To arouse sexual energy is to also arouse psychic energy; the two are intimately entwined, and the soulful capacity for love is the greater capacity. In that love, soulful being reaches out to unite with others through the medium of feelings and shared perceptions, thoughts, and intuitions in an empathic and co-creative interaction. While soulful being infuses body with sexual energy and responsiveness, it also infuses our relationships with others in a direct, interactive, erotic way. It unites us in common concern and intimate passions whose expressions flow into the world through the creative joining of souls and a uniting of hearts and minds.

For love to take root in the soul means that the quality of our relationships with others is manifesting an intimacy and sharing that comes from a spontaneous depth of feeling, not from a critical evaluation of the role or importance of others in seeking our own goals and concerns. This spontaneous feeling of relatedness is Spirit-born and flows out of the heart of the creative process, linking us with others as co-workers in the great work of mutual development and self-realization. We are all instrumental in the creative process and this capacity to share and to work together for the actualization of positive goals reflects a quality of soul. Its potential is to open and to feel the empathic influences of spiritual inspiration and to ground those inspirations in meaningful, caring human (and not just human) relationships. This opening to others, this sharing and participation in mutual exploration, is a soulful quality, and when fully developed, it leads to a deep and abiding compassion for all other beings as co-creators in a mutual becoming. Spiritually, we are linked with many, many others—now and in the past and future. This linkage is made manifest when love opens the heart to others and reveals clearly the intimacy that draws us toward the full realization of our human potential. This is a process of expansion that also has its stages of contraction in order to give birth. We contract when the process pulls us toward its natural conclusions and reaches that critical stage where full commitment and full presence requires all our energy and awareness to give birth.

When we contract without giving birth, or disengage and cannot attain depths, cannot share and co-create, being fearful, arrogant, or confused, then soul diminishes. This pulling back and pulling in can become so habituated, that the individual is no longer aware of sympathetic bonds or empathic connection. Life becomes a series of external relationships, seen only from the "outside"—that is, seen only as indistinct interactions whose depths are vague, impressionistic, and inseparable from the murky waters of an enclosed self-awareness. This pulling back, habituated by constant struggle and the failure of others to recognize the unique differences between individuals, leads to isolation, depersonalization, feelings of loneliness, and a fragmentary self-knowledge. Then comes jealousy, division, conflict, and separation—all the contracted currents pulling against the deeper waters of self-affirmation and mutual joy in sharing. The tide pool of isolated self-awareness, cut off from the greater ocean of mutual relatedness, simmers with all the reflected heat and crystalline salts of a lost sea of possible transformation—bitter, sharp, quarrelsome, angry, encrusted like the shells of lonely hermit crabs snatched from the rocks by predatory gulls. Soulful being in this process dies a thousand deaths, each stroke of the knife cutting some small link with the other. Then, storm-driven, comes the fearsome depths of a darkening sea whose currents pull downward toward death, complete submergence, and a suffocating weight of dark, cold, unseeing depths.

Yet there is always the capacity for redemption, for resurrection from this dark, cold, contraction and a slow resurfacing to light and warmth. A return to this light and rebirth occurs through new relationships, new openness, and new hopes born out of actual encounters "unbound at the edges" and thus receptive to the healing powers of love and mutual discovery. Those who lay, deep and dark, in the lower currents of murky waters are those whose inner capacity to rise is so injured that they must seek the aid of others, the light and air of those willing to descend into that cold and dark in order to help those in isolation to recover an inner capacity for expansion and new buoyancy. Such is Spirit, always leading us into the depths where our own transformations are only a prelude to the transformations of others, for in Spirit, the transformation is more than personal. It reaches out and encompasses the many, all those in need of light and love and awakening, all those lost because of soul's contraction, all those wandering blindly in the depressive tempests of floundering relationships. May Spirit bless those contracted souls; may it open our hearts to their pain and injury; may it show us the path toward healing and self-becoming, opening our eyes and mind, revealing to us the many byways of renewed transformation. And may we have the courage and strength to accept into our own pathways the needs of all those injured and in need of healing, that our co-creating should not exclude but include the suffering of those whose needs are greater than our own self-sought attainments.

The compassionate aspect of love, in the soul's opening to Spirit, is not a demand that we must enact a particular pattern or obligation as a formal sign of personal commitment. However Spirit moves us is the way we must follow—some in service, others in love and family, others in creative expression, in whatever pathways call us toward our soul's awakening. The "harmony and sharing" is in the greater community of diverse individuals with diverse ability and attainments built slowly toward a comprehensive realization of potential. The task of love is to explore capacities and to include in that process the many diverse talents of others; to explore within ourselves a richness of possibility and to see emergence in all the creative forms that love can take. This love is not bound, not confined to specific form or obligation, but flows out into the world, an inspiration for the soulful transformation. In this way, it is possible to find many means and expressions of soulful being, all communicated with love for the healing and well-being of others. This is our spiritual freedom—the freedom to love deeply, with passion, and to explore in every way the currents of that passion for the transformation of the world. This is Spirit's calling, and this is our mutual task, to awaken potential and then to realize its power and depths through shared healing and communal rebirth.

Freedom to love means letting go, not denying the worth of others, not refusing their freedom; love is not confined to one-dimensional relationships, or to one person—love is not possession but creative and shared exploration. (5.8)

Meditation: Love involves sharing, finding the many ways in which sharing enhances individual experience and makes life richer and more complete. This can only happen through a genuine and receptive affirmation of others and the development of a more self-aware sensitivity that harmonizes with the needs and aspirations of the other. This balance, between self-needs and the needs of beloved others, is the primal testing ground of love. A creative, developing love is not "selfless" because there is a recognized and valued center to personal identity that has its own needs, aspirations, and ideals. This is true for every person, regardless of maturity or spiritual development—every person has some inner sense of self in relationship to others and the Whole, however widely the values may differ. And, spiritually speaking, this self seeks not sublimation to the Whole, but an affirmation of individual worth through a unique focus on spiritual ability and real character, individuality, and graceful coexistence with others. The balance and harmony between individuals in a context of shared spiritual aspirations does not negate individual worth, but enhances that worth through the capacity of the individual to love and love deeply without losing the salt and savor of his or her own character and identity. This other is a unique vessel of Spirit, having his or her own form and contents, and valuing others means valuing them "all the way down" to the foundations of their own personal and unique abilities and accomplishments.

Often there is a struggle in love for self-definition that recognizes the legitimacy and value of the other perspective and yet also values self-perspective and difference. As we move forward in love, we move through all the stages of deepening awareness in the face of life challenges and the "trials and tribulations" of developing social commitments, family obligations, and communal responsibilities. These challenges confront us at every turn with new perspectives on partnership and loving relations. In this process love is crucial, revealing as it does a depth of strength and mutual support for meeting and integrating all those challenging circumstances. But strategies differ, and among many alternatives, some are more and some less appealing in terms of the consequences and impact on the relationship between those working to meet such challenges. Yet love is the deepest commitment; the primary challenge is to meet life's trials with love, and giving love to others when they need it and not simply when it is convenient or easy. Often this means giving it in a form that is helpful to the other, not always easy for the giver, and giving it freely without demands or future expectations. It is not a matter of increasing debts or obligations, but of a free gift, Spirit-given, for the benefit and support of others. The reciprocal response is not a matter of debt or necessity, but flows out of the heart as a thankful return, a willing gift whose fullness is in part built through the gifts of others.

Failure to understand the gifting of love, the spontaneity and generosity of Spirit in the loving response, leads to contraction, to patterns of demand that rely on habit, cycles of dysfunctional dependency, aggressive attitudes of control, self-centered pleasures, and a shallow and unpleasant egoism. Such a shallow "love" denies the worth of the other by constantly subjecting the other to the emotional demands and imbalances of an immature, unhappy, often confused individual (or community) whose needs blind it to the natural reciprocity through which love works to heal and create. Love is *reciprocal*, a constant sharing, not simply an excess in giving or an abundance of receiving. There is a co-creative bond in all loving actions that links the giver and the receiver into a microcosmic image of the Whole, the giving and receiving of Spirit, and the circulation of that love through a creative process of emergent becoming. The higher demands of love require us to love where love is impaired, where a loving response cannot flow but contracts around the inner injuries that keep the capacity bound and isolated. The healing of this condition flourishes through love and deep connectedness to Spirit and its overflowing fullness, such that this abundance can flow through and beyond the individual in reanimating the world with more healthy, reciprocal being. This healing presence, in deep empathy, gives that love without demand or expectations, knowing that in true health, such love flows out to others to heal and reanimate spontaneously.

To affirm the worth of the other means to affirm that worth regardless of the personal struggles, injuries, or hurt that the other carries. But this also means not becoming caught in the demands and expectations of others that emerge out of their internalized injury, hurt, and need—abuse is easily transmitted through patterns of expectation and in love can violate the integrity of even the most healthy relationship. This means we must always balance love and compassion with a degree of self-knowledge that affirms and values the individual perspective while not compromising that affirmation through excess in fulfilling the needs of others. Love is not about simply fulfilling the needs of others or living up to the expectation of others. A mature love is grounded in Spirit and in spiritual principles that guide love toward a more complete, creative expression in the processes of *mutual* growth and development. The refusal of a partner to recognize the spiritual grounds of this transformation, one who clings to unhealthy patterns or excessive rationality, only lays down the pathway for retreat and withdrawal from love. The spiritual ground of love also requires letting go and not clinging to relationships whose tensions can not sustain a creative process of mutual transformation.

Love is not a one-sided process, but a shared process of gradual emergence into a deeper and more self-aware spiritual sharing. Letting go in this sense means not clinging to redundant patterns of interaction that lead continually to stalemate, dead ends, or denial of possibility for new growth and transformation. Often, this means letting go of our limited ideas and attitudes toward another whom we genuinely love and to realize that it is often our own prejudice and habituated, shallow thinking that occludes the potential of the other and inhibits their possible growth and becoming. Reciprocal understanding involves a constant self-awareness capable of seeing the other in a new light, of making the changes with them and keeping up with the inner processes of a long-term love relationship and thereby avoiding the habituated response that only sees the other in the light of old thinking and old mental attitudes. Seeing the other, loving them, requires an ongoing inner sensitivity for their changes and new directions and discoveries; it means valuing those changes and not clinging to an outmoded, earlier idea or attitude that binds who they are or who they might or "should" be. Reciprocity in love requires a consistent revaluing of the other in terms of changing aspirations and goals. It also means inner changes within the one who perceives these changes in the other; there is a need for partners in love to be "in process" and each a part of the ongoing currents of spiritual transformation. We each have our own rhythms, interests, directions, and concerns, but in the depths of spiritual love, these interests and concerns are influenced and mutually conditioned by reciprocal choices and decisions whose consequences affect all concerned.

Fulfillment in love means a deep trust and openness, a complete sharing, with no positive desires unexpressed or unexplored; it means

loyalty, enduring companionship, and continued growth through creative insight and understanding. (5.9)

Meditation: Because love is shared and known through relationships, trust is central to its maturation and full expression. Trust is not always easy or immediate—every wound and injustice, every denial and false justification, detracts from our abilities to trust or to understand that trust is inseparable from deep love. Healthy and lasting love is not based only in feelings, in shared ideals or goals, or in mutual commitments or external obligations. Love, in the spiritual sense, is based in a genuine openness and sharing, in a concern for the well-being of others, and in a willingness to adapt, change, and develop as persons through mutual sharing. Yet this sharing opens us to the differences that we hold as our own, to the feelings, beliefs, motivations, hopes, dreams, or ambitions that we hold as crucial for individual existence. Opening our inner life to others implies trust, that is, a willingness to respect and appreciate the personal quality of individual values and aspirations. Without this trust it is very difficult to know the deeper life of others; however much they may share and communicate, they may also hold back deeper feelings and perceptions out of habits of closure and inner protectiveness.

This closure is often a consequence of earlier ridicule or denial, of being "shunned" for failing to live up to external criteria and expectations of insensitive others. This diminishing of self through closure is a common tendency among those whose inner life is richer and more active, more individualized than conventional social norms. Often there is a tension between collective norms and individual perception, between social custom and resistance to that custom as unjustly coercive or blind to another kind of seeing. This tension between normative social patterns, based largely in unexamined social conventions and unthinking communal values, and individual perception and disagreement or resistance to those unexamined norms can easily reduce openness and trust in love. As children, we may have experienced this closure to trust by having those most responsible for our care insist on conformity to conventional norms of social behavior and communal interactions. This false patterning, based on the wholesale adoption of external values, can quickly subvert a child's trust and leave him or her feeling vulnerable to the criticisms of those who hold an external social orientation. Such vulnerability is often a prelude to a growing inner division within self between personal perceptions or feelings and outward conformity. Once this division is advanced far enough, a loving relationship may be difficult, particularly if the beloved other is more conventional in thinking or perceiving the world.

To trust means to willingly convey to the other the real motives, values, and concerns that motivate us in a passionate and genuine way regardless of how nonconforming or individual the values. Love is a basis for such trust when it creates a mutual dynamic of sharing, each person hearing the other, feeling their concerns and acting to honor those concerns in ways that do not violate the integrity of either person. This is not always easy! Inevitably, there are disagreements and tensions over how to respond to a particular circumstance that genuinely concerns one or more parties in a loving relationship. Trust in such a case is a matter of not devaluing the concerns of others even when we may deeply disagree with those concerns. The point at which we resist difference is the boundary where action or intention becomes inhibited by the other, where active resistance involves acquiring the freedom to act in accord with values we hold even when we know such action may be resisted by one deeply loved. Such a circumstance carries trust to another level—to trust the other in carrying out their own projects and aspirations in a way that is nonharmful to themselves or others. Creative explorations, individual eccentricity, nonconformist behavior, or attitudes that are nonharmful may be a necessary aspect on an inner actualization long blocked by a divided inward condition. Embracing the whole self may mean exhibiting all the inner nuances of individual being without shame or contraction in order to actualize a more free and permissive life of self-expression and authenticity.

Love fosters this kind of growth because it expresses deeply the actual conditions of emergent being by flowing outward into expressive life, into actual form and manifestation. What guides this process beyond simple self-need is a community of loving relationships within which love and honesty function to express the boundaries where respect and appreciation for others may needfully co-condition each participant's actions with respect to the balance within the Whole. In balancing relationships, mutual respect is crucial and pivotal in the development of a shared space in which each person's needs are met, where each person can cultivate creative relationships whose reciprocal love is a fostering of inner development and not a matter of conformity to the demands of dominant others. To truly explore all "positive desires" through love means the creation of extraordinary circumstances and conditions that allow each person to maximize inner potential through the realization of multiple potentials and mutual needs without overriding one need for the expression of another. This is why simplicity is valuable in the process; and yet complexity certainly has a place, as do eccentricity and uniqueness. In this emergent process, love plays a central role of providing the emotional, connective condition for emergence in which our capacity for love is tested by our ability to simultaneously accept the creative needs and desire of others and also honor, within ourselves, our own unique needs and desires.

Only when love and trust work together with genuine commitment to a mutual process of development can this creative process flourish in the lives of all members of a spiritual circle. And as each circle connects with other circles, this same balance of love and trust acts, Spirit-guided, to ennoble the loving process with joy, spontaneity, and open, creative expression. Over time, this process creates a sense of loyalty and devotion to well-loved others whose mutual support and reciprocity in love create those conditions in which trust and companionship may flourish. Loyalty involves long-term commitment and a deep recognition of the value and worth of the other as part of the enriching, full life of spiritual development. The "enduring companionship" of long-term relations is a great accomplishment, one to be valued and deeply appreciated as part of the process through which Spirit transforms the world. These long-term relationships bring stability and teaching into the world of transient human encounters and offer the stability and shared memories and experiences that have enhanced a life of mutual spiritual transformation. We are not working alone but together in a great work of world transformation and all the friends and lovers we have are part of that process, each contributing to the richness and value of the emergent Whole. Life partners are highly valuable as intimate others whose sharing and love have made the journey memorable and worthy and without whom we would each be poorer and less aware.

In sharing the ups and downs of our different spiritual paths, we come to realize over years of love and creative interaction, how valuable the other is in opening our hearts to subtleties or mysteries we might never have seen had we been alone or lived without the "joyful turbulence" of a lifelong partner or beloved other. The healing of our injuries proceeds through these long-term relationships when new levels of trust open us to insights and understanding that we can share and mutually explore. The emergence of creative insight, Spirit-given, has a mutual ground for expression and communication whose application is directly related to our most intimate relationships. It is in those relationships that we can test within ourselves the full responsibility of our insights. Our capacity to enact our spiritual values is nowhere better realized than in these long-term relationships where another's honesty and openness to our growth can provide an alternative view. This view, when shared with love, can help us to more fully recognize where development is yet necessary, where growth must be modified through sharing and where, under conditions of deep trust, our own lack of seeing may be transformed through the knowing perspectives of a beloved other. This process is mutual, a shared awakening to spiritual capacity, and leads each partner toward a more refined and balanced wholeness in which male and female perspectives harmonize to create a fuller and more complete sense of understanding and becoming.

Without understanding and trust there is no love, only routine, habit, and false expectation; without understanding, there is censure, blame, or an unspoken hardness of heart. (5.10)

Meditation: Understanding in love means fully taking into account the differences between those who love. It means recognizing how these differences act to create tensions and seeing how these tensions require our full attention and sincere consideration to work out an equitable and co-creative solution. Sometimes, it is simply necessary for each person to follow the path as it unfolds before him or her and to do so without impinging on the freedom and direction of a beloved other. Often this requires a mutual sense of independence, a freedom for each to pursue different directions in different rhythms while deeply loving and sharing in gentle and mutual ways. Love is not a merging of identities, as much as a merging of feeling and concern; it is not a loss of self, but a heightening of self as co-related and yet independent. Love is not about sacrificing independence but about attaining independence without denying the value and importance of creativity for beloved others. This balance of independence and mutuality means having a view and holding to it and yet being also receptive to the perspectives of those we love. It means allowing love to act as a medium of interconnected concern that helps shape particular and evolving perspectives. In this way love unites and yet it individuates; it spiritualizes by valuing and enhancing the difference-in-unity.

Independence is not the same as indifference or inattention; a spiritual love requires concern and attention, a very alert caring awareness that is sensitive to the moods, feelings, and needs of loved others. Love takes us out of ourselves and into a more complete realization of how necessary loving relationships are in working through all the challenges and stages of personal growth. Mutual independence is an extroversion of a shared love whose introversion is mutual interdependence—together they represent the inward and outward tensions of love, shifting and exchanging perspective through a wide range of feelings, moods, and intentions. As we engage the wider world of human relationships, expanding our circle of friends and loved others, we also acquire a need to have a primary center based in long-term relationships that fosters stability and a sense of deep relatedness. The health of these long-term relationships is based on an alert sensitivity to the experiences of others who, while giving us support, also look to us for support. In these relationships co-developed memory plays a central role: there is a history, a continuity, a journeying together, even when apart, toward similar goals, or journeying in a way that touches each deeply. We have independence but we also have our lifelong shared experiences and our deeper continuities in love that is Spirit-blessed.

However, when this history flattens out, ceases to be a creative sharing, and is no longer able to maintain intimacy and shared intentions, then habit and routine become a substitute for authentic depths and sensitivity. Tension becomes combative, expectations lean toward demands, patience begins to evaporate and leaves only an increasing restlessness, a low current of agitation, a feeling of abandonment, or an increasingly sad sense of loss. In a contracting love, expectation is not a mutually constructed way of understanding the relationship, but an independent way in which one perspective tends to dominate over another. The artifact of an ideal lover begins to take on an increasing numinosity, and inner projection of something "more" than what really is in any actual relationship. An inner conflict arises—the beloved other as imagined in contrast to the real other as experienced (but often, not really known). This idealizing process, by no means a feature of only young love but quite active at various stages of older relationships, is a common feature of the struggle for readjustment. The task of love is to clear away these artifacts of imagination in order to know a real other and then to find ways to share love with that other in an imaginative and creative fashion—to love them with panache, verve, flair, passion, and not with just patient detachment and self-restraint! The ideal other is an artifact of a misguided love; it does not embody itself in real relationships with all the contours and rough edges of real individuals seeking self-development.

In a more contracted sense, love turns bitter and becomes aggressive in confronting the inadequacies of the beloved. A disappointed lover whose anger is fueled by indignation and an insecure sense of self-worth seeks to justify those feelings at the expense of the other. This anger and disappointment only increases the tensions between independent perspectives; like an arrow shot into the heart, it cleaves in two the once delicate union and merging. Out of this injury, the hurt engendered by an increasing disparity between an ideal other and the actual other, there is a rending of soul. This rending is an inner fluctuation that feels keenly the disjoining of two, the reforming of one as truly separate, the sense of a lost love whose spiritual contents no longer act to inspire but only to inhibit. In this condition "censure and blame" frequently become part of a defensive strategy, a way of disarming the other through pointing out the inadequacies of another's love and caring. This despiritualization of love, this judgment against loving capacity is a further step toward a collapse of love, when love becomes a criteria used to measure another's adequacy or effort. This is a perversion of love; it is a shallow means by which we often hurt the ones we love most deeply. By denying another's efforts to love maturely in an imperfect world of immature beings, we create the circumstances leading to mistrust and closure. Blame only drives the hurt deeper and creates a sheltering of feeling from others, sometimes driving that sheltered self deep into the inmost center where echoes cry out for recognition and help.

In separation between loving partners, blame and censure should play no role; a mature recognition of limits, of ending, however painful, should also work through a respectful loving. In a willing and spiritualized love, the process of separation, painful and difficult, is best helped by an ongoing commitment to the value and worth of all that was gained and received through the relationship. This recognition includes the freedom for each individual to chose a different life-path, to make the decision to go a separate way; not lightly or because of inflated desires or surface restlessness, but out of a deeper sense of needing to follow a path of development that cannot be actualized within the context of a particular relationship. In such a case, we owe a deep debt of gratitude to the beloved other in letting us go; or, conversely, we demonstrate our generosity and humility by letting go and still loving. We all have many partners in the network of loving relationships, many relationships that act on us differently to enhance or bring forth a nuance or quality perhaps unemphasized in other relationships. In honoring all these relationships, we need to respect the individuality and differences while also rejoicing in the nearness and sharing that is possible. There are always limits or boundaries in relating to others in terms of their needs or intentions—the harmonizing of intention is a joyful enhancement of capacity, but a genuine sharing of intention even briefly can also stimulate growth and positive change.

In this process of separate loving, blame and censure are only contractions that lead to harm and injury; without them we are freer to give and share what we most value. If others receive it, well and good; if not, let each go his or her own way with respect and appreciation. An inward "hardening of the heart" is only a sign of closure, a reflection on the one who contracts, creating a barrier of detachment from all the frailties of love and feeling. This is an artificial pose; a stance that has never successfully known love in its fullness. It reflects not detachment, but inadequacy; it suggests an incapacity to love and to undergo all the turbulence of real, committed loving—of being open to the other through the intimate causality of deeply shared feeling and closeness. Understanding in love is open to the other, and real openness means taking in the other as an influence in our own understanding. It is sharing, not pretense or simply passion, but a mutual exploration, a working together to find a deeper potential. The balance here is to love deeply and without reservation and also to explore all those paths and possibilities that are part of an individual vision. The vision is an individual encounter, but its sharing is part of the emergence of others,

interactive, and conditional in helping each of us realize the fullness of our shared potential.

**With understanding, love becomes a staging
ground for wisdom and insight, establishing positive conditions for tolerance and empathy, a
basis for maturity in valuing alternatives, however alien or strange. (5.11)**

Meditation: Sometimes, the "alien or strange" are the very persons we love and live with! This might also be a child or a friend who
is going through a life crisis; a co-worker or acquaintance; a practitioner of a different religion; a member of another culture, place,
time, or world. In many ways, love is a form of amelioration, a "making better" that opens our world to the world of another without
being vulnerable to the tensions that make those worlds so different.
The very concept of the "alien and strange" is grounded in an unknowing, a lack of familiarity or understanding in terms of what motivates, inspires, or excites a particular life way or commitment.
Easily enough, the other may become that which is "exotic" or alluring while still being known only in the most superficial way. To love
the other means to take into one's self that strange difference and to
respect and value it as meaningful and significant for the other, particularly when what makes the other alien is simply a consequence
of our own ignorance, denial, or stereotyping. In the processes of becoming, there is always a challenge to love those who are truly different and yet worthy and enhanced by love. Loving in this way, as
a spiritual practice, does not proceed through rational agreement or
through compromise; it proceeds through accepting the value of difference and then nurturing the differences in positive affirmation.

Can we love the snake that bites us, the spider that poisons us,
the dangerous or threatening? Can we do so with respect and a mature understanding of the capacity, temper, or tendencies of the alien
other? Such love is a nonsentimental, existential love that fully eval-
uates the worldview and tendencies that give coherence to another's
life or being. Love is not value-free, or unconcerned with ethical or
spiritual questions with regard to how others act or coexist. There is
an inner correctness in positive loving that allows for difference and

yet also seeks a harmonious and creative relationship with the other. Such a relationship requires knowledge of what motivates the other and how those motives can be enhanced by loving relationship and how, when necessary, those motives (including our own) must be co-adapted and modified or reevaluated. In the spiritual sense, this is a dynamic process of interaction, not a static attitude or simple one-dimensional affirmation. It is an ongoing process of co-adaptation, a two-sided interaction in which respect and appreciation acts creatively to open new possibilities of positive interaction. Sometimes, this requires stages of growth to overcome hostility or fear or aggression; in such cases, respect is a matter of seeing where the limits lie within one's self as well as within another, and then acting to overcome those limits.

In this process "the positive conditions" are those conditions that allow for a careful exploration of alternative ways of relating, of allowing others the freedom of their own self-expression. Patience is part of that positive condition and an ability to recognize where another has been hurt or abused, become mistrusting or skeptical, arrogant or misleading based on past conditions that have denied the value or worth of love and affection. Love as compassion or as a genuine caring about the other does not proceed through imposition or control, but through openness, dialogue, and considerate listening.[31] Compassion engages the other with a passionate interest in a shared well-being, in a mutual coexistence that values the intrinsic worth of the other through receptivity to new and often unknown concerns, projects, or goals. Integrity is certainly part of the positive conditions—such love is an affirmation of other and self, an understanding proceeding from diverse centers that intersect at the boundaries without closure, censure, or denial. This requires gentleness and humility, the capacity to take in what is alien and make it more knowable and comprehensible through attention and concern. There are many such conditions—curiosity, joy in sharing, the need for wider horizons, the value of complexity, the processes of continuing nuance and subtlety, the enriching of self through the enfolding integration of the no-longer-alien—all of these are conditions that can lead to understanding through love.

In a more developed sense, love is a "staging ground for wisdom" because it allows us to see through the eyes of another how a world might be, or might become, apart from our own personal views. In turn, it fosters an ever-deepening tolerance for diversity, change, and a more enhanced mutual becoming. By tolerance, I mean something more than passive acceptance or a detached (usually nonloving) disconcern. I mean an active engagement with the other, a compassionate, well-intended caring, an openness to difference as a means for personal growth and communal development. One "insight" generated by such loving is a very powerful kind of self-enrichment through a becoming-with-others, a sense of joyful appreciation that enhances a mutual life gift. In loving others, our own lives becomes more full, more charged with possibility, more complete through a deepening psychic extension, an enrichment of soulful being that participates more completely in Spirit. Such a Spirit-enhanced loving also gifts us with insights about the qualities and capacities of Spirit in the lives of others, as a foreground for a deepening wisdom about the capabilities within human communities for diversity and loving relationships.

Setting aside our own views for the views of others, as an act of love, does not mean abandoning our own world, but gaining insight into the ways in which others construct their worlds and make sense of their actual circumstances. The healing of alienation is another attribute of a positive love—when we understand another's pain, struggle, frustration through a simple affirmation of their worth to us—we open the process of self-affirmation to others. This is a means for healing. It is transformative because it creates an existential circumstance that counters the self-doubt and self-denial that too much suffering induces. Loving interaction can transform alienation by a direct affirmation of the worthiness of a normatively unloved other as an act of spiritual healing. If we remember the first principle is the principle of life, then the spiritual potency of love is an affirmation of each life, itself Spirit-given. Through a cascade of loving relationships, an alienated other can touch the inner presence of the life gift, reaffirming the transformative values of awareness into a more complete spiritual understanding. It is an understanding born through love, matured through increasingly positive, long-term relationships and fully actualized in moments of joy, deep sharing, and mutual celebration. It gives stability and inner security that allows for truly creative exploration of the yet unrealized potential in Spirit.

In valuing the other, we enrich ourselves; in enriching ourselves, we have more to offer the other. The "staging ground" for continued human development is the heart—the circulatory center of our life blood, our becoming through a heart-centered receptivity to the worth and centrality of the other. Our concerns for others are an en-noblement of human character that works to break down the nor-matively self-absorbed and defensive barriers that keep us from actualizing deeper potential. It is not only the other that is alien-ated; each of us carries a degree of alienation within us—from fam-ily or friends, co-workers or lovers, from the young or very old, from the poor or wealthy, from the educated or uneducated, from the racial, ethnic, or cultural other who is actually our neighbor or a member of the global society. Love cultivates a slow integration of the diversities that remain alienated within each of us and that, if healed, would make us more capable and creative in enhancing our shared responsibilities. Often this takes a great deal of self-honesty and openness to our own wounded condition and then an intensifi-cation and determination to move *beyond* that wounded self-protec-tiveness. The quality of our empathy, Spirit-enhanced, can be a remarkable basis for opening to a deep transpersonal wholeness that understands love as one of the most creative capacities we have as il-lumined, healthy beings.

Spirit manifesting through love is very rare, very fine, subtle, and pervasive; it elevates without words or actions, it uplifts through presence and inspires renewal and hope, it knows no bound-aries and has no limitation. (5.11)

Meditation: Spirit has many manifestations, innumerable and minute, vast and encompassing, beyond measure and counting. Of all these manifestations, love is one of the most primal and most cen-tral to Spirit's many becomings and creations. Yet, for a manifesta-tion to attain its fullness, to adorn us with radiance and presence, we must harmonize our intentions to love without resistance to the Whole in all its many aspects, beings, and conditions. The qualities of love most admirable—warmth, compassion, spontaneous care for others, depths of feeling, genuiness of regard, a harboring that gives a sense of worth and deep appreciation, a healing and regenerative touch that embraces and feels the suffering of others—are the very qualities that give us life and higher awareness, the very qualities that are Spirit-born and blessed. But they are not given to compel us toward a rigid standard of behavior or belief. Rather, concealed within being, they manifest through those whose hearts are open to its influence and direction, whatever their way of life or circumstance or condition. This is one of the mysteries of love. Its manifestation is not a compulsion or a demand, it is rather a fulfillment and a joyful attainment of an inward harmony in Spirit.

The intention is only to love, to be capable of love, to express and communicate love; the fulfillment is a spontaneous overflowing, a fullness of being whose expression deeply affects the world and others. This gifting of love, Spirit-born, is rare in the sense that our capacity for expressing and moving within the currents of this love is often contracted by our many fears, doubts, denials, and by our sense of an unloving and uncaring world of contracted others. To open to this love means to set aside these doubts and to open the heart to the full depths of Spirit in becoming a vessel for that overflowing fullness. This is the ecstasy of love, to let it flow through us like a river, with tremendous depths of feeling and powerful currents of connection and relatedness that draw us to the ocean of all-being and becoming. This is largely a matter of intention, of how we direct our will toward the actualization of our deepest values. Do we value love? This is the critical and central question within being. If we say "Yes!" then how do we enact that affirmation in the rounds of our everyday life? Our becoming within being is intentionality linked to our capacity to love, and that capacity is a means for the realization of being. Why? Because our mutual becoming, our loving relationships that work to co-create the world in a positive way, are born out of our ability to harmonize intention, to work together to actualize our full creative potential.

Love is also "fine and subtle" in the sense that its full expression is not a matter of simply intense feelings—though intense feelings of love are certainly valuable in teaching us about the depths and fullness of feeling. Yet the full expression of love engages all aspects of our awareness. Love can permeate the will, the mind, the imagination, psychic perceptions, dreams, visions, mystical states. It can pervade the entire soul and raise the capacities of soulful being to a finer and more subtle, pervasive seeing and knowing. This is the interconnective quality of love, refined through spiritual practice and discipline, to acquire a luster whose presence opens every horizon that we are capable of perceiving. This is because love works through connective currents; it is a primal energy within Spirit that pervades relationships between all beings in an enlightening and illuminating way. As a fine and joyful fullness, it is the Ananda or Joy within which all creative activity unfolds its deepest potentials. The very joy of the illumined mind is the same joy that opens the heart, awakens love, or engages the deepest feelings. This "joyful fullness" is a deep quality inherent to spiritual awakenings of many different kinds, a spontaneous overflowing and ecstasy, a magical sense of immediate relatedness to all life and all beings. And it can be very fine, very subtle, not at all overwhelming, simply a deep sense of the Whole that lives and breathes and has life in all its magnitude and fire.[32]

The spiritual qualities of love can elevate the mind to new insights quite spontaneously and without effort on the part of the thinker. Inspiration flows forth with abundant energy and impression; imagination is opened to new dimensions. There is a sense of psychic connectedness with others whose own thoughts and feelings affect us from afar. This opening to love, to its higher qualities and capacities, moves us into the transpersonal horizon, where all that is personal and individual is retained, and yet the loving presence lifts us toward a fullness that exceeds individual expression and reveals to us the full extent of love within Spirit. This visionary aspect of love is a threshold that expands beyond the temporal limits of personal love relationships and into the vaster horizon of a more expansive, incorporative sense of being and becoming. It is an inspirational opening, an uplifting of self to a more profound loving presence, a presence whose nature and fullness exceeds description but that encompasses each and everyone of us. This visionary realm of love is an excess of being, an expressive and loving joy that holds each being as a jewel-in-the-net, the sea of which is without precise form or qualities and from which every quality in born and bred. And in the heart of this formless abundance, are the many currents of love that act to gather all beings into that net of interconnection, into the multiple worlds, into the expressive manifestations of Spirit-born beings.

There is "renewal and hope" because there is no inhibition against love; no necessary boundary that love may not overflow. Such love is inspirational by lifting us to new visions of our own path, work, or becoming. The renewal comes through a direct experience of that higher love, an opening of the heart to its sacred presence, an inner realization of the real depths and fullness. This renews and regenerates because our limited capacity in love is largely self-imposed; our concepts of love must be opened to a new horizon of loving possibility. Love is not simply a "human phenomena" but much more and much deeper in linking all the creative moments of becoming within a greater continuity of being. Our "love and being" is enhanced by realizing that the fullness of our individual potential is greatly enhanced through our capacity to soulfully love others and to incorporate their concerns and insights into the unfolding of our mutual capacities. This mutual becoming through love is a precondition for our full recognition of the many influences of love that act to stimulate new spiritual expression throughout a multitude of realms and worlds. Our renewal through love is a function of opening to co-relationship, co-creation, co-awareness—all enhanced by the currents of an emergent closeness and sharing within being. Our hope is that others will also open to the loving current, that the soul's capacity to love will lead through actual relationships to a higher transpersonal horizon in which love swells to its full energy and convection.

Such a love "knows no boundaries" because it has no boundaries. The boundaries are only those we draw within our own minds and hearts, the necessary protection of sensitive areas that, over time, become bound and bind us with our own self-created fears or uncertainties. Love unbinds. Its power is to open us to new possibilities, new frontiers within our becoming that injures none and respects all. Yet it moves us past our own limits and opens us to mystery, power, and transformation. There are "no limits" because the higher aspects of love include all without exception. This is the challenge of love: to fulfill the capacity to embrace others without qualification or resistance. Still keeping our own center, we learn to see where the limits are in the loves of others and to help them to move past the fear into a deeper openness. The spiritual depths of love call upon us to truly revere the qualities of love that make us more human, open, receptive, and more able to be vessels for that openness. Within the context of our normally closed lives, it means overcoming the resistance to love others and to realize that the rewards of love are in the giving and the gifting—from that gifting flows all the reciprocity and creative energies of love that can carry us far beyond our self-imposed boundaries or immediate needs.

The Sixth Principle

The Sixth Principle of Spirit is the manifestation of wisdom and illumination; from the illumination of the heart to the illumination of body, mind, and will. (6.1)

Meditation: Spirit manifesting as wisdom is like the Divine Sophia, like the spontaneous birth of Athene from the mind of Zeus, like the Babylonian Siduri Sabitu or the "great name that belongs to God only," the Chokmah of the Holy One, blessed be She. Such wisdom is the "wisdom of Illumination" (*hikmat al-ishraq*) taught by many esoteric traditions—Neoplatonic, Hermetic, Sufi, Christian— and is personified as a feminine manifestation within divinity that acts to communicate understanding and spiritual awareness. The Divine Sophia symbolizes the quality of a caring and compassionate presence that embraces all worlds and all beings within them, gifting each with the holy spark of her presence.[33] In many ways, Spirit is that Wisdom, is that divine feminine presence, like the Shakti of the various Indian gnostic schools, the active principle that embodies the world process through creative expressions of the great reservoir of potential that lies deep within Mystery.[34] The reflective depths of Spirit mirror the actualized forms of the creative process, imaging the pure imageless awareness of the higher gnosis; actualizing the cyclical, processual involutions of all species life under the protective mantle of a deep and inexhaustible, loving, heart-centered Wisdom.

Wisdom is not necessarily feminine. I express it this way only to emphasize a nuance among the attributes of wisdom, to underline that wisdom is not impersonal, detached, or abstracted from feeling. Spiritual wisdom is highly empathic and relational, involved in the processes of thoughtful relationship to a world of living beings whose concerns and aspirations reflect intelligence and insight. Wisdom is not a content or a mental construction, not a specific "idea" or a specific philosophy. It is not a matter of a particular definition or logical construction. Wisdom is a complex set of qualities and insights that cannot be reduced to a spiritual goal or ideal easily summarized, yet it is recognizable. The feminine aspect of wisdom so long symbolized in many different traditions refers to those qualities of spontaneity, immediacy, and sudden clarity of understanding that is immediate, intuitive, and deeply perceptive. Like the Buddhist female images of Tara or the Prajnaparamita, it is wisdom that cuts off doubt, cuts through mental confusion, and liberates the psyche from its ordinarily contracted state of fear and sorrow. It is an encompassing, intuitive wisdom, joyful, luminous, and bright.[35]

We start with the "illumination of the heart" in the development of wisdom because it is the center of a living relationship to the Whole. Like the alchemical retort, the heart is the place where the transformative experiences of life unite with the passions of feeling-desire and with the clarity and mental calm of reflective, stable awareness. Wisdom is the full synthesis of life experience transformed through inner processes into luminous insights about self, others, world, and being. In a personal sense, I regard a "heart-centered wisdom" as best epitomized in the symbol of the Divine Sophia. We must each seek out those signs or symbols of wisdom, those images and forms that lead us to a personal awakening of the qualities of wisdom we most desire and approve. A soulful wisdom arises from feeling of the heart, from passion and intensity in living and relating; it also has calm, stability, and a centered sense of self, an openness to love, a sense of its own limits and boundaries. Wisdom is not omniscience, for, as the ancient gnostic story of the Divine Sophia tells us, wisdom cannot find the origins of the Deep, cannot overcome the actual content or qualities that give her specific form and meaning. Thus, she is reconciled in the higher world of the other Aeons, with other divine qualities that reflect the unchartable depths of Being and Mystery; she is one among many, yet often epitomized as the "first of all creations."[36]

As the first, incipient wisdom was there in the beginning, that is, an intuitive feminine wisdom sprung from the mind of God fully active and aware. Such wisdom is born from the energies of Wholeness, from first reflective awakenings to bright illumination in spontaneous bursts of revelation and gnosis. It is not something out of nothing, but something more out of something great, where the "more" recedes and the "lesser" takes individual form to represent the synthesis of qualities we call "wise." She is "wise." She understands how it is with human life, with sorrow and pain, with joy and aspiration, with wanting and needing and seeking. And she sees with clarity how it came about and where it leads when you follow this or that path, and how to heal a misperception or change a misguided idea. It is a deeply experienced wisdom whose seeing is more than psychic. It is a seeing that unites with the foundations of mind, heart, and soul, and knows those foundations as a stable center within self uniting her with unbound Mystery. Yet this is only an image of wisdom as a specific invocation or image of an archetypal maturity. It might be a Yogi, or Sufi, or Saint, a singing poet, a dancing ecstatic, or a mother, or a child who is wiser than adults still caught in old patterns and endless, internal debates.

From the heart we can move to the body and say, "the body has its own wisdom." This means that the processes of wisdom are not all mental or emotional, not just psychic or "above nature." Wisdom pervades the created world in every living being and acts at every level, from the subatomic to the cellular, from the cellular to the organ, to muscle, nerve, or body as a whole. There is a "knowing" that occurs which in ordinary consciousness is rarely seen or accessed, but that in a higher kind of seeing, reveals these qualities of wisdom as not simply "human", but as manifest in every living being, from the most minute to the most complex. There is wisdom even in pure energy, as in the great pranic energies that are empowered through various kinds of solar and astral light, all imbued with subtle qualities of wisdom. In the body, we feel it in the spontaneous reactions and coordinated responses that guide us to act, eat, rest, sleep, or renew ourselves, with particular consequences when we ignore this inner, bodily wisdom. When we listen to the body, when we pay attention to its processes and inner reciprocities, we are guided, through spiritual transformation, to follow those healthy inclinations and break through the habituated and learned responses that so often choke and suppress that bodily wisdom. The free flow of energy, following the subtle pathways, can teach us a great deal about the body's wisdom, a wisdom very little known or appreciated in a strictly materialist thinking of body as machine.

The wisdom of "mind and will" is far more subtle insofar as the mind and will are more susceptible to external conditioning and processes of socialization. This influence of the external, of the outer world's impingement, the "cultural milieu," is easily embodied in the collective thinking and believing of others. That milieu often masks the inner manifestations of wisdom by formulating images that contract and compress social ideals into stereotypes whose functions in the human psyche only reinforce the collective, normative interaction. Disparate images, disassociated from those norms, and romanticized as "ideal," often reflect a tragic alienation. Such images as the heroic male who faces all odds and triumphs, the heroic female who subordinates herself to the needs of others and endures, the mythic starship captain that solves every problem in a single brain-storming session, are not expressions of wisdom, but the stereotypes that blind us to a deeper and more individual, complex, and creative insight. The wisdom of "mind and will" goes far beyond stereotypes and collective images. It encompasses all human endeavors and all cultures and is bound only by the limits of our own capacities, which we often deny under the influence of collective attitudes that inhibit individual growth and maturity. The manifestations of wisdom are actualized through the processes of focused effort and aspiration, through a stripping away of stereotypes, through an inner transformation of the individual into a more aware and wise being.

To transform the "mind and will" and to awaken the inherent potential for a wisdom-guided intentionality requires opening the heart to the full splendor and intelligence of the cosmos as a living Whole. Wisdom is not simply the accumulation of experience, not just the consequence of living a rich and varied life, of travel, education, or exposure to what is other, unique, or challengingly different, though all these can effect the process of development and maturation. But such experience may fall into a collapsing horizon of repetitious, shallow interactions, into a superficial "skimming" of surface life. What is required is to open to the depths and heights of the yet unrealized potential, to acquire a more expansive awareness and to do this by breaking through the stereotypes, the accepted patterns, the inherited ideas without denying the original value of those patterns or ideas. Wisdom proceeds through mutuality and relationship; it acquires substance and form through reflection and interaction with others and builds on those relationships to seek out its own unique manifestations. The wisdom-guided mind and will seek attunement with a more coherent and integral life, one not reducible to stereotypes or collective norms, but one that flourishes because it seeks to cut through those stereotypes and actualize a vision that goes deeper into the yet unrealized potential.

The illumination of the heart proceeds through love to accomplish the first opening, the irradiations of expansive joy and sharing, the unfolding of mutuality and trust. (6.2)

Meditation: The illumination of the heart is simultaneously an expansion of soulful being, an opening to greater awareness and a felt, participatory sense of the Mystery. The key to wisdom is love, the capacity to feel deeply the concerns of others, to enter into their lives as a way of being more informed about our own life. Letting the influence of the other impact and modify perceptions and thinking, letting the feelings of love guide and direct a response that is deeper and more aware is part of the process of a true awakening to wisdom. Such love is not a matter of superficial feeling or passions of the moment, even when those passions are genuine and heart-felt. Such mature love is guided by understanding and insights arrived at through many long years of loving and feeling the reality of others in all their searching and longing for maturity and self-actualization. A soul-guided love is one that takes that initial passion and wonder into an alchemical transformation where, in the heart, with others, it acquires a different and deeper luster and illumination.

It is not simply feeling, but understanding as well. It is a deepening guided by a sincere intent and care to be loving, to be caring, to be mature. Such loving evolves from the processes of life encounters and the inscriptions we make within ourselves and within others, marking our journeys, our sharing, our mutual learning. These inscriptions are impressions and habits of mind, thoughts and words, feelings or behaviors conveyed through communication in acts of all kinds. It is not a matter of writing over the same surface, words over words, creating only an obscure, difficult script of unfinished promises or half-realized hopes buried beneath unsifted layers. It is more like an alchemical reduction, a refinement, or boiling down that leaves not simply a trace, but golden qualities of maturity and insight. This process of refinement and deepening, of concentration and increasing clarity of intent and congruity between thought, words, and deeds, is the beginning of wisdom. The deepest intent of such wisdom is to create through loving relationships a stimulating and meaningful life with others.

In this process, the "first opening" is the capacity to feel deeply the needs and wants of others distinct from one's own and to fully value such feelings without letting them supplant the valued inner intentions of an authentic self-awakening. Authenticity involves conscious choice and a willing receptivity to the concerns of others as a means to clarifying and developing an inner sense of meaningful relationship to all others. The "opening of the heart" requires us to move past our own inherited limitations—biological, cultural, or however acquired—to embrace a deep ethic of co-relatedness. This is a spiritual task whose roots descend into the primal life of creation, whose branches include every life form, and whose fruit is the continued life of that process in the progeny of all emergent beings. It is an opening to the life process, not simply to some few other human beings, but to the various magnitudes of joy to be found in the wonder of ongoing life in all its diversities and forms. This opening is a recovery of wonder through authentic experiences of love for the creations emergent on every world, in every sphere and interdimension, through all forms and subtle transformations. It is a willing participation, an intentional decision to be fully participant in this loving emergence.

In turn, this opening leads to a "joyful wisdom" that recognizes natural limits within which that joy may actualize similar joys in others. There is joy in sharing as much as in creating, for creations in solitude may go out into the world and touch many. Thus, wisdom is born of a mature attainment of positive human relationships that encourage growth and new perceptions and clear, committed action. It is not a limitless wisdom or an "all-knowing" understanding. It is a particular, individual knowing, one that corresponds with the inner processes through which we, as human beings, acquire resonance and attunement with the deeper currents of Spirit. In a more superficial sense, it is a recognition that we are not alone but in-relation, thoroughly immersed in all the interactions with others that affect our own self-perceptions, that we are inescapably part of the human drama. However, such an immersion gives no mandate to the collective either to legislate our rights as individuals or to determine the extent of our freedom to seek alternative visions and new spiritual paths. Such seeking is inherent to the life process, embodied as the aspiration for a wider horizon, the need for a more complex and developed world, one no longer stratified by prejudice, intellectual myopia, or restrictive patterns of faith.

The birth of "joyful wisdom" is found in freedom from the restrictive consensuality or communal thought or belief, in an opening of the heart that illumines a new way of thinking (or being) or that throws its light onto what was with deepened nuance and meanings. It is a joy that comes from recognizing the past, the present, and the future in correspondence with the thoughts and perceptions of others no longer bound by strictly normative thinking. Yet the collective gives stability and constancy, a grounded sense of having been before, and having lived a certain valued way of life. Thus there is *mediation* in this wisdom, a need to balance what has been for others with what is now, in the individual present, an authentic yet mutual self-becoming. The joy is in finding correspondence, in feeling the inner connectedness with others, however distant in external time or space. It is an "overcoming" that exceeds a limitation without violating the perceptions and aspirations of others, that recognizes the differences, rejoices in freedom, and respects deeply the variation and alterity while yet pursuing what is most authentic and real in the personal, transformative sense. The joy lies not in conformity but in creative variation with correspondence, in having identity, not in surrendering it to an external collective norm.

This opening can lead to more expansive states, punctuated by contractions and a pulling inward, away from others, in order to see more clearly, the emergent character of alternatives not yet actualized. This is why love is so crucial, so that in pulling back we do not lose our sense of relatedness to others and to the warmth and support they offer us. It is not simply a matter of continual expansion, continual openings of the heart; but more a process of growth with all the stages, plateaus, stumblings, backslidings, recoveries, and renewed determinations to continue on, even in the face of the opposition or disapproval of others. Wisdom requires courage—this is a critical point. The processes of spiritual development are not set according to external criteria (which is why paths with set stages or stations seem so artificial), rather these processes are born out of a lifetime of compassionate seeking, with others, in the immediacy of present life trials and unexpected challenges, crises, and all the unexpected turns and intersections on the path. Yet every turn is an opportunity for new perspectives if we can open to that possibility with genuine love and trust. This is love born of Spirit, of the deep currents that pull us toward new experience and challenge, that put us into just those circumstances that we must face in order to move past the plateau or beyond a rocky ledge where we stopped for fear of falling. The key to such experience is to face it with a heart-centered love, an inward trust in presence, a sense of mutuality that unites us even in the most intensive moment of conflict or denial.

We are each capable of "mutuality and trust" but only to the degree that we purify and sublimate our own self-serving needs, desires, or aspirations. The "joyful wisdom" is not egocentric nor is it selfless; rather it is an integration of the self-other paradigm into actualized, creative human relationships. It requires self-honesty and a willingness to change, to give up old ways, to modify attitudes and actions, to graciously recognize shortcomings and unhealthy dependencies or clinging demands made of others. It requires taking full responsibility for attaining spiritual goals that have been self-selected and not imposed by others. It requires creativity in resolving and moving past old problems, conflicts, or struggles—through love, through affirmation, through acceptance of limits without denying the potential for self-awakening and positive illumination. We each learn from one another and we can each share what we attain without impositions or demands. Such is the way of Spirit, to give utterly and yet to never cease to be fully in possession of all that is given. What flows out, flows back, with joy, into its own self-realizations. It is out of this reciprocity that trust is born and mutuality actualized for the benefit of all those participant in the sharing. This trust is a bond of mutual concern to actualize self-other potential without denying the uniqueness and difference that makes each creative relationship possible.

We each have a story, perhaps many, and these stories teach us the meaning of wisdom. The stories of science can never replace the human stories that, in dramatic form, represent the lessons we learn in struggling to attain the actualization of higher potentials. Our lives are filled and surrounded with stories and those teaching wisdom require the greatest study and appreciation. Stories of science, about impersonal law or principles of nature detached from human awareness, do not give us, nor will they, the guidelines we need to evaluate clearly the possibilities of wisdom. The inscriptions of personal, existential, dramatic encounter is where we find Spirit guiding us in the fullness of our being human. When the stories of science begin to integrate themselves into human stories, where principles of life merge with human motive and aspiration, with epitomes of excellence reflected in compassion and love, then such stories will truly endure. When the stories can show the intimate bonds between individual aspiration, collective maturity, and a deeply spiritual science of nature, then will our stories create the mutuality and trust necessary for a full flourishing of unrealized possibility and shared illuminations. Until then, we must each seek to image the stories we know in the medium of our own lives so that others may glimpse there, the joyful wisdom of the heart and be inspired.

The second opening of the heart comes through compassion for all life, in all diversity of form, in both essence and manifestation; this is the source of peace, stability, and creative exchange. (6.3)

Meditation: If the first opening is an inner acceptance, a letting go and opening out to complexity and difference, then the second opening is an embracement, a process of incorporation by the unbound totality of all life and being, without exceptions or qualifications. The first is recognizing the capacity to relate well to others, through love and by letting go of inner resistance to the shared needs we have as mutually co-related beings. And the second is allowing the self to be gathered into the panorama and multidimensionality of all forms of conscious being, into the full plurality of the Mystery, without being overwhelmed or self-negated. It is an opening, unlike the first, initiated through a breaking down of the normally sheltered life of enclosed self-perception. It is the discovery of compassion as no longer rooted in human concern alone, but as a permeating and encompassing attribute of all life and all becoming. Wherever there is life, there is compassion; wherever compassion, then life; the initial form is buried or rooted in the preservation of like to like, or adult to child, or companion to companion. Where any species thrives, there is care for the related other and for the symbiosis between species, for the biodiversity that necessarily creates partnership and co-relatedness. Yet we are inescapably part of a greater interwoven web, of Gaia, mother spirit, earth-soul, holding within her life fields, the great work of all becoming together. It is to this harmony of interactive relationships, as they extend even beyond our planetary homes, beyond our star systems, and out into the immeasurable expanses of intergalactic energies, that the second opening refers.

This opening, as an acceptance of the diversity and plurality of all created life, from the smallest microbe to the most subtle expanse, is a counterpoint to the doctrine of "emptiness." It is a recognition of the profound "fullness" of all-that-is, of the abundant, overflowing life presence in every niche and nook where life might become. It is a reference to the Pleroma, the spiritual fullness of the world, rooted in its material manifestations but enwrapping that world with all the psychic qualities birthed through interspecies relatedness. One symbol of this fullness is the world-soul, the collective psychic influences of all life forms, centered on the pivotal star around which our many worlds turn and encompassing potential life on the farthest reaches of its energy. Every world is a potential home, either now or in the past or future; and every home a place where life may manifest. Every world system may be itself embraced by the galactic energies of Spirit manifest, in stars, moons, planets, cometary bodies, or stellar configurations yet poorly understood, each with its own subtle forms and dimensionalities. It is life-within-life-within-life, as an endless spiral inward and a vast uncoiling outward, even to the spiral arms of our own galactic home where we, embodied life beings, may reflect that stellar energy even in the molecular depths of our bodied chemistry and neural well-being.

In the midst of the vast plurality of the second opening, the depths of its complexity are saturated with a deep compassion rooted in the heart of our own individual being. It is a "love for all that lives" and a "reverence for every life form" as manifesting the fullness of Mystery from which we ourselves have been birthed. We are not self-created but the consequence of a long birthing through slow, multiple processes of interactive transformation millions of planetary cycles in duration. There is much that precedes us and much that will endure when we are no longer visible in our present human form. At the heart of this process is a deep nurturing of the life gift, the preservation of species through an embedded life of co-related and mutually dependent becomings. The life gift, Spirit-given, is inseparable from the multitude of other beings with whom we share our world; their transformed ancestral being is our ancestral being as well. Let us honor and revere these co-related ancestral roots as a mark of our deep thankfulness for the gifts that have been passed on in the love and preservation of all species. Let us also look on the coexistent life of other living creatures as an intrinsic part of our own self-being, as part of a shared coexistence that enriches all. Compassion in this sense means a deep joy in the very existence of the other, and not a particular attitude meant to change them according to our own "human" image.

By "essence and manifestation" I do not mean a reduction of manifestations to some particular set of abstract qualities or to a mental paradigm espousing some quasi-eternal or universal form or content. By "essence" I refer to inner qualities that makes up the complex intentional, motivational, and imaginative-emotional world of humanity. And by "manifestation" I mean a visible form, however subtle or immaterial. In turn, symbols may be said to have meaning only insofar as we are able to relate them to the intentional, motivational, imaginative, and emotive worlds of those for whom the symbol represents or expresses. Thus the symbol of the world-soul is meaningful only insofar as it represents a certain intentional understanding of relatedness to others, be it those who hold such a symbol to be valid or those who may contest a host of diverse meanings for the symbol. Every created symbol must, to some extent, represent the world as the author of the symbol knows that world and thus it incorporates to some degree what is seen or known "essentially" by others. As beings-in-relation, every symbol and every set of intentions participate to some degree in the symbols and intentions of others, linguistic or not. And in language, we find that words mean only insofar as they are apprehended by others in a meaningful way. And the more one wrestles with manifestations in word form, the more competent they become in reading various intentions in the words of others.

How important it is to read with compassion! To read with openness and receptivity, to open the heart to the words of another and to take in the meanings in order to find the inner intention or essence.

Every creative manifestation, every genuine word, is yet another effort to open the world to meaningful interaction and alternative interpretations. It is not only the reading of books to which I refer, but to the reading of others, to the reading of life experience, to the reading of a dream or vision, to a Spirit-born reading of our interdependent being. The world is an embodiment in symbolic form in which the manifestations are visible in every aspect of every life, meant to be read more deeply, in a more essential way than simply through the medium of its material or externally formed appearance. To read with compassion, to interpret with compassion, to understand with compassion, means to be open and receptive to the other in terms of what they value as essential or critical for a meaningful coexistence. As a spiritual discipline this means opening the heart to the reality of others for the purpose of enhancing self-understanding and communicative awareness. It is not an abandonment of individual perspective, but an enhancement, a receptive search for correspondence in valuing life and in preserving the worth of difference-in-mutuality. This requires self-honesty and a willingness to be changed, even in the most subtle and allusive ways.

A compassionate receptivity to the full plurality of mutual coexistence sets the stage for a peaceful, stable, and creative exchange. In a human sense, this is a nonreductive relationship. As essence is a matter of relative individual intentions or perceptions and motivation, the goal is cooperation in a noncoercive and creative way and not a search for identity through sameness or authority. We are not the same and we differ in many ways, even though we may share common goals and work together for valued ends. A peaceful sharing requires deep respect for these differences and a recognition that a willful imposition subverts the processes of a healthy and well-balanced mutuality. The second opening of the heart requires stability, a sense of inner poise and commitment to a valued way of life that seeks to comprehend the fullness of cosmic diversity and difference. This means learning to nurture others in ways that foster tolerance, love, compassion, and shared goals, assisting others in actualizing the value, potential, and capacities of each individual. In this process we foster our own growth as well. It is normal and essential to form well-intended relationships as we engage in processes of mutual becoming. The wisdom born out of this process is creative, interactive, and yet has self-meaning and unique, individual form. Each seeks to find his or her higher capacity and to embody it in a deep compassion for all such authentic self-becoming.

The third opening of the heart comes through Spirit, when the "eye of the heart" sees directly the presence and power; when penetrated to the bones, the will is transformed. (6.4)

Meditation: Wisdom is born of direct experience no longer limited to a material or strictly sensory account of the world. Spiritual transformation begins to penetrate beyond the sensory and visible world, begins to transform that world and to make it into something new. This transformation takes us beyond love and compassion by moving through compassion and empathy into the very heart of that loving response. It is a grounding in Spirit through direct awareness and visionary encounter—not through belief or faith, not through argument or abstract ideas, not through a psychic receptivity—but using all these, it is even more so a grounding in presence, a direct seeing, an experiential witnessing and affirmation, a gnosis.[37] It is that special meeting of all that is within with all that is without, such that boundaries dissolve and a deep sense of participation opens on all horizons. Yet these horizons do not collapse or fuse; they each retain the uniqueness of their respective autonomies while becoming transparent through mutual congruity and shared correspondences (or differences). They open to each other, mirroring alternatives, between and through which new possibilities may emerge.

It is not a presence that "obliterates" differences but preserves them in fullness and diversity and yet opens to a self-becoming no longer bound by exclusive or contradictory ideals or by a particular set of relations, ideas, or beliefs. It is a presence through which horizons of embodied openness become the ground of a new seeing. This ground is deeply personal and yet leads to a seeing that reaches out beyond the personal. While preserving personhood, it offers visions of a profound transpersonal becoming. It is among those visions that the "eye of the heart" is stimulated to fully open and to see what truly *is*, to learn how much overflows out of the nurturing heart of nature to fully actualize all living beings to new awareness and seeing. This does not refer to theoretical insights or abstract ideas, but to a "direct seeing" in the most vivid and experiential, immediate sense. It is an opening of the "wisdom eye" to alternative horizons of being, increasingly comprehensive and incorporative while leaving, in quiet congruity, the actual structures and forms of alternative pathways.

It "comes through Spirit" insofar as all such becoming is Spirit-guided and Spirit-inspired. All occurs within Spirit, within the nurturing presence that gives birth to embodied life, as life process seeking to attain an ever more adept comprehension of self-development and spiritual growth. It is a gift, a constant sense of grace that accompanies all forms of life, continually nurtured through difference and correspondence, through shared needs and mutually competitive desires, through continual processes of world actualization. This "coming" is part of the process of emergence through difference or through individuation that seeks to actualize, in a specific way, the potential gifts of Spirit. The "eye of the heart" sees according to the capacity and abilities of the individual actualized through the influences of new spiritual awareness. The individual is the grounding center of the manifestation, transformed and opened to vast horizons of meaning and being, yet the nature of that seeing is shaped by the life experience, capacity, and context within which it occurs. As beings-in-relation, such seeing is created out of the perceptual horizons, beliefs, attitudes, and mental sets that predispose any individual toward deeper spiritual awakening. It does not occur "in a vacuum," nor does it necessarily override individual awareness with a collective revelation or specific meaning.

The "direct seeing" is not an unconditioned seeing. It can act to deeply confirm a spiritual worldview or it can, by degrees, deconstruct that worldview. It can open the heart and mind to a vast comprehensiveness, to an all-inclusiveness that, nevertheless, requires interpretation and translation into uniquely conceptualized forms for the benefit of others. This process of "symbolization" is a recasting of experience into visible form, a creative activity of meaningful expression seeking to epitomize the value and intent of the experience. The "transformative value" of this process is threefold: it opens the heart of the individual to new horizons of unbound possibility; it allows for the establishment of new forms of symbolization and interpretation through interaction with others; and it sets up the possibility of diverse interpretive patterns as an interactive ground for others to draw out implicit nuances and alternative meanings. But such "interpretation" is not simply a function of reflecting on the symbolizations; it also requires a direct participation in Spirit as we move through those interpretations into a more self-aware being. Opening the "eye of the heart" refers to a seeing that is not individual but shared, an opening of many diverse kinds, individualized according to receptivity and context.

This seeing goes deep and is more than simply opening, it becomes a transfixation, a momentary encounter of being grasped, not of grasping. The third opening is a penetration, a penetration from within bursting outward, an overflowing fullness from the heart magnified against a cosmic multidimensionality in which every life form is an enstatic realization. Like so many suns bursting, then contracting into diverse forms, are the inner awakenings, Spirit-prompted, according to the magnitude or potency within each and every being. We are encapsulated by the immediacy of sensory-emotive life and mislead by the abstractions of mind insofar as we see only the outward life made visible, the manifestations, entangled in the lives, beliefs, and thoughts of others, in the collective, the normative, consensual minimum. But the maximum potential far exceeds the narrow entrapments of habit, pragmatism, or having a "safe harbor." The wild seas and depths of night in all their visionary contexts, swim with life potential awaiting those willing to dive deep, called to recognize the fullness of our individual being. Then is that will transformed in encounters that grasp and penetrate the core, soulful being laid open to the deeper seizures of a transfixed seeing far beyond norms, pragmatism, or the consensual minimum.

When "penetrated to the bones" the will is transformed. This means, first, allowing that penetration, not from without, but from within, to fully penetrate the whole of the individual, not just mind, or thought, or feeling. It means letting go in an interior sense, allowing for surrender and release of all defensive inner postures. It is an unraveling, an opening up that allows what was hidden, concealed, or bound to manifest in all the diverse forms correspondent to our individual circumstance, predisposition, context. This is not always easy or without risk or dangers; emergence is never simply "guaranteed" even by the most sincere intention. But Spirit-led, through nurture and gradual, natural process, this emergence can transform the will into a fine instrument of sensitive responsivity and flexible creation. It becomes will in the nonaggressive sense, an integrated, balanced will able to respond by context and inner intent strengthened through commitment and purposeful seeking. A compassionate and caring will, not a will enwrapped in its own self-seeking, oblivious to the seeking of others, nor is it traumatized, impotent in carrying through to completion, the purpose. A reformulation of will is found in clear intentions actualized according to conscious decision and purposeful action, and arises as a consequence of ever more meaningful heart-centered realizations leading to a deepening wisdom.

The wisdom of this "third opening" is reshaping the will, clarifying spiritual intent, moving more fully into a disciplined spiritual life for the purpose of actualizing spiritual potential. It involves "surrender" to inner experience nurtured through Spirit in the devotion of the individual and tested in self-other relations of respect and tolerance. Even in the transfixed state of enstatic experience, the perceptions of others are valued, correspondent, affective in the processes of sharing, shaping, and symbolizing new understanding and insights. The "transformed will" is fully awakened to the reality of spiritual experience as a ground for personal becoming, takes its formative intent from that experience, and shapes itself according to shared and mutual becoming in a celebration of diversity and fullness. The surrender is not a self-denying or a disavowal of personal responsibility or identity, but an affirmation of the need for articulate sharing and communication in a noncoercive, respectful, and receptive manner. The will is actualized through such seeing, illumined by presence, and sparked to creative action, care, and responsiveness to further actualization and relatedness. But such relatedness sees, with the eye of the heart, the panoramic potential and diversity of ways, knowing thus, the multitude of paths, forms, and possibilities as each having distinctive and particular consequential goals.

The transformed will seeks only to actualize the impulses of Spirit, to flow into the deeper channels of life—with the current or against the current—to manifest its joy and renewal. (6.5)

Meditation: What are the "impulses of Spirit" other than the inner arising of aspirations and desires for a more fully human and more fully actual being? They are the specific intentional decisions we each make in determining how we will act, live, value others, and seek the realizations we are most capable of attaining. Such impulses, urging us to awaken to our full potential, are a healthy sign of spiritual vitality and well-being, not because we have yet actualized those potentials, but because we are aware of that potential pressing against the heart, seeking expression and manifestation. Yet the formulation of that potential into actual expression is not simply a matter of "personal will" or striving; it involves a recognition of the deeper sources of that aspiration and a turning inward to affirm and to listen to those sources. This listening means creating the circumstances in which that inner prompting can surface and become articulate as a source of direction and intentional shaping. At times, these circumstances may involve risk or exposure to new ways of acting or behaving, an encounter with others that stimulates growth. Or such circumstances may arise in seeking quiet and solitude, through disciplined reflection or a more tranquil, meditative approach, or in the passions of prayer and devotion.

Many times the insights arising from these activities becomes deconstructive insofar as they lead to changing our views, or habits, or goals. There is a "confrontational arena" in the processes of spiritual growth and development, sometimes involving others and sometimes arising from within, which seeks to impel us toward a new horizon of self-understanding. The confrontation arises within the context of a narrow self-other awareness and opens out into a wider arena of human relationships inspired by spiritual understanding. The individual learns to see the self in relationship not only to some others, but to a multitude of others through the correspondent relationships established within Spirit. The transparency of alternative worlds and their actual inhabitants confronts us with the limitations of our own bound world. The "transformed will" seeks to enhance that correspondence without surrendering the value and integrity of the known and familiar—yet remains open to the influences of the "other." This often occurs through the cultivation of deeply positive, loving human relationships grounded in respect and mutual honesty. The more participants engage in authentic dialogue, loving action, and healthy exploration of alternatives, the more space that is cleared for mutual development.

The "impulses of Spirit" are often the most subtle and most far-reaching in the sense that they impel us, however gently or dramatically, toward the realization of yet unknown capacities. Often, it is Spirit manifesting through our relationships with others, not simply from without or strictly from within. This shared, interactive impact through which the actualizations of one are met with the actualizations of others creates a potential opportunity for development in every human relationship. Such a potential stands in contrast to the isolated, repetitive, and habitual processes of relationships fixated in static patterns of conventional interaction. There is a "quickening" affect in Spirit that allows the responsive will to open up to the positive realizations of others while also sharing the self-realizations of authentic seeking from within. This reciprocity, this spiritual sharing, is a vehicle for the manifestations of Spirit in the development of creative wisdom. Such a wisdom of the attuned will, opening to the wisdom of others through inspiration and integrity, is the fertile ground of true gnosis, of authentic, illumined understanding. The lucidity of such wisdom is what flows between beings, between each of us, in our interactions with each other in seeking to embody an enlightened state of understanding.

The "deeper channels of life" are not separate from the many currents that have shaped those channels through the living earth and through embodied forms of life. Those channels are not merely present but extend far into the past and future as a vast network of spiritual connections whose full potency is barely visible. The nontemporal nature of spiritual realizations extends the reaches of human capacity across a wider horizon than the immediate present, such that those realizations become nodal points within a new fractal cosmology. The gaps and interstices between or among those realizations are filled with potential not-yet manifested but pointing to the realizations attained as signs requiring new understanding. It is not a single fractal pattern, but a multitude of patterns sharing reflective features and similarity but each functions in a context of particular limits and conditions. The gaps, like "dark matter," sustain the abundance that is yet unrealized, while visible life goes on reiterating the known patterns and making unsteady modulations in the collective. The deeper channels are not the "known" historical interpretations, the great historic persons of spiritual history, or the acceptable interpretations of traditions and history. They are, instead, the unrealized capacities that reside interstitially "between" the known realizations and the yet unknown possibilities. Spiritual seekers are, when authentically seeking, "between" the known and unknown, seeking to inhabit and actualize a yet unrealized potential.

This process of seeking an illumined wisdom can come through conformity to a traditionalized pattern of development under the guidance of an already actualized human teacher. But such an actualization seeks to epitomize a known channel by which humanity may celebrate a given potential and its concomitant interpretations.

Other seekers may choose a less known path, a way into the mountains that has not been well trod or marked with recognizable signs. They may choose the gap between the known ways and risk the dangers of becoming lost and "fallen" through confusion, misdirection, or the turbulence of an inauthentic duplicity and self-falsification. Yet even that is a "proving" of a certain kind, a proving of what must not be done, or at least, avoided after a bad fall or slip into a barely escapable crevice. Or they may successfully explore the unknown alternative and thereby open a new channel for being and becoming, create a new fractal pattern, a new visionary reality. This is not simply a matter of sincerity, but far more a matter of deep commitment to genuine spiritual principles enacted and realized in authentic living. This requires abandonment, a willing suspension of the known, a release from the tangible expressions of the social contract that binds us to a less individuated, collective humanity.

Thus "with the current or against the current," each must plunge deep into the capacities of courage and openness to Spirit, to flow where the currents lead into darker, less known waters of transformation, baptism, and rebirth. These "life currents" are the currents that carry each of us through the great and small moments, the crisis and the joy of attainment. And do we flow with the majority or aside from it or perhaps, like martyrs, against it? A spiritual standard is not indexed by collective or traditional thinking or beliefs. It is indexed by Spirit through authentic living and a wise and compassionate life. This is a metaprinciple: however we may arrange the patterns of our life, nevertheless, it is the qualitative difference that gives nuance and depth to Spirit and best fills the gap. Rebirth requires that we each die first, to the old way, to the less sufficient, to the inadequate and obstructive and then find the courage to go on into the not-yet known and to make real the vision that leads us beyond the insufficiency—to rebirth our deeper identity as intrinsic to the fractal cosmos, to image the joy of renewal through the pains of birth and the contractions of uncertainty and hard times. The "joy and renewal" does not come without sacrifice; we must give up artificial creeds, inherited dogmas, received opinion, and mass consensus for realizations more luminous and fluid.

This is not always easy or obvious and sometimes; it requires tremendous courage in the face of unknowing, a plunge into depths that have no measure and no promise of safe harbor. The transformed will is a consequence of touching and being touched by Spirit, through the world, others, in dreams or visions, through trial or heavy burdens, though responsibilities transformed into an exploration of potential. In this process, the "world" cannot retain its normal face, cannot be sustained as a one-dimensional index of the known, but must instead become a place of unknown possibilities and spiritual opportunities. The "masks of the world" must fall. Its convenient forms and faces must shed the outer forms and chance the realization of a naked seeing, a dying to the old world, a rebirth into a new, less bound, less certain, and more aware possibility. In this way, we can each flow into the deeper channels and thus manifest joyful possibility, each discover a new wisdom born in the gap between what has been and what is yet to come.

> **To touch the heart of another is wisdom; to lift the veil, to uncover the presence, is to share the host, for the true host is Spirit in all its diversity, plurality, and perfection. (6.6)**

Meditation: Touching the heart of another means being touched; it points toward a shared spiritual life no longer bound by exclusion or fearful of alternatives. To touch and be touched, to love and be loved, to see and be seen—these are aspects of a joyful wisdom no longer bound by the necessities of a fixed mental horizon. The intersection of our individual search for understanding lies in heart-to-heart communion, in an openness to Spirit in all the diversities of evolving form and emergent becoming. The wisdom that emerges from this openness to others is a creative wisdom, not an exclusive or conformist, consensual kind of thinking or believing. There is belief, not in a particular credo that justifies loving or admits to only a narrow standard in love, but a belief in the value and worth of the other as enhanced by mutual understanding. Nor is it a belief in extremes or unmoderated passion that has little or no regard for the feeling, hopeful other. Such understanding moves forward through respect and compassion, a desire to reach the other, regardless of their illness, or confusion, or denials. It is a reaching out to that otherness as the not-self coming to be and meeting somewhere between, in the gap that represents an unrealized relationship.

In part, this sharing can only succeed to the degree that what is yet unrealized in-between has been already sought within or through other caring relations. Many have been touched with ill intent, harmed, wounded, abused, controlled, oppressed, and deformed by the relentless uncaring of those also wounded and deformed. The reality of human prejudice, bias, disregard, rejection, and out-and-out denial has created great harm and left a multitude of incomplete and struggling beings all in need of a better, more caring world of loving, wise relations. Distrust, alienation, fear, anger, and a closed, withdrawn attitude is common, and in many cases, considered an ideal defense against the indifferent, dominating worlds of self-seeking others. In such cases, Spirit is buried in the folds and collapsed contours of a painful, hidden withdrawal and takes the form of an inner cry for a more authentic, self-liberated life. And in the oppressor, that buried spark burns most dully, enwrapped in the energies of an aggressive determination that sees only myopically, the "one" reality of its own cause or need. And there, Spirit becomes distorted as an inflated ideal in which mastery is nothing more than control over the perceived weaknesses of the unloved other, however loving that oppressor may appear.

Wisdom, in this case, is a search for the successful means of healing both self and other, whatever the past consequences of unloving circumstances. Such wisdom grows out of a determination to find the healing wells and springs, the waters of life that heal those wounds and open the enclosed soul to a new life of more authentic being. In the deeper channels, the circulating currents seek a release of inner tensions that contract, opening by stages, the inner capacity to newly manifest real, receptive being. Those currents must flow freely through the entire person, through bone, muscle, organs, blood, nerves, psychic and spinal channels, and into a fully aware feeling-consciousness open to the ultradimensionality of diverse spiritual manifestations. This happens slowly, suddenly, progressively, and with lapses and leaps. Until stabilized in a deep-seated healing of the whole being, Spirit-guided, the manifestations are a joyful process of self-awakening. Our mutual healing in such circumstances is a long-term process of recognizing the nature of the illness and acting to release the trauma and strain of an inauthentic, unloving life. To drink deeply from the healing source, to share the cup, to accept the grace of a new becoming means to also accept the love offered by others in that process, and, to know the flow of Spirit in-between. This is the

alchemical cup, the elixir of the golden Grail, that renews and restores vitality, uplifts, and opens the eye of wisdom to a new seeing,
a new becoming.

To "lift the veil" means to see into and through the external form
of things to the heart and inner workings, into the depths of an infinite expanse. The "veil" has many diverse meanings, including the
blind unseeing of material preoccupation, the denial of diversity, the
assent to only a single paradigm or a dominant worldview unreceptive to its own inadequacy. Falsification is also a veil, as is a critical
counterreading or an indeterminate ambiguity whose contents cannot be fixed accept in unending nuances of meaning. It is not simply
"difference" that matters, but qualitative distinctions capable of flexible expression and reconfiguration beyond the simplicity of dualistic or dialectical models. The "veil" is our own limitations, our
particular way of seeing in a reductive sense, a search for exclusive
definition, or an operational logic set apart from the nuances of real
embodied life. The "veil" is what we draw over Life in trying to limit
the meaning to serve a particular way of thinking detached from authentic being. Our real being toward Life is a process of incorporation and correspondence with all life forms, as such, inseparable
from all those other living beings. To lift the veil is to see with our
full being all the relationships that make "us" possible in the
processes of an expanding and evolving cosmological becoming.

To "uncover the presence" is to find what already resides within
us through a process of increasing self-awareness, and to find what
lies without us through the discovery and exploration of alternative
worlds. This enhancement of awareness through increasing sensitivity to the energetic worlds of others, as well as to our own dynamic potential for change, marks the threshold of a profound
transhistorical horizon.[38] In opening to that horizon, the lineal
processes of historical learning or development are encompassed by
a macrocosmic plurality of possible new directions. We are no longer
bound by a strict causality or past conditionality but become co-creators within that presence for the emergence of more capable, actualized being. Emerging out of spiritual dialogues, explorations, and
transitive, expressive forms, such realizations are part of the celebration of spiritual rebirth. Such is a true "making of history"—
rather than being a consequence of historical conditioning, it is a
conscious, enstatic actualization that gives rise to new historical possibility. The manifestation of presence is a profound sharing of ca-

pacity not yet actual or real in the ordinary world of conditioned, his-
toricized consciousness. No longer a product of society, the spiritual
seeker becomes a maker and co-creator (with others) of emergent, visionary worlds whose social validity and concretion must engage
those others in a shared commitment of actualization.

In that process of actualization, inevitably, there is coalescence,
a uniting of abilities, skills, aptitudes, of those drawn to the realization of a shared remaking of the old world. It might be few or many,
but the criteria for an authentic engagement with shared values,
ideals, or visionary worlds, is the capacity it bestows for positive, loving human (or other) relationships. The "host" is a symbol of that
shared love and that birthing wisdom that shines forth as inspiration for the full actualization of communal effort, for co-creative engagement. What is shared in this engagement, through love and
lucid understanding, is a more alive, more vital awareness of
Spirit—its presence, activity, and hidden potentials. The "true host"
has no particular form, or may be any form, insofar as it genuinely
shows the fullness and flowering of a spiritual realization. A lotus
blossom, a golden fire-petaled rose, a handful of pure water, cedar in-
cense, or white sage, the feather of an eagle, or a white, translucent
stone might all be seen as "host" and thus symbolize an awareness of
how Spirit manifests. It might be the smile of a lover, a child's eyes,
a woman on the threshold of birth, or dawn on a cool spring morning.
All these are living expressions of life shared, made concrete in perishable form, enlivened by Spirit in the eye of the heart. It is said
that all living things are the signature of a holy creation—such a
thought bears remembering.

Thus the "host" cannot be confined to a particular form, sign, or
symbol, to only one rite, practice, or reification. It is prevalent
throughout the world, a effervescent bubbling up from the heart of
life in the sharing and love that coexists between all loving beings. It
purifies and distills all granual thinking still caught in material
forms and subtilizes our felt relationships to the created other, drawing out of us a more refined and pervasive awareness. To "lift the
veil" means first and foremost to do so with deep respect, love, and a
receptive will, flexible and responsive to the beloved yet concealed by
the veil. To kiss and to be kissed means to do so unpossessively but
with full sincerity that love be a catalyst to understanding, to the attainment of true seeing, to self-mastery for the benefit of a greater
shared wisdom and insight. The union of the bride and groom, the

Hieros Gamos, the alchemical union, the *conjunctio oppositorum*, are also signs and symbols of this uncovering, the unveiling of life-in-death beyond simple mortal pleasure or joys. Whatever comes, must pass; what emerges must live and then, die, fall into the earth, germinate, and be reborn with variation, change, and new fortitudes. The symbols are always transitional; like human beings, they live, endure, die, and come back, never the same and always "in process," always bearing potential for new birth and death.

When the "eye of the heart" has seen essences and manifestations, has actualized the flow of presence, has been both uplifted and cast down, then wisdom begins to truly give birth. (6.7)

Meditation: There is no becoming without pain or suffering, to some degree, as necessary for learning and differentiation. The learning of wisdom is a lifelong task whose goal is not the accumulation of knowledge but of insight into the human heart, into the needs, sorrows, and longing that impel human beings toward their ambiguous destinies. Such insight should be active and not passive, engaged and not detached, concerned and not indifferent or tainted by cynical conceits or cold dispassion. This necessary suffering is not always negative, not always to be avoided or escaped through detachment or rational disdain, nor is it a devaluing metaphysics of ascetic transcendence. Suffering is often a product of a false aspiration or a misdirection of will or desire; but the discovery of such misdirection is a step toward new being, toward a refined, more flexible seeking. In this sense, suffering is often the means by which we overcome our own inauthentic patterns, by which we confront the inadequacy of sought goals or habituated, self-serving tendencies. Being "cast down" is a normal part of opening to new awareness and discovering depths no longer obscured by surface attention and shallow collective attitudes. The "false consciousness" of the superficial seeker will inevitably shrink back before the full import and impact of the unactualized potential. The suffering involves letting go through the development of a grounded and centered receptivity no longer bound by immediate needs and grasping. This is one kind of suffering.

Another kind of suffering is that imposed by others, the demands of others that make life difficult, static, habitual, repetitive, stifling, and contracted. Cast down by those more intent on external life, less receptive and sensitive to the refinements of Spirit, by unconscious tendencies of daily routine and comfortable habits, suffering becomes a goad impelling change. And there is suffering in change, in loss of the ordinary or habitual, or of the once confined but contracted world now shattered or disassembled. There is suffering in the loss of those once loved, in death, accident, tragedy, and ruptures of all kinds, unexpected and consequential. This is suffering born of an absence, of a loss of support, of a new isolation and loneliness, an absence no longer reflected through the immediate reciprocity of mutual care and love. There is the suffering by abandonment, by giving up a world, a home, a life, a pattern or old way no longer sufficient. Suffering has innumerable forms based in human bias, ignorance, and petty self-admiration. Inevitably, human beings project into the lives of others their own fears, sense of superiority, imbalances, and pathologies—each grafted onto issues of race, gender, age, culture, ethnicity, religion, ideology, social rank, or supposed rights of inheritance, privilege and education. Through these many biases, suffering comes into the world through enactments from within, through impositions from without, and through the tedium of incessant negotiations motivated by the maintenance of position, influence, and private gain.

Such is the "thrown" state of the world from the perspective of a contracted struggle for compassion or from an awakening to the wisdom of the heart. The ignorance and suffering of the world is an inevitable feature of actual existence, as it now is, in the real lives of a multitude of beings. To be "uplifted" in Spirit is to find inspiration, the healing breath, renewal, and contact with the life source, the affirmation of potential in the face of the suffering other. It means to experience both the "expansions" and "contractions" of spiritual life, the rhythms of opening and closing, of receiving and holding within, of giving and holding back. This is a growth process, not a lineal progression, but a cyclical phasing, a turning of the wheel, the inner spiral deepening within and the outer spiral reaching out to encompass and be transformed. In this process, wisdom seeks to constantly recognize the states of others, their sorrows, joys, aspirations, failures, and becomings. This is what it means to be human—to have limits and to overcome them, to fall back and then to go on, to collapse and yet to hold firm. In this sense, there is no ideal perfection and no necessary pattern or goal; instead there is only the individual path overcoming inner resistance and outer misdirection.

In this process, the "flow of presence" acts at times as a stabilizing energy that gives direction and continuity and at other times, acts to push forward or to push back the precipitous leap. At times we run a straight course on open ground toward our goal; at others, we wander in night and fog, groping forward but, perhaps, moving in circles and in retreat. We plunge into unknown deeps, contemplate visionary forms, are overwhelmed by magnitude or potency, then find our weaknesses in everyday habits and resistant attitudes instilled early and hard to release. The flows are many and constricted or opened by the uncertain thermodynamics of spiritual growth and development. But in moving through all the stages, expansions and contractions, losses and gains, we become increasingly enriched, given character and increased dimensionality, enfolded into a multitude of suborders, made implicate, and more aware and understanding. The more complete the journey, the more rich in experience, encounter, contrast, and difference, the more able each seeker is to comprehend the journeys of others, their struggle, suffering, and joyful actualizations. From this enrichment, compassion flows more easily, out of the opening into new being, out of the transmissions of an actualized life, out of the guiding presence of Spirit.

When the "eye of the heart" is opened, it sees quite clearly the sorrow and suffering of others. It sees the manifestations, the intentional and unintentional consequences of interaction, the shaken foundations, the cracked and broken enigma of human potential, the distracted lives of a multitude in conflict. Through this forest of shadows shines an indistinct light, a flickering of sparks, auras of dawn and twilight, of midnight suns and astral planes of luminous action. That light is a dawning wisdom, a glimmer casting new color on cloud edges, a harbinger of expansive horizons and rebirth, a promise awaiting actualization. In that light, attained through the gradual or sudden progression into alternative worlds, into visionary horizons no longer reducible to common miasma, is revealed a vaster panorama in which human suffering need not be a way of life but only a rite of passage into rebirth and joy. Human life and embodiment is that rite of passage, marked by the stages of a dawning wisdom, leaving the tattooed marks of stages attained and then transformed for new learning and becoming. Every soul is marked by these rites, by alchemical and Hermetic transformations, by the ashes of transformed passions marking flesh and bone. That light, dawning through a multitude of beings, brings peace and world renewal but through the necessity of each of us having made an individual journey, having attained the goal, able to manifest a compassion fully potent and alive.

Then "wisdom begins to truly give birth" to her many daughters and sons, her children of life and becoming, light and dark, her sparks of presence, in bright auras of new-found affirmation. And what is born must grow and mature to a full and complete expression, shared for the benefit of others, offered without pride as a gift, received with joyful thanks. Having given birth, wisdom remains, quietly prompting and guiding, setting forth by example, making real the living currents as intentional acts of creation. The "essences and manifestations" cannot be counted or reduced to a known quantity or fixed qualities, to a particular set of attributes, or to a recognizable and bound articulation. Always, they exceed expectation and knowing; never measurable by external means, they are nevertheless enacted by real beings in real becomings. The heart, opened to inspiration, allows those manifestations to guide and direct the processes of self-awakening without grasping or holding onto them. Such inspirations are markers of the passage into a more complex, aware life now filled with the ambient auras of alternative realized beings. The heart becomes a source of healing, the energy flows throughout diverse realms, and the guidance of those energies is Spirit-born. Life flows into life and enhances the contracted form, flushes out the weakness, and unfolds into diverse potentials, each grounded in particular abilities or gifts. This gifting of Spirit is the means for a profound healing if only we open fully to that deep, abiding presence.

Then mind is subdued, enters calm, and perceives the Source; when the will is enrapted it cannot differentiate; but will resolved in Spirit's nurturing, knows both its purpose and its consequence. (6.8)

Meditation: Wisdom is not, after all, strictly a matter of "mental development," external learning, or "intellectual ability." The over-intellectualized attitude, cultivated through constant mental stimulation, tends always to overvalue the mental life partly because of its tendencies toward complexity and partly because of the obsessive, somewhat hysteric attitudes (hidden behind a veil of detachment) with which many intellectuals cling to their ideational constructions. Such intellectual development is all too often horizontal. It consists of a constant spreading out into a particular domain of mental concern, a constant following of mental tendencies conditioned by a limited, often overly rationalized patterning whose potential for complexity cannot compensate for the lack of depth or maturity. Intuition is harnessed to serve only interpretive goals predefined by restricted mental attitudes. Epistemology is reduced to an invariant horizon of theoretical constructs whose parameters block out alternative modes of mental perception, empathic awareness, or, often, imaginative thinking no longer bound by such a reductive episteme. Such thinking is reduced to a limited intellectualized horizon, emotion is suffocated, sensitivity for other mental-emotive perceptions is arrogantly rejected or denied plausibility, and very commonly, a passive-aggressive intellectual stance creates an atmosphere of intolerance, suspicion, and shallow skepticism that, in the end, is a defense against novelty, unconventionality, and creative transformations.

The search for authentic being and becoming can be enhanced by a creative, intellectual life, by openness to new ideas, thoughts, or insights no longer bound by a social conviction that certain schools of thought are the most valid or rigorous. Scientific methodologies may be a useful way to explore the problems of science, but the problems of science are not identical with the problems of authentic human existence. Critical rationalism may have important applications to a wide variety of problems and intellectual issues but it may also prove woefully inadequate in developing human relationships, understanding deeper human motivations, and in providing ground for a creative freedom in the exploration of alternative ways of seeing or understanding. Historical arguments may be useful in revealing some aspects of how we interpret the past, but may also reduce that past complexity to a simplistic picture replete with narrow historical concerns and overly determined theories of causality. The problems of confronting the internal inconsistencies of real human self-existence far outweigh the speculative consistency and ideal imagery so often projected to represent the other in the detached mental space of intellectual construction. The spiritual challenge is not simply to embrace an intellectual perspective (however rigorously), but to actualize human potential that far exceeds a strictly intellectual life.

Spirituality is a union of diverse capacities and abilities in the context of an energized, creative life inseparable from the full extensions of higher awareness and the embodiment of that awareness in deep commitment and worldly actualizations. The Gnostic-Hermetic perspective on this transformation is an ever-deepening commitment to the actualized real world of corporate beings whose responsibilities include a careful, respectful attention to physical life as the means for real transformation and spiritual development.[39] This requires calming the mind, knowing how to bring it into a restful state of receptivity and relaxation, no longer preoccupied with mental activities but allowing those activities to subside into a focalized, alert awareness imbued with attentive listening and deep openness to inward spiritual depths. Such a state is memorialized in the precept of "body as temple"—that is, body as a valued and profound source of transformation, as *mater materia*, the mother substance through which potentials are given authentic form and content. From such a perspective, there is a full reciprocity of Spirit born through bodily life and bodily life born through Spirit. This is the ongoing cycle of the double spiral, inward and outward.

The enstatic aspect of this realization infuses the entire being of the seeker with a plenitude of being, a fullness so intense as to immobilize individual consciousness and to annihilate difference. As a mystical state of authentic self-being, it is a realization of profound possibility emergent through the various subtle and increasingly more material aspects of embodied life. The spiritual dynamics of this awakening and transformation proceed quite differently for different individuals; the enstatic rapture of a fully luminous awakening may be quite mild or gentle or it may be a rapture of great intensity and even overwhelming power. But it is not birthed intellectually, nor is it a consequence of simply thinking (or believing) in a certain manner. In the initial stages of self-awakening to this deep potential, the will, the emotions, the mind, imagination, and awareness in all its psychic correlates become infused and completely surpassed by the sheer abundance and depth of the open horizon. Spirituality as openness refers to the unlimited capacity that we as embodied beings have for experiencing the extensive life ways that abound throughout a multitude of visionary worlds. At the heart of this multitude of visions and becomings, Spirit infuses and enwraps them all within the embrace of a constant, purposeful unity through the self-realizations of each unique being.

But the enstatic state, the enraptured will, is only a stage toward more flexible and expansive realizations in which the individual functions in and through a more gracious continuum of infused presence. The original "lack of discrimination" is a function of complete immersion in the enstatic encounter, in being grasped by dynamic energies that subtilize into an actual, operative physical life of joyful, embodied living. Moments of being overwhelmed by such manifestations may come and go, but the long-term affects of this process are to subtilize the will, feelings, and mind by intending them toward a more conscious, self-aware life of related interactions. In part this involves "surrender" in the sense of no longer maintaining rigid or fixated patterns of behavior (mental, emotional, or physical). It means following the currents, adapting to the flow of giving and receiving, engaging in a self-aware reciprocal becoming. It means accepting the nurturance of Spirit as something other than principle or ideal. It means actualizing the real currents between beings as the interconnective medium for awakening to a more extended way of co-seeing and co-being. It is a new responsiveness to the dynamic patterning of perceptions as they open to new horizons of meaning and interrelatedness. It means bringing the will into attunement with larger patterns of being, no longer motivated by a strictly ego-conscious self-concern.

This opening to Spirit, as a vastly incorporative domain, in no way denies us the individual capacity for unique and personal contribution. In fact, it is an enhancement of individual identity, a joyful realization of human capacity actualized in specific patterns of real expressiveness. This is the wonder and joy of the process: nothing is lost; everything valuable is preserved and taken to a new level of self-actualization. What falls away is only the petrified habit, the "old way" of entrenched thinking or believing, the unnecessarily rigid attitude or "unconscious" regressive tendencies. There is nurturing in an unhurried and graceful opening, without panic or fear, without excess and imbalanced extremes. The "middle way" is to follow the process through all the stages, individualized by temperament, and to accept the necessity of pauses, regressions, backsliding, confusion, and uncertainty as completely natural and normal. Going on means not giving up, not turning away, not denying the need for greater development or the necessity of tracking through former patterns in order to more clearly essentialize learning. The will, guided by an unfolding purpose, grounded in spiritual intention, becomes a creative source of solution to the innumerable problems facing every seeker. This is an enacted wisdom, a responsive engagement with the world as a place of transformation where, Spirit-guided, the individual becomes a center for the realization of a higher, more inclusive wisdom.

From this, the body heals, irradiated from the heart; it dissolves conflicts and contradictions, releases fears, angers, or hidden anxieties and no longer cushions itself in habits or denials. (6.9)

Meditation: In awakening and illumination, there is a flowing movement toward ever more expressive being, an unfolding no longer occurring in isolation from cosmological wholeness. There is an opening to deeper patterns of co-relatedness with other spiritual seekers, a resonance with all life and organic embodiments. In such a context, the Source is everywhere and each of us is a center, a manifest complex of internal forms seeking self-expression and functioning in a new context of intimacy. Yet there is an inner stillness, a quiet reserve, a tranquility that preserves a deep respect and awareness of the invisible mirror, a reflective presence that gives depth and fullness. Such presence is an increasingly subtle sense of interrelatedness with other life forms, with an ultradimensionality that infuses life and awareness with a compassionate and caring, quiet resonance. It is a pervasive, qualitative and incorporative life field, an expanding fractal correspondence between all forms of impassioned life seeking wisdom and luminous insight. It has no recognizable horizons other than a specific inward concatenation of individual tendencies, desires, or aspirations and an outward cosmological context of the unbound universe organized according to complex intersection of alternative visionary worlds.

Between the cyclical unions of these horizons, the individual acts as a catalytic center for transformation, enhancing the jewel-like refractions of a shared species wisdom. This interactive, mutually reflective involution toward ever more complete understanding has its complement in an outward creative, peaceful coexistence. The illusions of conflict, aggression, war, and violence all stem from a closure of those horizons, an isolation of the individual and a reduction to a self-contained, bound, defensive ego-existence closed to all but immediate personal needs or desires. The oppressive mentality arises through closure, through denial and suppression of alternatives, through an aggressive insistence on a contracted will meant to compensate for insecure feelings rooted in low self-worth or inflated personal values, enacted with a blind unconsciousness that overrides a more sensitive, empathic, responsive becoming. The infusions of Spirit incorporate all types of contracted being, opening them to new responsive sensitivity, and providing a dynamic context for further development. There is no exclusion in this pattern, only increasing receptivity directed toward the healing of any being through the instrumentation of a well-disposed other. In this process, Spirit acts to create the healing context through a nurturing presence meant to unlock the closed and isolated worlds of the contracted other.

In this process, we must first seek to heal ourselves, to purge our limiting tendencies, hidden anxieties, suppressed fears or angers. By "first" I mean that self-healing should be a primary concern, a healing that does not proceed in isolation from others but works with and through others to attain the desired, healthy life. We must work to heal the wounds, the collective deformations of contracted social life, the generational patterns that only serve to suppress healthy new becoming. This requires wisdom, a deepening understanding of the processes of healing, of self-recovery from abuse and ignorance, of purifications from the harmful affects of unconscious behavior or conformity to limiting and suppressive attitudes. Spiritual life requires an inner openness to being, a stripping away of buffers and habituated tendencies for a freer and less driven, less compulsive, less defensive life way. This process of reorientation is facilitated through direct participation in the dynamic transformations of spiritual awakening. The contracted habits of mind, body, emotion, self-other perceptions, and the limiting beliefs of a strictly externalized or material worldview must be released for a freer and more flexible, responsive, intuitive relatedness through Spirit. Such becoming is part of the joyful wisdom, the loving concern and insight that opens the heart center to a richer, more shared life.

The "dissolution" of habits and negative tendencies occur because there is a willing release of old ways, a dropping of mental or emotional attitudes that retard personal development. The identification of these tendencies is part of an inner awakening by which the luminous qualities of a more enhanced seeing show clearly the shadow forms of former restrictive habits. These tendencies are not suppressed in this light, they only stand out as bas-relief, the "leftovers" of old psychic organizations (complexes) in need of transformation. The ruse of these tendencies is always to appear as necessary aspects of personal habit and identity, as resistant to change and entrenched against any shaking of mental foundations. And yet they are often, on closer inspection, superficial tendencies formed early and encoded within the parameters of "permissible" personal behaviors. They are all those areas of self-indulgence by which we ease the stress of a harried life—habits such as dependencies on alcohol or drugs (legal or not), certain eating patterns, fixated sexual interactions, as well as a multitude of defensive-aggressive emotive and intellective patterns, all contributing to a retardation in spiritual development. Such tendencies, often deeply intrinsic to normative behavior, need to be released and transformed to allow for a freer circulation of inner potential.

All the deformations of childhood, adolescence, sexual awakening, early adult responsibility, and the search for social, maternal, or fatherly roles are transformed through a healing inflow and upswell of inner spiritual potential. The facilitation of this process of awakening is heightened through positive, loving human interaction and an open receptivity to Spirit. As a process of individuation, it leads toward a deepening of sensitivity inwardly and outwardly and is "irradiated from the heart" as a healing presence communicable to others. It is not simply an individual development, but an interactive, comutual evolution engaging many others and working through various contextual, social circumstances. It may be a variety of communal formations forging new perspectives, or a form of communal seeking meant to develop a positive, creative visionary world. In affirming the life process as the foundation of spiritual transformation, it becomes an opening to the value of others as creative partners in a process of mutual development. In such a circumstance, the capacity to love, as a positive healing presence, takes precedence over intellectual or cognitive abilities so often truncated emotionally and unable to value the loving response of "alien" others. This loving response is neither passive nor self-denying, but a creative, wholesome, stable inner clarity Spirit-born and shared in joyful wisdom.

In turn, the "body heals" not in the strictly physical sense as a complex of organic, cellular, and genetic compounds, but it is maintained in good mental-emotive health and positive bodily habits. This means releasing deep muscle contractions, inner tensions, the cramps of earlier trauma or assaults from outside. It means clearing the inner channels for a clear flow of neural-psychic energy, where the "spiritualization of the body" becomes a development of preserved and respected habits, well-disciplined and resulting in a vital, physical, sexual, emotive life. In this way, the mind becomes more settled and attuned to the inner currents of spiritual impressions (inward or outward) giving rise to visionary horizons and to a noetic development of a more lucid and illuminative thinking. Such thinking becomes a means for the expression of an inner wisdom and seeing, no longer disconnected from higher cosmological horizons and intimately part of the conditionality of emergent, shared becoming. Open to the emergent energies of being, Spirit-guided, the individual lives in a sensitive matrix of complex relationships, flowing with interactive, intentional possibility. It is the responsibility of each person to organize that intentionality into the real patterns of authentic life and to actualize them through an honest, creative, and joyful wisdom. This is the calling we each have as real beings whose evolution and higher realizations may all contribute to a more wise and self-aware species life.

The Seventh Principle

The Seventh Principle of Spirit is ecstasy, the union of individual life with the eternal, with the ultimate source of renewal and transformation, with unextinguished Light. (7.1)

Meditation: The seventh principle is twice three plus one, a double trinity with an added musical fifth: life, awareness, understanding, plus unknown mystery, loving compassion, joyful wisdom, and in consummation, unity, ecstasy, oneness. The seventh conjoins activity, seeking, and aspiration with rest, renewal, and an expansive consciousness. Its ancient sign is the astral cosmos, the seven heavenly bodies, visible symbols of a celestial harmonic balance born long before our present human self-becoming. Yet this ecstasy takes us far beyond the confines of a single star, far beyond the most distant moon, comet, or space rock hurling in eccentric orbits toward our planetary home. It takes us out into the vaster seas of plasmic, energetic, star-seeded, dark-mattered, galactically clustered radiances from high-band to low-band partice-waves, into the blue shifted light of an energetic sea without boundaries, horizons, or measures. Expansive in all directions, it seems to have no end; contracted into a spark over the top of the head, it bursts with a radiant burst of mental, emotive, and psychic illumination. Settling to the heart level, it opens a multicosmos of undefinable proportion, complexity, and beauty.

The progressive opening of the psychoneural centers moves from the lower presexual through sexual awakening, to will and expansive, heart-centered relations, up into spoken songs or words, to a psychic unveiling of new spiritual latitudes, and finally irradiates forth in the seventh center as luminescent, expansive mind. This most precious and rare event traverses a full spectrum of possible stages and stations, all of which collapse into the unbound, interdimensional fullness of the unknowable Mystery. Such ecstasy is neither ultimate nor final insofar as we can never exhaust the interpretative fullness in which it arises. What emerges is simply an affirmation of potential, a formulation of perspective (possibly tied to specific mystical techniques) and a communication of felt and known horizons. It may be articulated as profound, holy, sacred, awe-inspiring or as a lucid, clear, all-pervasive, unbound unitary wholeness linking all beings in emergent revelations. Such a perspective in no way exhausts the possibilities for yet greater realizations or new expressions of wonder or attainment. It is not a matter of a closed universe embedded in fixed ontological signs or a cloistered metaphysics of fixed stages or stations, nor is it a hierarchical ladder laid against the walls of sociobiological history or intellectual determinism. It is far less bound than what human beings crave through their insecurities; it is far more than a known universe of mystical becomings wedded to a limited horizon of possibility.

The vastness of possibility manifestations through continual variation and diversity of life forms and their adaptive relationships to a shared ecology results in a tendency toward constant variations and alternatives. Yet there is a deeply conservative collective tendency that manifests even in the most ecstatic states of spiritual realization. There are certain well-traveled pathways that, when followed, end in sanctioned realizations promoted as the goal of a particular spiritual practice. It is as though the psychic world of a spiritual tradition bound the individual to only sanctioned patterns of actualization. The more the individual participates in a certain way of thinking or believing and follows a structured spiritual guidance, the more likely that the realizations will conform to the ideals held as mystical goals. This existentialization of a spiritual, visionary world resonates with shared realizations or transmitted psychic patterns that collectively define a mystical condition or attitude as a stratum within being, a possible way to spiritual illumination. The good of this principle—that a particular path leads to a particular pattern of realizations—is that it provides a formal means to direct others toward that realization. That which is less good, is the tendency to absolutize that pattern and to extol its virtues as final or ultimate.

How can there be an ultimate or final spiritual "state" or goal beyond the continued creative actualization of potential that does not reduce the Infinite to a human scale? We should have the species humility to recognize that we are not the measure by which All That Is can be known. We may know it as best we can, in the best possible ways, constantly seeking to better our understanding, but where ecstasy leads is beyond a quantifiable measure, beyond a particular human account of actual transformation. Nor are such spiritual realizations simply quantitative, a kind of additive universe of multiple experiences together equalling what Is, for that Is is a human Is, a cluster of qualitative perceptions inseparable from a vaster, transformative cosmos of multiple becomings. The "eternal" is an unbound, ever-existing Whole, without end or known limit, a limitless expansive of multilayered coexistences with innumerable, necessary others whose own seeing adds to the qualitative nuances by which we know who we are, or might become. I call it "eternal" simply because I can see no real beginning nor end, no real limit to the possibilities inherent in species transformation, and no necessary goal that we, as incarnate, embodied beings, must seek or actualize beyond creative, peaceful, exploratory, and compassionate coexistence.

We may choose to explore the vertical dimensionality of "higher or deeper" strata of the neural-psychic mind in an attempt to define a full-spectrum awareness. We may indeed enter the depthless sea of Mystery and fully immerse our limited self-identity in utter ecstasy and mystical illuminations, thus bringing forth new understanding and insights. We may engage fully in soulful explorations of deep psychic potential for the good of our shared well-being. But in this process we will not exhaust the capacity for the embodied mind to yet reconfigure, reformulate, or completely revise and restructure our understanding of the depths of mind in relationship to the Whole. Spirit-guided, we will discover the vast reaches of life as primary and limitless, eternal in the most enduring sense, a cosmic constant whose manifestations cannot be limited to purely human constructs, thoughts, or belief patterns. Like light poured into the vessels of creation, they burst asunder with the radiance of a deep intensity of being, overflowing those vessels to a magnitude inconceivable or containable in their glassy, transparent forms. This is "transformation and renewal" in the most cogent and personal sense, through the direct encounter to realize the enstatic embrace of the Beloved and in that embracement, to fully surrender to ultimacy, limitless beauty, and a fullness beyond recounting.[40] Such a renewal surges through the entire emotive-mental-physical being, completely captivating the attention and focalizing awareness through the lens of a luminous, transpersonal horizon. This may occur while waking, sleeping, dreaming, quietly praying, in mediation, walking in nature, making love, or in any number of unexpected moments of revelation and expansive openness. The deep affirmation is one that grounds the entire complex of psychic tendencies in an overwhelming immersion in Spirit, and then leads beyond into pure Mystery and Ineffability. There is no "promise" or even "necessary end" to such experience. It simply continues to unfold into ever more diverse possibilities of expression and creative corelatedness. It takes us into the dark as well, into the shadows, into the deeper unseen side of our own potential for distortion or misunderstanding, into all the unresolved tensions inherent in embodied, undirected will. It is not merely a shining surface reflecting essential light, but also an alchemical vessel absorbing energy and heat to dissipate that acquired urgency into new inner forms born out of a dark, warm, creative womb. It is only the suppressed and unexpressed energy, entrapped in the unrealized contours of unrealized potential, that tends toward a more contracted and ill-formed manifestation. This is why there must be purgation, letting go, a release of inner tension, a realization of deep inner capacity to birth forth tha limitless beauty still hidden within each of us.

Light within Light! Where there is neither light, nor life, nor unknowing! Where all is known as inexhaustible Infinity; as sourceless Source, as Spirit's inner formless form. (7.2)

Meditation: It is inevitable that language is inadequate to the task of a full and precise description of mystical states and experiences. This is because such experience utterly surpasses the mental-constructive formalisms of linguistic habits and joyfully manifests as

ineffable qualities of Spirit. Like lovers arising from the bed of a joyful sexual union filled with loving presence, an expansive union of
souls, a deeply felt communion in the unified wholeness of interpen-
etrated and interpenetrating being, words cannot transmit the fullness of the experience. Nor are words adequate to the task of
substituting for that experience through description or abstraction,
not now, not ever. How much more so the depths of a soulful union
with Spirit where words become a pale reflected image like a hiero-
glyphic painting on a wall meant to signify a divine glory but unable
to convey even a small portion of the real being whose image the
drawing seeks to represent. This is not to say that words have no
value in communicating experience or meaning, but only that their
value is derivative, dependent, nonautonomous, and secondary in establishing the reality of being through direct encounter.[41] There are
inspired words, songs that are like prayers, images that language elevates to a simple glistening of inner visionary forms, even words of
power that can transform and elevate, like mantric hymns and
prayer-songs. But enter the circle of light, stand in the presence, experience the upswell of Spirit, and words dissolve like so much dust
before the rain. It is in the rain that one finds renewal, not in the
dust that the rain settles and soaks back into earth.

The "light within light" is no mere metaphor or external sign. It
is an actual description of real being, experientially grounded in a direct personal seeing. Within the inner light, I see yet a deeper Light
that the inner light reflects as an enstatic image resonant with the
greater, oceanic Light without. Wave on wave that Light submerges
all self-consciousness in an endless sea of all-conscious life filled
with sentience, inextinguishable, eternal in a noncorporeal sense,
beyond mere imagining and far beyond abstract mental ideas. And
yet even that Light is not an end or goal. It is rather a phenomenal
sign of the pervasive currents within an ambient sea whose life
forms are incalculable and whose depths are immeasurable. It is not
only the external, visible cosmos that symbolizes this Infinity, but
also an inner opening that reveals all the hidden, fractal, multidimensional reflected orders of the *Mundus Imaginalis* yet awaiting
discovery and full expression. Inner light and outer light are in
many ways the same; they resonate with qualitative brilliance, reverberate with energetic life, interpenetrate within a single continuum of neural-psychic perceptions across a threshold of shared,
concomitant being. It is not mere hyperbole to say the sun (and all

stars) have consciousness. They indeed do reflect an energetic medium of lifelike currents, beaming down on us with exquisite joy in times of darkness, and energizing our entire state of well-being.

But how is it that there is "neither light, nor life" within that Light? This is a trick of language, an inversion, a reconstellation of meaning meant to direct mind away from words and toward something more than words. Neither "light" nor "life" are truly adequate representations of that-which-Is, of the full meaningful significance of either "light" or "life." Like broken vessels, words cannot contain that to which they point, cannot convey the full meanings that are irreducible to a linguistic sign or symbol. They can suggest, urge, prompt, encourage (or discourage), perhaps persuade or even "prove" points. But they can never engender the direct actual experience in all its fullness, nuance, and being. And it is in mystical experience that lies the truth of the words. Being "alive" and seeing the "light" must inevitably track to the baseline of personal experience and various kinds of personal and transpersonal encounters. Yet words are also a kind of witnessing, a testimony, an offered account of real being, and in authentic speaking, they become a form of visible sign vouching for real life and meaningful awareness. The authenticity of the speaking means giving an honest account, a genuine presentation of experience through an act of interpretative commitment, as a persuasive embodiment of real being actualizing itself, word by word. And yet, neither bound by those words nor determined by them, we struggle to transmit in dialogue, those experiences that may confirm, to some degree, the value of the words heard and remembered.

The "light" is not metaphorical but a phenomenal description of actual experience, firsthand ethnography, part of my own visionary anthropology embodied in words that can only symbolize what I cannot truly convey. This "light of being" has no phenomenal boundary, no measure above or below, but presents itself to me as a supersaturating presence within all life and as irreducible to any particular life form. My spiritual anthropology is based in just this kind of experience and encounter, as real transformative awakenings to alternative states of being and seeing. It is not a theoretical construction, yet I give it theoretical interpretation by translating it into verbal summaries meant to isolate significant features of experience as contributing to a wholistic view of human creative, spiritual development. It is a "spiritual light" that appears as nonabsolute and yet all-pervasive, beyond my ken and yet deeply informative. It is intuitive but phenomenally visible, enstatic and yet diverse and multidimensional. Within, there is a deep "knowing"—not in the specific, informational sense, or in any revelations of law or didactic guidelines. This light shines as a direct awareness of profound cosmological intentionality, all-pervasive and embedded in the actualizations of real, specific, embodied life forms whose autonomy and creative capacities are fully real and meaningful. It has been for me based in almost entirely nonverbal, visionary experiences. Thus, there are few words or verbal expressions associated with my experiences of that deeper, eminent being. Yet I write eulogistically because it is so life-filled, so deeply brimming over with life presence, so utterly conscious and so abundant and beyond qualification, so intimate and worthy of respect and reverence.[42] That light is shared; it is "nature nurturing" as the enfolded order of multiple beings cohabiting a living planet, sheltered within the creative matrix of all-conscious, Spirit-given life. The death of even one of these life forms sends a small shock wave of loss, while the birth of another sends also a small tide of enhancement (though too many births can turn that tide into a counterforce, suppressing the basic potential). It is in the "light" of this constant genesis and reabsorption that human beings must find their way to contribute to the meaningfulness of the whole. If we live valueless lives, we can expect not to thrive but only to fade, diminish, and become less in the overall genesis of an evolving, emergent, more valued matrix of multiple, creative becomings. At the heart of the process, there is a creative urgency, an inner unfolding of potential meant to actualize real being as inseparable from the vast potential capacity. Where that potential is maximized through creative actualization, it thrives and nourishes and is nurtured; and where it contracts, penalizes, concretizes around a selfish desire or need, it fades because it cannot connect, cannot relate to the emergence of the Whole in its ongoing evolutions toward greater self-manifestations. Spirit does not merely abide, it draws us out, persuasively, toward a more complete expression; it authentically confronts us with the limits we must overcome and challenges us to move beyond a limited intellectual, emotional, or moral horizon.

The "sourceless Source" is that deep spiritual potential that remains as yet unrealized in actual occasions of real being. Our search for authenticity is nothing other than a search for an actualization of potential that is not only within us, but about us, around us, freely circulating within the cosmic matrix beaming its life energies with an unrelenting stimulus to realize the yet residual, latent, passive life-potential. This is an "inexhaustible source" that cannot be reduced to any particular project but can find its fulfillment only through the total engagement of all beings in all worlds forever— without end, now and always. Yet such a source is reducible to the most minute project, to a child's play or the fall of leaves into still water, to a single snow flake reflective of harmonic forms, to all the natural proportions of nature signed with cosmic potency. The inner form is "formless" (as "formlessness" is itself a form), and points us toward the unbinding of metaphor, toward a release from images, words, ideas, thoughts, perceptions, leaving only the vast expanse of an undefinable vibrancy, profoundly translucent, transparent, transpersonal, transcendent, yet immediately present and thoroughly real, nurturing, and vivid. Such is the paradox of real being, infinitely expressible and yet never containable or reducible to the expressed.

> **Thus the world is turned inside out, the perceived becomes perceiver and the manifestation, the essence; individuality ceases to construct and is constructed by the all-absorbing flow. (7.3)**

Meditation: Such an inversion is not atypical, but reflects a tendency within consciousness to turn the object of perception into an internalized subject, and in this case, on a cosmic scale. To behold the "infinite in a grain of sand" is a similar precept. It reflects the need to behold the universe from within and not from without, not as disjoined observers but as immediate, deeply involved participant-creators. It is quite possible to perceive from multiple unitary perspectives as in the old Chinese line drawings in the *Secrets of the Golden Flower*, and in that state to turn the subjective position into numerous alternatives seen from without.[43] This emergence into multiplicity, the manner of its sudden inversion, is quite mysterious and difficult to describe. Consciousness seems to no longer inhabit a particular being, body, or position but is seen as simply part of a greater wholeness in which the "individual" no longer has a privileged point of view. Such an experience transforms the "I am" into something more than a single, embodied, isolated consciousness and is converted, quite suddenly, into a multiplex of equally conscious alternative perspectives, more of a "we are" that has no one center. This "dissolution" of self is yet an affirmation that consciousness is more than a particular form of embodiment and is not reducible to a single form, however personal and immediate.

The shared life of interrelated becoming is not reducible to embodiment in a strictly physical form. From the psychic and spiritual perspective the creative matrix is far more incorporative and pervasive than any individual account of consciousness can offer. In fact, every individual account, in the strict sense, is a truncated view insofar as it has not yet recognized the incorporative aspects of species-wide emotive-mental life. Consciousness as a shared matrix, a world-saturated awareness, is inseparably part of a greater self-becoming, rather than any particular account of personal development. Yet personal development is deeply contributory to that matrix, to the spiritual affirmation of a world-transforming process. The "inversion" refers to an awakening of this potential as an actual occasion in which consciousness suddenly "spreads out" into a vaster domain of self-realizations and alternative perspectives. Such a domain is embodied without closure in an enveloping, emergent condition, in a responsive, creative "leap" to new understanding and insight. This "spreading out" is not simply horizontal, though occasions on the horizontal plane may be its most dramatic expression; it is also a process of interiorization and has, subsequently, deep connectedness with the more vertical dimensions of being and awareness.

One can go "up" into increasingly more subtle forms, increasingly more potent, archetypal, and noetic (as in certain types of dreaming). Or one can go "down" into the inner workings of physical embodiments, even to the atomic and subatomic plane where consciousness still remains subtilized in a pervasive, horizontal sense. That inner physical world is distinguished by a vast number of concurrent structural features, themselves subject to manipulation though conscious intent (symbolized in alchemy as the conversion of lead into gold).[44] These vertical dimensions cannot be exhaustively identified because such identification is itself a creative occasion of becoming creatively more conscious. Through identification, classifying, comparing, analyzing, and so on, we each contribute to an emergent, creative perspective that subjects the world to new partitions, more or less adventitious, useful, or significant. Consciousness cannot be separated from observation or participation in the creative processes of "knowing"—how much more so, in knowing spiritually! The reciprocity between the knower, knowing, and the known is inseparable from the creative actualizations of becoming more conscious; therefore we are as much objects of perception as we are perceivers. What perceives us is the other, the yet unamalgamated alternative other that acts as a creative goad to move us forward into a more co-related seeing. Then, suddenly, we become that other, we see as they see and in that seeing recognize the limits of what we once saw so incompletely.

But this "being seen" is not simply a human process, it involves all other life forms—the visible, the not-yet-visible, and those seeable but not always obviously so. Our being seen directs us to allow the respectful other to respectfully see what we have seen and to see through them what we have not yet seen. This reciprocal seeing moves us beyond the ordinary horizontal plane of external human relationships and opens us to the more vertical planes by which the "other" takes on increasingly spiritualized form (upward) or more specific embodiment in minute differences energetically constructed (downward). Yet there is a third perspective, the incorporative view that unifies these horizontal and vertical directions within an incorporative cosmological process, seen in a direct, participatory sense. Here we must pass beyond a strictly constructive view and become participants in a spiritual ethnography of observing the simultaneity within which all our creative occasions occur. It is "participant-observation" in the sense that the creative actions of others inform my own understanding, enhance my own awareness even as I may enhance theirs, be they human, animal, plant, or even mineral. The construction of "self" flows through the neural-psychic being with increasingly subtle influences, correspondent to the realizations of spiritual potential in others.

The "leap" in consciousness is simply to experience the totality of this transformation from a unified perspective no longer overvaluing the individual point of view—yet to do so without denying the value of individual contributions. This is not, I must stress again, a mental constructive view, but an actual experience, spiritually induced, through which one surrenders the autonomy of self-identity to the greater magnitudes of Spirit. It is not simply an additive feature of "spreading out" into the world of all conscious beings, but an essential feature of spiritual transformation. The action of Spirit on the sensitive and receptive heart is to unfold the wings of perceptions in such as way as to allow individuals the opportunity to know directly the being we all share, to soar hawklike, eaglelike above our ordinary self-preoccupations and see across the entire globe into the mother country of all soul-related beings. And in such seeing, there are currents, a high, clear pressures that lift our wings to where lucidity reigns far beyond the normal conditions of a caged existence, limited by preconceived thought or narrow beliefs. That current is one that requires the greatest skill to ride, Spirit-driven, while yet maintaining balance, effectiveness, and responsibility to others. It is a current as wide as the sky and even more pervasive, incorporating whole worlds into its embrace and actualizing in those worlds the necessary occasions through which such a seeing becomes actual.

Thus "manifestation becomes essence" and the inversion is a counterreflection that images all occasions as essential expressions in the continual overturning of alternative worldviews, visions, and all religious, philosophical alternatives. Such a work is never complete, it simply goes on, seeking the higher values through which the many occasions contribute to an ongoing, real becoming within being. The currents flow from the essential dynamics of transformation, into and up through the receptive psyche, embodied in existential commitment and authentic perceptions, to manifest what is already there in a visible, viable way. That actualization is a subtilization of essence, always drawing out of itself, Spirit-guided, alternative possible forms, occasions, or circumstances in given, embodied forms. Essences are themselves simply more subtle occasions awaiting actualization and are, as such, inseparable from the evolutes that they precipitate. That precipitation has a reflux, an effect able to resubtilize the source of its own arising and thus become mutable, reciprocal, more than adventitious. What is above is also below and what is below is also above, and neither is separable from the other, and both are mutually influential in the creative process. Though what is below appears more contingent and less essential, it may become, through inversion, more necessary and formative, even to the degree that what is below becomes, indeed, that which is above.

Where silence reigns, where thought and image have no face, words no sound, gesture devoid of

**signs, rapture-filled; there Spirit uplifts and re-
veals the deep foundations of our ongoing visionary dreams. (7.4)**

Meditation: It is not a "bottomless" universe in the sense that
there are no currents that carry us through the cycles of multiple becomings, explorations, and actual attainments. Yet these currents
are not impervious to human intention, creative actions, or thoughtful reinterpretations. In fact, the currents flow through these intentions, actions, and interpretations to actualize the unrealized
potential yet concealed in a lesser, more preoccupied seeing. And at
the heart of this transformation is Mystery, the unknown depths
that cannot be well contained in words, signs, or images. Where "silence reigns" is that place that has no adequate descriptions and yet,
truly *is*. It is the imageless, nonessential-essential, the irreducible
fullness, the plenitude of being that overflows multiple bound worlds
of discrete beings inseparable from the process of creative transformation. This is an emergence from the normal cocoon of self-aware,
constricted, bound existence into the vaster, freer space of an all-
conscious expansive totality beyond the bound categories of thought,
word, and ordinary concepts. It is enstatic when described from the
perspective of the subject, but from the perspective of that which
grasps and holds us in stasis, it is only a more conscious moment of
pure intentional union, a synthesis of aspiration and realized being.

This flowing of one-into-other, this union and dissolution of difference, this mergence that is emergence, signifies the awakening of
a deep potential resident within being as a solution that dissolves all
discrete entities into a single continuum of luminous potentiality.
Here the salt doll is dissolved into the salt sea, the rain into clear
streams, the light into its own reflected energy, the wind into an infinite sky. And yet there is meaning and purpose, intentionality intending a creative outcome, something far more than mere passivity
or inactive awareness. It is a dynamic quietude, a fullness overflowing its boundaries, an upswelling of possiblity pressing outward toward continual expression, manifestation, and actualized being. The
swelling heart of the cosmos overflows through the fullness of all its
manifest life forms in all degrees of being, becoming, and the yet-to-
be. Throughout all, Spirit abides, a creative impluse toward a more
actual realization balanced within a billion billion expressive acts.

At the still center of each, there is a depth immeasurable, an ineffable presence whose nature cannot be adequately described. I call it Mystery—a plentipotent source, nonreducible to essential qualification and yet containing all qualifications. Mystery is uncontainable in any attribute but is the primary ground of all attributes, descriptions, words, meanings, or intentions.

It is Mystery, for me, because I cannot comprehend or encompass its reality in any expressions that would truly represent it fully to others. While I can write abundantly about its manifestations, relations, and potential capacities, I cannot say I comprehend or understand in any way, all that Mystery *is*. Therefore, able to enter the stream, dissolve into the stream, become the stream, I still cannot say I know either its origin or its end, or even its purpose in streaming forth, other than to give rise to all embodied life. As all is alive, so too, is Mystery a very fountain of life, an overflowing plenitude, spiritually active and life-giving, inherent at every level or plane of discrete being or becoming. Yet Mystery refers to something other than discrete manifestations; the term becomes an enigmatic symbol of the not-yet-comprehensible, of the hidden pearl, worthy of great price, even to the selling of all we possess for a greater possession yet. To be Spirit-grasped, however gently or ecstatically, is to enter into the luster of that pearl, into its inmost luminous joy, and to pass through that joy into a vast, expansive multidimensional horizon of endless seeing, where "self" and "other" have no context and no recognizable contents. Here, all is vibrant, deep quietude, peace, and imageless calm, and yet it brims over with inherent possibilities, brightly luminescent with constrained energies of valued capacities awaiting actual expression.

Each of us embodies any number of "visionary horizons" as the guiding imagery, emotive tendencies, intellective constructs, tacit assumptions, beliefs, values, or responsibilities through which we engage the world in all its complexity and contradictions. The "foundations" of this horizon are not to be found only in individual or collective formations of personal identity, or in the eccentric qualifications we make to justify or differentiate ourself from those who live or value differently. These deep visionary foundations are Spirit-born from the very heart of the life process. As discrete individuals, we find our capacities inseparable from the evolutions, devolutions, and punctuated leaps, through which an entire world seeks an enduring balance and place within a transforming cosmos of multiple others.

Always the visions press toward horizons that expand outward, beyond the individual visionary, and into the intersecting visionary worlds of others while creating a deepening sensitivity within for the possible unique and individual contribution we may each make to the unfolding of the Whole. Transpersonal visionary dreams are a creative occasion through which Spirit acts to realize the yet unexpressed possibilities of Mystery. They dissolve previous structures and dismantle old ladders and every raft used to cross from the island of self to the mainland of the more than collective realization. And they lead, beyond the collective, into the primary currents of unbound Mystery, into the swelling seas of life-giving, enhanced, luminous, all-pervasive being.

In that "rapture-filled" moment, there is no commanding voice, no necessary action, no messianic promise, no compulsion toward action that must confront or demand. I find ecstatic energy, luminous vistas in all directions, multiple worlds or multiple beings, a deep inherent unity, a perfect oneness or integral wholeness whose parts refect and self-reflect all that is within Mystery, boundless and unexpressible. There is also deep intentionality, purpose, direction, and meaning, but none written plainly on the walls of the temple other than those we seek through the realizations of our specific individual needs. Living a spiritual life is not a matter of following some transcendent "master plan" necessarily guaranteed "from above" to produce a certain end-result. Certainly there are plans and pathways we each may follow, but these are only abstractions from the direct immersion in real being. The authentic life, seeking spiritual renewal and transformation, is a continual search for authenticity in living, a deep commitment to follow the intuitions and actualizations that arise in seeking greater fullness in health, well-being, compassion, love, and understanding. If a "plan" helps, well and good; but no plan should be taken as an adequate subsitute for actual, authentic realizations, in Spirit, fully open to the creative horizons of emergent being. The opening to ecstasy is more often a stripping away, a giving up, a release of external structures and a willing reception of the inflowing creative potential.

Thus the "deep foundations" are not reducible to only one particular intellectual formulation or philosophy of predetermined ends or necessary precepts. Any number of such theophilosophical ontologies may be articulated, some perhaps more meaingful or interesting than others, but none can be taken as either final or truly adequate in a constantly emergent cosmos of creative beings, each seeking to actualize co-related possibilities. Human beings will often only see what they want to see and no more, regardless of experience. Thus there is little doubt that no particular articulation of spiritual truth will ever be adequate or even acceptable in part by disengaged others. Yet, for me, those foundations are real, vivid, mysterious, pervasive, and actual through my own direct experiences and, in part and in whole, teach me that the creative awakening of potential in others will take a great diversity of perspectives in order to satisfy the needs which, Spirit-born, constitute the complexity yet inherent to emergent being. Subsequently, the principles in this work are nothing more than a contribution to that greater dialogue through which Spirit enacts the dramas and dreams of a multitude of beings all compelled to seek insights in the bound and limited conditions of traditionalized teachings. It is up to each of us to throw off the bindings of conventional thinking and believing in order to find those deeper foundations through which we can build a more authentic spiritual life.

How is it possible to divide it into "steps and stages," into progressions gradual or sudden, into expansion and contraction, into higher and lower, into inner and outer? (7.5)

Meditation: Of course, it is possible to make such divisions, of this we have abundant evidence in every spiritual tradition from the most primal to the most urban and contemporary. The spiritual path can be articulated into any number of steps or stations, parsed out into hierarchies of numerous levels, planes, mystical stages (like purification, purgation, illumination, and unity). Or stages may be more subtle, according to the various states of consciousness, as in the higher and lower *jnanas*, the various forms of *samadhi*, each associated with a multitude of divinities, esoteric symbols, and so forth. This is a "psychic tendency toward elaboration" that reflects far more the predispositions of the makers than it does the "necessary" structures of being. Inevitably, all such divisions are subject to reabsorption and reconfiguration, to an ongoing process of creative construction and reconstruction. This does not mean that such structures are merely arbitrary or only a matter of "appearances." Within the esoteric traditions, many of these configurations are highly efficacious, that is, they work. Following a particular technique, or a graded path toward the actualizations of real being through the directions of a known path, can produce remarkable states of psychic and spiritual attainment.[45]

A known path can be a formal means for the instrumentalization of those states or goals toward which the path points. The very nature of intentionality is manifest in its capacities to give specific form and content to being, or to realize the capacities within being through the solicitation of a structured means. This process of instrumentalization is something more than a "conformity" to latent or subliminal structures. It is far more a process of exploration, intentional focus, and the creation of a consistent, patterned method meant to guide others to a similar end. This is clearly part of many traditional paths and teachings, expressive of often many generations of refinement, development, and successful application and practice. As many traditional teachers have pointed out, the means should not be mistaken for the goal, nor should it be seen as a substitute for a mature and complete attainment of the spiritual ideals toward which the path points. These "ideals" are something more than merely ideas or "types" of experiences, though they can be symbolized as such. From the perspective of emergent being, "ideals" are a crystallization of spiritual tendencies, an integrative or archetypal synthesis meant to facilitate actualizations of being through authentic practices, commitments, and training. They are not merely mental constructs but actually embodied realizations reflecting the transpersonal predispositions of real beings, transmitted through often traditionalized patterns of thought, belief, and cultural practices.

The actual spiritual realization, however, does not always follow a prescribed course, as so often witnessed in a multitude of mystical traditions whose practitioners have found themselves in conflict with the more orthodox followers of their respective faiths. The "unbinding" of the individual through a transformative process of spiritual awakening can have, in fact often does have, tendencies toward innovation and personalization that reflect the authenticity of real experience. In those traditions less bound by external orthodoxy or collective rule, the experience simply adds to the richness and complexity of the tradition. But in those traditions clad by conservative institutional frames of references, such innovation can be deeply threatening or "heretical" and are often regarded as anti-authoritarian. Subsequently, many experienced followers of the mystical life have found it necessary to create formulations of their experience that conform to a ruling hierarchical model of collective thought or dogmatic belief. There is a constant tension within the more authoritarian traditions to dogmatize the inherent structural contents of an idealized spiritual life that pulls toward the authoritative, institutional representative as the final arbitrator in judging the value of innovative interpretations. In less dogmatic traditions, the pull is toward a consensual model of the spiritual path in which the innovator may (or may not) contribute various teachings, usually affirmed (or denied) by the outstanding, usually elder members of the community.

No tradition is static and each evolves and transforms over the course of time, at the very least, through the sheer impact of multiple encounters with other alternative spiritual teachings. The very nature of spirituality involves transformation, an awakening of potential, an affirmation of the yet unrealized capacity of each and every being. While some traditions may enact this transformation slowly from without, through the constant application of laws and guidelines judiciously organized to direct everyday life, other paths are more inwardly directed toward the immediate awakening of potential for the purpose of affirming and exemplifying the highest degree of spirituality possible. And between these two, there are a multitude of degrees admixing the inner and outer life according to individual circumstances (married, unmarried, male or female, and so on), various institutional alternatives (a priest, a monk or nun, a renunciate, a lay follower, an esotericist), and a host of cultural and social conditions—each contributing to or inhibiting the processes of spiritual development. And throughout all, there is an inner urgency toward transformative horizons inciting aspiration, creative visions, and a restless, exploratory search for affirmation and fulfillment. Thus all structures are subject to change and realignment, to cosmological, social, and metaphysical adaptations, in a constant search for a more fully realized and global synthesis.

In this process, the spiritual seeker must find his or her way and make it a direct, personal, authentic commitment, susceptible to change, resistant to constant qualification, and centered in a genuine opening to potential inseparable from the deepest realization. In seeking to maximize that process, it becomes clear that while the means are not the end, the means do, nevertheless, instrumentalize and direct the seeker to predictable experiential consequences. Yet the depths and heights of spiritual realization are not simply the products of traditionalized actualizations or ideals. The open horizons within being are, and remain, unqualified in any absolute sense, though the qualities are many, and each of them a way and a path, they are each relative to the capacity, inner disposition, and character of the motivated spiritual seeker. The creative realizations of the individual may emerge as consequent to the practice of any number of "traditional" teachings, but those teachings by no means represent all that being is or might become. No tradition is "ultimate"—each is relative to the truths of the other, even when the truths they claim refer to what is, indeed, ultimate. That ultimate continues to pour forth a vast array of possible becomings out of the infinite heart of an unqualifiable fullness.

As such, all ways, paths, divisions, and structures are more than adventitious but less than inherent; they spring forth into form as a consequence of human interpretation and practice and become authenticized through repeated spiritual attainments. Made on earth, they are reflected in heaven; reflected in heaven, they are made on earth. The reciprocal processes of creative transformation make all the "steps and stages" simply attributes of a particular pathway. Such pathways may be valued according to their consequences, in terms of the real human beings who actualize those stages and the kind of human beings they truly are. Such steps are a "fractal array" revealing the possibilities within being for authentic, multiple spiritual transformations. Each images within itself some minor reflection of other such images, creating the jewel net that continually spreads its floating strands over an infinite sea. The process requires expansion and contractions, a deepening inwardness and a more explicit outward incorporation, a referencing of higher and lower conditions—all relative to the actual experience of real practitioners seeking to move through and beyond the conditionality of a structured and explicit pathway. Eventually, there is a bursting forth, a death and rebirth whose consequences are beyond adequate description. It may be either "sudden or gradual" or, most likely, it may proceed through long gradual periods punctuated by sudden breakthroughs and sharp, pervasive insights and illuminations.

Such is the way without a way, the path that has no name but can hardly be called nameless.

There is no ecstasy greater than another; no unity less than all; no enlightenment that is complete, no extinction of the soul—these are only metonyms, a part standing for the whole. (7.6)

Meditation: The constant judging of the spiritual attainments and realizations of others is an inauthentic practice, one that only reduces the complexity and lives of others to a quantifiable mental scale. Mystical experiences are not authentically reducible to external criteria by which they may be evaluated in terms of either significance or meaning for the mystic. It is, to speak metaphorically, like someone who can neither paint or play music trying to determine the value of a painting or musical composition for the artist or composer. As many painters and musicians know, the value of someone else's painting and compositions are entirely relative to one's own accomplishments, interests, and skills. There is, of course, a long history of literary, artistic, and religious "criticism" that aims at making value judgments about the merits and defects of the accomplishments of others. Generally, this is a reductive practice whereby examples become quickly subject to external criteria often irrelevant and secondary to the motivations and concerns of the artist or mystic. In spiritual development, it is not a matter of evaluating the practices or accomplishments of others in order to determine their merits; what we must seek to evaluate is our own accomplishments with an eye to improving what we may contribute to the development of others.

The critical aspect in human relationships always requires self-criticism as its authentic base; otherwise, difference is eroded and the unique is seen as alien and insignificant. By harnessing the critical attitude, we can still make qualitative judgments, but without denying the value and importance of individual perspective and contribution. What is the purpose behind such judgments? It is not to determine the value or worth of the mystical text in comparison to social or economic consensual existence (as often the case in science, and unfortunately, art), but to offer a qualitative description of human possibilities in the realms of Spirit. Yet most criticism of mystical experience has been based in the consensual and "orthodox" religious attitude, specifically as embodied in authoritative institutional representatives (priests, ministers, upper-class Brahmans, empowered officials of all types, almost exclusively male). Such criticism seeks primarily to maintain the consensual character of its institutions and laws and to enforce social order by suppressing developments that might threaten that power. In a more contemporary setting, criticism has been identified with academic scholars of mystical texts, few of which have either experience or inclinations toward such experience and who are often arrogantly dismissive of "experience" as in any way meaningful to the formulation of an enduring spiritual outlook. Yet such criticism adds almost nothing to the enrichment of our spiritual understanding from the perspective of a living, cosmically centered receptivity to altered states, visions, dreams, or any of a myriad of possible psychic enhancements intrinsic to our basic human development.

The decontextualized, atheistic, reductive critic who wishes to stand "outside" the phenomena and to use a similarly reductive logic to assess such experience creates a profound bifurcation in conceptualizing the human situation. The denial of human experience, its primary and supportive function in human life, must include the mystical and spiritual as intrinsic to and inseparable from the reality of being a whole person. We all stand within the embrace of an inclusive unfolding of human potential and those who choose to stand outside this embrace, isolated in dead matter, denial, and a rationalized disbelief, only contribute to the deep alienation already active in the collective human psyche. Just as those who would dismiss the "unorthodox" from the circle of the believing majority, so too those who reject the value of the subjective experience as intrinsically worthwhile, contribute to the divided, polarized, and closed ranks by which a human community heads toward ever-deepening conflict and self-derision. This is why evaluation needs to be rooted in self-evaluation. We each need to understand that "spirituality" is not about conformity to someone else's theories, but is about the actualization of Spirit in a direct personal sense. In that deep actualization, these largely petty arguments about intrinsic worth or meaning are dissolved in a very immediate encounter with our own limits and capacities. Spirituality is about affirmation, not denial; about commitment and self-honesty, not detached observation and rationality; about transformation and casting off limits, not in applying limits for the preservation of autonomy and authority.

The further we go into the heart of our human potential, the more it becomes clear that normative thinking (and language) is not adequate to the task of articulating what is revealed in bursts of illumination or insight. All mystical reports and texts are emblematic—they suggest and point, in a minimal way, to the breadth of the horizon as it *actually manifests* in real beings in multiple worlds of becoming. The experience is qualitatively real, and this is the "real" that matters. It is the actual, self-awakening transformation, Spirit-given "real" that leads to a deep equality within the heart of being. In every case, divine potential exceeds by a vast degree the actual capacity of even the most "enlightened" individual, who, in that individual sense, may indeed fully realize the possibilities of a specific, self-transcending illumination. Light to light, all lights are dissolved into that one Light in which all light is surpassed. There is no difference, no "higher or lower" and no "less or more" when deeply entered and utterly dissolved. Not in diminishment of self, but in a greater fulfillment of self, is that transparent, transpersonal self now made luminous and bright. The words "no unity less than all" means that the absorption of the individual leads to confirmation of a shared, integral, unified continuum of unbroken continuity and wholeness. This wholeness is capable of infinite expressions and "descriptions" without in any way diminishing its capacity for diversity in actual, manifest becoming. All such becoming occurs from within that continuum, including manifestations of denial, doubt, rejection, dismissal, and any particularized, isolated metaphysics of the material.[46]

The words "no enlightenment is complete" mean that however much the individual may attain to an utter and full sense of illumination within being, such an illumination is only a refracted ray of that Light. This is a metonym, a part-for-whole analogy; it means that each individual's capacity for enlightenment is qualitatively different, and that every path followed has its own special limitations and intentionalities that gives it formal properties of excellence and attainment. Such attainment is not all possible attainments, or all possible excellence, but may be, nevertheless, completely real, genuine, and luminous. The dissolving continuum within higher spiritual experiences brings all seekers into a vaster and more profound holo-universe of mystical expansion and proportion. There, in that greater resonance, the harmony of many souls may be felt, the immaterial forms of celestial entities recognized and appreciated, and beyond, the complete dissolution of all forms, substances, and distinctive energies leads to a vast, ineffable totality. No enlightenment, illumination, mystical encounter, or profound awakening can capture that full totality; always Mystery exceeds our conceptual, experiential, qualitative grasp. Grasped by the ungraspable, we can only surrender to that dissolution in order to be reborn, reconstituted, and reaffirmed through the meaningful communication of that rebirth in limited, partial, emblematic reconstructions, in words, images, movements, music, or sounds. And yet there can be completion, fulfillment, utter repose of attainment in a deeply personal, immediate sense.

The "part standing for the whole" is not the Whole; it is still a part even when the part knows that Whole as inseparable from its own deeper self-identity. Yet the part may "stand for the whole" in the sense that every manifestation of life is such a part and each may offer a more full and complete actualization of that Whole. Individual identity becomes a lens through which a focused light may shine, may burn with intensity, or simply offer a warmer, more receptive, gentler hallowing of other life within its ray, or become a ray like moonlight, a shimmer of cool luminosity in an otherwise dark world. If that circle of luminosity only encompasses a few others, then that life has been a true contribution to the life of others. It is not a matter of magnitude but of purity, genuineness, and openness to the healing of the world of loved others. There is no need for "extinction of the soul" in the sense that we may each choose to maintain the part we represent within the Whole, even following a complete dissolution and union with the Whole. There is no demand or need that calls for total relinquishment of identity. That demand is an old, poorly understood teaching of men who have given up the value of individual existence as irrelevant in the face of that All. I see clearly that such a teaching is by no means accurate, more a convention than an attainment, though in rare cases, a final dissolution may be willingly elected. For most, even the most advanced, there is a going on, an "ego-of-devotion" or a personalized self whose continuity and habits are by no means valueless and which reflect, inevitably, the eccentric character of one being. What ends, is a need to judge others, and what is born, is a deep appreciation of the value and worth of the unique other.

Ecstasy is a moment of eternity, a permeation of body, mind, and soul, a radical revisioning, an inward-turning outcome, a realization of endless paths and possibilities, where no joy exceeds another. (7.7)

Meditation: How is it possible that "no joy exceeds another"? This is because there is a point where all "joys" are part of that one, integral continuum of joy that is constantly reaffirmed by subsequent immersions in luminous states. The enstatic condition is a return to an experiential constant, even though it may take a variety of phenomenal forms in visions, dreams, mystical intuitions, various types of enlightenment, and so on. This constant has no name or qualifications in any fixed or determinative states, and yet there is within the multitude of experiences, a consistency that unites those experiences in a single continuum of Spirit-sustained reality. It is the consistency of affirmation, of a joyful immersion in alternity, in deep, unbound Mystery where even a touch is joyful and poignant with life and hope. The joy of this touch may be followed by other such joys, but they do not in turn "exceed" each other; they only continue to confirm the reality of a joyful presence, an underlying sense of ecstasy, a maturing sense of depth and connectivity. It is like the continual weaving of a tapestry whose pattern and colors become more and more obvious and in which no single aspect, color, design, or form can be deleted without diminishment of the whole. It is not, I suspect, the moment by moment weaving, or the transient moods of one particular weaving moment, as much as it is the completion of the pattern as a whole, the communication of the vision in as much clarity and detail as possible. Even then, it is only one picture among many, the value of which is simply to be seen with the weavings of others.

The deeper we go into the multitude of possible forms and colors, into the various visionary worlds of even one individual, the more complex and multifaceted the whole of the process. In a sense, the further we go in this process, the more necessary it becomes to recognize the parts within ourselves that co-extend to a multitude of perspectives within the world. It is not a matter of fusion or of a simple perception of an obliterating unity. Rather there is an increasingly individuated sense of relationship to complexity, to the world as maintained through dynamic, creative processes whose activities correspond to various interests and facets of individual attention. As creative individuals, the "endless paths and possibilities" far exceed the capacity of any one person to explore and, in fact, a single path requires whole communities of persons in order to bring out the residual, potential actualization. These communities may be widely scattered across the face of the world or joined in actual living environments dedicated to the exploration and solving of particular types of problems or concerns. We have a multitude of capacities, many diverse abilities, all coexisting within the framework of our self-chosen occupations, commitments, and social relationships. Spirituality is a means for the enhancement of our capacities, in the full sense, and not the subordination of any of them for some greater good. And yet, in the same spiritual sense, such a development proceeds through a process of creative respect and appreciation for the limits and boundaries within which others may choose to work or live.

Such development is not simply mental or emotional but involves the entire human capability: "body, mind, and soul." The deep experiences of mystical encounter and enstatic being, Spirit-given, permeate the whole of the individual, brimming over and flowing through every neural-psychic channel and thus awakening new perceptions of the world, self, and others. The "inward turning outcome" refers to that inversion through which the normally hidden reality becomes the explicit, all-containing present, the truly real in a self-surpassing moment of timeless eternity. It is no longer a matter of the hidden pearl, the inward, private experience, but of a remarkable overturning of perspective in which the whole of the outer or external world is suddenly internalized and held within an infinite frame. It is not seen through a glass darkly, but through the bright splendor of a shared light resident in every being, in all life forms, throughout nature and yet, so much more than nature—an overspilling, outward pouring abundance of grace and beauty that is normatively the inner, hidden potential of surface life and distracted alienations. The "outcome" is a redefinition of the world as such, no longer isolated by mental abstraction or emotional fears and anxieties. The horizon of the everyday suddenly expands far beyond ordinary perceptions and takes on the luster and depth of more spiritualized motivations.

We each must work according to our own special capabilities, in various areas, without bias toward the worldviews and beliefs of others. It is not a matter of a particular philosophy or "school" of thought or belief, but of authentic and effectual real being in the world. The transformations invoked by spiritual awakening and attainment are themselves a confirmation of each healthy path. In that awakening complexity of difference and diversity, what matters is cooperative, shared efforts to manifest a more balanced, integrated humanity, whatever forms it may take, whatever schools it may reflect. The most effectual being is found through the manifestations of Spirit and communicated through a principled, balanced life of positive, human (and animal) relationships. The test of any spiritual path is the quality of relatedness and receptivity that is revealed through its practitioners, as well as the depth and maturity of its practices and resulting spiritual transformations. Without these, a teaching quickly becomes an externalized shell, burdened by outward appearances and impoverished within, however exotic the outer forms may appear. Thus it is better to strip away outward forms, to live as simply and authentically as possible, without pretense or illusions, with great commitment and yet, with an open, loving, and sincere heart.

To be receptive to Spirit means to open to the possibility of radical change and reorientation, to whole new ways of thinking or seeing, sometimes at the cost of abandoning long-held beliefs or biases. One who has read or studied mystical teaching may have developed many artificial and incorrect attitudes or emotional imbalances based on overvaluing certain kinds of teachings or techniques. While mind is developed, the heart, emotions, and feelings may be immature and repressed through false spiritual idealism. Or one may have a tremendous emotional passion that inhibits a deeper, more critical thinking about issues in need of careful discrimination and reflective balance. Another may have adopted a particular adherence to a traditional school of thought, a kind of "Zen intellectualism" that seeks an identity-in-difference but at the cost of denying the necessity of complexity beyond simple unity. Our freedom within being and becoming is vastly misunderstood when it is reduced to a single perspective, however sophisticated or worthy. In seeking "liberation from ignorance" it is useful to remember that ignorance is a human condition that pervades all paths, ways, traditions, or innovations. The human condition is always capable of obscuration through adherence to a single point of view, as though no other mattered or counted equally as one's own. Such thinking is a form of spiritual immaturity in a cosmos of incredible complexity crying out for a multitude of various self-expressions, from the most local to the most universal, but never at the cost of negating either.

The "moment of eternity" is always with us, never separate from our immediate circumstances, always hovering with expectancy right in the midst of our greatest trials and struggles. These trials very often act to catalyze the correct attitude, one that drops a defensive, closed mentality or lifts the troubled mind toward a more stable and enduring horizon of relationship to spiritually minded others, to the primal sources of spiritual awakening. This "moment" is not simply found in times of rest or meditative calm. It can be found in every kind of human experience, even in the most stressful and soul-wrenching confrontations. It is like a sudden burst of light that reveals a whole horizon of possibility in a single flash, like a lightning storm on a dark and foggy night—suddenly there is light and we see where we are and how to avoid further danger and distractions. But such a seeing takes preparation and an inner determination and commitment, an openness to Spirit and a willingness to surrender a long-held view for an unknown intuition. This takes courage and ever deepening reverence for the life processes, a willingness to follow the currents, even in the face of opposition of a more conservative preservation of known values. The "moment" is there right now, even as you read these words, waiting for your own ascent, your own courageous willingness to move beyond a known world and to embrace what has not yet come to be—the creative moment of self-emergence, of a true coming-into-being.

All the paths, philosophies, dogmas, rules, and paternal hierarchic guides are only moments of engendered power seeking to direct; the footsteps of ecstasy are free to fall or rise wherever they may. (7.8)

Meditation: First, we must break the hold of the spiritual dialectic and then abandon its polarities for a more nuanced, dialogical, feminized disclosure of relative truth. The "dialectic" refers to the simplistic reduction of spiritual horizons to a strict dualistic frame: God without qualities over God with qualities, impersonal over personal, knowledge over love, spirit over matter, and so on. This is not an accurate picture of what *is*, only a formal way of articulating a primarily male, dogmatic, traditionalized stance, a dialectic structuralism that is strengthened by polarized institutionalized power, dualistic texts, or ranked social orders. The usual asymmetry of these pairs, privileging a dominant motif over subordinate secondary values reflects a strictly hierarchical way of thinking in which what is above is superior to what is below—yet another asymmetrical dialectic. While it is without doubt possible to cognize the world in terms of these dialectical patterns, in a simplistic "black-and-white" mentality, it can only be done at the cost of losing all the nuances and subtlety of the full spectrum of human encounter with the unknown potential. From the point of view of the mystical encounter, it is also quite possible to experience an inherent and de-theologized unitary continuum in contrast to an experiential personal, loving, theologized (or thealogized) personal divinity. But the *valuing* of these experiences, the interpretative weighing and categorizing of experience is a quite different enterprise.

Interpretation does not occur in a vacuum. It is always contextual, and always relative to a particular era, time, place, social reality, and spiritual context of a particular people, often as a strictly gendered speaking. The spiritual interpretations have tended toward authoritarian models, an often excessive emphatic voicing that may, under certain circumstances, speak even as the "voice of God" or from a critical prophetic stance. In this process, there is a deep tension in resolving the authoritarian tendency toward absolute, didactic, utterly autocratic speaking (framed in threats, violent predictions, and condemnations of those who refuse to "hear") and a more personalized, loving, nurturing, complex spirituality valuing specific qualitative differences and attributes (but also capable of dogmatic expression, collective ethical norms, and a rigid denial of values of a more "polytheistic" type of thinking). Neither of these perspectives are adequate in the realm of direct experience unmediated by traditionalized thinking or an overdependence on external authority to confirm or value the subjective realizations of the individual. We must each take full responsibility for the interpretation of our spiritual development, experiences, and interpretations. To do that means to move beyond the dialectical models, to liberate spiritual potential from reductive thinking, and to find the fuller and more open horizons in which spiritual differences, individuality, and personally nuanced interpretation is contributory to ongoing dialogical processes between diverse individuals and communities.

Whatever has motivated the formation of so many hierarchical models in so many diverse social, historical, and cultural contexts has arisen out of male intellectual styles organized around dialectical habits of mind. It is these mental habits that need to be abandoned for more open, complex, and diverse forms of thinking and interpretation. The reductive tendency to organize experience around dialectical processes no longer serves to illuminate but only to obscure the underlying complexity emergent through authentic individual spiritual commitments. This emergence "into novelty" requires a more refined epistemology, a more nuanced way of thinking through the diverse manifestations of visionary encounter. As in the interpretation of dreams, it no longer serves to reduce them to "structural polarities" as a reflection of "deep mental structures" when dreams are far more complex and meaningful than any such polarization or reduction can grasp. The processes of creative self-becoming involve multiple intersections of meaning and relationship uncontainable in a strict spiritual dialectic. The new epistemology of creative emergence requires more subtle, interactive models of intersubjectivity, of mutuality and dialogue, as a more meaningful frame of reference than simple, isolated, often emotionally alienated, dialectical logic. The new epistemology is a fractal art of embedded sets of meaning intersecting the embedded sets of others in a creative, interactive way, making diverse interpretations possible from any one frame of reference. And this must be carried out in a highly reflexive, self-aware, and nuanced way.

One criteria for the "authenticity" of spiritual values is the way they are actualized in the intersubjective realm of meaningful human relationships. It means bringing the full weight of personal experience to bear in any human situation as a means for subtilizing and enhancing the potential of that relationship. This has very little to do with "authoritative dialectic claims" and much to do with qualitative perceptions and the character of the individuals who willingly share alternative perspectives. It has to do with a receptive spiritual attitude and not a particularistic interpretive stance or an inflexible way of interpreting religious experiences. There is certainly room for great diversity in perspectives but such a diversity can only flourish where no one perspective tries to claim a greater worth at the cost of denying the values and perspectives of those who think, feel, believe, or experience differently. While there may be a potency and a directness found by those who accept and submit to an external authority in spiritual direction, the real authenticity of spiritual transformation is far more than an affirmation of directed spiritual norms. In a less regulated and authorized development, or even in a directed development open to dialogical interpretations, the individual becomes a creative seeker after the as-yet unrealized potential resident within his or her own authentic self-awakening.

While the "emergent self" must always risk the disorientations of sudden spiritual awakening, nevertheless the fullness of our human potential continually presses out beyond known forms and into the Mystery, which can only be known through direct encounters. The insufficiency of the dialectical model becomes quickly apparent when the horizon truly opens to its far-reaching fullness. The male tendency toward a structured, codified, traditional interpretation or strictly constructed intentional process for spiritual development fades rapidly in the face of a truly infinite and open horizon of possible becomings. A more feminized, nurturing, caring, interactive style can carry forward the work of transformation with less dependency on hierarchical thinking and with the cultivation of greater shared reciprocity in the explorations of spiritual potential. The value of the male structural model is relative to the preservation of certain core values, or systems of thought, that epitomize a more structural approach to spiritual development. But these models are themselves relative to the meaningful relationships they engender between real, diverse human beings. The more exclusive the model, the less sufficient and contributory the teaching. The feminized model is a "grassroots" perspective that values the ordinary person, the real human being immersed in situations of struggle, coercion, sorrow, and shared hope. This is spirituality from the bottom up, from the position of immersion in the world of real being and not an elite perspective, arrogating to itself a restricted, authoritarian, "correct" teaching.

Nor does such a dialogical interpretation result in an ascetic rejection of the world or the human situation—instead, it builds on a deep commitment to fully embodied life, awareness, and understanding through positive commitment to real human relationships in the most substantive sense. The "footsteps of ecstasy" are not bound by human law or dialectical thinking; we are each free to dance the dance we hear in the rhythm and music of our soulful awakening. Having danced our dance, we must then "walk our talk," that is make comprehensible the value of the experience through a concerted effort to communicate, share, and discuss the meaningfulness of spiritual awakening in authentic human relationships. Such relationships need to be healthy, interactive, and by no means cloistered in private communities or special, isolated communes built on a "we-they" dialectic. The intersubjective processes of world engagement may involve a communal life, but not one isolated from the world or closed to full, interactive sharing and free choice. The "both-and-other" model is primary to an open, interactive epistemology in which sharing relative perspectives makes possible a greater complexity of understanding and a deeper valuing of others as intrinsic to our own self-awakenings. There are underlying harmonies in the continuum of our dances, new ways of bodily, emotional, psychic, and mental expression that reflect a cosmos more diverse, alive, and active than simple duality can comprehend. Joining hands and dancing together, even in solemn splendor, is only a first step into that unknown.

Do not be bound by law or tradition, by consensus, comfort, family, or nation; throw off your bounds of consanguinity and language, for Spirit is not bound and ecstasy is its norm. (7.9)

Meditation: It is ironic that the teachings of so many traditions present spirituality as though it were a revelation of iron-clad law or inflexible norms of social, customary behavior. It is particularly ironic that these laws only articulate the most obvious kinds of social norms necessary for minimal, though positive, cooperative human solidarity. Further, this irony is compounded with tragedy when in the name of some universal God privilege is stratified according to gender, age, ethnicity, and social positions—as though these were divine concerns rather than the obvious creations of human beings in very specific communal, cultural, tradionalized contexts. It seems that over and over again, religious thinkers, primarily men, have been utterly unable to think apart from their immediate social structures and context. Inevitably, that social context becomes divinized, that is, integrated into a "status quo" model sanctified by those most in a position to value their own privileges (at whatever rank they hold in the social scale). On a more subtle level, spirituality is further codified in numerous "esoteric" teachings that have also tended to privilege those who conform to a particular pattern of spiritual practice or belief, even though there is greater diversity in such schools than in the more normative orthodoxy of conventional religious teachings. Even so, most of these esoteric schools also participate in the broader cultural biases of their natal social milieu. Men, for example, are privileged over women, elder over younger, and more educated over the less educated, and so on.[47]

Without doubt it is true that these traditions have, nevertheless, crystallized various patterned approaches to spiritual life and maintained a long continuity of practice, teaching, and techniques supportive of the goals those traditions hold as ideal in the advancement of spiritual understanding. And certainly these teachings lead to real experiences that confirm the validity of those practices. Every tradition offers a diversity of spiritual paths, all of which might be traveled authentically and realized in the committed life of a genuine spiritual seeker. Yet, without denying the validity and indeed ancient wisdom and authenticity of those teachings, we can also seek spiritual fulfillment "outside" of those codified and conditional paths, moving into a more contemporary frame of reference congruent with a process view of creative self-emergence. We are all, including all members of every "world religion," engaged in a process of rapid awakening to a collective global identity. In differentiating ourselves within that global collectivity, it is important and necessary to formulate meaningful perspectives that fully value the individual contribution, not to a "tradition" but to the human community at large. Inevitably, every spiritual tradition will undergo the continuing processes of globalization wherein the uniqueness of each tradition will become increasingly relativized by the possibilities offered in alternative traditions, including secular "traditions" in sciences, both physical and social.

In the global context, we must not lose sight of the individual contribution—specifically, the genuine spiritual contributions. What constitutes the "genuineness" of that contribution is the long-lasting effects, the ways in which even the most subtle realization acts to enhance the quality of shared, communal life. Even on the scale of a single family, friendship, or in a human dyad, such genuineness is meaningful and contributory. Like ripples in a pond, the waves may spread out in an increasingly connected world to have far-ranging consequences, even as in the flapping of the wings of the butterflies of Beijing. The more conscious and self-aware we become, the easier it is to see these effects in the broader scale of a shared, communal life, as intentional acts meant to celebrate and heal our fractured and too often divided humanity. To embrace a global perspective in the process of spiritual self-awakening means to see individual development as an inseparable and necessary act inherent to collective transformations. This is because, Spirit-born, these acts reverberate through an open horizon of shared realizations, disseminate through a dialogical context, and actualize in the intentional decisions and commitments of like-minded others. Those like-minded others may be far removed from immediate family or childhood friends. They may be resonate with shared concerns no longer bound by consanguine or consensual relationships. They may reside in other language cultures, other times, other places even nonexistent in the present or past. The waves go out, and bounce back, a returned echo affirming a presentiment or intuition even on the threshold of its first lucid articulation.

Not to be bound by "comfort, family, or nation" means that often our spiritual journeys into newness require a setting aside of normative values, and, while not denying the value of persons, we need to let go of inherited and socialized expectations. Not infrequently, we seek a way that is a "comfortable" one that fits and does not cause too many waves, too much disequilibrium. And there is nothing wrong with that more conservative, cautious approach; indeed, those who throw themselves passionately into a completely alien worldview often risk radical disorientation, confusion, and in the end, a loss of identity and purpose. The very nature of the heights and depths of spiritual possibility require some sense of cautious and moderated explorations. Yet, all too often, it is this very conservative attitude that undermines the creative aspect of the enterprise, hedging it with increasing strictures and guidelines until, eventually, these very guidelines become an enclosure, a fence, a wall, a defensive stance against alternatives, openness, and difference. This is why, on a global scale, we must start with openness and difference, proceed through openness and difference, and arrive at openness and difference as a shared, worthy, spiritual goal. This means, at the beginning we do not bind spiritual experience to set norms or idealized states or the authoritative censure of others.

It is truly written: "You will know them by their fruits." That is, regardless of religious claims, what matters is the positive, loving, creative outcome of a committed spiritual life. It is not the experiences per se, those are the personal, incommunicable depths that only affirm the reality. But the consequences of those experiences are found in creative manifestations, however simple or complex. It is the *qualitative life*, the capacity for spiritual action in the immediate, everyday circumstances of ordinary human living that show most clearly the depths of genuine actualization. A life informed by Spirit is not always obvious or immediately recognizable. It may appear as nothing extraordinary or unusual, but look closely at the quality of human relationships and how those relationships are informed by spiritual values and a sense of presence, and there you have authenticity. And here is a crucial point: the "ecstasies" of Spirit may be very quiet, very calm, almost entirely subtle and inward, not at all visible or obvious. Yet there is real spiritual awakening and a sense of openness and loving presence that is more than ordinary, more than convention or habit. Thus the "norm of ecstasy" must not be taken as some dramatic, obvious, externalization of Spirit (though it may be exactly that). Rather, consider it as similar to intelligence or emotional sensitivity, as a subtle quality that enhances awareness even in others when they interact. This qualitative life may be infinitely enhanced, either by slow degrees or by sudden leaps, or by both. What matters is that the qualitative experience deepens and arouses appreciation and understanding of the inner consistency from which difference and diversity emerge.

In "throwing off bounds" it is wise to do so in stages, and to secure those stages as integral to a creative life, in a natural, unforced, and spontaneous enactment. This takes time, even an entire lifetime. It is a long process of ecstatic moments blended with everyday concerns and deep intuitions seeking expression through habitualized ways of thinking and acting. Spiritually, we are always *medias res* (in the midst of actions) and even when we make a dramatic alternation, a break, a new beginning, it is still part of a larger continuity of creative transformation. Such "stages" are really only moments of realization that new patterns need to be formed and old ones broken and restructured. There is no one formula for this process, no external guidelines in a creative advance. There are only real efforts, real commitments, and the willingness to hold on to spiritual values that seem most effective in catalyzing the necessary transformations. Sometimes we leap ahead into a whole new perspective only to have it slide away in the confines of everyday preoccupations; then, it comes back, and eventually, with care and attention, it can be made fully actual and real. Other times, we work hard to attain a spiritual goal, but always it slips away from us unrealized. Often, only when we stop trying does it start to actualize perhaps in a different form or mode we have not yet seen. In this process, Spirit-given, we cultivate our own special skills and abilities and through this process of respectful appreciation of natural gifts, we come to see more clearly the path we must travel.

The Eighth Principle

The Eighth Principle of Spirit is freedom from constraint; the wild grasses of the field know nothing of the plow, their seeds are scattered by the winds, not by human hands. (8.1)

Meditation: It may seem impossible to live without constraint, conditioned as we are by bodily, emotional, social, and cultural life. And yet this is the very challenge of authentic spiritual transformation—to unbind ourselves from the bindings of others, from our own self-bindings, from the accepted and inherited bindings of class, gender, ethnicity, age, or social milieu. We must avoid living like mummies, bound by external wrappings and lacking in internal integrity! The grounding presence of Spirit does not bind us to live our lives in a constricted fashion, nor does it compel us by habit or circumstance to live according to only past dictates or norms. Spirit is the overflowing inwardness that surpasses the conventional boundaries of inherited life form and presses us toward a creative possibility through incarnation and embodiment. Our quality of life, our capacity to adapt, respond creatively, to be imbued with imagination and freedom, is a primordial characteristic of good health and openness to possibility. When we deny our capacity for change, take on crippling attitudes of doubt, skepticism, or a rigid fixity of mind, then we lose our most precious and primordial gift: our capacity to grow and develop beyond the limited horizons of inherited belief or commonly held attitudes.

In learning to live creative, adaptive, fluid lives, it is necessary to embrace the deep truths of our capacity for imaginative, Spirit-inspired living. Our potential for change and self-awakening is not limited to a strictly individual capacity, but arises from a deeper and more compelling source. Creativity is not a burden but a gift. To live creatively means to embrace that deeper potential that lies within each of us as a primordial source of self-renewal and self-other discovery. The "creative process" reduplicates the fractal, cosmological principles of restless, emergent, self-surpassing becoming. Even in the depths of the prehuman world, the restless, compelling energies of nature constantly work through the labyrinths of co-relatedness in constant adaptation, adjustment, and responsive, adaptive self-realizations that reflect a continuing expression of possibilities. It is the urgency of natural relations pressing toward unrealized expression that reveal the constants of creative, evolutionary transformations. This is a far cry from a minimized, contracted idea that creative life is a strictly individual responsibility. Not at all! We are co-creators in a vastly complex, natural process of spiritual evolution from lesser to greater awareness. Whatever contracted, resistant, antilife philosophies may spring up, they are only contracted examples of a failed ability to surrender self-preoccupation for a larger, more profound process of co-creation.

The transformative energies of nature surround, enwrap, stimulate, and encourage us at all times to break through the shell of our isolated, self-limited thinking to act as instrumental creators in an already thoroughly creative universe of limitless potential. Our responsibility is to awaken our sleeping sense of relatedness to the whole of this process, to the constant inflow of creative instances into our daily lives, into our relationships, into our sense of who we are and what we hope for and desire. The instrumentalization of these creative instances is not simply reducible to isolated examples of insight or sudden realization, but thoroughly enwraps us in the joyful wisdom of living creatively moment by moment. Every breath offers us a precious moment of awareness to recognize a shift toward a more creative living and being in the world. The foreground of everyday life is the normative stage for creative, spiritual expression; the moment of sudden insight is the background, the luminous moment when there is a congealing of insights into a new pattern of awareness. And in between, there are all the lucid moments in which we seek to redress past insufficiencies, to improve the quality of our relations to others, to open the possibility of new patterns of behavior, thoughts, or perception. Creativity is not some form of artistic action other than living life well with artistry. By living as creators and co-visionaries, as a source and resource, we maximize our capacity for ongoing "adventure in ideas" and a continuing adventitious realization of creative possibility in authentic living.[48]

The words "seeds are scattered by the winds" refers to the principle of Spirit in action. Through nature, through human expression, through connectedness with the inhabitants of nature, through the unfolding of inner dreams and visions, we realize an inner self-awakening. The causalities of human inspiration are many and the consequences far too complex to map onto a simple, one-dimensional, or truncated metaphysics. In a co-creative universe of multiple beings, embedded in the creative energies of nature and aligned with the deeper principles of self-emergence and a multitude of transformational horizons, creativity becomes a vastly complex matrix of intersecting influences irreducible to rudimentary sociocultural or psychobiological models. Materialistic models strain for meaningful parameters within which to capture the creative, impressionistic spontaneity of emergent being. Subsequently, they lapse into a didactic rhetoric of the most limited sort, hypostatizing the social and biological worlds into a fantastic mélange of hybrid causes and consequences. And yet social and biological influences are indeed part of the matrix in which creativity seeks to enact a transformative awakening. The bindings of a materialized concept of creativity need to be unwrapped in order to expose the naked flesh to the light of a more pervasive and spiritualized resuscitation. In this awakening, biology and social conditioning play their role but by no means define the territories that extend into the primal energies of nature and into a living cosmos.

The whole world is a teaching. Not "world" in the limited, self-obvious sense, but "world" in the greater cosmological fullness of its immeasurable multidimensionality. Creativity is the norm by which this vaster scale incorporates into itself, the limited worlds of biological and social existences. Those lesser worlds are not simply "causal" in a material evolutionary sense, but far more the receptacles within which highly potent natural expressions of being come forth. Like alchemical transformations in the crucibles of creative self-surpassing, these expressions materialize through viable flesh. Psychically, incarnate flesh seeks to reduplicate creative ideas in virtual social and cultural forms. These forms are "virtual" in the sense that they can only be maintained by the willing cooperation of a multitude of other embodied, intentional beings. Psychically envisioned, these virtual forms become embodied in all manner of institutions, social structures, and cultural norms. Each and every embodiment is virtually maintained through an ongoing semiotics of interpretive discourse in a multitude of forms—written, visual, plastic, or enacted. None of these forms are "eternal" or "everlasting"—all are conditional, relative, and valuable only insofar as they function to maintain a particular psychic order or transient stability. The processes of this embodiment are engendered through Spirit and as such, reflect even at the minute material level, an inherent density of creative influences far more extensive than the visible or virtual forms.

The "wild grasses of the field" are not entirely unlike those growing in a more cultivated area, but they share a closer connection with a multitude of other plants and animals than those found in the more sedate and controlled settings of a well-gardened world. The winds of Spirit blow where they will, carrying the seeds of many inspirations into new ecologies of possible emergence. However humble or quiet those settings, however noisy or booming with action, they settle and act to inspire new ideas and insights, resting in potential, awaiting the right circumstances to flourish or flower. Where they wither and fail, life is too pressed into routine thinking, unconscious action, and limited preoccupation with inherited ideas, themselves limited by generations of conservative resistance and fear of change. The creative matrix, the stimulus toward emergent being requires us to attend to those inner urges, those seeds, that press for new expression in a less bound, less self-enwrapped world. Our freedom lies in Spirit, is Spirit-birthed, and requires that we remove the binders and blinders that keep us from seeing into the depths of a thoroughly creative universe. These "wild seeds" are natural potencies, awaiting discovery through a reverent process of illumination and self-awakening. We must always be alert to those moments when one of these seeds drops onto our heart and stimulates there a quickening vibration, a burst of hope and vision. Fulfilling that hope is the direct way to a deep and lasting joy.

This requires courage, humility, and patience— the virtues of the untrammeled, those liberated spiritual seekers who have renounced all coercive codes of law and never injure or harm another. (8.2)

Meditation: Following such a vision, into the creative matrix, is one of the greatest challenges facing a human being. A successful response to that challenge requires self-discipline, effort, joyful excitement, and the wonder of cognizing new horizons open to possibility and change. It also requires humility, patience, and perseverance to follow the vision through to its natural conclusions, only to set the stage for yet more such emergence. The gift of creativity is transformative, and transformation requires courage, change, new thinking, and perception. Meeting this challenge is a lifelong process. There is no final goal other than continued emergence, no resting place other than those we choose along the way, no conclusion but the ones we make when looking back over a life well lived. Freedom from constraint does not abrogate responsibility or the need for discipline and a focused life. If anything, it draws more deeply on our capacity to live meaningfully as mature, caring individuals. The responsibilities of freedom are manifested in processes of refinement, illuminated by Spirit, and require the highest degree of mastery and excellence. It is far easier to live in conformity and accept the lesser discipline of meeting inherited ideals. Surpassing those ideals, the horizons open and in that vaster space, self-mastery and clear, responsible living establish the patterns through which creative advancement proceeds. In that process, a prayerful heart and a deep thanksgiving provide wings where once there were only feet of clay.

Who are the "spiritual seekers"? They are every curious individual after something more than a simple conformity to established norms and social expectations. The true "fakirs" (Arabic, *faqiir*) are those willing to throw off the cloak of respectability and success, or the promise of such, in order to pursue a path less well traveled or acceptable to those enamored of tradition or social authority. The breaking up of foundations does not require a revolution of violence as much as courage and determination even in small things. A tap at a point of weakness can easily reveal the fractures and fissures normally hidden in imposing structures meant to awe or subdue. There are too many bones in those foundations! Too much blood in the mortar! Too much coercion in the building and clearing of ground, too much pomp and ceremony in the maintenance of its perpetuated life. The quiet revolution is pursuing a vision and living it, however distant the goal, however demanding the perspective. Personally, I cannot value violence as a means to social, cultural, or spiritual transformation. There is too much violence in the buildings of the

older order, in the temples of gods who demanded sacrifice or exclusive, rigid allegiance. The true "fakir" is one who, of whatever gender, seeks to move beyond these more collective norms and into the
creative matrix of spiritual adventure and exploration for reasons of
the most positive and preservative kind.[49]

It is not the strict denial of past values that contributes to an
emergent spiritual horizon, but the careful sifting, appreciation, and
sorting of those values in the context of how they may contribute to
a more full and complete spiritual life with others. Not all positive
values necessarily contribute to an emergent horizon of spiritual development: marriage may or may not contribute, having children
may or may not be part of the path, the role of sexuality, solitude,
and community may all be diversely interpreted. The degree of social action in comparison with contemplation or time alone cannot be
inscribed in a permanent metaphysics of transformation, both are
valuable and differ according to temperament, mutable occasions of
possible enactment, and the needs of others. There is no one template, no one configuration that necessarily applies to the emergence
of a truly creative life. The creative synthesis that results in spiritual well-being for any one individual reflects a broader interpretive
field. What works for one may not work for another and what works
for many may actually inhibit a genuinely individuated self-awakening for one. The interplay of the one and the many (OM) occurs
constantly on an unbound human playing field whose possibilities of
play have yet to be realized in actual, creative occasions.

In such circumstances, past values may be regarded as already
actualized occasions whose intentions may or may not contribute to
a richer, more conscious life. The many "codes of law" created by men
are only reflections of those past occasions, often entrenched in the
momentum of an earlier vitality now largely spent and no longer
fully capable of meeting the complexity of emergent, present needs.
The origins of those laws are found in the human tendency to insti-
tutionalize codes that protect a valued way of life, but that may also
enshroud deeper, less obvious social inequalities, unjust privilege,
certain paradigms of unequal power, or out-and-out bias against out-
siders and those identified as marginal or alien. Such rudimentary
laws are not adequate to the task of fostering the necessary diversity
and pluralism of a truly creative interaction between cultures and
peoples who hold differing laws and allegiances. To live the creative
spiritual life, we must be willing to set aside our inherited codes,

however revered by ancestral precedent, and move into new frontiers of dialogue and interpersonal relations. In those circumstances,
the pledge of nonviolence is critical. All paradigms of forced conversion are an inadequate means for the necessary transformations of
others. The task is *not* a preservation of a way of life, but an interaction leading to emergent creative insights that draws the best out of
all engaged parties.

Should any community choose to insulate itself from such dialogue, which in a metaphysics of freedom must be possible for the
preservation of a valued way of life, then so be it. No community has
the right to enforce its ideals and traditions on others, and such an
attempt must be resisted in order to preserve what is most valued.
In turn, this leads us to a world in which the valued other is distinguished by something more than simple tolerance. There must be
deep commitments to the right of every community to maintain its
own standards in a nonviolent, peaceful coexistent pluralism with
positive intentions. Coercion calls for response that is willing to risk
its own integrity in facing the problematic challenges of overcoming
that coercion, not by a greater coercion, but by a more creative, loving, well-intended strength that allows for the necessary struggles
and contractions. This healthy birthing occurs through positive example, loving commitment, and a deeply spiritualized way of life.
Nor does it require martyrdom, or an unwilling sacrifice to some collectively imagined greater good. What is needed is a grounded reciprocity, a shared concern to reach concord, a tempered, well-forged,
hammering out of difference in an arena of positive support—without blood, castigations, or denials of the rights of others. What is required is a Spirit-born sense of the unfolding complexity of the
Whole and each community's place within that wholeness.

To "never harm or injure another" means to live with integrity,
by well-founded principles, in a context of sharing insights with
those who may think or believe differently. It means to recognize
the intrinsic values of others as more than adequate for their own
way of life and to resist the temptation to devalue those other ways
simply because they differ from one's own. A creative wrestling with
ideas and beliefs is not a permit for imposition on others, or a li-
cense to validate a superior understanding. Joyful wisdom flows up
from below, stands on the margin, and seeks to encourage others to
attain their own highest potential. It does this without seeking to
substitute one persons's understanding for that of another, however

profound either person's understanding may be. This requires patience, humility, and courage—patience in not pushing forward, humility in allowing others to have their own beliefs, and courage in learning to articulate personal insights and understanding with respect and genuine receptivity to alternative creative views. Such a dialogue, many-voiced and harmonic, seeks the appropriate counterpoint to allow for the voices of others—at whatever pitch or intensity seems right for a fuller, more comprehensive speaking. All this evolves through respect and not clinging to narrower, more contested ways of thinking or seeing. Every voice seeks a choir if it only once resonates with the unseen harmony calling each of us; and in that harmony there is place and moment for every kind of creative singing.

There is still life and death, still sorrow, joy, or pain, but in the reborn context of a dynamic present, not inscribed as a static "moment of creation" nor determined for all time. (8.3)

Meditation: The horizons of our self-becoming are by no means predetermined or simply a consequence of social enculturations or "conditioning." Nor are we entirely free from past and present influences. We are all influenced by others, by parents, friends, or foes. And yet we are also fully capable of overcoming these influences through a dedicated and determined effort to reach beyond the immediacy of interactive life and into the deeper, less obvious potentials we each carry within us. As relative beings, subject to the conditions of language, culture, historical embeddedness, a certain genetic heritage, a certain social location, influenced by a variety of referential frames, we are yet able to move beyond these immediate influences and open ourselves to a less conditioned, more expansive development. None of these influences are necessarily determinative: we can learn new languages, live in alternative cultures or learn from them, live as creative agents in the midst of historical alternatives, choose to emphasize select aspects of our genetic inheritance over others, radically alter our social location, become more sophisticated in seeing and negotiating diverse fields of meaning. The paradigms of social conditioning may be turned on their heads:

we may become social engineers, agents of creative transformation, a source of inspiration for the evolution of new consciousness.

The creative principles of Spirit invite us to engage as active co-creators, to throw off dogmas of conformity, and to accept the deep responsibilities of emergence and spiritual awakening. Many times this involves struggle and an inner willingness to dismantle inherited ideals, habits, or mental-emotive dispositions, to resist social neurosis and pathological tendencies masked by collective ascent or custom. It is not simply a "live and let live" world. From a global perspective, there remain many pathological tendencies in every culture: deep paranoias of distrust, aggressive militancy, a lack of caring for the impoverished, hording and greed of every sort, local destruction of ecologies, rapacious tendencies toward excess, self-indulgence and alienated indifference, as well as a troubled sea of violent, naked hostilities and many contracted fears. All of these are buffered and sustained by the inadequacies of cultural form and social inequality, mediated through entrenched mentalities dedicated to the preservation of a certain social order. It is not a spiritualized world and no ideals of spiritual transformation will be effective unless they become embodied in responsible, creative human beings dedicated to healing the wounds, conflicts, and tensions that surround and support our current malaise.

First, we must each take the path at our feet that leads to personal transformation and follow it through the labyrinth to the healthy, illumined center. Then we must journey out of that labyrinth and take with us the knowledge gained in order to be mature, creative partners in the healing of others. Finally, we must, together, work for the healing of the world, the planet, and all co-related species, for all beings to coexist in spiritual health and interconnected well-being. This means turning over the paradigms of contracted, biased living for more comprehensive, noncoercive, intersected paradigms in a pluralistic world of many diverse, co-creative, mutually respectful beings. The "preservation of species" depends on this overturning. We are no longer the unconscious inheritors of past values; we have now become the co-creators, fully responsible for a conscious, well-intended making (with others) of a healthy, evolving world. In such a world, there is no "dominant culture" and no place for privileged leadership based on inherited rights or inequalities in wealth. Every person is a co-creator, without exception. Every person has the opportunity to choose an inner path to self-development and every person may contribute to the unfolding of the Whole because, indeed, every person does so now! It is only the retrograde mentality of the opportunist who refuses to recognize this intrinsic capacity in every being. It is only the narrow boundaries of cultural prejudice that keep it from being actualized in the fullest sense.

There is still "sorrow, joy, or pain" because the spiritual paths to illumined states require that we dive deep into the sources of our sorrow in order to heal them, deep into our longing to be heard, deep into our hope for redemption and rebirth. And we must dive deeply into the pain and suffering of others, to hear them, to be with them in their own transformations, to assist in the rebirthing of new found belief or emergence into being. This does not mean that we "take on" that pain and suffering of others; vicarious suffering is itself a paradigm that has oppressed many. But we can stand ready to respond as loving, caring others in a mutual work of healing. The healing of wounds is no easy task, and in the deep sense, such healing is a gift of Spirit, guided by ability and intentions of the most dedicated kind, and realized in a deep relief and a soothing of uncertainty, ambiguity, and doubt. The joy is found in the workings of Spirit, which are abundant and continuous throughout all created realms. The sorrow springs from the deep wounding of the past, the contractions of the present, and from fears about the future. The pain is not only the personal pains of ordinary life, but also the pain of the world as all beings struggle to realize their inner potential often blocked by the ignorance of others. Creating a center of calm in the midst of this stormy sea is a great gift; healing the turbulent waters, a prelude to even more miraculous actions.[50]

There is still "life and death" but in the context of throwing off the inherited past (while still honoring its worthy values) there remains the possibility of rebirth and the reincarnation of former ideas and beliefs cast into a new context of self-aware living. The themes of death and rebirth are a constant counterpoint to themes of enhanced awareness and self-awakening. They entwine together like dual snakes on the Caduceus (the winged staff of Hermes), symbol of health, spiritual awakening, and sacred illuminations. The contracted states of less-aware being require a willing surrender of self to the internal processes of death and rebirth, to the reconstruction of preformed worldviews or vaguely assembled beliefs rooted in collective miasma or pathology. Metaphors of spiritual growth all point toward the need of the individual to heal those deep pathologies within him or herself in order to open to a more healthy, radiant world. This involves letting go of those parts of self that have become a refuge from the more challenging frontiers of self-examination. We are not static beings, nor need we live by habit alone. The creative challenge is to let go of our bondage to contracted ways of living, to open to the deeper energies of creative well-being in order to attain a more mature understanding, a more lucid seeing and sympathy. Like the snakes of the Caduceus, we must shed outer skin and renew our life force through the infusions of Spirit in order to attain the full realizations of our potential.

In this process, many inherited ideas and practices fall away, only to recirculate through the refining fires of spiritual awakening, each adding its nuances to an expanding awareness of interconnected being. The "context of the dynamic present" is a process of continual growth in which we shed, layer after layer, the confinements and contractions of a limited seeing. We do this through loving relationships, not simply solitary explorations; we do this by exposing to others, our inner worlds and understandings in order to learn from them, how we are seen or known by others. The self-other context is the most salient testing ground of long-term development and maturation. Dialogue is a creative ground, the place in which emergent being is tested through communicative exchange and reciprocal perceptions. These may be nonverbal expressions, artistic or mathematical forms, bodily gestures or poetic reveries, scientific theories or technical innovations, but all are taken into the shared worlds of others for further refinement or simply put forth as an alternative view. In this process, there is no "eschatological goal," no predetermined end toward which all moves. The dynamics of transformation, Spirit-born, are embodied in real beings whose freedom is indicated by the quality of their relationships with others; the emergent result of those relationships is increasingly determined by an intentional co-creating.

The "moment of creation" is now, in the reader's present, not in some previous time or instant, but in the expanded "now" of a more illumined awareness that incorporates into itself, a fullness of both past and future. In that process the past is redefined, the future cast into alternative perspectives, the present enhanced by a plurality of possible views. This present absorption of past creative occasions is itself a creative challenge to not simply embody a past occasion, but

to take in that occasion and transform it in relationship to the totality of other occasions. The relative being of such a process acts to inhibit a static, hierarchical view. It forces us to adapt, to evolve
beyond our earlier ancestry, to move past the denials into a deeply
affirmative appreciation of past creative occasions, yet one that
seeks to surpass those occasions for a deeper and more integrated
life. Much of what is past is deeply significant and valuable, and all
of what is past is part of our species inheritance and revelatory of
species bias, predeliction, poverty, or brilliance. And all is Spirit-born
in the free concourse of our interactions with cultural others; in the
deeper stratum of Spirit, even these past occasions can be altered
and changed. Time is subject to psychic alteration and the visionary
synthesis of many diverse paths leads to new interpretations: we are
not subjects of past conditioning but co-creators capable of altering
our entire history, becoming and being.

**The traditions are like chains made of gold and
silver strands, jeweled with the lives of "saints
and martyrs"—how brilliantly they enwrap the
soul, how subtly they bind and constrain the
heart or mind. (8.4)**

Meditation: By "tradition" I do not mean simply religious or
spiritual traditions, but any tradition. This means any patterned,
multigenerational behavior passed down as a meaningful characteristic distinguishing a particular group of people as socially and culturally related. This involves everything from weaving baskets to
hunting techniques, including art styles, behavioral codes, moral or
philosophical systems of belief, scientific methods, legal and economic practices, or attitudes toward death, reincarnation, or psychic
phenomena. Even more basically, it includes inherited ideas about
the body, the emotions, the mental life, the importance of reason or
imagination and what constitutes the correct standards for excellence in education and happiness in living life. And it includes all the
various spiritual and religious systems transmitted orally or in written form to children the world over, as well as all vehement denials
and dismissals of religion and spirituality by the more empirically
rational and materially minded. Human beings the world over pro-

ceed by imitation; one of the most fundamental characteristics of learning is to repeat the attitudes of parents and previous generation teachers often with little or no critical appreciation of the inherited biases being thus transmitted. A thousand years of repetition may be too little to eradicate a multitude of inherited ideas and practices all transmitted as valued by past generations, and all enshrining hard-won privileges at the expense of denying the rights of others.

The "chains of gold and silver" are all those traditions we hold to be sacrosanct; these chains are not necessarily heavy or awkward, but ones we may wear lightly, like those around the waist of a dancing *houri*. But they are chains nevertheless, binding us to past revelations, teachings, promises, and ideal glories and rewards. Some people are happier wearing chains and knowing their place than living without such knowledge, without chains, on an expanding frontier offering no future rewards or promises other than those revealed through direct personal encounters. All religious and spiritual traditions have these chains, the "chains of transmission" by which one generation approves the teaching of the next and by which former generations receive the appreciation of those they once taught. There is the "chain of enlightened teachers" that connects with spiritual aspirants far beyond the immediate context of a particular life, now recorded and captured in texts, photos, video montage, and all the communicative media that reduces a life to a few brief moments or images. There are also the chains of the teachings: codified, polished, processed, and institutionalized over thousands of years, and passed on as irrefutable, inviolable, transhuman in origin, and divine in all aspects, each a form of binding to particular ideas and beliefs.[51]

Then there are the many chains of the institutional embodiments of the teachings: special classes of "ordained" persons empowered by cultural, social, and spiritual sanctions, to propagate the "truths" embodied in their own investments. Each has its special buildings, places, times, rituals, life rites, codes of behavior, laws, expectations, demands, and ingrained resistance to those refusing to believe in the requisite way. These same expectations are found in a multitude of secular institutions, in the most materialist dogmas, and in the most vehement political actions, however conservative or revolutionary they may appear.[52] And many people rejoice in wearing these chains as the way to a better, more fulfilling life, wanting to link with like-minded others in terms of the most idealized goals. As one grows older, these chains become more and more stoutly linked, until like Marley's ghost, the forged links are heavy in dragging one down to the most common denominators of conservative, normative life. Heavy, even after death, the old are not renewed but continue to live bound by chains of their own creating. Such is the chained life, one bound by obedience, inflexibility, authoritarian credos, little self-knowledge, and even less knowledge of others. Many a battle has been fought in chains and many a chain used to flog others; and many lives have been bound by those same chains because they refused to accept the burden but were captured, forced into chains, or paid the penalty and died, sometimes hideously and without pity, by the linked propagators of the chained life.

I do not believe in chains. In many ways they are the most potent sign of slavery and control exercised by others in the name of their own particular truth. And those who wear them, inevitably seek others to wear them as well (even while secretly hoping for liberation and reward). What we must learn is to cut our chains, to find the right circumstances to liberate a lesser self from a contracted way of seeing or being. This refers not only to the chains of inequality, prejudice, or social denial that we all struggle against, but also the more subtle chains that bind us through traditions of inherited spirituality or the teachings of those we admire or would emulate. Throwing off chains does not mean abandoning responsibilities, obligations, or familial commitments. But it does mean reformulating those same responsibilities in terms of a more open and expansive way of life. Such a life is one dedicated to the personal search for illumination and spiritual well-being and not simply to obedience or conformity. It means a deep, inner commitment to a higher value life in which the illumination of "heart and mind" are direct personal attainments. This does not mean that we cannot learn from past teachers or traditions; indeed, they are primary resources for personal self-awakening. Without such resources, we would be deeply impoverished and far less able to attain the positive realizations that beckon us.

The lives of "saints and martyrs" are exemplary in showing us the possibilities inherent to a committed spiritual life; the realizations of the "sages and enlightened ones" surely provide directions along the way. But we are not those persons, and we are not living as they lived, nor are we sharing the same communal world or values that shaped their experiences into rare formations of spiritual attainment. Even the most enlightened teaching has its bias, boundaries through which the filtered light of Spirit takes on a particular visionary form. And many of these forms are worthy, noble, impelling, authoritative, epitomizing excellence in spiritual fullness and flower. But they are not absolute or final; nor are they suitable for all beings or even a majority of beings. However much they attract, they are only bright lights that help us find our own individual way to a new realization of potential, a new emergence, another nuance of Spirit seeking to manifest itself. The brightest lights, such as the Christ or Buddha, epitomize the tendency to create a luminous ideal out of a real human life; however brightly that light shines, still it is necessary that we not substitute an ideal for the real.[53] The real work lies in throwing off these idealisms, these distant promises or past glories, in order to cultivate new changes, in the present, for the immediate good of self and others. We may hold the ideal within as an image of what can be, but the real challenge is to actualize it fully in the real world of enchained beings.

The "subtle bindings" are found, layer after layer, as internalized, introjected ideas, teachings, images, aspirations, all acting as a substitute for self-actualization in the authentic sense. Arousing the intention for enlightenment and illumination, we must strip away our introjections and inherited beliefs. We must clear space within for a real dawning and awakening that follows no prescribed path other than that deepest inscription we can decipher in the utmost depths of soulful being. Such an archaeology of soul requires detachment from past obsession, a deeply calm clarity and reflection, an openness to being shown, a receptivity to newness, creative insights whose origins are not bound by past teachings or realizations. There is a need for inner surrender to Spirit, to the guiding impulse toward new synthesis and creative discovery, a letting go of fixed ideas or attitudes, and an opening up to the arousing energies of a more luminous life. Often, we must throw off inherited teachings or customs, a male or female bias, or a narrowly restrictive dogma that holds us back from a direct, authentic seeing. Often, we must give up an image or idea of self, or of others, that restricts our view from attaining the full vista of our shared potential; often we must let go of everything we hold dear, only to reclaim it in more comprehensive realizations of illumined life.

Spiritual insights are often deconstructive in nature: they dissemble a pattern, or dismantle an introjected view of self or others. The re-creation of understanding emerges out of an overwhelming sense of a greater, more complex horizon. And this is good! There is constant renewal within the process that draws us out to a more incorporative, inclusive understanding; it stimulates us to enter more fully into the processes of co-creation and the birthing of worlds. In the process, we can preserve everything valuable and at the same time, notice and observe everything in need of healing and repair. Many are wounded, hurt, even crippled—many need healing, a new vision, a way to proceed without further harm or injury. These ways are born out of the committed life, out of the refining fire of a passionate quest; a quest that removes, layer by layer, the chains that bind us to a less realized life. In that process, Spirit is the great liberator, the gentle presence that dissolves, at a mere touch, the heaviest of chains. Her wings hover over us, her breath infuses us with life, and her presence is a felt reality; her embrace is ecstasy and her kiss, a profound awakening to new life and awareness. Therefore, let us open ourselves to Spirit, to the embrace that frees us from past error or ignorance, and allow those chains to fall away, gently, one by one, until finally, we can stand embraced in purity, integrity, and naked joy.

It is the work of a lifetime to be truly free, not bound by tradition, not enslaved to the past, not conditioned by futurity, not entranced by images of contracted light, present, past, or future. (8.5)

Meditation: There is no freedom without effort and a sacrifice of less mature ways of thinking and acting. Further, this process of transformation cannot be rushed or set to a fixed pace or pathway. Our freedom is relative to our understanding and requires a consistent and enduring effort to refine and mature. The ways of Spirit are beyond calculation; every path has its own challenges that bring into focus those aspects of freedom most highly valued by that path. My own path has always emphasized creativity, self-knowledge, imagination, dreams and visions, the natural ecstasies of real experience, and a lifelong study of world religions, esotericism, and indigenous cultures the world over. All this has combined with natural sensitivity for altered states of perception, certain psychic abilities, and strong, positive love relationships with others, male and female. In the processes of spiritual development, I have continually been faced with the ongoing challenge of seeing the insufficiencies of my own thinking, my misinterpretations of experience, and the inadequacy of my knowledge in the face of the vastness and complexity of Spirit. Yet I have actively pursued authentic knowledge in the face of Mystery as the greatest and most enduring challenge, as an inexhaustible frontier of possible awakenings, each of which blends its light with all that has preceded it and, sometimes, radically overturning mind and soul. As a spiritual seeker, I am not a member of any religious tradition, but having studied most, I have been influenced, to various degrees, by all traditions.

It is a "work of a lifetime" to genuinely cultivate inner presence and a direct sense of Spirit daily, waking and sleeping, through all the ups and downs of ordinary life. Ordinary life is the palette from which we can take all the necessary colors need to sketch out our inner vision of that presence. The forms are mutable and the colors can be blended to create new shades of meaning. The freedom sought, from tradition and the past, is relative to our efforts to transmute ourselves into more receptive vessels of Spirit. Spirit, freely working, enacts within us the magical awakening to a more related and attuned life. The harmonics of spiritual transformation are played out within the psychophysical complex as we attain to a more and more integrated life—the body inclines toward greater purity of habit, deeply positive mental-emotive states, greater focus and creative energy, a deeper, more resonate inner peace. As an open-ended process, we simply respond with increasing sensitivity to a deeper, more pervasive presence; the pace depends on the individual and the outcome is a reflection of individual capacity, circumstance, and relative being in the world. The source is Spirit-conceived, Spirit-carried, Spirit-born. The consequence is a continuous process of spiritual development and maturation, through all the suffering and joyful byways of the embodied psyche, constantly related to a multitude of others.

The adaptive challenge is to find the inner balance that allows the maximum in personal development while also meeting fully our obligations and responsibilities to others. Yet these obligations, flowing out of the inner awakenings of Spirit, are often recast into altered forms that require restructuring of past or present relations. Always, Spirit presses us to honor our relationships without violating love or trust; to work through all the processes of honoring others without denying an inner need for self-development. As we grow and develop, we sometimes outgrow old patterns of relationship and in turn, this leads us into crisis with those we love. Yet Spirit presses us on to find new ways of relating, to explore areas too long denied, to release old resentments, frustrations, fears, or desires through a process of spiritual honesty enacted for the purpose of a preservation of the good and a purging of the insufficient. Sometimes, this leads necessarily to compromise and a common recognition of boundaries beyond which only love can continue the work of sustaining lifelong bonds of affection. It is natural that in a world of differences, compromise must act as a means for establishing commonly accepted boundaries. The quality of that compromise is best enacted through a loving respect even while there may be creative debate and the ongoing challenge of validating to others the viability of a deeply held view. Where such compromise cannot be attained, separations should fully honor the right of others to their own view (while the oppressive view should be fully resisted and challenged).

Relationships are a spiritual ground, a context in which we can validate our insights with others and receive from them alternative perspectives that may enhance or alter our own. This includes relationships with those who are masters of a tradition, or a traditionalized way of enacting a spiritual path. Personally, I do not see the master-disciple relationship as the most viable spiritual model. We are all teachers and we are all students; and while the privilege of age may carry with it a certain luster in experience or practice, nevertheless, every person has a potential to contribute insight into processes of spiritual development. The bonds of dependency, of covert authoritarianism, of rigid thinking and narrow perspective, or an out-and-out inflation and arrogance are all possible in the more structured teacher-student relationship. A better model is that of *kinship*: that is, how I related to others as a brother, sister, father, or mother based in deep ties of relatedness and loving concern. Rather than students, I have brothers and sisters; rather than teachers, mothers and fathers, all of whom I can honor as part of a larger kinship embracing all human beings and extending into the world of animals and even plants. This is an old teaching well rooted among ancient peoples the world over, a deep ancestral image of co-relatedness and species harmony. A model far deeper and more grounded than any master-disciple tradition; a way that extends beyond the very margins of human communities and offers us a way that respects all members and all relationships.[54]

To not be "enslaved to the past" means seeking liberation from the inherited bias of a multitude of beliefs and practices that have stained the bright potential of our species evolution. Racial hatred, sexual discrimination, class bias, political entrenchment, overdetermined rationalism, or spiritual arrogance unwilling to recognize the validity and equality of other faiths, are all examples of past enslavements. These patterns of bias and false discrimination are bred, generation after generation, in the uncritical transmission of parental attitudes to children through the propagation of unquestioned assumptions concerning local status, rights, or prerogatives. Aggressive and violent practices must be resisted wherever and in whatever culture they may appear; practices such as infanticide, forced mutilation, the torture or torment of others, and all forms of militant aggression, must be resisted through resilient, nonviolent means. The ways of Spirit are many, but they all point to species preservation through the cultivation of a higher value life—to free ourselves from enslavement to the past means to cultivate an attitude of deep respect for the rights of others to choose for themselves (and not for their children or the elderly who are dependent upon them) in a context of loving, nonviolent practices, their own customs or traditions.

Circumcision should be a matter of free choice, not a "medical practice" imposed on male children; the brutal custom of clitoridectomy performed on young females—a practice rooted in male fear and deep discriminations against the female body—should be resisted through teaching the integrity of the body, born in the whole and complete sense. These and many more such enforced and violent practices are part of the *spiritual* concerns that involve all human beings in seeking to actualize healthier, more well-balanced global cultures. The spiritual counterpoint to these forms of enslavement is to offer, through example, alternative ways of authentic living, grounded in nonviolence and free, informed choice. Care must be taken not to impose a "conditional future" on others in the name of a nonviolent practice. Spirituality is about the present, the immediacy and quality of choices we make that enhance and give greater depth and meaning to the expansive "now" of spiritual awakening. Whatever "prophecies of doom" we may project into the future, innumerable factors can intervene and change those tendencies into something quite unpredictable and unexpected. The most potent of those factors is an authentic spiritual life, lived in an exemplary way, validating a creative synthesis through actual manifestations. The "future" should be an outgrowth of actual practices, themselves subject to constant scrutiny and reevaluation—the goal being to live, step by step, the most authentic life possible.

This includes the recognition that past light is emblematic of present potential, attained not through imitation, but through venturing courageously with humility into the yet unknown realizations. The past does not represent simply exemplary or ideal types of spiritual development, as much as the primordial, paradigmatic forms in evolving cultures whose foundations have been thoroughly compromised by limited attitudes and beliefs. This includes all present cultures as well and, in particular, those most dominant in the twentieth and twenty-first centuries. Past lights may indeed represent or epitomize the purest examples of a particular cultural milieu or historic moment, but those lights, as real historical individuals, reflect a depth neither fully known nor understood. Let us honor those individual examples, revere the valuable teachings they offer, and then, continue on in the demanding work of direct personal attainment. In this process we may very well receive help from those lights and other sources less visible or well known. We may indeed, seek Spirit directly as guide, teacher, or Mother. But in that process there is no need to negate the value of the present in overdetermining the value of the past. Those past lights are with every generation, present to their need, and they all work to encourage the deep realization of higher value in every soulful being. In this way we must each seek the freedom of the present as the highest ground for self-realization, however thankful and receptive we are to those past lights.

Learning to see with both eyes is difficult, as many have only learned to see with one eye, one path, one way; both eyes must open, to compare one image with another, to not surrender to sentiment and habit. (8.6)

Meditation: From a global point of view, there are a multitude of ways and there is no "one way" for all human beings; in turn, this truth liberates us from all forms of totalitarianism, however truthful the path we choose to follow as individuals. It is always possible to choose "one way" over others and to take that way as the supreme example of how to live or how to enhance the quality of life. But the fatal step is to presume that such a choice is also good for others, or even worse, to insist that unless they imitate your choice, they are condemned to a less sufficient life or, even more arrogantly, condemned to a life of ignorance and suffering, even beyond the grave. These are teachings from humanity's adolescence, from a period in which religious persecution was a norm and religious bigotry was uninformed by the scope and history of alternative spiritual paths. Over the generations, increasingly, every spiritual tradition has impacted the traditions of others and this impact has continued to relativize the absolute claims of those traditions. Secular traditions (like those in science) whose authority rests strictly on human efforts have "secularized" majority populations throughout the world. Subsequently, there is no "one way"; if we choose a way and make it the exclusive path for our spiritual development, well and good, but only insofar as we are able to let others also freely choose.

The problem of seeing with "one eye, one path, one way" is the tendency to imagine or believe that such seeing is validated by the similar seeing of others, as though numbers and collective assent were a sign of truthfulness. But collectivity can be an inhibition to spiritual development and collective beliefs may be deeply prejudicial even to point of fostering profound mental-emotive imbalances and deep-seated social pathologies. The "collective will" has led to violence, oppression, authoritarianism, and the denial of the rights of others. This is exemplified in the oppression of the masses by political revolutionaries, the colonial destruction of indigenous peoples, the enslavement of whole races, families, and peoples as well as in the persecution of those regarded as marginal critics of such practices. Collective assent is no sure sign of truthfulness or validity other than in the ways it reinforces existing norms that tend to privilege the many over the few. It is the breakdown of such collectivities that reflects the movement from human adolescence (and peer pressure) to adulthood and mature, individual choice. There are many spiritual paths and many ways and some are better suited to particular goals than others, but all exist because some human beings have considered them necessary for the cultivation of a better, more mature life.

The human learning process increasingly involves learning to "see with both eyes" that there are alternative paths for spiritual development, some more intrinsic to a particular way of life and some more adaptable to a specific cultural setting. All these paths offer insights into what it means to be human and to develop; and some are viable alternatives for anyone willing to pursue its goals, while others are closed to just those members who truly qualify though birth, culture, or inheritance. These many paths lead to many diverse goals and epitomize many diverse ideals, some of which contradict or at the very least, severely challenge even the most basic assumptions of other traditions. Such is the "divine milieu" in an increasingly global culture of diverse peoples and traditions. There is no grand conclusion that summarizes these traditions in a way acceptable to all members of those traditions, and it is doubtful that such a summary would contribute anything more than simply an abstract perspective added to the whole. In a creative global culture, pluralism and diversity are normative; they are signs of health and complexity congruent with the deeper currents of cosmological life.[55]

The higher value cultures of the present are not those perpetuated through collective assent or popular mood or current intellectual fashions. Such cultures are emerging out of the communal formations of creative individuals working together to consciously actualize a shared vision in a very specific, grassroots effort to develop new creative forms. This process is well underway and provides the creative testing ground for a multitude of culturally sensitive individuals to relate their gifts and abilities to the maintenance of communal living through emergent models of social life. Such "experimental communities" are presently found the world over, and the underground currents of these communities are deeply global and "international" in the noncorporate sense. The best of them are free from the tendency to idealize their own values as models for other, alternative communities. Such communities study teachers and teachings from many diverse spiritual traditions, as well as creative thinkers, artists, and scientists whose values are seen as contributive to an emergent global richness in complexity and higher values. In such communities, it is necessary to see with both eyes, hear with both ears, and to use both halves of the brain. In such communities, dogmatism is regarded as an older form of coercion; and exclusive beliefs, a constrictive form of reductionism. What matters is creative dialogue, continual learning, and the freedom to explore alternatives.

In this process, "sentiment and habit" must be transformed; the tendency to cling to past ideals or the sentiments of earlier learning or adolescent experience, must be released for the dawning of a more complex and spiritually mature life of dialogue and communal living. Seekers must proceed at their own pace, to find the rhythm that best suits their temperament, the style of life most compatible with their emergent spiritual awakening. Where visible community is not available, the mature seeker must live with others in a "community of Spirit" through the invisible connections of like-minded affinities and intentions merging in creative projects, meaningful spiritual occasions, and deeply loving relationships. These occasions are fostered in whatever context offers the possibility for a meeting of diverse individuals on the grounds of common spiritual interests. A "community of Spirit" may be highly eclectic or more focused on particular issues of concern, but the goals of that community are focalized through a willing recognition of the value of spiritual alternatives and the importance of diversity in exploring spiritual potential. The cohesive center of that community is the reality of Spirit as a viable presence in the life of every individual member.

The processes of spiritual maturity require that, to whatever degree we can, we engage with the comparative values of alternative spiritual teachings, paths, and practices. The process of learning more than the basics of diverse spiritual teachings is proportional to our willingness to devote serious time and energy to the processes of spiritual transformation (in contrast to simply affirming a particular set of values). The more deeply we engage a variety of spiritual teachings, the more deeply we are able to see the capacities, values, and limits of the teaching. The goals of such exploration is to heighten the understanding and to deepen compassion so that a mature spiritual response grows out of an informed and knowledgeable grappling with spiritual alternatives. Should the occasion arise that a seeker selects, through this or any other means, a particular spiritual path as best providing the grounds for fulfilling spiritual needs, then well and good. As long as such a seeker remains open to other traditions as viable alternatives in spiritual development, as equally viable and meaningful as one's own, they remain in dialogue with emergent spirituality. Should such an occasion result in closing off to other traditions, or to a denial of the reality of those traditions for others, then this is a regression to a less mature understanding. Such a position will no doubt resonate with all the extreme claims of past generations whose intolerant attitudes resulted from an unwillingness to meet the challenge of diversity and human equality in differences.

The greatest challenge is to recognize our own limits and to see that our motivations to attain a worthy goal are not definitive of what is best for others. Nor does our attaining the goal give us any special right to judge the accomplishment or commitment of others. The goal is not to judge, but to *value* every positive contribution to the actualization of creative occasions. In such a process, it is always necessary to see our own limits not by devaluing them, but by seeing their relative merits in relationship to the worthy merits of others. In that process, Spirit is the guide to a better kind of seeing that seeks a compassionate and joyful participation in Spirit's teachings to others as well as to self. The emergence through Spirit is universal in the sense that all beings are Spirit-endowed and Spirit-gifted; and such emergence is individual and "local" in the sense that it involves real relationships, circumstances, and conditions in the actual life of particular, discrete beings. This means we must open our eyes to what is immediately in front of us and to those we know and love; and we must learn to think and see globally and historically in valuing what is loved and valued by others. In this way we can overcome the tendency to use only one eye and even that one, poorly.

> **Freedom is born of curiosity unrestrained by artifice or "moralities" of the past; the "eye of the heart" sees clearly life as it is—a gift, a challenge, a plurality—not as a constraint or a demand for conformity but as a joyful wisdom that gathers together and celebrates. (8.7)**

Meditation: In the heart of Spirit there is ample room for all spiritual paths and teachings, and those awakened to Spirit understand that there is also more than ample room for emergence and newness. To live a Spirit-guided life means to live a higher-value life whose respect and reverence for the well-being of others is paramount. Such a life reflects not a lesser "morality" but a greater ethic of adaptation and creative, respectful interactions no longer encoded in narrowly literal laws. Many older moralities are marred by exclusive and prejudicial attitudes to those who are not members of their community. Community membership is not a guarantee of a better way of life; the teaching of having "no other gods" than the god of one people or one cultural minority can be oppressive and arrogant. The gods (and goddesses) of others are denied, believers in those gods oppressed, attacked, and violently forced to alter their beliefs on pain of death, imprisonment, and marginalization. The followers of Judaism, Christianity, and Islam have all practiced this kind of "morality" and the history of these oppressive tactics have all been justified by sanctioned codes regarded as the highest sources of spiritual guidance. Indigenous peoples the world over have been the victims of such "morality" through forced conversion, legal oppression, and a failure on the part of the "dominant majority" to recognize the validity of indigenous spiritual practices.

The greatest perversion of these older moralities is the concept of "holy war" or a direct attack and assault on others who refuse or resist recognizing the exclusive, totalitarian claims of a particular religious tradition. Such persecution is still practiced, as in the Shi'ite persecution of the Baha'i, the Chinese oppression of Buddhists and Daoists, the bombing of African-American churches in America, and so on, all done in the name of a "superior" ethics rooted in "one way" morality but distorted by the exclusive human tendency to overvalue inherited prejudice and to devalue difference and resistance to any and all forced conversion. I do not believe in the "god of war" and regard such belief as atavistic and regressive, as an archetypal entrancement with the inflated powers of a particular god-complex. The mental attitudes of such oppressive believers is rooted in a deep and dark egoism that wishes to see the world reduced to a subservient model of obedience to the "ways of the fathers," to a continuation of generational abuse and enslavement by aggressive male competitors seeking to create an absolute hierarchy ruled over by a militant, wrathful god of judgment and condemnation. Such teachings are based in an ethic of terror and justified as a guide for the oppression of others. A collective mentality of conformity and submission has perpetuated these tendencies in all "monotheistic" religions; the histories of those religions are inseparable from a history of oppression, violence, and the denial of the rights of others to believe differently.

The nature of our collective spiritual freedom is not contingent on one pattern of belief nor on submission to a single hierarchy of ruling authorities (either religious, secular-political, or scientific). Our spiritual *freedom* lies in the fullness of living a mature, creative life, deeply respecting others, and living with integrity in actualizing the deepest stratum of our spiritual potential. From a global perspective, this means that we must surpass that older morality that justifies war and oppression of others in the name of some violent code of collective self-glorification. What is necessary and inevitable for the emergent pluracultures now being birthed, is an ethic of deep respect, tolerance, and a willingness to adapt and coexist peacefully with genuine concern for the preservation of differences. In that difference we can find the true measure of our capacities and potential. Through dialogues between spiritual perspectives, we can learn and grow toward a more mature understanding that will allow for even greater emergence and creativity. The "gift of life" is the freedom to become more self-aware and more able to read the complexity of creation in the depths of our collective well-being. It is not one gift, but many; not one way, but many; not one truth, but many. Our tolerance for diversity is a measure of our maturity and our capacity to formulate a coherent, integral point of view, a measure of our creativity.

In the process of development, curiosity is a central and valuable, even crucial attribute and should be encouraged and developed. By curiosity I mean the freedom to explore, search out, investigate, experiment with, all aspects of human life that promote health and well-being. In this process of exploration, inevitably, there is an attraction that draws the innocent (and experienced) toward more dangerous, dark, and destructive sides of human capacity. It does little good to suppress curiosity out of fear of perversion or harm; far better to temper curiosity with good judgment and positive values that give form and substance to the ways in which curiosity may be satisfied through positive learning. We always want to protect those we love from injury or actions that might lead to harm or emotional trauma or obsession. Positive values like nonviolence (to self or others), respect, kindness, generosity, compassion need to be balanced with alternative positive values like courage, strength, determination, self-discipline, and commitment to provide a context within which curiosity can function in a healthy, productive fashion. Virtues are holographic or interdependent and like the many qualities that make up a whole person, develop in relationship to each other.

The whole person is a complex of mental-emotive-psychic abilities and the development of any one of these tendencies reflects the state of all the other qualities. These other qualities are resources for the development of any one quality. We constantly moderate our development by enhancing our ability to integrate all our abilities into a healthy, focal awareness that moderates the choices we make in exploring alternatives. This wholistic model of the human psyche reflects the larger scales of nature as an integration of a multitude of cosmological influences in the evolution of the Whole. Curiosity is not an isolated response, but a very natural consequence of being self-aware and sensing, however remotely, affinity with a multitude of ways to live, to know, and to be human. Curiosity is an index of our receptivity to other ways of thinking or being and, as such, is moderated by the internalized values we hold that delimit certain areas as more healthy or positive than others. As healthy-minded beings, it is extremely important that we understand all that contributes to ill-health, imbalance, and the darker, more destructive passions or motives. The wholistic approach to self-understanding requires a genuine knowledge of human capacity as well as insight into the causes and consequences of imbalanced, distorted, or negative antilife behavior or values. Such exploration, to be healthy, must be paced with internal spiritual development that is prepared to bear the consequences of exposure to those more negative tendencies.

In this process, the "eye of the heart" is that capacity that allows us to develop through deeply positive human relationships; that sees into the heart of the other and allows that seeing to guide us into deeper interconnections within Spirit. This is a challenge and a gift. It means becoming heart-centered, responsive, and receptive to the feeling states of others and it means purifying our own emotional life so as not to distort the perceptions that flow through Spirit to us. In moving beyond conformity to unsatisfactory or unreflective collective attitudes, we move into new relationships with others through the "community of Spirit" and through the joyful recognition of others with whom we are intimately related through spiritual affinities. The formation of community is a great good and represents a means for the fulfillment of intrinsic spiritual needs. The "eye of heart" is a means for sensing those others with whom we might most authentically live and share our lives. This joyful gathering together may occur in the most spontaneous and free-form manner without any external influences beyond those of a natural sympathy and attraction. This is what I call the "Eros of Spirit" or the attraction that works between individuals to draw them together in dialogue and community for the development and the exploration of creative abilities.

In this process, respect for others is paramount but so too is the need to follow a certain inner guidance and inspiration. "Life as it is" is not a fixed quantum or a completely knowable process; it must be lived and lived fully to give us even rudimentary insight into the vastness of the processes involved. It is a lifetime commitment, this exploration of what-is, and in the process not all will be known. Always there will be limitations, boundaries, and capacities that we chose not to develop as we developed others. Like the Divine Sophia, we learn that the full depths cannot be known and that we must rest within limits and give thanks for all that we have learned, Spirit-guided, by living positive, creative lives. And it means transforming ourselves by learning from the past, the limits of which are so often self-created and perpetuated on the basis of prejudice and an artificial discrimination. The expansion of the human spirit into a truly spiritual life can move far beyond that history not by denying or ignoring it, but through a careful study and appreciation of all that history reveals. To escape the cycles of past error and prejudice, we must understand the origins and causes. Only then can we have some hope of a more liberated and balanced life in which we do not repeat these past errors but live as mature and responsible beings in an increasingly creative present.

There is no system that adequately explains the whole, no morality that recognizes every exception to the rule, no theology justified in the totality of its claims, no authority deserving respect because it wields power. (8.8)

Meditation: There may be elegant theories that claim to give a comprehensive overview of the Whole. They may be scientific, psychological, or other sociologies of human development, or various spiritual philosophies, that present themselves as "complete" summaries of human potential. I personally regard these various theories as incomplete, regardless of whatever claims they may make concerning wholeness and completeness. I say this because while some of these theories may be helpful in understanding the human experience, or may contribute to a particular insightful view, there is simply too much territory that is unknown to have really comprehensive maps. Like the old maps of the thirteenth and fourteenth centuries, most of these maps were projective in ways that seemed congruent with what was then known (or valued) but most missed by large degrees the actuality that had yet to be seen and understood. In the realms of human potential, I see clearly that there is much that is denied, distorted, and re-imaged in accordance with ideas that are too confining and often a gross distortion of what is possible or on the threshold of manifesting. As a species that is just growing out of adolescence, we need to accept the limitations of our understanding and be more receptive to alternative ways of thinking about similar phenomena. The issue is not which of these ways is "right" but which of these ways best applies in certain, specific circumstances. Subsequently, any number of theories may apply to identical phenomena because the goals sought differ in terms of the means used to attain them.

There are any number of "right" explanations for the human experience, depending on the kind of answers being sought. The very questions asked will shape the nature of the goals attained and the presuppositions used to structure an argument or theory may well determine the outcome of their application. The circular nature of human thought and belief relies on the tensions between the needs and thoughts of the individual over against the mutable dynamics of a creative evolution, driven by those thoughts and needs. In this process of negotiated reality, Spirit abides as the inner stimulus for coherent transformation and development without necessarily predetermining that development. As such, no particular system, morality, theology, philosophy, or scientific theory fully represents the life process in all its actual, creative occasions. Every actual occasion contributes to the dynamics of future evolution and change; even the most marginal occasion acts to influence the Whole, however slightly, and thus, there are always unseen influences at work. Thus, it is highly unlikely that any "theory of everything" will be actually adequate, however interesting or creative. Possibly, if we reach a plateau in which there is a deep stability and inner cohesion on a species-wide basis, such theories might be more enduring and accurate, but only as long as that stability lasts. Inevitably, the "next crisis" will shake those foundations and give rise to yet new theories.[56]

While there may be "no morality" adequately inscribed to cover all exceptions, a coherent set of principles can act as resources for living a creative, nonviolent life. But even an ethic of nonviolence must face the challenge of aggression and the oppressive tactics of the violently motivated (as in acts of criminal violence, terrorism, or emotional or political aggression of all kinds). It is spiritually necessary to resist violence and oppression, and it may be necessary to defend one's life or the lives of others against such aggression. Such nonviolent martial arts as T'ai Chi and Aikido reflect just this ideal of a strong, disciplined ability to defend against life-threatening aggression with an ideal of disarming and immobilizing rather than simply meeting aggression with stronger aggression. Further, nonviolence as a principle may require intervening in the aggressive acts of others in order to stop cycles of aggression that might threaten others, even tangentially. It may mean offering protection to those under assault or initiating actions to remove someone from a violent situation, thereby contesting the values that permit such abuse (for example, animal experimentation). Following a nonviolent ethic does not mean living passively or accepting norms that permit oppression or perpetuate social imbalances and aggressive norms. It means living a creative, nonviolent life that actively engages the problems of a violent world through intelligent, disciplined strategies that require courage, training, and a deep sense of the preservation of life.

However, the value of nonviolence does not function in isolation from other values; and these other values are themselves emergent and creatively part of ongoing spiritual development. It is important to distinguish clearly between the ideal value and the actual integration and development of that value in day-to-day living. Most human beings have a very poor sense of the values they hold as intrinsic to their own (and others') well-being; even though they may accept in an unconscious way, the inherited values of their culture of upbringing. The life we choose to live, as conscious spiritual beings, involves more than simple conformity to inherited norms of behavior. It requires a deep thoughtfulness and an ongoing effort to refine and develop by "shedding old skin" and thus constantly seeking to deepen our individual understanding, compassion, and wisdom. Spirituality, as an emergent, creative occasion, engages the deepest potentials and shapes that potential according to our intentions, values, and aspirations. Step by step and stage by stage, we can grow beyond more contracted ways of thinking and acting. We can become more spiritually aware and we can throw off self-limiting attitudes, which brings a greater sense of participation in the Whole, with others, in creating a more vibrant spiritual awareness. We can attain states of illumination that bring us into direct, participatory encounter and union with Spirit in moments of profound spiritual awakening.

In following the creative spiritual life, all guiding principles are subject to refinement, redefinitions, new complexes of meaning or relationships and no "one morality" is sufficient to cover all creative occasions. The refinement of spiritual principles is ongoing and open-ended, but these principles are foundational in the sense that they can act as guiding intentions to establish lasting and meaningful relationships with others in conjunction with a creative self-development. Each step we take leads to greater responsibility and inner self-discipline; and each time we fully embrace that step, make it part of our real being, it becomes a conscious, integral aspect of our actions and thinking. In this process, we can evolve through any number of moral pathways, but in most cases, the limits of those pathways also become apparent in the rigidity of their application or in the aggressive ways in which they are propagated by others. The actualization of spiritual principles requires an adaptive, relative clarity of circumstances and the appropriate responses congruent with inner values—a testing of integrity and flexibility in creating a more receptive world of co-related others.

There is "no one theology" whose claims can be seen as adequate to the theologies and spiritual philosophies of others; all "metatheories" are relative to the parameters and exclusions chosen to articulate a particular perspective. Among relative worldviews or cultural particularisms, no one world or set of particulars can be said to be thoroughly adequate, even for members of that culture or worldview. Always, there is an inner sense of inadequacy (or cultural underdetermination) insofar as it is possible to conceive of or envision ways to enhance or alter a cultural perspective to bring it more into alignment with individual needs or aspirations. Among emergent pluracultures, that is, a culture in which a multitude of global cultural influences are embodied in diverse members of that culture, there will be numerous pathways by which creative potential may be actualized. The values of those pathways will be relative to the values of other such pathways, for example, in vegetarianism, gender relations, the rights of children, animal rights, in attitudes toward global ecology, in any variety of spiritual disciplines, and so on. Subsequently, each individual must take responsibility for embodying a coherent set of principles to guide his or her spiritual life, among a wide array of possible alternatives. This requires courage, thoughtfulness, and commitment to actual, existential practice of those values, and a continual shaping of them into an integral, spiritual life.

The issue of choice, Spirit-inspired, rises above collectivity and norms of institutional power or influence. To "wield power" through identification with the social institutions by which that power has been formulated is not an adequate means for living a creative, spiritual life. I regard the saying, "Render unto Caesar that which is Caesar's and unto God that which is God's" (Mt. 22:21) as misleading insofar as it is interpreted to mean that spirituality requires conformity to existing social and political norms. The creative processes of spiritual development require that we question everything demanded by Caesar and, where necessary, that we resist and refuse to recognize that power when it inhibits and denies our individual right to live creatively according to alternative spiritual values. The guiding principle of creative spiritual life is Spirit, not conformity to human institutions, ministers, priests, masters, or the institutional leaders of any cultural forum. Some of these leaders may offer genuine spiritual guidance in terms of the traditions they represent, but there are alternatives, and for responsible seekers in an emergent cosmos of creative self-becoming, Spirit is a primal source for a multitude of alternative spiritual pathways and becomings. The integrity of the individual is to realize the pathway of his or her individual life and to transform that life into a worthy example unimpeded by the norms of a collective and less individuated way of thinking and being.

Through freedom, let us respect the views of others, accepting alternatives and other means and ways; but let us cast off our gold and silver

chains to live freely together by choice, with reverence, not by demands, or by gross conformity. (8.9)

Meditation: In the most basic sense, we are all free to choose our spiritual path to the degree that we liberate ourselves from unconscious assumptions, inherited prejudices, and strict social conformity. Insofar as we reject the challenge to become increasingly self-aware and motivated by conscious, clear choice, we are subject to continuing submergence in inherited patterns of belief and cultural bias. The spiritual challenge of creative emergence requires that we question deeply our own cultural norms, practices, and institutions in an attempt to formulate a more adequate and luminous spiritual life. With a questioning approach, we can move pass the inhibitions of inherited prejudice through the formulation of creative principles and spiritual practices leading to a higher value embodiment of alternative lifeways. This requires something more than intellectual abstraction; it requires deep commitment and a fully engaged, passionate search for spiritual maturity. In this process, it is deeply important to respect the values and practices of others without abandoning the capacity to think critically or the ability to see how limitation and bias may limit an alternative way of life.

The dialogical approach involves interaction between worldviews and perspectives for the purpose of species development in a conscious, self-selecting process of gradual maturation. Respect for the views of others does not mean an acquiescence to biased thinking or prejudicial values that result in the oppression of others. Nor does it sanction aggressive attack or dismissal of others; instead, it requires a thorough, patient, committed determination to bring to light all those inadequacies that inhibit human freedom and responsible, loving coexistence. The principle of "freedom from restraint" refers to the need we each have for the free pursuit of spiritual life that does not impinge on the freedom of others. This mutual freedom requires a direct, conscious, dialogical interaction whereby we can mutually agree to differences and then move past those differences through mutual care and healing. There is room for a multitude of perspectives as long as each perspective is purged of its totalitarian claims and tendencies to dismiss or deny others. Such abuse and denial must be resisted in order to attain a mutually free climate for present and future development. The pluracultures of our shared emergent spiritual horizons will be increasingly diverse, multi-ethnic, and globally complex. As such, there will be an increasing need for greater and greater tolerance, free independent development, and mutual access to the historical richness of all spiritual traditions.

Such a rich diversity of perspectives will inevitably create a climate of intense interaction and debate. In this process of global awakening, individual integrity, clarity of vision, and a passionate concern for mutual creative life can provide any number of alternative pathways. With many "means and ways" the issue becomes, not which is right or wrong, but which best suits individual needs or aspirations and is most conducive to creative development. Others cannot make this choice for you—the challenge is to work out your liberation with diligence, to pursue with deep commitment, the alternative that beckons. Then, to test that alternative in dialogue with others through respectfully honoring differences and boundaries, while seeking to transform those boundaries through mutually creative ideas, practices, or insights. Where there is little or no mutuality, there is little or no development; throwing oneself against a wall does little good, better to go elsewhere and, with others, to mutually take walls down while still respecting the boundaries. It is never a matter of crashing gates or forcing on others a particular view; all such "evangelicalism" is a sign of profound misunderstanding of the rights of others and reflects a pride of belief that is generally immature and unaware of the larger, global context of spiritual development.

The need to "respect the views of others" as a spiritual principle has a context, that is, to engage the other as part of the process of mutual development. It is not a credo for distancing oneself from unappealing views, nor is it a rationale for ignoring the counterclaims of alternative beliefs. The context, as I see it, is to participate in the development of any spiritual perspective as necessarily engaging others in creative, exploratory dialogues. Partly, this is a matter of temperament and social location. Certain social circumstances offer more opportunity to discuss alternative views than others, and certain persons are more inclined to put themselves forward as spokespersons for a particular view whereas others are less public and more private in sharing beliefs or exploring alternatives. Partly, it is a matter of the degree of social or cultural resistance to new ideas or alternative views. Some cultural climates are more receptive and others more resistant to emergent views. And, partly, it is a matter of finding an appropriate forum for the sharing of ideas, in alternative communities, electronic media, writing and publishing, and so on. Sharing one's own view is part of the process of creative development and the effort of articulating beliefs and principles is itself a creative occasion. The context of respect flows both ways: respect for the views of others and respect for one's own tradition or the influences of others as they are embodied in one's own life.

In the above parameters, social location is secondary to inner commitment and the degree of self-development. Spirit moves in unpredictable and often marginal ways to bring forth a particular influence or spiritual perspective; the history of religion is filled with innovation arising from the marginal and the relatively humble individual. Often, persons with strong social locations have abandoned those positions in order to affirm a more authentic life in a less central social circumstance. Yet innovative individuals have been mocked, denied, socially harassed, threatened, or excommunicated because they offer an alternative view. Creativity tends toward the margins because it challenges normative assumptions or conventional attitudes, and as "marginal critics" there is a tendency to polarize emergent views over against conventional norms. This is a tendency that has distorted a great deal of creative effort in the struggle to survive hostile criticism from those representing themselves as cultural icons of a particular religious climate. This contestation of beliefs is not the central issue, nor is the challenge to "prove" to nonbelievers the efficacy of a spiritual path.

Only in walking the path, do we understand its demands, potential, and rewards. In "walking our talk" the primary challenge is to embody a way of life, not convert others to it. The issue of respect grows out of the recognition that personal freedom requires an unobtrusive space, a social and cultural location free of conflict and defensive living, a place that represents a center, a *temenos* within which spiritual potential can flower undistorted by the argumentative, aggressive criticism of others. The "alternative community" is just such a space; the "community of Spirit" is a transcultural community with embodied cultural roots. The sharing that takes place is cross-cultural and alternative without the rancor and abuse of hostile criticism and the one-dimensional thinking of those resistant to pluralism and relativity in a world of creative emergence. The hard boundaries in religious and secular-scientific worldviews are created by real human beings espousing aggressive and resistant attitudes fundamentally unreceptive to the alternative values of others. In the process of species development and maturation, those boundaries represent the areas of human development most retarded and regressive. These inflexible, didactic, overly assertive (usually male) conflicts only illustrate the lack of adaptation and the resistance to change that indicate an incapacity to grow beyond old ways of thinking and living.

In Spirit, nothing is static and everything is subject to transformation, development, and modification. What fails to adapt will die out and what adapts will continue to adapt, seeking an always more complete and thorough self-expression. The "gold and silver chains" must be cut and even the most illustrative examples of spiritual transformation must not be made into static icons or inflexible ideals. The semiotics of transformation include ongoing processes of reinterpretation, new interpretative horizons of meaning, some created entirely out of contemporary concerns that reflect alternative ways to understand past lives and examples. This is natural and necessary. We do not have to abandon those ideals or examples, but we must continue to examine them in the light of every emergent concern and new perspective in order to fully value their contributions and limitations. The chains may be cut slowly, link by link, and some preserved as part of a new linkage, and even the most brilliant jewels honored without excess or false inflations. Inevitably, even the most worthy examples have their limits and even the most brilliant light has only partial refraction and often diminished expression, all subject to diverse interpretations. The "truth" lies in the living, in the quantum of personalized energy and consciousness, Spirit-given, that results in a positive contribution to creative emergence. Such a contribution might not appear in any visible form, but be more a matter of living a spiritual, exemplary life and validating spiritual beliefs through compassionate, caring human relations.

The Ninth Principle

The Ninth Principle of Spirit is peace, nonviolence, and creative joy; the birth of new worlds, the opening of horizons free of fear, uncontaminated by possessive lust, lies, or confusion. (9.1)

Meditation: Perhaps the greatest challenge to spiritual development is learning to overcome the many internalized contradictions generated from the clash and contestation of alternative worldviews. The development of pluracultures on a global scale will mean an increasingly rich diversity of spiritual pathways in the midst of a potent, developing technological materialism. Further, ethnic identity and historical connectedness to local cultures also contribute to the problem of framing personal identity in terms of a global relationship to cultural and spiritual others. These various interpretative frames, including technological dependency and the "scientific" way of thinking, will all impact even more primary issues of identity such as age, gender, sexual orientation, language skills, and familial or peer group influences. The individual challenge is to work through the necessary stages of self-development in all these areas through a positive affirmation of self-worth and a deep concern for the well-being of others. The impact of diversity and pluralism in a postmodern world requires the development of a stable, mature creativity, open to the influences of Spirit through natural processes of learning and exploration. The challenge is to overcome internalized confusion (or cultural contradiction) through a committed, creative exploration of alternatives.[57]

Exploring alternatives is only a first step toward reintegration and spiritual emergence. Nevertheless, the more thorough the exploration, the more committed the individual to a global perspective, the more likely the possibility of diverse, meaningful connections with a wide range of others. The "community of Spirit" is not bound by any specific credo other than a free exploration of spiritual alternatives in a creative context of dialogue and personal synthesis. This dialogue is ongoing and essential to creative development while also recognizing the need for solitude and meditation as integral to a creative life. Such dialogues involve also sorting through the many monologues of past teachers, writers, poets, artists, and social-scientific theorists. Inevitably this means reading (and writing) as well as speaking and bringing the voices, concerns, and thoughts of others into our inner dialogues as referential guidelines to an emergent creative view. Individual development is a shared concern that can impact a multitude of others through whatever means we may choose to communicate insights. Being-in-dialogue means breaking through the constraints and conditioning that resists a more global way of thinking and acting. Exploration is a critical aspect of spiritual emergence and should be undertaken as a central aspect of creative maturation.

The "confusion" in this process is found in the way human beings tend to internalize values in an unthinking, unreflective way. These values (often inherited) do not form an inner coherence but simply surface under various circumstances to provide an often unthinking guidelines for "correct" (but biased) behavior. Or under other circumstances, contradictory values may arise simultaneously creating mental confusion or emotional uncertainty and doubt. Or even more confusing, some values may flatly contradict others, paralyzing individuals and fixating them at a certain stage, a condition that may retard development for an entire lifetime. From a perspective of creative emergence, the commitment to self-development requires a constant review and reassimilation of positive values through the context of real-life experience (that is, through *enacted* values). This means a continual "working out" of values and principles for the purpose of guiding self-development toward the highest degree of creative enactment. In the immediate sense, it means thinking critically about those values held as central to a genuine spiritual life and then enacting them in meaningful human relationships with a receptivity to the (noncoercive) values of others.

The "opening of horizons" is part of the continuing process of spiritual development, the ways in which a diversity of horizons intersect to form a coherent view of the world. In the postmodern world of global pluracultures, these horizons far exceed the capacity of any one individual to fully integrate or to even fully explore. The process of development is *selective*, conditioned by observable external factors as well as inner capacity, interest, motivation, or abilities. What we elect to study, explore, or master can be seen horizontally in terms of the culture of birth or childhood, in education, gender emphasis, and the restrictions or possibilities inherent to a specific cultural context. From a perspective of vertical potential, what we elect to study is deeply conditioned by attitudes concerning human potential and undeveloped capabilities. From the perspective of an emergent, creative metaphysics of transformation (as articulated here), all human beings have a capacity for profound spiritual awakening and illumination that is deeply participatory in the natural spiritual processes of species evolution. The capacities of the vertical horizon are neither predetermined, nor limited by a strictly material (horizontal) account of social or spiritual development. The vertical horizon symbolizes the as-yet unrecognized capacity(s) for self-development and species-wide transformation within which our global pluracultures are only reflections of a far more profound diversity of cosmological potentials.

The "birth of new worlds" is already in process, from the discovery of distant planets beyond our system and other world's life forms within our planetary system, to the very archaic life forms of our own planet as well as through a multitude of alternative spiritual and material cosmologies. I regard the birthing grounds of the Mother Spirit as thoroughly pervasive throughout all worlds, beings, and cosmic becomings. These worlds are also birthed through human imagination, myth-making, creative storytelling, artistic expression, musical inspirations, and all the melodies of a heart-centered way of living. They are also birthed in a plurality of creative theorizing and credible scientific explorations, more fully enhanced when they are wedded to an awakened spiritual sensitivity and dedicated self-development. These opening horizons of possible meaning are all potential for spiritual exploration, and yet the inner life of the explorer also needs cultivation and development. Interpersonal skills and emotional sensitivity are by no means secondary to this process; the lack of such skill or sensitivity all too often results in a contracted, competitive-aggressive, or isolationist mentality unable (or unwilling) to relate well to others and thereby truncating the positive, developmental aspects of self-other maturation.

This resistance to the centrality of relatedness to others, to a healthy, mature emotional life and the requisite sensitivity for the feelings of others, tends toward a more manipulative mentality where the "other" becomes either a supporter or a detractor (the old dualist mentality). This can lead easily to a divided self, in which feelings and emotions are repressed or pushed into the background and the intellectual or cognitive life becomes overdetermined and blind to other ways of seeing. An overidentification with the emotions and feelings of others can lead to distortion and a self-denying vicarious life that actually needs a greater critical ability to think independent of the emotional claims of others. But the tendency among many males is to distance themselves from feeling and emotion in order to justify a particular intellectual claim or belief (which is itself strongly rooted in largely unrecognized emotional constructions). In turn, such denial can easily lead to a "possessive lust" for truth and to assertive, inflexible truth claims. If by "truth" we mean an accurate description of what-is (either in the realm of the observable or in the realm of nonobservable beliefs), then "truth" is relative to personal experience, education, and methods of investigation.[58]

What is true for me may be contradicted by others, and I may be fully able to falsify my own truths, but the claim that someone else's truth should also be mine simply by consensus or by status or social location, is an unacceptable assertion. As I see it, we do not, as individuals or as a collective, "possess" the truth; it is not a thing and cannot be owned by anyone. It is not "intellectual property," nor is truth the province of specialists or some unique class of truth-seekers. From the perspective of a creative metaphysics of self-development, "truth" is a current of shared evaluations that influence how I or others live in relationship to our recognized limits and individual capacity. It is not "out there" in nature or in some abstract world of intellectual essences or in so-called "objective facts." It is an interpretive framework shared with others that makes more or less sense and has the consequence of shaping how we think about our own lives and the lives of others. Even the most abstract scientific truth can have a profound social dimension, and every such truth has a social context, however limited or isolated the thinker may be. As soon as that "truth" enters the social, relational world or others, it is subject to immediate and far-reaching reinterpretations in an ongoing process of shared worldviews. As such, no one person "possesses" the truth, at best they only hold a meaningful interpretation of how that truth works in relationship to basic human conditions, all of which are subject to alternative interpretations.

This does not mean that all such truths are simply relative; some interpretations are better and more meaningful than others, some reflect greater maturity, insight, understanding, or are more aesthetic, more valued by a greater majority, more focused and directed to specific questions or particular, sometimes very minute, concerns. And some truths are simply transmitted, generation after generation, as "more true" than any other alternative explanations. In general, human beings are extremely prejudicial in clinging to what they believe constitutes their "truth" and, in too many cases, this "possessive lust" has led to the persecution, denial and marginalization, imprisonment, and death of those who believe differently. And threaded throughout this tangential weave of ultimate claims and obsession with exclusivity, is the lie, that is, the tendency to perpetuate a half-truth or partial truth as though it were altogether true. The denial of relativity is perhaps one of the last great barriers to a more truthful living and a more honest sense of our own relative limits. When we regard truth as a matter of relative interpretations with a strong, determinative social content, then it is possible to value those truth claims that most deeply satisfy personal understanding without denying the validity of alternative views. This seems obvious and in no way does it impede creative development; it clearly points to truth as a means toward development rather than as an end-in-itself.

Out of the opening to Spirit, comes the fruitful life, creatively in dialogue with others, centered in nonviolence and noncoercion, at peace within and at peace without. Such is the ideal toward which Spirit inclines through human creativity and co-creation. This does not mean there is no competition or struggle to reach new horizons of understanding, nor does it mean that some adequate truth must be eliminated in the face of new insight and understanding. The fruitful seed is put back into the earth; old truths must be constantly evaluated and those that hold honored, but not extolled in an exclusive sense. Always the possibility for radical transformation is there, on the next horizon of spiritual awakening, awaiting spiritual seekers whose capacity for truth is not diminished by the strictly known.

To be "free of fear" means to live within Spirit as an inspiration for greater development and self-awakening. It means to live peacefully and creatively with others, however they may differ. It means to encourage others, their growth and development, without imposing one's own ideals or values. It means loving others and valuing their difference, their creativity, and their unique gifts, and sharing with them creative interpretations that lift self-and-others into Spirit for ever fuller expression and realizations. It means understanding that truth is relative to our maturity and experience, and that all "facts" are subject to alternative interpretations.

Out of Spirit, everything flows and moves and has life, is aware and immersed in the webs and fields of others; it images and we respond, it provokes and we question, it vanishes and we doubt. (9.2)

Meditation: Perhaps the reader will think that when I say that truth is relative that I am suggesting that we live in a "bottomless" universe in which truth is whatever we care to make of it. But that is not what I mean. The world in which we live has coherence and functions according to diverse principles that include human thought and belief but are not dependent or determined by such thought or belief except in the local, relative sense. This means that what we believe or hold to as true reflects what I will call a strictly "human perspective" often highly influenced by identifiable cultural-historic influences. These influences, which are local and relative, are constructs based in human experience, observation, and theorizing all of which are integral to a particular way of life, in a particular milieu. That milieu, in the larger sense, is part of a process of species maturation, itself inseparable from terrestrial ecologies of connectedness that, in the elemental sense, are also determinative of how we see or understand what it means to be human and aware.

As carbon-based, oxygen-breathing beings, with a certain evolutionary history and a mammalian tie to species interaction, with specific cultural and linguistic ties and a dual-brained way of thinking, we inevitably see things from certain conditioned perspectives. In this context, that is the context of our species'way of thinking and acting, we hold a large variety of "truths" as intrinsic to our relative ways of living and indeed, these are "truths" as some human beings see them. Artists, poets, scientists, mathematicians, philosophers, theologians, musicians, and so on, all hold to truths they regard as fundamental to their own well-being and self-development. And in the context of their individual milieu, these truths are certainly valid and may well reflect "truth" in a more pervasive context than simply human. Yet the human aspect will always be there, the "human way of thinking and believing." These insights come forth from Spirit, which is inseparable from our humanity but not bound by it. They flow out of the deepest stratum of Spirit as "nature nurturing" in and through all psychic, mental-emotive, physical development and in the most lucid noetic insights constituting authentic self-becoming and genuine truth-seeking.[59]

In this process of "nature nurturing" Spirit abides as an inner motivating coherence, as more than a simple unitary principle, as more than a primal source of the materialization of all concrete ideas into actual, creative occasions. In this process, the human tendency is to form collectivities with passionate attachments to specific truths or systems of belief. In turn, this gives rise to competition, conflict, and, tragically, warfare and often violence (of many subtle forms). Spirit does not impose truth or intervene to stop human beings from destroying themselves and others in the name of some passionate attachment to collective thinking and acting. But constantly Spirit acts to inspire new alternatives and emergent perspectives more deeply compatible with the inner coherency of human potential for a higher value life. This occurs, not through the imposition of a particular form, but through the stimulus of a *principled way of living* that fully recognizes the inner coherencies of planetary evolution in the context of relative truth claims. This is because, as I understand it, truth is multidimensional, complex, capable of transformation and bound by neither material laws nor immature thinking nor unrealized fixations in species evolution.

The "inward turning out" as the principle of psychic manifestation, that is, of spiritual intentions resulting in actual occasions, leads to a continual process of embodiment by which earlier truths are overturned or revivified. Impacted by the manifest intentions of diverse beings, individuals are nurtured in Spirit according to their gifts and through the specific influences of their actual historical-cultural setting. Those intentions are co-related and part of an emergent process in which all "truths" are constantly processed through diverse interpretive frames, resulting in a plurality of views whose intersections represent matrices for creative species development. Diverse intentions are inseparable from Spirit, from the "webs and fields of others" that act to influence our understanding and maturation from the context of our (naturally) evolving humanity. Such truths are existentially grounded in the lives of real human beings whose passionate intentions give form and meaning to their lives. Thus it is anything but a "bottomless" universe. The actualization of potential through the embodiment of relative truths is a primary source for the evolution of core values in an authentic spiritual life.

This embodiment of truth as relative values in an evolving cosmos has a qualitative context. A life able to value the lives and insights of others, to creatively assess and interact with alternative perspectives, gives the highest index for further species evolution. We have long passed the threshold where the mechanisms for species development are determined by unconscious (or semiconscious) biopsychic influences. We now stand on the threshold of an emergent horizon of self-determination based in conscious choice and intentional purposes and goals. This means that our present and future species development will emerge out of the choices and goals we purposefully set and be qualitatively structured by the values we each consciously choose to embody. The higher value life can only be actualized because we consciously choose to embody values that express a coherent understanding of a developed spirituality. The spiritual transformation is not simply a faith-project but an expression of a conscious, intentional determination to actualize the highest degree of illumination in the context of a single lifetime. Such realizations contribute directly to the enhancement of species awareness through a deep attunement to Spirit in a context of creative exploration and individual articulation and sharing.

Spirit is inseparable from all psychic development as it is intrinsic to our natural evolution from the very beginningless beginning. Through the multifold processes of "nature nurturing" our collective development has reached an increasingly critical series of thresholds. Each area marks out new territories for conscious development: the control of reproduction, the issues of self-selected death (euthanasia), disease control, genetic control of plants, animals and humans, and increasingly complex issues of social development through emergent pluracultures in all areas (religious, economic, political, sexual, aesthetic, or intellectual)—all of which "flows and moves and has life" and is therefore in transformation, nonstatic, restlessly pushing toward even more fullness and self-expression. In this process, Spirit acts to inspire and reveal more cohesive, co-related interpretations in which the "preservation of species" (all life) is a higher value whose worth is relative to the quality of life sustained. Like the phoenix rising on new wings out of the ashes of its old life, so too humanity has the capacity to rise out of the old mythologies, monomyths, and constrictions of passive-aggressive resistance and theories of dominance for a more spiritually mature, dynamic life of co-related explorations and shared relative truths.

In this emergent process, the quality of life of the individual is critical to the embodiment of those higher values. The illumined life is not an abstraction, but an actuality that leads to a more profound understanding of the life process. Spirit acts to image for us the new potential, the new pathways of emergence, the creative actions we need to embrace as spiritual intentions in the continuing reformation of human potentials. The inner provocation of Spirit is the felt urgency, the inner sense of arising new insights and ideas, the expanding horizons of psychic awarenesses and intuitions, the opening-into-being that is the transformative ground of species development. The individual grounding of those relative truths, their "transubstantiation," is the work of Spirit in concourse with a willing, conscious intention seeking to maximize the quality of life as we actually live it through committed dedication and loving human relations. The presentiments of Spirit, when denied or ignored, result in a turning away that denies a more cosmically whole context to the processes of human evolution. This is a process of great subtlety arising on a continual flow of creative opportunities whose actualization requires a willing receptivity to the subtle, the intuitive, the visionary. In the denial of Spirit we banish receptivity to the unknown potential in a living, animate cosmos and reduce our potential to strictly material causes, skeptical intellectualism, and a profound doubt in the very meaningfulness of life itself. This too is an alternative within Spirit, but not one I choose to embrace, nor is it one I can recommend for the preservation of species.

To survive and flourish, there must be an expansive heart, an uplifting power, an inner unfolding

flow; adaptive, responsive, fluid honesty and exchange. (9.3)

Meditation: Life, from the perspective of higher spiritual values, is more than survival, more than just meeting the needs for daily existence. Spirit presses us to maximize our quality of life, to attain a more complete vision, to attune ourselves with more expansive horizons not only for ourselves but also with all those with whom we intersect. The concept of "spiritual influence" is based in a subtle receptivity to the attainments of others, in a developed psychic capacity to take in those influences and to allow them to act as directly as possible on the psyche. For this process to be mutually affective, there needs to be an intrinsic, deep-seated receptivity to the positive outflows of others. This requires a certain degree of training and psychic development, but such receptivity is rooted in inner attitudes toward the values and experiences of others. There is a certain balance between deep stability and receptivity to others that is best maintained through the cultivation of love and care in all human relationships. This nonpossessive love, even when erotic, is like a current of relatedness that creates energetically sensitive correspondences between individuals by opening mutual partners to new insights or experience through shared perspectives.

This "fusion of perspectives" occurs where there is a genuine sense of receptivity to the relative understanding of experience. My insights may not be identical to yours, they may be only relative to others, but they may be fostered and developed through a loving interaction that fully values the difference as a creative ground for further development. My insights may be incompatible or even contradictory to those of others and may not be easily reconciled with those other insights. Yet we can still each care about the other and cultivate a loving attitude regardless of our differences. It is only when we close our minds and hearts to others and refuse to care about them or to practice loving concern that we contribute to alienation and conflict and the "closing of the mind." Alienation is primarily fostered by a stubborn refusal to recognize the validity of other ways of thinking or believing and then denying the importance of loving others who are, indeed, different and differently motivated. The healthy spiritual life proceeds through positive human relationships without denying the integrity of individual insights or creative efforts to synthesize an emergent understanding. The "fusion of perspectives" is a fertile ground for further development and emerges best in an atmosphere of trust, respect, and receptive concern.

The "expansive heart" is one that is open to others such that the more subtle psychic influences of Spirit can act to create those deeper correspondences that make life and human relationships a joy. This type of "expansion" is tied to the development of an ever deeper openness to Spirit that allows us to feel directly the warmth and fire that burns away all our clinging to earlier, more contracted states. It is more than merely metaphoric, it is an actual feeling of expansion, a direct perception of a more subtle field of spiritual activity that embraces the self-other relationship. Passing beyond empathy, this state leads to a deeper sense of relatedness to all others. It is an opening to Spirit in a genuine mystical sense; it is an enhancement of awareness that incorporates self and other into a single continuum of co-relation, as intrinsically related, joyfully immersed in Spirit and fully alive to the living presence of Mystery. The normal contraction of the detached observer is far removed from this living presence, so animate and so alive in the flowing exchanges between loving beings. This expansion extends into and through nature and all the inhabitants of nature, as participants in the living processes of ongoing spiritual co-evolution. The "inner unfolding flow" is a consequence of such an awakening, working through cycles of expansion and contraction, slowly leading us into more connected, animated relationships.

Our ability to "survive and flourish" depends on the cultivation of those values and embodied ways of living that will open us fully to Spirit. The process of actualization moves through the various cycles of expansion and contraction by cultivating a genuinely adaptive sense of balance. In many ways, it is not a loving world, many live contracted, oppressive lives. Therefore, each person must take on the responsibility through his or her own life, to create those occasions that will introduce a more loving practice into this world. Only by cultivating love, can love flourish; only by engaging in long-term loving relations, can love attain stability and presence. It is not a matter of momentary passions but of long-term commitments and determination to live a genuine, loving life, open to Spirit and guided by inspiration and the expansions of the heart. To keep balance in this process means to go step by step through all the stages, to thoroughly master each stage to prepare for the next. It means cultivating inner stability without creating barriers to others because of differences or disagreements. It means living a positive, creative life through a continuous inner maturation whose fruitfulness reveals itself in loving human relationships.[60]

In this loving process, honesty is a critical threshold for establishing trust and long-term relationships. Not "brutal honesty" that disregards the feelings of others or self-serving criticisms masked as honesty, but a loving honesty that seeks to maintain the highest quality of relatedness by giving voice to deep-seated perceptions about the self-other relation. Such honesty begins with self-honesty and seeing our own limits and the relativity of our own understanding or values. And it proceeds not by compromising those values through unspoken conformity to the expectations of others, but through an articulate sharing of perspectives in which each person seeks to hear and respond positively to the other. Honesty proceeds best through respect and appreciation of differences, rather than through an artificial expectation that the goal is an uncompromising conformity to an inflexible ideal. The relative values we each seek to actualize in our own lives are enhanced and developed through positive human relationships, open to discussion, compromise, and adaptation. The integrity of an individual view, through processes of spiritual development, undergoes cycles of reexamination and continual sifting and pressing down, only to be poured out in honest, loving communication for the examination of others.

Such a sharing can only proceed where there is healthy respect and love on the part of each person. Where there is only harsh criticism or cold denials or overly rational demands, such sharing is crippled by false expectations and an unreceptive rigidity. Uncontrolled emotionality, destructive rages, depressions, anxiety, and emotional imbalances of all kinds also obscure and block positive, loving relations. The adaptive response, the very necessities of species development, depend on receptivity to alternatives, differences, and the creation of supportive, emotionally positive, nurturing communication. Without such communication, each party only retreats into the isolation and enclosure of a defensive-aggressive emotive-mentality increasingly closed to dialogue and more likely to abandon the relationship altogether. In turn, this leads all too easily to whole communities of people closing themselves off to others in the name of preserving a more rigid, less receptive standard of "truth." This leads to collective neurosis and pathologies of a bound and self-destructive alienation. The healing of this alienation can only proceed through an ongoing concurrence of positive intentions and spiritual honesty and self-discipline.

Love is a spiritual gift; it flows out of Spirit and through the human heart-mind-soul and into the world for the betterment and enhancement of human relationships. The furthering of love requires positive, receptive communication, a soul-to-soul willingness to talk out differences, to seek compromise that does not violate individual integrity, and to promote growth that moves beyond a particular, more limited stage of development. We are all in process, all engaged in growth cycles of expansion and contraction that require each of us to moderate those processes in cultivating more loving, lasting relationships. In order not to be so vulnerable (though a positive vulnerability is part of a genuine loving), we may cultivate those principles that best represent our own sense of spiritual identity, within Spirit, and then consistently practice those principles so others will more readily perceive the nature of our spiritual commitments. By this I mean a consistently *enacted* way of living that clearly demonstrates a loving, positive commitment to human relations. This enactment should also demonstrate the nature of personal integrity through consistent disciplines directed toward spiritual development and growth, and not simply a mere speaking of such or an empty theorizing that somewhat vainly imagines spiritual growth to be strictly a matter of intelligence or mental abilities.

Such exchange requires no violence, no oppression, no anger or denial of the other; it values others, the perspectives of others, their struggles and their search. (9.4)

Meditation: The ways of Spirit are many and beyond knowing in the full sense, but central to those ways are the ways of peace and peaceful determination in living a spiritual life. Such peace begins within and is the result of cultivating a deep reverence for life in all its forms and varieties. It proceeds through a recognition of the rights of others to their own point of view and perspectives; it culminates in a deeply loving, consistent attitude rooted in peace and nonviolence in every confrontation in which truths are tested through human relationships. Such a life is not passive or indifferent to suffering. It is not "detached" from the real exigencies of real beings struggling to make sense of life in a confusing, competitive world of clashing values. The "peaceful warrior" is not one shrouded in detachment from worldly concerns, but an engaged, skilled, committed individual whose energies and abilities are honed and sharpened through real-world experience and a wide range of human relationships. This requires training, a multitude of diverse skills and mature abilities, and a richness in learning and education that opens all the diversities of global coexistence. It is not a passive way, but an active, engaged praxis of alternatives best suited for specific situations and drawing on a wide variety of skills and abilities.[61]

The "struggles of others" are also our struggles, because as human beings we are all engaged in a higher value search for better ways of life, more grounded appreciations of the worlds of others, more enhanced means for fulfilling the potentials we each carry. The specific struggles are part of a larger archetypally structured process in which certain dramas and confrontations emerge as a human way of overcoming our own limitations through a resistance to the ways of others. But the ways of others are part of our way, our shared species evolution toward a more mature means for actualizing potential through a cooperative and skillful, nonviolent struggle to uncover or unearth hidden capacities, ideas, techniques, psychic abilities, or any number of residual abilities awaiting the right stimulus for development. If we fail to make this transition into a more mature practice of species interaction, we will all suffer through the repeated insensibilities of more violence, abuse, and mismanagement. The old credo that "competition" was the means to the survival of the fittest is now dying as a fossilized construct of a largely aggressive understanding. In a more wholistic world of deeply related others, survival becomes a matter of intense cooperation, emergent integrity, and a variety of alternatives that can each add to the conscious richness of the whole.

On an individual level, we each embody a multitude of others, ancestral roots are diverse and varied. The influences in an increasingly mobile and intercommunicative society are highly multinational and culturally diverse. Each person struggles to make sense of this circumstance in an increasingly complex world of demands and expectations. Each searches for those values and the appropriate synthesis to contribute a personal quantum of loving energy to the emergence of a more creative, mature awareness. Or seekers find a place in the process to sustain values worthy of holding, or oscillate between values seeking clarity; or they grasp the authoritative claims of others as a refuge from confusion, or barricade themselves behind a wall of fear and anxiety in embracing a code that sharply separates "us from them" and thereby perpetuates the ways of violence and isolation. The artificial closure of self to others is rooted in fear, an unwillingness to change or grow, or to truly recognize the insufficiencies of past ancestors and past generations wrapped in miasmic, inherited illusions. How long will human beings continue to suffer these fears of their own self-making? How long will we be enslaved to the inadequate mythos of "past greatness" or to logotherapies that justify the denial of others?

We all need the freedom to explore our whole capacity to be human, and we need a safe, nonviolent world in which to carry out those explorations. We also need the pluralism of alternative worldviews to overcome the shortcomings of a dominant majority (or a hostile minority) that would insist on the validity of their views as adequate for the needs of others. Diversity provides a foreground for creative development and the background is a woven tapestry of primal truths drawn from the collective human heritage with care and deep appreciation for their origins, colors, and designs. And our individual weavings may be a piece that fits with the weavings of others and contributes to a larger self-becoming in species life and evolution. Our connections are not simply physical, but also psychic and not bound by the materialist laws of Cartesian space-time coordinates. Psychic life, in a more exoteric sense, is interconnected through a variety of subtle continuums relative to the intensity and effects of personal development and creative spiritual efforts. Consider the long-term effects of the Buddha and the Christ, still reverberating through the psychic life of millions of human beings. Such reverberating effects show clearly that human freedom can result in consequences of a global magnitude over thousands of years and planetary revolutions.

The phrase "no anger or denial of others" does not mean an uncontested acceptance of every alternative, including those that threaten others with harm, manipulation, or impositions of a more subtle or overt kind. It means a willingness to debate, to interact, to seek a more satisfactory answer, to think critically but with empathy and imagination, to engage in the distillation of our own truths for the emergence of even more far-seeing illuminations. It also means where necessary, to intervene and to protect those more vulnerable to harm or manipulation. Thus we need courage, skill, and determination as well as humility, positive evaluation of the skills of others, and a deep sense of loving commitment to the higher values that motivate others through creative actions. It also means accepting others in terms of the degree of their maturity and not expecting or demanding of them an understanding they are not yet capable of attaining. I say this because it is a great illusion to imagine that genuine knowledge is immediate and easily attained. To learn higher math requires study, as in learning any developed science or art form; so it is with spirituality. There is a long, curving arc in learning that takes many, many years to fulfill in terms of actualizing full potentials and finding the appropriate lines of development to express that understanding.

Like Mother Teresa in the slums of Calcutta, many years passed before the world and others were awakened to the value of her very down-to-earth concerns. And it took years before she fully realized her dreams and potential in the formation of a new spiritual order with new spiritual goals. She "valued the other" regardless of their religion, attitudes, beliefs, negative proclivities, bad karma, or nasty habits. And she offered a worthy model, to use our spiritual gifts and capacities for the healing of those most in need, asking nothing in return other than a means to perpetuate the work. The real work is the transformation of human consciousness on a global scale that preserves differences and values creative, imaginative insights in the context of emergent technologies that can free us from obsessive drudgery (but that also have their tremendous dangers). The goal is to encourage others toward a more illumined, self-aware, other-aware life in the context of a more cosmically oriented understanding of the human capacity for transformation. This is the Hermetic circle, a transformation that follows alchemical pathways and practices that lead to an emergent visionary reality in which all life is valued to the highest degree as an instrument of Spirit manifesting. It is not the "loss of self" that matters, but the *transformation* of self from the murky unseeing of a turbulent life of misdirected passion and intellectual confusion to clarity, light, and inner luminescence. In that illumination, passion is actualized in a healthy eros of loving others and intellect discovers the bright noetic connections to a more harmonic, psychic world of diverse spiritual being.

**Inflexibility, rigidity, unmoving and falsely moti-
vated care are signs of illness, confusion, and
contraction; the strength of peace is its power to
uncontract, to restrain without force, to redirect
and to channel through permissive concern. (9.5)**

Meditation: As in the old Daoist teachings, we must learn to
bend but not break, to move the energy through and around without
creating walls of resistance that only invite greater aggression. In
this process, the need for a grounded flexibility is foundational;
rooted in the earth, in the fully incarnate, self-transformative life,
there is a constant need for clearing out the old, internalized static
energies. These old energies, bound in psychic habits, attitudes of
mind, emotional conditions of defensive, dependent, or vicarious living, need to be released, freeing that bound energy to flow into emergent patterns of creative response and adaptation. Through the
"community of Spirit" we can each learn to receive the love necessary for healing and the encouragement to drop old habits and mental tendencies that bind us to one-way thinking or believing. The
narrow range of emotional and psychic responses that bind most
lives is a consequence of long-term ancestral patterns presently up-
rooted in the turbulence of conflicting worldviews and alternative
values. The reknitting of these ancestral patterns is a multigenerational task that requires a substantive rethinking of the past and an
ongoing reevaluation of the good of that past.

To carry out that reevaluation, it is necessary to be flexible and
empathic, to cultivate a sense of relatedness to all past conditions
and to seek in those conditions a better, healthier response. There
are many inherited illnesses, particularly those transmitted down
family lines permitting abuse, prejudice, and the negation of others as normative within a particular familial context. Or these
lines perpetuate obligations of dependency, or victimization, by
teaching values that are unhealthy and centered on the unhealed
wounds of even older generations of abusers or of the neglected and
dependent. These norms are not adequate for a creative, healthy,
spiritual life and are the very impediments that keep individuals
from attaining their full potential. Some family lines promote an
imbalanced, aggressive competition where being the first of the
first, best of the best, is far overvalued. Such values diminish the

more comprehensive dimensions of Spirit by failing to recognize the value of finding a place through more cooperative and less competitive means. Subsequently, the deconstruction of any "hierarchy of values" requires a loving attitude aimed at the preservation of the good and a careful sifting of the less valuable for every grain of worth and positive contribution. The healing of the past is a slow process of granting recognition to every good and directing healing energy toward the past illness.

The psychic transformation of present generations requires a healing of the past through the dismantling of inadequate or partial values inhibiting a more cooperative, co-creative way of life in a global context. Just as individual healing proceeds through the "healing of memory" and the working through of all past trauma and conflict, so too, the health of our collective species life depends on a creative healing of our species past. We must cultivate a new understanding that values the good and seeks to heal old wounds, contractions, buried trauma, and all the vast consequences of centuries of rape, pillage, and molestation. We cannot turn our backs on the past and imagine that we have no need to understand (and heal) it without blinding ourselves to collective imbalances deeply in need of transformation. We are each a living witness of past trauma, such that, for example, the history of arrogant persecution has left its mark on everyone who is truly conscious of that history. Centuries of abuse cannot simply be swept under the rug and ignored! It has to be cleared from the human psyche and healed in all its incarnations in the present. Its primary manifestations are in the familial lines, now thoroughly broken and severed by generations of conflict and disagreement. As these lines dissolve even further, we need to embrace a spirituality that allows us to thoroughly review the illnesses transmitted down the generational lines that are still active within the psyches of the inheritors of those illnesses.

The necessary healing begins with self-healing through the cultivation of positive loving relationships in which there is a mutual recognition of the wounds each partner carries. A direct healing of those wounds is a vital part of a creative relationship in which each partner is healer and healed. The medium of that healing, Spirit-led, is a loving consciousness that seeks to facilitate the growth of the other in a mutual process of exploration, encounter, and support. Then, we must learn to give up our attachments to our wounds and move on, into a healthier context of loving. This requires something more than a genuine acceptance of the other; it also requires a challenging exploration of mutual boundaries and the deep inheritances of the past—of those inherited biases that are themselves in need of healing. The positive psychology of such a relationship proceeds through a process of encouragement to change and grow beyond old patterns, not to remain stuck in defensive living or to assume a right to a criticism of others. The dropping away of past inheritance proceeds through its healing in a context of nonviolent exploration and by cultivating a thoroughness in understanding. The peaceful warrior uses her energy to attain balance in a context of confusion in order to illustrate a pathway out of that confusion. The healing power of Spirit is channeled through the healing of the individual into the healing of the generations; every spark of illumination is another light that reveals a possibility for transformation.

To "restrain without force" is a higher value principle; it means knowing how to capture attention and direct it without coercion toward positive awakening and insights. The strength of nonviolence is the manner in which it acts on others to encourage a more principled life. To teach by example means to fully embody those principles "all the way down" without reservation and with full commitment. The embodiment of spiritual principles acts spontaneously on the psyche of others to induce a sense of purpose or direction, without force, toward a higher value life. The "restraint" stems from memorable actions embodied in the world as a counterimage to past trauma or aggression. Such principled action offers alternative ways of becoming and embodying healthy relationships with others; it illustrates the creative occasion through which Spirit acts to enoble the quality of life. The impact of such an occasion can be far-reaching in its effect on others as exemplifying the very principles they themselves would choose to enact even while they are searching for appropriate expression. To restrain without force means to model alternative principles and to do so clearly and spontaneously, with flexibility and suppleness. I am speaking of creative adaptions, not fixed behaviors or rigid codes, of embodied principles by which life proceeds through spontaneous actions illustrating deep spiritual qualities, not simple conformity to proper codes or moral rules.

The "falsely motivated care" refers to the tendency to present a façade of compassion as a mask over a more deviously motivated aspiration toward power, influence, or the adulations of others. The deep wells of care and love draw on Spirit as a primal source of fulfillment in self-becoming, and pour themselves out through vessels whose motivations are genuinely directed toward loving others. The psychic principle of attraction is only a weak attestation of this deep love; underlying even the most violent disagreement or conflict, there is a current of loving presence capable of being lifted into consciousness through a sincere and purely motivated occasion. This connection is Spirit-born and bred in all beings as the life principle and, as such, remains incipient in even the most conflictual situation. To access that creative, loving joy means dropping the mask, seeking authenticity of motive, and being open in espousing a genuine compassion and loving concern, even in the most nascent form, as a means toward truly creative awakening. Such genuineness of motive creates an activation of that current that flows throughout the life world awaiting those occasions to better actualize an underlying psychic continuity whose forms are highly diverse but whose consequence is to create stronger bonds and more lasting joy in life quality.

The Spirit of nonviolence is also the source of life; it procreates through its many manifestations by forming a Whole, not by bartering a fragmented patchwork of conflicting views! (9.6)

Meditation: This does not mean we live in a nonviolent world or that nature is free of violence! Death through violence is a part of the creative process: the lion rends the lamb and the snake poisons its enemies, even whales eat smaller life forms. But Spirit is the *source* of life in its perpetuation through species continuity of credible lifetimes and processes of development. It is also a life source through our interconnections to all nature and the potencies of nature as the birthing grounds of new understanding and species development. The heart of that preservation is a nonviolent principle of positive loving concern, not just toward one species but toward all life forms wherever and however they may exist. Only through a reverence for all life can it reach its fullest expression in diversity, difference, and divergence. There are limits and boundaries whose transgression may threaten other species (or our own) or whose violation may result in a destructive mutilation of life. Those boundaries are not rigid or fixed in any permanent metaphysics of soul or necessary patterns of spiritual development. They are all semipermeable, open to creative possibility, capable of expansion, contraction, or reverberations with the intentions or evolutions of others. However, the creative ground of our species becoming is inseparable from our capacity to preserve species and species relations as an enrichment of our own understanding within Spirit.

In many ways, the Great Work goes unseen because of the spectacular effects of occasional eruption and violence—as in a hurricane, tornado, or volcano, or in the death of a star or the sudden swooping threat of a comet or other tumbling space rocks whose impact surely threatens life. But these are the dramatic punctuations of eons-long cycles of relative stability whose nurturing balances gave rise to life in all its varieties. These potencies of nature, Spirit-bred, are undergoing constant change and realignment, resulting in the actual occasions we call life forms and linked hereditary species ("nature nurtured"). This process is not simply a planetary process, but a cosmological process in which the term "nature" must be stretched to include all visible and invisible spheres. The Great Work is the evolution of life throughout the cosmos on all worlds, planes, and spheres as multiple aspects of Spirit-imbued becoming linked through the correspondences of soulful being and spiritual maturity. We hardly know the contours of that Work, we barely see the contributions each soul makes in living its psychic life as part of a greater wholeness. The "life of the soul" is a life of intrinsic relations to past-present-future beings whose lives also act to impact our own. The visible violence in this process is a minor scale within a greater harmony that allows for life in the first place.

To live in that wholeness means to accept our vulnerability as part of the fragile conditions in which such evolution is possible as sensitive, vulnerable, creative beings in a vastly complex universe of tremendous power. And yet, in Spirit, to see that this vulnerability is only a temporal condition relative to a more soulful being that cannot be fully manifested in only one lifetime (except under the most sublime conditions). Species continuity carries within it the templates of all past occasions, buried sometimes in the most unobvious ways, but capable of recurrent manifestations, for the reanimation of future soul-life. We can draw on these archetypes, of the Christ-spirit, the Buddha-spirit, the Dao-spirit, as meaningful sources of spiritual empowerment for further development. These templates of

Spirit in human form are constantly undergoing processes of creative transformation as human understanding and wisdom grows and becomes more deeply rooted in real human beings who are themselves spiritual examples. Human beings are vulnerable, fragile, and limited by the very nature of their incarnate life, while that which they incarnate can be carried on through a deepening of soul and its reincarnation in alternative manifestations.

Spirit is inseparable from nature and the natural processes of species evolution, but more than incarnate life, it is also the primal source of all thoughts, feelings, ideas, and emotive-noetic insights. The gnosis, or illumination of self through spiritual transformation, reveals a context in which all life forms are co-related, creatively linked, and whose life processes are inseparable from the quantum effect to the most macrocosmic vibration. Embracing Spirit at deeper levels of coherence reveals the underlying, nonviolent currents of life preservation that makes co-evolution possible. On a conscious level of participation, it becomes possible to create a world in which there is only minimal violence and restricted expressions of aggressive energy or competition without in any way denying creative potential for further development. Without such nonviolent intention, violence can and will become an option whose effects may sever the lifeline to the ancestral past (through destruction on a global scale) and blind its adherents to future peaceful coexistence (as in acts of terrorism or through violent wars). The underlying currents of creative, peaceful life must stem from the cultivation of loving respect for others and a deepening awareness of the inner continuities of Spirit.

The Whole is not known or recognized, even though it is knowable and may be, over time, more thoroughly understood. We are not working through the creative occasions of self-development because we know the Whole in which we become. In fact, we do not know it anymore than those early explorers who first traveled the globe with all their restricted maps and bound presuppositions. It is largely an unknown universe of possible becomings, the psychic dimensions of which are hardly seen or taken seriously. There are many "levels of reality" yet to be discovered and explored, some of which will alter forever human presupposition and understanding. To enter those realms will require a far more developed sense of our own individual psychic abilities. Those abilities will not evolve through the assimilation of diverse systems of thought, nor through the "patchwork" of knitted together metaphysical schemes. They will evolve, Spirit-led, through the natural opening of new potencies in the processes of co-evolution because we, as fully conscious human beings, choose to explore those dimensions as meaningful and intrinsic to our real human capacities.

In making that choice, in creating that intention to fully explore psychic capacity, we open ourselves to new revelations and insights regarding the relationships between many diverse fields of knowledge presently bracketed and often closed to each other. Emergent wholeness, slowly expanding outward in psychic senses, just as mind was expanded outward in material explorations, will encompass a vast reserve of natural potencies awaiting actualization through creative disciplines and committed spiritual exploration. In a context of nonviolence, those potencies can unfold a masterful panorama of possible techniques, disciplines, practices, arts, and sciences, all capable of leading individuals to a more spiritually complete life. This plurality of spiritual alternatives, born through the development of an enhanced psychic awareness, will produce radical transformations in social and scientific disciplines. Inevitably, the recentering of spiritual life will be a consequence of actual attainments by a multitude of others who also affirm the emergent templates of spiritual well-being through visible lives and manifestations.

Plurality in such a context is only relative, not absolute. It means that unifying principles of diversity work through processes of cooperation and nonviolent peace. These are self-selected by intentional human beings seeking the maximum in creative diversity without surrendering mutuality or loving relationships on a global scale. The wholeness is not found in "one interpretation" but in the qualitative excellence of a multitude of views whose common themes support creative life and continued emergence. The Whole is not finished but in the process of continual amplification and enhancement, such that an inner coherency may shine forth through a multitude of expressions irreducible to one form. This richness in diversity is the very heart of the life process held together in the creative tensions of species coexistence. Our interpretations are not merely additive, they are qualitative manifestations of natural potency. They are the creative projects by which we, as creative beings, manifest the universe in its most spiritual forms. In doing so, we draw deeply on natural potencies whose sources are Spirit-given and Spirit-guided. With a thankful heart, we become co-creators, primal sources for species advancement and the celebrants of that even greater Mystery, the very act of creation itself.

Freedom from conflict means not espousing popular opinion or a party view, not taking the part for the whole, not being entrapped by "impartiality or objective claims." (9.7)

Meditation: There is a certain seductiveness about "objectivity" that tends to mislead its proponents into a position that subverts the subjective nature of such claims. Observations and perceptions are relative to the mental-emotive condition of the observer, and the belief that such perceptions are immune to subjective bias creates a barrier between observers whose subjective attitudes are discredited or denied as relevant to meaningful observation. The functional relationship of the part to the Whole depends on a coherent relationship between individuals seeking to understand their meaningful place in that Whole. This relationship goes "all the way down"; it does not simply engage our mental ability, or only our rational capacities, but draws on the full and complete range of perceptions and sensitivities that we each have as healthy, joyful beings. The part-whole relationship includes subjectivity at the very core of what it means to be "in relation" to the Whole. Subjectivity is the primary medium of relationship; it is highly valuable and manifests the very qualities that make the understanding of the other possible. Further, subjectivity pervades the nature of all we do as human beings; it colors our every thought and shapes the nature of our emotional and perceptual capacities for observation. Those who tend to emphasize a dominant intellectualism often fail to recognize the profound emotional and subjective qualities that motivate them to cling to a highly rational or "objective" point of view.

The emotions, feelings, intuitions, and imagination are all critically important factors in cognizing the world around us and the role of others in relationship to our own roles. But the subjective problem goes further than this. The depersonalization of the observer through an artificial dependency on a highly rational attitude breeds rigidity and inflexibility because it limits human perception to a very narrow spectrum of cognitive abilities. Our knowledge of the world is highly dependent on a wholistic experience that fully actualizes *all* epistemological means: feelings, intuitions, aesthetic sensibility, imagination, and the full spectrum of our inherent psychic abilities including such phenomena as dreams, visions, mystical experience, altered states, and all "extra-sensory" capacities. The fact that many of these abilities are latent and basically undeveloped is a direct function of the denial of these means as valid ways of knowing and understanding the world. The dysfunctional consequence of this rational denial is that the part becomes increasingly isolated from the Whole and increasingly limited in understanding that Whole. In this sense, "objectivity" becomes another example of "one-way seeing" resulting from an overdependency on rational means and a denial of alternative epistemologies. The dysfunctional disorders resulting from this repression or denial of alternative ways of knowing manifest in an increasing intolerance for other ways of knowing and an increasing denial of alternatives as "false" and "superficial" by individuals whose own lives are severely limited and truncated by an unappealing defense of objectivity as "the only means" for the advancement of species life and wisdom.

There are many ways to advance human understanding in a living cosmos of diverse, gifted individuals whose abilities are in no way limited by the authoritarian discourses of either religion or science. There is no "one way" but the way we each choose as individuals in a world of multiple choices, rich in alternatives, and brimming over with unexplored potential in human capacity. The enhancement of humanity through emergent creative occasions may take a wide variety of approaches some authentically more "subjective" than others; the theory of "objectivity" may result in creative additions and insights moderated by a more positive, subjective attitude. The problem lies in the polarization of consciousness into an artificial dialectic between subject and object. This dialectic itself is a manifestation of polarity within a consciousness as yet unable to integrate a thoroughly subjective point of view with a creative and dynamically interactive engagement with "facts, events, or things" in the world around us. Such a polarity inhibits creative development by limiting the means, expression, and contours of what constitutes valid and acceptable areas of knowledge. Everything incongruent, at-odds-with, and consensually marginalized by those embracing such a polarized consciousness is left unexplored and inwardly repressed. The world conforms to the way we think it. It becomes the very image we have internalized and stands out in the exact contours we attribute to it as relevant to our own interests and concerns. And this focal attribution of objectivity gains a psychic reality through the collective assent and energy of those dedicated to propagating a worldview conducive to their own interests and beliefs.

The mediating reality between subject and object is Spirit in the most comprehensive sense, engaging as it does all subjects and all objects into a continuum of wholeness whose dimensions and fullness we have yet to realize in a full species-conscious way. The mediating reality of Spirit works through the potencies of nature and engages human beings at the deepest and highest levels of awareness. It is inseparable from either subject or object and is the revelatory medium through which all creative relations become actual. Inevitably, this emergence involves a unitary context diversely interpreted and even more diversely experienced. The diverse creative energies of Spirit work to stimulate and facilitate the continual process of coming-into-being. This inexhaustible process draws on the most primal conditions of relationship between stars, planets, cosmic energies, and other potencies of nature, to actualize and integrate each and every individual consciousness into that greater Whole from which it is inseparable. To "objectivize" these potencies is simply a means toward understanding them; but stripping those potencies of awareness and life means denying the life-giving qualities that have emerged from those potencies. Life breeds life: through the most subtle means, life stirs in the wombs of creation because life abounds in all dimensions and directions. These lives, Spirit-nurtured, are a testament to the life capacity, its profound subjective character as those potencies act to facilitate constant diversity, development, and resonance within and between life forms. The human task is to understand our role in this process of life development and to become conscious contributors to that process through living principled, spiritually healthy lives dedicated to an enhancement of the Whole through a profound understanding of individual human worth.

In part, this means avoiding a "party view" or the tendency to accept the teachings of previous generations because they have been accepted, validated, or popular in the lives of others. What is valid for one generation may not be valid for another and what was once thought to be adequate may prove to be profoundly inadequate. Every generation needs to test the truths of previous generations, and calling accepted tenets of those truths into question is part of the natural process by which human beings creatively evolve and adapt. Alternative explanations are thoroughly possible in all areas of human knowledge, and the tested truths of the past must stand the scrutiny of every new generation to prove their worth and value. The relativity of these truths means that there will always be new ways to contemplate the whole of things as it related to any particular set of parts or elements. This testing should be carried out in a manner, congruent with spiritual values, that holds the preservation of all species knowledge and experience as crucial for continued development. It is a criticism that seeks the good of the past while also seeking to facilitate yet a further transformation. Every creative occasion has some debt to the past; as inheritors of that past we must not be bound by it but we also have a responsibility to appreciate and value its contribution to an ongoing development. The "party view" tends to embrace the past with an uncritical attitude and to see in its progenitors, the examples most relevant to the maintenance of those values. But this is often far from true—many historical founders would shutter at the consequences of their original teachings and the ways later generations have perverted or abused those teachings.

The goal is to seek a free and permissive environment in which values of nonviolence can guide development without having to embrace party values simply because they are current or in vogue. This is as much true in science as it is in literature, art, or music; and it is certainly true in philosophy, religion, and spirituality. Constantly, Spirit presses us to move beyond didactic teachings and into the free and uncluttered space of an emergent creativity that fully values the teachings of others without becoming entrapped by the collective tenets of such teachings. And yet the need for continuity and relationship draws us toward those norms as a common meeting ground for explorations of new ideas, beliefs, and insights. The part-whole relationship is a dynamic testing of individual perspective relative to the perspectives of others and how those perspectives best emulate an evolving, emergent creativity. Collective views are the normative parameters within which this process of exploration is carried out but those parameters are permeable, fluid, subject to transformation through direct personal experience. Out of that experience can come new guidelines, principles, and expressions for species development, only to be tested over and over in the creative fires of future generations also seeking renewal, insight, and spiritual fulfillment.

Such freedom comes from the heart, through a reverence for life, based on inspiration, trust, compassion, and maturity; wisdom unites, then divides; it is free and then, chooses. (9.8)

Meditation: Wisdom unites because it seeks correspondence and postulates differences based on relationships rather than on logical contradiction or strict negation. Strict negation is largely an illusion based in a tendency to absolutize relative points of difference. Day is not the "opposite" of night any more than love is the "opposite" of hate. The same may be said for the positive and negative charges of a single magnetic field; they are not opposites, only relative points in a single continuum. The dualistic mind tends to think in these categories as though such thinking emulated natural phenomena, when in actuality, natural phenomena represent integrated fields of complex energy and not isolated events unrelated to each other. The wholistic mind tends to see things in terms of patterns of relations in which each part plays some significant role in influencing the totality of events in which it participates. Twilight, dawn, ten in the morning, or three in the afternoon are all equally part of the equation "day and night." In the continuum there is only a rotating planet and a constant source of light and energy sometimes fully reflected by the moon and at others, less reflected. These relationships are all constantly in motion and there is no "one point" that is more valuable than some other except in a pragmatic, relative sense.

The point is only a relative concern that helps to focalize or diffuse attention for purposes of generating creative insights, actions, or results. All dualisms may be dissolved into a higher and less bound unity-of-relations, into a more complex way of thinking and perceiving. In such a case, a female-male and male-female synthesis is quite possible and the relationship is by no means "more real" because it is more typical or more conventional. A full understanding of the female is inseparable from understanding the male, and knowing the male means understanding the female. Soon these polarities dissolve into complex relations that refract a continual series of nuances and shades, all subject to differing valuations. The same is true for the "good-evil" paradigm: it breaks down into shades of difference, into grays or darkened whites, under a variety of circumstances, each requiring thoughtfulness to determine the values best suited to the circumstances. "Reverence for life" is a higher value by which any polarity may be scrutinized for its relative preservation of life forms in determining how "good" or "evil" any action may be. It is a relative good and evil, and our evaluation of its qualities depends on the higher values we hold to assess its degree of vitality or harmfulness.

There is no final or absolute scale other than a relative understanding motivated by degrees of maturity and insight into the multifaceted dimensionality of the Whole. The limits of our understanding are reflected in the limited standards we use to make valuations. The more rigid the standard, the more likely the limitations or possibilities for creative occasions. A creative and joyful wisdom may emerge through a thoroughly relative process of development in which intuitive, inspirational awareness works through a variety of symbols, systems, or schemata without claiming absolute allegiance to any of them. Each teaches something different, each reflects truth in its relative nature, and whatever claims are made with regard to absolutes are relative to the merits they seek to promote. A particular system or symbolic discipline may lead to transformative results, and those systems deserve to be honored and respected. The full appreciation of such systems, as in Buddhist Tantra or Jewish Qabbalah, requires a full and authentic commitment to the practice and philosophies of those systems. Each has its own goals and attainments and these goals and attainments can be self-fulfilling and provide a sense of genuine spiritual guidance. Yet they represent diverse means best suited to particular systems of valuation that lead to deeper awareness without in any way inhibiting the possibly of alternative, equally effective means.

Wisdom is "free, then chooses." This means that while we have the freedom to explore alternative paths and a wide range of spiritual disciplines, nevertheless, we must choose some path to actually follow. Wisdom "unites and then divides" is the process of first comparing alternatives and seeing similarity and then seeing difference. The challenge of difference is to develop an appreciation for correspondence without seeking to merge those correspondences into a single, abstract interpretation. Let differences stand. These differences are creative sources of tension within the global community that reveals the diversity of our different understandings. There is a balance between the wholeness of our communal relationships and the tensions created by difference and divergence. Such tensions are an inevitable feature of species life evolving through creative explorations. The danger is when any one perspective is proposed as a solution to the entire human situation. The imposition of a single perspective on others is a history of repression and denial—a "colonizing" mentality whose ideals become a substitute for authentic dialogue, sharing, and a responsible freedom. These tensions in perspective must not be erased, denied, or dismissed, but, rather, moderated by a sense of respect and an ethic of nonviolence. Wisdom is free to choose a path and to follow it to its highest conclusion knowing all the while that there are many other paths, equal and perhaps superior to one's own.

Seeing the similarities, seeing the differences, still we must choose the path best suited to our individual nature, one that leads to a fulfillment that is meaningful without being absolute. This does not limit our capacity for higher awareness or illumination. In fact, it only opens more pathways as possible means to that illumination. A "heart-centered" path has many alternatives and is rich in symbols, techniques, and practices. Such a path involves primarily an ethic of deep concern for the preservation of species in the most spiritually developed and diverse sense. Our strength lies in diversity not conformity, but we also need to genuinely cooperate and work through positive, loving relationships in order to attain the goals that diversity implies. Our unity lies in our capacity to love and care for others in the most authentic ways; our diversity lies in intellectual, artistic, and expressive freedom in seeking to understand the complexity of the world at large. And our creativity is a fractal pathway in a greater wholeness whose opening into being is furthered through the actualization of all creative occasions. The spiritual challenge is to fully actualize the pathway that is our own life, one lived in meaningful, loving relations to others but also free in its capacity to choose an untrod, unseen way.

Where intuition arises, in health and in a context of loving relations, Spirit prompts us to fully realize an individual capacity for excellence and spiritual illumination. This is the Great Work: to inspire growth and development and to enhance that growth with deep and genuine mystical insight into the creative foundations of all self-becoming. We are not alone in this process, we are co-creators along with a multitude of others throughout the generations who also valued creativity and healthy, individual attainments over conventional norms and well-trod pathways. The necessary ethic is one of peace, nonviolence, and creative respect that fosters permissive and flexible mental and emotional development without insisting on the narrow parameters of only one interpretive pathway. All these pathways are viable and reflect human capacity, the task is to be informed and capable of selecting those teachings best suited to the development of a higher awareness. This is an individual challenge, for children as well as adults. The undercurrent of authentic choosing is the cultivation of a meaningful ethics of relation, one that fully values the gifts and insights of others as an enhancement of species life. We are each free to choose and to break out of the narrower confines of inherited ideas and beliefs. We can also choose to hold on to those ideas and beliefs in a context of receptivity to others. As the heart opens toward those others, their thoughts, concerns, and aspirations matter and thus lead to a context of sharing and mutual growth.

Let Spirit guide, let the life force flow into thoughts, words, heart, and actions of nonviolence, to liberate every life from its contractions, sorrows, pains, and fears. (9.9)

Meditation: The goal is not simply personal enlightenment or illumination. It also includes working with others toward the fulfillment of their potential and capacity. In this process, the "postponement of illumination" may be a necessary feature of creative engagement in projects directed toward the alleviation of suffering, confusion, illness, or social needs that are paramount in transforming our collective circumstances. The alleviation of "sorrow, pain, and fears" is itself a creative occasion and such healing provides a basis for further developments often cramped and restricted by negative mental-emotive or social conditions. The transformation is mutual, though not identical: the healing of others is also a healing of self. It leads to a deepening wisdom and appreciation of the human condition and it shows us the shadowside of our own potential. By engaging in the processes of healing, by practicing a spiritual ethic of human concern and empathy, we engage Spirit in an authentic and dynamic way that creates a deepening reciprocity with the needs and aspirations of others. The ways of healing are many and highly diverse, requiring special training, study, and inner development. But the foundation of that healing process is a loving concern for others that opens itself to Spirit and seeks the most effective means for facilitating spiritual transformation.

A principled healing is one motivated first and foremost by a love of others, a genuineness of concern for their well-being and a genuine engagement with them as persons. This includes the principle that all animals are also "persons" and deserve equally our full compassion and humanity in treating them. Successful healing flows out of that motivating love through various channels of ability and technical expertise as the instrumental means by which spiritual motivation is actualized. Healing is not a technical skill, even though technical skills may be involved, for every skilled technician is first a person and then a person motivated by desires and aspirations that have a direct effect on the quality and success of their healing capacities. The most direct and powerful healing is a spiritual act of deep intention guided by natural potencies whose actualizations are inseparable from a developed psychic ability. This cannot be learned from the study of external techniques that obviate the value of subjective ability and inner development. The successful integration of learned technical skills need to be amplified and correlated with equally developed spiritual capacities that, in their fullest form, go far beyond technical skills. The materialist paradigm in healing is simply not adequate to the task of a full-spectrum healing that fully engages our wholeness as beings in a living and evolving cosmos.[62]

This is why spiritual development is a critical factor in the success of healing others. Its moves through natural, implicit capacities into an actualized, creative use of those capacities directly affecting others in an empathic way. These capacities reflect our primal, most grounded psychic abilities channeled through right-minded intentions and guided by Spirit for the well-being of others. The healing capacities of Spirit are profound and deep and far more capable of catalyzing direct transformation than any mechanical act of technical repair. But in a thoroughly materialized culture closed to such healing, it remains in the most nascent phase of its evolution and acts only in and through those few marginalized individuals most able to bear the responsibility of healing gifts in a context of collective denial. All the world seeks healing; every individual desires a more soothing, gentle means for living in complete health and radiant well-being. The needs we have for healing are great, and of central importance to our collective well-being. The most critical area of that healing lies in emotional health, in a healing of the turbulent currents of counter emotions and deep conflicts that give rise to violence, hatred, and indifference. The need is for a deeply spiritual healing, for the arising of a spiritual ethos dedicated to the healing of all the ills that divide and fracture the human communities.

The healing abilities are there, Spirit-given, as natural capacities working through individuals dedicated to the healing arts (including the art of prayer) for the good of others. The development of healing skills requires a high degree of self-knowledge and inner work to be a clear, positively motivated, healthy healer. The saying, "Physician heal thyself" is certainly a valuable guideline, but such healing requires a deep emotional and spiritual healing as well as appropriate habits in physical and sexual life. The concept of a "postponement of illumination" is a relative truth and must be tempered by a critical self-evaluation as to the degree of maturity and psychic health of the individual. To put it differently, a certain degree of illumination is critical and necessary for the actualization of deep healing. There must be real awareness and gnosis, some actual awakening to the reality of Spirit as a viable medium and presence. The degrees of gnosis are many and, as such, all coalesce in the cultivation of a loving attitude and a deep receptivity to personal transformation through spiritual disciplines and a creative life. While the higher degrees of gnosis constantly draw the sensitive psyche toward continued spiritual awakening, the actualization of creative engagement in worldly life also beckons. In the end, it becomes a matter of personal choice which tendency we choose to follow. But without doubt, the need for effective healing requires a mature balance between individual capacity, inner awareness, and outer expression.

The emphasis on individual development should not be undermined by an external pressure to engage in healing others. Some are much slower to develop than others and healing abilities may not manifest in a genuine spiritual life accept in minimul ways or they may manifest only very late in life. This is a matter of natural development guided by a lifetime of intentional living and spiritual commitment. The gifts of Spirit are many and diverse and only some of them involve healing—though every person may practice healing and contribute their abilities to healing the world communities. There is no absolute scale by which the abilities of others can be evaluated; these spiritual abilities are all relative and may reflect any number of gifts or capacities. Perhaps it is a gift for music or mathematics, for art or analysis, for imaginative story or poetry, or for technical innovation or skills. Whatever those gifts, their value lies in a capacity to contribute to the enhancement of what it means to be human in a deeply relational sense. To liberate life from contraction means to open ourselves to deeper, unrealized potentials that can enhance the quality and richness of living. The more open and developed we are as individuals, the more far-reaching and subtle the impact on others, an impact that has infinite variety in effecting transformation.

Each individual must find the balance between an authentic self-development and direct engagement in the transformation of others. The effects of transformation are found not just in actions or words, but also in subtle, less visible ways. As the life force flows with ever greater fullness and currency, it reaches out to link us with others we may never speak to or even meet. This is why so many reports exist about the "influence" of various spiritual individuals whose very presence is an inspiration and subtly impacting, even in a smile or simply in passing. This flow of current is a healing current, peaceful, deeply integrative, calm, yet dynamic, joyful and inspiring. The impact, Spirit-given, is not bound by ordinary four-dimensional space-time, but reflects a transpersonal influence quite capable of affecting others at great distance and far removed in generation and history. The subtle impact, for example of a Buddha or a Christ, resides in psychic potential that may blossom forth through archetypal encounters that are deeply transformative of individuals far removed historically from the original life of the progenitor. This is a spiritual principle: the manifestations of Spirit through individuals act as a matrix (or reservoir) through which others may access higher degrees of spiritual development in their own lives. We are being-in-relation and the creative occasions of others act to enhance the occasion that is our own creative life. Those occasions we chose as models or teachers will in part determine the degree and quality of our own development and engagement with the world. Therefore, we must choose carefully and in the light of understanding the needs of the world we inhabit those models best suited to its healing and transformation.

The Tenth Principle

The Tenth Principle of Spirit is solitude, calm, and repose; everything grows old, matures, deepens, and acquires the luster of age; this is natural and good—every death is a new beginning. (10.1)

Meditation: Death is transformation, not an end. The continuity of spiritual well-being precedes birth and extends after death just as the disequalibriums of life act to impede death and rebirth. Even though materialists may deny the reality of life-after-death, or life continuing through death, I see it every year when the leafless trees of winter sprout new leaves and the dead grass revives and the fields flower. I have already written that I do not regard the soul or psyche as eternal (or absolute) but as a relative continuity within the fabric of being. It can and does endure beyond one bodily lifetime. We must open our minds to the great continuities of nature and the natural capacity and potencies that allow even a very small part to reconstitute the whole as in genetic reconstitution. Spiritually, similar processes act on the psyche to invest it with a vision of the greater continuities beyond the death that act to preserve the psyche in a transformed state. What is preserved is not an image or an idea or essence, but a *complex* that coheres according to the quantitative experience and conditioned emotive-intellectual life of the individual. In a superficial sense, identity is preserved as memory; that is, the sense of self is conditioned by recurrent attitudes and beliefs engendered in the past and acting in the present to give coherence to ordinary awareness. But in a more complete sense, the "ego-identity" is no more than a persona over a deeper complex of qualities whose relative integration stems from core experiences garnered over many lifetimes.[63]

There is also "death in life" through very profound and powerful emotional experiences that can radically change a sensitive individual. The transformative stages in spiritual development are themselves part of the ladder by which we climb out of a narrow perspective and slowly learn to incorporate a vaster cosmos of beings, energies, and possibilities. These transformative experiences are often extremely powerful and grip the entire psyche with the energies of death and renewal insofar as the individual is able to choose those pathways most conducive to renewal and personal growth. Personal intentions toward growth and health are crucial to this process. Allowing emotional release and full consciousness of feelings is only a preliminary step toward making the necessary changes in life and attitude that will facilitate continued growth. Otherwise, there is a tendency for the more entrenched, habitual mentality to allow experience to propel it toward some repetition of past experience as the individual chooses not to face those inner challenges and clings to a more outmoded and regressive way of thought or belief. As in life so in death; by embracing the death experience (in life) we prepare ourselves for transformation in death that in turn may lead either to a repetition of old patterns or to an ongoing-within-Being toward a renewal of creative occasions.

This choice is not a function of the superficial ideas of the persona, as much as deep intentions springing from core attitudes and deeply ingrained habits. Those that live wholly in a materially bound framework can easily succumb to the illusion that life-after-death is nothing more than a reflection of ordinary life, that is, a perpetuation of the world in its most recognizable forms. Psychically, this is a source of profound illusion in after-death states where the individual reports nothing other than a direct continuity with the previous life in terms of form and appearance. The after death state is far more than an image of the personal psyche. It is an opening into vaster realms of experience that far exceed the normative life-plane and open to interdimensionality of the most arcane and esoteric kinds.[64] However, the normatively bound psyche of the fully conditioned and consensual, collective individual knows only that most recent incarnational world as a basis for any psychic realities. Thus are co-created representative worlds whose inhabitants vividly imagine the reality of their world as nothing less than equal to the incarnate present. And all the psychic contents of this world, in beliefs, attitudes, and mental patterns, are transferred there and reconfigured according to the deeper passions and attitudes of individuals to create an image of their own illusory containment—in some cases, severely limited by pathological tendencies, and in others, more normatively structured according to commonplace beliefs and personal idiosyncrasies. Subsequently, there is no real death, only transformations and the continuing processes of possible creative renewal.[65]

Facing death requires calm and acceptance. It requires a willingness to die and to go through the death experience as part of the ongoing continuity between this life and the next. Even with the hard-core materialist, death still requires calm and repose in valuing the experience as a final opportunity for insight and spiritual awakening to deep potentials. We can grow in dying and we can develop right in the moment of death by facing it with love and courage, both in ourselves and with others. It is perfectly natural to feel loss and pain and sorrow but these emotions should not blind us to the fact the life continues and change is an inevitable feature of the incarnate life, the very basis of growth and renewal. Out of sorrow and loss, we are challenged to find the continuity and current that leads to the next plateau, the one we have yet to reach in this lifetime, the one that beckons us past our sorrows and into new light and warmth. This transformation can be a form of healing and renewal, or it can drag the fearful into terror and deep confusion. The best preparation is a lifetime of effort dedicated to growth and the cultivation of a loving consciousness. Love is the great wave that can carry us through death and beyond. It is the love of others, our love for them, the love of Spirit, our receptivity to that boundless loving concern that animates nature and all becoming. In that loving current there is no fear, no anxiety, no dread or guilt or denial of self. There is only the positive current of creative self-becoming held in the embrace of a loving lifetime of devotion and service to the well-being of others, Spirit-inspired.

We all grow old, and it is our choice what the quality of our maturity will most clearly emulate: genuine spiritual commitments to higher values and simple, sincere living; or a less focused life increasingly contracted and removed from others and, in the end, isolated and seemingly alone. The "luster of age" is a spiritual luster that strips away all the ambitions and aspirations of a more youthful period and leaves only the marks and lines of a face joyful in being an instrument of even the smallest spiritual gift. There is a need for solitude, for reflection and quiet inner realizations of the mature life no longer in bloom but now heavy with the fruitfulness of creative actualizations. It is a solitude in preparation for death, a quiet waiting, by no means passive, but active with all the projects and creative joys of a slower and more well-paced activism. It is a time when the many strands of the past should be rewoven into a meaningful present rich in insights and understanding, integrating and progressively releasing what *was* for what *is becoming*. It is a time of more than memories; it is time for the most creative actions drawing on a full life of creative synthesis and long-term habits of inquiry and meditation. It is a time of ripeness, of fullness about to drop onto the earth and be renewed through a reseeding and a regrowing and not a simple repetition of the past. It is a time of dying and rebirth, a time of shedding skin and living with utmost sensitivity and humor.

> **Maturity is a gift of Spirit as is calm and repose; they are the fruits of compassion, love, and trust, the manifestation of depth, the immeasurable links between lives. (10.2)**

Meditation: Maturity is an expression of intentions realized, of actions producing fruit, of conscious aspiration fulfilled in real relations and attainments. It is not a function of idealizations or of intellectual theories divorced from actual practice and real transformations in growth and awareness. In many ways, maturity is a process by which the world and a personal vision of the world come together in synthesis and harmony. As a creative spiritual act, this synthesis requires more than intellectual or emotional commitment. It requires a willing surrender to Spirit, to a principled life whose core values direct self-transformation toward congruity and correspondence with the inner harmonies of Mystery and Being. These "harmonic values" are not fixed or predetermined within being but emerge in a species-determinative, often individual, way through well-intended actions, aspirations, and intentions. There is infinite variety, as in an expansive, microtonal musical scale that allows for a vast range of creative possibilities in fully exploring musical (and atonal) potential without denying the basic principles of harmonic resonance. Certain natural vibratory relations between notes, such as thirds, fifths, octaves, and other harmonic overtones, represent common structures within a wide variety of musical expressions. Between and among spiritual interpretations, there are various common principles and harmonies, such as nonviolence, compassion, love of divinity, kindness toward others, and so on, that represent shared principles between widely divergent faiths.

It is the actualization of such principles that leads to maturity because these actions result in deep correspondences with Spirit, with the life source, with the very heart of reality. Rather than living on the surface, in a material and superficial, immature sense ("at odds with self and nature"), we are called to actualize those potentials that will best bring us into accord with the creative principles by which life itself evolves and thrives. Maturity is a consequence of deepening correspondence with principles congruent with creative development and increasing awareness. Such correspondence brings us into maturity because we come to recognize our relationship, our resonance, within the Whole, with the deepest possible sources of empowerment and understanding. This type of maturity, spiritually based and evolved, is very important in illustrating what a principled life is, what a creative, loving person can be and do that contributes to the development of others in a convergent world of increasing challenge and confusion. Such maturity is by no means "all-knowing" and in fact may be quite simple, unpretentious, and dedicated to very down-to-earth concerns. It is neither lofty nor abstract in character, but is grounded in a loving presence and a caring sense of relation to others and to the healing and preservation of all beings, human or not.

Maturity may be imbued with understanding that is philosophical, aesthetic, intellectual, or esoteric; but that understanding is not itself maturity. The maturity comes through a well-integrated life that embraces all aspects of self in congruence with Spirit and lives to actualize those capacities in an exemplary, healthy way. There are many immature intellectuals, artists, and scientists whose accomplishments are quite remarkable and who reveal unusual gifts and abilities. Yet the full maturation of those gifts is not found in an overexaggerated attachment to a particular kind of thinking or creating, but through a capacity to bring those gifts to a rare synthesis of full humanity and deep spiritual values lived with integrity and great self-honesty. In that synthesis, the gifts find their appropriate place as expressions of spiritual capacity well-attuned to basic spiritual principles, creatively interpreted and succinctly lived within a context of positive, healing relationships with others. In some crucial ways, maturity is deeply inhibited through failing in our human relationships, regardless of our education, social background, or access to knowledge of any type. Maturity is not an "accumulation" but an *integration* that lifts awareness to a horizon in which other beings become the key to a more full and complete creative life. In this horizon, love is not a theory but a practice; compassion is not an idea, but an actuality that swells up and enwraps you and world in a spiritual embrace whose survival depends on free-will offerings of the heart, a healing touch, and a welcoming receptivity to the creative concerns of others.

In this process of maturation, "calm and repose" are a mark of a deeply rooted soul, one that knows how to draw nourishment and sustenance from the richest soil. This calm is not a function of enforced practices of meditation or the maintenance of a particular state or mental condition. It is more than a certain mental continuity; it is not a detachment from feeling or a consequence of suppressing affective states. This is a calm full of joy and inner light, a calm based in a sense of place and a response resulting from deep relaxation and a restful ease in carrying out day-to-day life. It is not always calm and in repose but that is the condition toward which it returns in an inner attunement with Spirit, no longer driven by the compulsion to know, but already knowing, already being-in-relation as the actualized continuity of the creative spiritual life. It is a calm concentration on the tasks at hand and a calm and repose in the midst of action and creative work. It is a calm arising from the perception that the full capacity has been engaged, that the gifts have been shared to the fullest extent without denying the need for renewal and restoration. It is a gift because it is not self-created (as those attached to spiritual disciplines might claim) but a manifestation of deep attunement with the stable inner currents within and through which the world coheres and makes sense. These spiritual currents are all about us and surround us constantly with the potential for a deep, luminous awakening.

By living a compassionate, trusting life with others, one free of betrayal or disloyalty (or healed of such), the fruits of that life manifest in natural congruency with age and the cycles of growth and development. It is impossible to force maturity on oneself or on others. At best, we can only model that ideal of maturity that represents our finest attainments and the fullest life expression of who we are and how we have chosen to live. This maturity is not found in the formulations of a social persona reflecting static images or superficial attitudes of maturity (such as a way of dressing or behaving, or a certain insouciance or a flouting of such codes). It is not based in an imitation of any kind, in adopted patterns of an ideal type, or in the embodiment of cultural icons (or images) representing an external appearance as a model of social accomplishment. Spiritual maturity comes from within, and may be conjoined with great innocence and openness to others. Or it may be more worldly through contact with others but not formed out of that contact, only enriched by interactions catalyzing insights intrinsic to a spiritual path. It is the spiritual path that acts to give form and character to personal development; the critical aspect is the spontaneous arising of insights based in authentic living according to principles and core values. These insights, when followed by genuine reformation of character based in the actualization of potential, lead to creative occasion in which new personality structures can emerge as indications of a maturing process of self-awakening.

The "manifestation of depth" is a progressive feature of such maturation, a continual deepening into Spirit, into Mystery, into full potential. There is a growing sense of connection and relation not only to others and the visible world, but also to the unseen worlds of those who have died or lived before, as well as to other spiritual beings who are part of the collective psychic spectrum. These various stratum reflect a diversity of worlds, beings, and visionary realities irreducible to material or physical causations. The "macrocosm" is a vast network of related beings whose powers differ dramatically from those of a more materially oriented individual. The visionary worlds, the mythic and imaginative structures of the world-soul, the creative potential of heightened states of awareness and psychic connectedness with the life forms of others far exceed the visible physical cosmos. The jewel-net is cast wide to a degree that the physical earth seems to be like a drop of animate water in a living ocean whose currents and rhythms we hardly know. Maturity in this context means a deepening familiarity with these currents and the complexity of worlds so interconnected and active in the less visible spectrum of ordinary consciousness. There is bliss and joy in the higher gnosis that contribute their presence to the mature soul, giving it radiance, potency, and a magical sense of wonder and amazement. And always, there is the Mystery that exceeds a hundredfold, even the most mature and spiritually advanced soul.

Death is not to be feared, it is only transformation; if life has been fluid, so is death; if stagnant, cathected, blocked, or denied, then death is terror or confused by fear and ignorance.(10.3)

Meditation: Dying is not easy! And the difficulty of dying is a consequence of a patterned way of living, a certain way of thinking, believing, or responding to crisis or threat. The least effective response is to close off, to suppress feelings or fears, to deny the threat or the anxiety, to live only in the surface personality. Such responses lead to a divided self, to a continual fracturing of self, to fragmentation as various aspects of life are continually bracketed out and left isolated from the developing core of identity. Dying is an art and a form of transformation leading to self-knowledge and integration in the positively minded. Many persons who throughout their life have denied life after death are assailed by severe doubts and questions when actually faced with dying, questions they refused to consider, which they bracketed out while living a busy, surface life. When death looms in the direct, personal sense the patterns of the persona, the surface life of day-to-day identity can be easily threatened. In pain, suffering, or anxiety it can be dissolved and collapse, leaving the individual with a rootless sense of uncertainty, fear, and no clear intentions whatsoever.

From the impact of this inescapable fact of death, the surface personality can disintegrate and all the stagnant, unresolved tensions of a lifetime of denial can pull the conscious identity into a realization of its fragmented, undeveloped inner tension. That realization can itself be suppressed, leaving only an empty sense of waste, ineffectualness, and in more severe cases, of meaninglessness and despair. This kind of dying reveals clearly the immaturity of the personality and its fragmentary condition held together only by a constant projection of surface ideas and unexamined collective attitudes onto the resistant forms of the world. There is no depth or understanding of inner motives, of the spiritual currents of self and becoming, of the need for love and growth beyond limited beliefs or acceptable social patterns. The psyche turned outward becomes only a mirror of social, collective identity and, as such, shares all the pathologies and limitations of that collective. In the collective there is a deep denial of death, of its power, its reality and transformative capacity to awaken us to new understanding and insights. Death is treated as something to be avoided, denied, not thought upon, horrific and frightening. In fact, death is nothing more than a transition not unlike the many deaths we have all died in suffering loss, trauma, or the sorrows of others.

The psyche turned inward in a self-awakened sense, as spiritually sensitive to the art of dying well, can intend a transformative death through various spiritual disciplines (such as various forms of meditation or prayer). A life dedicated to gradual, consistent, creative living, one grounded in spiritual values and positive relations, can engage the dying experience as yet one more horizon for developing insight and giving the final touches to all those loved and cared about in living. To carry beyond dying and into the after-death planes requires some training and experience in order to consciously direct the process toward a continuing positive development. Unfortunately, many people lack the necessary training and sensitivity and, having denied the relevance of death, are in no way prepared for the actual dynamics of suddenly discovering that there is, indeed, life after death. I do not wish to suggest that the spiritual ideal is to control the processes of death and rebirth as much as to suggest that deep intentionality, cultivated over a lifetime, has profound consequences. An important intentionality to cultivate is the intention to remain conscious and aware in all transformative occasions. To speak metaphorically, it is like the differences between one who wishes to cross a river and strikes out in a disciplined fashion to land at a specific spot on the other side; one who, while swimming well, lets the current carry him or her to whatever spot seems appropriate; and one who, not knowing how to swim, falls into unconsciousness only to revive, she or he knows not where or how.[66]

Often, the most common experience in dying is one of confusion subsequently resolved in a dawning realization that life-goes-on and that, in fact, death is only a marker between distinctive types of existence. The types are many and the qualities of those types are directly related to the attitudes and psychic condition of the dying. The "stagnant and cathected" life is a type lived in an inflexible framework of rigid ideas and deep resistance to alternative ways of thinking or believing, one closed to change except in a very narrow, predetermined sense. In such a life, death too is rigidly defined, reduced in scope, and made into a nonconsequence. But in the face of dying, something quite different occurs, suddenly the repressions of life are no longer a means by which experience can be controlled. Death comes, unbidden or unwanted, but it comes and does not turn back or relent in carrying out the task of transformation. No repression can stop it and no denial can refuse it entry into the very core of one's being. There is a deep intimacy in death because death claims the whole person, their whole way of being. Then it opens that way to new roads and possibilities, to unseen horizons that in turn may also be repressed as old states reassert control over individual perceptions and enclose them in the limited world of their own psychic complexes.

The denial of death and its affects is similar to the denial of dreams and their affects; dreams reveal real transformative capacity, pathways that might be taken, lessons that could be learned. Instead, dreams are denied, ignored, and bracketed out, and the contents are never contemplated or absorbed into a more conscious way of living. So too it is possible to deny the relevance of death and the dying experience, to choose unconsciousness, a drugged state, anything to diminish the reality of facing the visionary world of death. For in dying, we go truly into our dreams, deep, deep, into the very psychic fabric of our being, and, there, in complete ignorance of the psychic factors involved, we weave yet again the webs of our own self-delusions, attitudes, guilts, ambitions, and general illusory wants. Having denied the reality of dreams and visions, many dreamers cannot see their own making and unmaking of the world. They take the dream for reality, until, having exhausted the psychic tendencies and patterns, they emerge out of their dream and begin to glimpse, however slightly, the more extended complexity of the macrocosm. Long before they can begin to master the higher intentions of dreaming, they are drawn into the causal factors that impel yet another lifetime where ideals of control seem more accessible or various passions more desirable or where the currents of past actions lead to consequences far different than those imagined or sought.

The "fear and ignorance" in this process is largely self-generated and a product of repressed experiences consciously ignored or patterns so deeply ingrained as to be beyond the control of the individual. Many people have a very weak persona, a surface identity so fragile and ill-constructed that the slightest crisis results in psychic dissociation and disorientation. The powers of death are great insofar as they reflect the deep processes of Spirit in ongoing cycles of creation-destruction-recreation. These processes cannot be halted and every individual is subject to them without exception. And yet these processes only index an external means for regarding the cycles. On a deeper level, these cycles are an embodiment of continuity and preservation. Yes, there is death, and yes, there is life after death, and yes, there is rebirth and yet further lifetimes. What is crucial is not so much the cycles of transformation as the continuity that is preserved and sustained. The creative aspect of that transformation is the continuing emergence of creative expression and a deepening manifestation of Spirit, and thus of the Mystery of Being. The higher truths of that Mystery are found in the preservation of life, not its destruction; in patterns of transformation to new and emergent life forms, not in the suppression of alternatives, but in their transpersonal variety and multiform continuities.[67]

To live a fluid life, means to adapt, change, grow, and evolve over the course of an entire lifetime, right up to, and through, the moment of dying. Maturity is not about stagnation or a slippage into regressive states, as much as it is about continued development, creative mastery, and the epitome of attaining a full and complete sense of being. It may also involve casting off the unneeded and the no longer necessary, of getting rid of old baggage and attitudes or emotional attachments no longer conducive to growth. There is a purging that is part of the process. This purging helps us to stay fluid and less burdened by attachment to the past or, at times, to others. Aging with maturity means making the cuts that liberate energy and capacity from old patterns, youthful patterns, now become a burden on self-development. It means giving up attachments to appetites and habits used to cushion life, to dull it, and make it less sharp, less clear, and less interesting. It means investing life with enthusiasm and not letting the wonder and magic be dissolved in a truncated, isolated redundant tracking of old ruts worn deep into the psyche and making it an endless loop of static, uncreative living. Those same ruts will be the very channels that act to create deep intentions in dying and after; those ruts are the very reason why death is necessary. It is the creative means to break up the old complexes, attachments, and habits in order to allow for new growth and development. Death is a liberator and translator, a source of life and renewal, not a negation, but a means to yet another affirmation.[68]

To live in Spirit requires many deaths, none less great than the body's death or denial; affirm the body, affirm death, and accept the transformation coming; then there will be calm and joy. (10.4)

Meditation: The body undergoes constant death and renewal as cells slough off and new ones regenerate, yet the continuity of the body continues. We lose someone we love, a part of us dies, that part enlivened by their presence and love; yet we go on, carrying both the death and life of that person. We undergo spiritual transformations, we let go of old patterns, habits, attitudes, yet there is continuity. We experience illumination and higher states and see our entire identity in the light of a more comprehensive being, and yet there is still a sense of self, of conditional self-awareness. In all cases, there is continuity that incorporates the lesser into the greater by changing perspective, through seeing the part within the Whole. Death is an entry into wholeness, into a more complete awareness and into alternative phases of becoming intrinsic to the ongoing processes of creation. What is left behind is the bodily complex, a multitude of intricate systems correlated with the even more intricate systems of the psyche, the subtle structures of which are hardly known or recognized. And even these subtle systems undergo transformation in the after-death planes where the processes of recreation remold an individual identity in concurrence with deep intentionality, habit, and attachments.

Bodily life, passion, feeling, sensation, appetite are all tremendously powerful and attractive; the very fabric of creation is focused in the synthesis of Spirit manifesting through natural potencies in innumerable life forms. There is no spiritual reason that we should not affirm the joys and capacities of bodily life, fully and completely. I regard monastic ideals as creative occasions for spiritual develop-

ment and as a basis for living a valuable life. But I do not believe
that they are the highest or best ideals for spiritual development.
They give more focus and purposely direct attention away from bodily life, but in a superficial sense. In a deeper sense, they only create
a schism and a denial of the creative incarnational processes of real
beings. The incarnate life is the means by which the potential of a
spiritual ideal is actualized; it is a testing ground for development,
and the means by which thoughts and beliefs become concretely
manifest in the actual and real sense. Only when the full capacity of
the idea or ideal is made real in the world is its deeper potency revealed. This means making the bodily life fully spiritual in the
world, in marriage, in sexual relations, in love and child care, in passionately seeking to realize actual creative occasions in the direct
physical sense.

The hermetic-gnostic ideal is the transformation of matter into
more subtle, potent, spiritual forms, not the denial or rejection of
matter in the archaic dualist sense. The so-called mind-body dualism is an artifact of a certain kind of thinking that either rejects the
body as an insufficient vehicle for higher spiritual attainments, or
rejects the spirit as a phantasmic projection of a strictly material existence. Neither of these views is adequate in articulating the complex relationships between the "physical and the psychic," which are
deeply intrinsic to each other and highly dependent on dynamic, interactive processes of evolution. When we drop the dualistic model
and fully embrace a relative, process view in which the greater continuity of the Whole is reflected in every part, then bodies become a
means for the actualization of the Whole through the development of
specific abilities and attributes. These bodies are intrinsically related to each other through ideas, feelings, intuitions, and empathy
such that their collective emotive-mentality in a complex field of relations supports the emergence of newness through specific, shared
actualizations. This means, real persons attaining real states and insights, real accomplishments as manifestations of spiritual principles under appropriate conditions for actualizing potential. This is a
complex web, not a simple dualism.

To "affirm the body" means to affirm the value of living a physical
life limited by actual physical and material conditions but not reducible to those limits or conditions. It means to affirm spiritual principles whose manifestations occur in and through the material world
in its transformation to a more spiritualized plane of coexistence. By

the phrase "more spiritualized" I mean a worldview that fully affirms the value of physical life in the light of principles capable of transforming the world. Like the caterpillar into the butterfly, this transformation is long and complex and involves psychic transformations inseparable from bodily existence in the physical world. But the physical structures of that world are malleable and subject to reformation and the alchemies of induced creative changes through a more Hermetic understanding of principled living. We hardly recognize these processes and our understanding of them is in the most nascent phase. We have yet to heal the divisions of the old dualisms and the old antagonisms between "spirit and matter." In the future, the transformative perspective will be based in a profound understanding of spiritual and psychic principles whose manifestations can elicit transformations in the most direct physical sense.[69] As in the transformation of "wine into water," the old destructive powers of a material physics must be reintegrated with a new, creative metaphysics of transformation engendered through a lucid, clear recognition of the role of bodily life as a basis for spiritual transformation. And spirituality must be seen as an intentional and principled life that gives direction and capacity to bodily transformations. And death is one of those transformative experiences, one that grips the bodily life and draws from it the yet unfulfilled potentials of an even more complete awakening. The web of life, the supportive matrix that makes such development possible is there also in death. It is not the life of one soul that matters, but the web of soulfully related beings that sustain the life processes on more subtle planes of being and becoming. Life on those planes is also transformative and nonstatic; it leads to a prompting to go on, to continue the process of immersion in the life fields, from more subtle planes to less subtle planes. Working constantly within the process of change, every plane has its own constitution and boundaries, but none are absolute and all are capable of transformation through focused, spiritual intentions. And all planes, worlds, dimensions, are interrelated and causally connected, though some only in the most tangential ways.

In the human world of real incarnate beings, the spiritual life is an adventure in exploring potentials that lead to an awakening of ability and understanding no longer restricted to a purely material model. That model is fully capable of being transformed without denying all the positive insights that have been generated out of it through a more limited but rigorous logic or methodology. So too in

death. The model of a physical life form lacking any continuity beyond dying is only a limited perspective bound by a certain rigid way
of thinking. In actuality, even the most hard-core atheist, utterly
convinced of the nonreality of life after death has nothing more defi-
nite than the strength of his or her convictions. There is no means
for proving the truthfulness of those convictions. An affirmation of
nonexistence may be highly illusory because it serves the needs of
the alienated believer. On the side of those convinced of life beyond
death, there is a wealth of clinical, philosophic, and spiritual litera-
tures describing various features of what the life beyond might be or
become. And there is direct witness testimony of millions of individuals who attest to some direct experience of those realms from the
earliest historical records to the present. My own beliefs are based
directly on personal experiences of those realms and the many encounters I have had with those who have died and yet still live.[70]

From the point of view of the collective mental and imaginative
worlds, there is also a wealth of information in stories, encounters, images, and archetypal visions resulting in profound transformations.
And death is part of all this, part of the process on every level of being
by which we undergo psychic development and leave behind the petrified worlds of our earlier beliefs or respectfully lay down the fossilized
inheritances of past generations. The afterworlds are not fixed within
being, they are evolutionary horizons, planes in which continual
transformation occurs and where nothing is static. These visionary
worlds are also subject to change and interactions within the webs of
life, they too are places of creative occasion and ongoing development.
There are no sharp divisions that keep these various worlds separate
and uninfluenced by other related worlds, particularly those of the
human scale, all reflections of the *Mundus Imaginalis*. Like a Tibetan
world mandala, these planes and realities are all projections of mind,
very powerful projections that cannot be extinguished by denying
them intellectually. Like the world mandala, each part, each realm,
has its place within the Whole and acts as a balancing realm to give
full expression to spiritual potentials. Death is the guardian at the
threshold that tests us and acts as the gate through which we must
pass in order to more fully explore those alternative worlds.[71]

**Solitude is healing, renewal, rest, and relaxation;
it is creative regeneration, a time of reflection,**

prayer, and reconsiderations; a time to redress
the past through present relations. (10.5)

Meditation: Solitude is an important part of spiritual growth
and forms an essential practice for the development of insights and
intuitions by creating a quiet and a calm receptive to subtle impressions. In the development of psychic abilities, in the more sensitive
person, the usual stimulus of ordinary life is overwhelming. The inflow of impressions, the psychic impact of others, noise, collective vibration, energy fields from a variety of electromagnetic sources, and
the continual booming and buzzing of daily life, all act to constantly
externalize or agitate the psyche. The "still voice" of Spirit is too easily lost in an outward mélange of impressions, demands of others,
and the complex responsibilities of a busy, engaged life. In developing psychic ability, the present collective mentality tends to flow in
recurrent patterns that restrict and often deny the viability of spiritual sensitivity. Those with pronounced psychic awareness find it
difficult if not impossible to maintain the clarity of their sensitivities
without frequent periods of withdrawal and solitude in which they
can reknit and clarify the inner voices of developing psychic ability.
In the mature psychic life, time alone and apart is a crucial part of
being fully aware and in touch with the promptings of subtle impression and the more far-reaching impressions of the psyche. There
is a need to pull back from the continual stimulations of others and
the impact of external stimulations of all types, from the sounds, vi-
brations, and multiple energies of modern life.

The value of solitude is its capacity to provide a time for introspection, self-analysis, and a more careful attending to perceptions
and a range of psychic impressions through visions and dream experiences. This time is not merely a time of self-absorption, though a
certain degree of focused, ongoing self-analysis is highly valuable. It
is also a time for clarifying the relationship to Spirit as a conscious
intentional relationship in which one cultivates (through various
disciplines or practices) an open receptivity to the Mystery and presence of Spirit. Practices such as meditation, prayer, visualization,
chanting, and other spiritual arts require a certain degree of solitude
to fully actualize their value. In being alone, one is able to open more
fully to the spiritual reality of the path and to actively seek renewal
and restoration of attunement with the primal sources of spiritual

well-being. The noisy distractions of the world are set aside and periods of solitude created as a means for deepening sensitivity and increasing receptivity to more subtle and far-reaching impressions. Such times are crucial for deepening inner awareness and are a normal feature of most spiritual paths. Attention is withdrawn from external relations and refocused through psychic sensitivities that bring the seeker into better alignment with his or her own developing capacities. The process of honing psychic and spiritual perceptions is a critically important part of the spiritual life and in a process of maturation should be a regular part of the life pattern.

Solitude also provides a time for "rest, renewal, and relaxation" in a context where there can be a complete letting go of external relations. This letting-go allows the psyche to reduce its more nervous and overstimulated excitations and return to a state of more settled calm and inward focus. The processes of creative development require a constant ability to relate the external happenings of the world to a clear, inward-focused perspective in order to gain a relative sense of the meaningfulness of those external events. The template is not the imposition of worldly life on the individual, but the transmutation of worldly life in the crucible of spiritual sensitivity and creative ability. Neither the world, nor the collective, nor other individuals can determine the qualitative response and spiritual interpretation of the seeker. Such interpretation is the very heart of the spiritual path and each individual has a responsibility to engender that interpretation through self-selected processes of spiritual development. In periods of rest and renewal, the psyche clarifies, like turbulent water settling into a still, lucid calm, bringing into focus higher values and perceptions in order to more clearly evaluate experience and worldly life. Solitude and quiet is the appropriate context for mature self-reflection as well as reflection on external relations and the actualization of higher goals.

Without a regular and periodic renewal through solitude it is all too easy to become swept up in external relations to a degree that thoroughly obscures and masks the inner potential. The "creative regeneration" of these regular times alone allows for natural processes of healing and spiritual renewal by opening inner sensitivities to new directions and psychic impulses that seek expression along lines of development often missed by a more routinized, external intentionality. The psyche has its own wisdom, a deep inner sense of direction or purpose distinct from the conscious intentions adopted by the surface persona. In solitude, the externalized social-self can be dropped or backgrounded to a more focused intent to fully actualize inner directedness to creative goals less shaped by the "outer world" and more shaped by inner spiritual impulse. Letting go of the rational mind is very important because the rational mind is a very limited aspect of full consciousness. The social persona, functioning under the influence of more rationalized demands, can reach only a limited sphere of actual spiritual capacity. In solitude, we can let go of those rational demands and drop the social logic of collective behavior for a more personalized, individuated, creative exploration of potentials. The limitations of "social logic," often functioning through lowest common demoninators and entrenched social patterns, cannot provide the necessary context for a personalized realization of psychic and spiritual ability.

We each need to learn to step back from our social and familial obligations and entanglements in order to give time and space for emergent perceptions and ideas. In quiet and calm, it is possible to examine more carefully past relationships and events and to understand their effects in the present. Such reflections on past relations gives a context for adapting to present relations by providing insights based on having seen ways those past relations may have been improved through more mature behavior and self-expression. The personal past is part of who we are in the present and reflecting on that past provides a context for reassessing behavior and motivating changes in the present. We are only "products of the past" when we refuse to look carefully into that past as means for creative transformation; not only to look, but to enact new ways of relating or envisioning our own responsibilities in the present. The past is a resource for personal growth as we learn from it by adopting new strategies and ways of improving the quality of our relationships to others. It is a resource for understanding our own limits, biases, and more youthful illusions. Failing to integrate that past with the present can only lead to a divided psyche whose more immature aspects remain a constant source of tension to the deeper self. Following a spiritual path means to take full responsibility for spiritual development, now, in the past, and in the future, up to and through dying and beyond.

Solitude should be more than a remedial rest and slowing down, it should promote a deeper awareness that dissolves the tensions of social existence and allows for a full surfacing of inner direction and motivation. Such periods of renewal should be a regular and a disciplined part of a spiritual path. To be more than remedial, they must engender a sense of spiritual intimacy that fully affirms the value of the life path or suggests ways in which that life path should be moderated or redirected in order to attain higher realizations. These periods of renewal should open fully to the "still quiet voice" whose speaking directs us to engage our whole being with Spirit, to the cultivation of inner awakening, and the luminous realizations of presence. The "presentiments of Spirit" may occur at any time or place or circumstance, but certainly, time alone is a vital period to cultivate such presentiments. The more sensitive we are to such presentiments in the privacy of our retreats and withdrawals from social life, the more apt we are to attend to those impressions in a more public sense. There is a special sensitivity that must be cultivated, an acuity of spiritual perception that allows for the manifest world to become a carrier of psychic impressions unobscured by social interactions—a clarity or clarion call that breaks through the social condition and reveals a depth of presence transforming the ordinary into a more-than-ordinary occasion, one filled with Spirit and heard by those capable of hearing beyond the normative chatter of ordinary thought. Such an ability is cultivated in time alone, in solitary listening, in prayer, mediation, and spiritual disciplines meant to heighten such hearing.

Share your thoughts and reflections if you desire, or choose silence and inner peace; do not be driven by the past; make peace, see your shortcomings and your gifts, give thanks for both. (10.6)

Meditation: Following a spiritual path does not mean teaching others or trying to persuade them of the value of your own practice or tradition. The most valuable teaching is through example and quality of life, not through persuasive rhetoric. Personally, I see no value in aggressive proselytizing or forcing one's views on others; and I see a great egoism in those who feel called to such activities. There is an unhealthy, aggressive tendency whose justification comes through collective assent and a feeling of personal empowerment built around the self-righteous collective claims of those who act to embody that assent. It is as though the number of believers determines quality or truthfulness (an unjustifiable claim) and as though spiritual development were built around the externalization of teachings as their full realization. In a disciplined path of self-development and creative engagement with a continually emergent spirituality, the realization of teachings is embodied in a higher-quality life and a deeper inwardness that fully respects the differences and uniqueness of each person. There is no urge toward conformity in this kind of spiritually individuated path, only the willingness to share ideas and insights with those who themselves initiate dialogue or interaction.

Spiritual seekers should be receptive to others, should make themselves available to others as a way of enacting an ethic of compassionate, caring love. But they should resist the inclination to assert their beliefs outside of a community of like-minded, interested others. The teaching is the embodiment of spiritual principles as a way of life, one whose qualities and fullness can act as a channel for creating relationships with others in a spontaneous, natural way. The "community of Spirit" is built inwardly and develops through principled living and sharing among those whose development acts to create positive influences and relations in the world around them, quietly, without excessive notions or dramas. The life of such a community is a consistently internalized effort to actualize the creative circumstances that will best result in a positive influence through community offerings and projects open to noncommunity members. All such relationships are dialogical, that is they engage in motivated relationships on the basis of shared concerns and goals and not by trying to substitute one's own goals for the goals of another. Those who choose a more silent path, one of inner peace and solitude are in many ways the best examples of such a community; and yet those more active and engaged in relating to others through spiritual dialogue are also important. There must be a balance between inwardness and outwardness, a synthesis that allows for both attuned with cycles of nature and longer and shorter periods of engagement and solitude.

In finding this balance between the inner and outer life, it is important not to be "driven by the past" in which everyone has made occasional poor choices or errors in judgment. We are not perfect beings and we should not strive for perfection. The goal is self-development and a qualitative life and not some image of an abstract ideal type. As limited, fallible human beings we all are subject to error and poor judgment and this is normal and often, unescapable, an intrinsic part of life by which we can learn through our own mistakes and self-centered decisions. First, we must recognize our poor choices, the mistakes or bad judgments; then we can reflect on those circumstances and seek the deep roots and origins in poorly formed habits or attitudes of mind. We must seek to reform those habits and overcome the negative tendency and allow ourselves to feel remorse, shame, or guilt if those feelings honestly stem from a realization of shortcomings. But then, having made the necessary changes, having actualized the reformed pattern and moved beyond a destructive or negative tendency, we must also let go of the guilt or shame and purge ourselves of attachments to negative emotion and self-doubt or unnecessary self-criticism. The clear, lucid mind moves beyond the reformation of character without denying the imperfections and destructive tendencies but is no longer attached to them or to the after-shadows. Without releasing these imperfections through positive growth and transformation, there will be a continual pressure to justify present actions based in past motives.

The present motives of present actions should stem from a clear integration of spiritual principles no longer held as a consequence of less mature motivations. The truthfulness of motives can only be known by a long and continuing look at all those shadow aspects of self that are so often projected into spiritual goals. Desire for the recognition of others, being seen as a model, the desire for personal power, the need to feel loved or appreciated—these and many more such motives often underlie the externally motivated self. The authenticity of the spiritual life can often be seen in the quiet, subtle influences that flow out of a person no longer enwrapped in either their personal past or their accomplishments. In this circumstance, it is important for the individual to know his or her "shortcomings and gifts" and not just one or the other. To know them in the light of a higher understanding, reveals the similar contours of others and results in acceptance of those conditions as natural features of any spiritual path. We all have our shortcomings and gifts. We each have our peculiar problems and struggles; we each have the capacity to move beyond those tendencies and into a more integrated, more spiritually luminous life. Some of this transformation we do for ourselves, Spirit-guided, and some we do with the help and love of others. Progressively, we can liberate past cathected energies and live more freely and more completely without attachment to that past or its shortcomings.

Why must we "give thanks" for both our shortcomings and gifts? Because in seeing both we see the real limits of our human condition and become sensitive to the struggles of others because we know those struggles within our own lives. Our shortcomings are a bridge to the suffering of others who also struggle to overcome past habits and failings. We should see these tendencies, desires, even in brief moments of possible behavior rejected, as a link with the very same tendencies that become actual in the lives of others. Anger, fear, hate, greed, lies, distortions, deceptions, misdirection, holding back, sloth, indifference, ignoring the needs of others are capacities within each of us. We need only attend very carefully to all that passes within us, however brief or momentary, to see real examples of human capacity. Sometimes in empathy with others, it is possible to feel what they feel and the intensity of such feeling is often loaded with negative contents and distortions of all types. These negative contents are not permanent features of psychic life but more an upsurge of collective tendencies and ingrained patterned responses. Each of us is a carrier of possible collective, undifferentiated, prejudicial response and the development of the individual in creative spiritual life is to work through those tendencies and to move beyond them through recognition and insightful understanding.

This means seeing the human capacity within oneself, seeing through the eye of the heart and through purifying motives and intentions to recognize the actual condition under which most human beings live. Sorrows, anxieties, intense emotional flux or rigid, fixated ways of thinking and feeling—all this is in us and needs healing. Through gradual maturation and processes of spiritual transformations it is possible to reach an open, loving state of receptivity to others and yet preserve a sense of integrity and difference as expressive of the creative occasion of our own personal life. This is a lifelong process and has no necessary end or conclusion other than that expressed through positive human relations and creative actions in the world. The "community of Spirit" is an ongoing process of natural development conjoined with intentional values and principled living and within that community individuals are at different stages of maturation. Yet each individual can contribute to the maturation of others through authentic relations and genuine caring, each individual can improve and develop one's own maturation by being receptive to the insights of others, younger or older. To do this, it is necessary to feel within one's own life the reality of the other and the realness of the other's struggle. In this way we prepare the ground for deeper and more peaceful realizations of the interplay of limits and potential, all as occasions for enhanced creative insights.

Self-knowledge sees the boundary, the horizon beyond, and knows the strength of the aspiration; it does not take comfort falsely, nor does it blame unnecessarily the weaknesses within self or others. (10.7)

Meditation: In following a spiritual path it is important to move beyond self-doubt and skepticism, beyond blame and fault-finding, while still retaining a certain critical ability. Dropping these negative tendencies requires seeing clearly one's own limits and accepting those limits as the creative ground within which transformation is possible and actual through committed, principled living. Intellectual skepticism and rational dismissal of ideas inconsistent with a particular way of thinking are more an impediment to spiritual life than an aid because such habits tend to be rooted in a defensive mentality closed to alternative ways of conceptualizing or cognizing the world. Too often, skeptical intellectuals are highly defended against alternative ways of thinking or envisioning a life path and overly identified with the social position that their "view" represents in the context of institutional affiliations or its link to culturally normative paradigms. But spirituality is not about culturally sanctioned ways of thinking or institutionally approved, collective consensus. It is about individuation, creative living, genuine human relationships, maturity in loving, and a deepening direct, personal transformation inspired by all the diverse and manifold possibilities within Spirit. In such a context, doubt too easily becomes an index of personal limitations and skepticism a reflection of intellectual rigidity.

Most human beings "take comfort falsely" through identification with collective norms, or by forming subgroups that reinforce particular views or attitudes toward living and co-relationships. Spirituality is largely about the search for authenticity and for a more authentic, genuine way of life rooted in positive spiritual values and less identified with overt cultural or collective norms. Specifically, it involves identifying and then actualizing those values most conducive to a higher quality of life and those more subtle states of awareness and illumination consistent with that quality of life. In order to do this, it is often necessary to break away from collective norms and subgroup identifications because of the many ways in which such identifications limit or inhibit continuing spiritual development. In growing older, this process of development requires an ever-deepening commitment to that higher-quality life, no longer inhibited by others and no longer caught in the critical denial of others (or in tail-chasing self-doubts or introjected blame). Always, we are thrown back on our own resources, onto the inner quality of life intrinsic to genuine spiritual transformation, onto the very inmost presence of Spirit active in motivating alternative ways and means to the realization of full potentials. To embrace that inner resource we must let go of our skeptical, denying, doubtful tendencies and move beyond the limiting criticism of others in order to open ourselves to the full spectrum of possible spiritual manifestations.

It is always important to see the boundary and to see the horizon beyond that boundary; seeing our limits as well as the limits of others is only a first step. Always there are horizons beyond any specific state of limitation; but to reach that horizon we must first recognize the limits and respect those limits. We must seek the creative means for transforming that boundary into a less resistant and more receptive condition permitting the inflow of spiritually creative energies. This takes a certain willingness to let go of limits that may be defensive, seemingly self-protective, or habitual in maintaining a certain posture in the world at large or with certain others. All these inhibit and contract the spiritual potentials; skepticism, doubt, intellectual systems of all kinds become inhibitions to genuine, creative development. Spirit overturns these systems, dissolves doubt, shows skepticism to be a pale shadow and an empty, formless resistance to new possibilities and directions. Certain emotional states, emotional patterns and habits, also become barriers to development by inhibiting the arising of greater diversity and complexity of feelings linked to the development of others. Emotional excess becomes a form of defense and a resistance to a more subtle, nuanced awareness whose many emotional tones cover a panorama of subtle perceptions normally blocked by excessive and limited emotional development. Our limits are the inhibitions and defenses we construct, intellectually, emotionally, aesthetically, or psychically to defend against the constant challenge to grow and evolve.

The "strength of the aspiration" is a means by which the limits are overcome. The cultivation of a deep and permanent desire for spiritual awakening and illumination is a positive, creative intention whose affects are the means by which we become more aware of Spirit. Such an awareness flows out of a deep center of individual spiritual aspiration through connectivity to the more subtle creative energies and currents through which Spirit acts to engender more conscious, aware being. This aspiration is something more than "belief in things unseen" as grounded in direct personal experience and self-development. We are all engaged in processes of maturation, and those processes involve a gradual (yet sometimes sudden) awakening to meaning and significance in life that, at a younger period, may have escaped notice or attention. Our maturation is guided by intentionality, by the values we hold, the goals we work toward, the quality of life we enact, the meaningfulness of our relations with others, the care we take to establish our way of life. All these evolve through conscious intentions. Spiritually, these are the means through which aspirations are realized. The aspiration for the full realization of potential is grounded in real-life habits and practices and not simply in ideas or intellectual insights.

The "strength of the aspiration" is a reflection of our intent and focus are on maximizing our potential as spiritual beings. It resonates through every aspect of life and relation to others and is not part of some bracketed arena of actions or closet disciplines, nor is it restricted to patterned social or religious behaviors. Such aspiration pervades the entire life way of the individual and infuses it with a qualitative awareness of spiritual values in every circumstance and acts to direct energy toward those patterns most conducive to continued spiritual awakening. Every step forward in development is a realization of that aspiration. The fulfillment of such an aspiration does not lie in some remote time or in future rewards or an enlightened state, but in the immediacy of daily life brought ever more consistently into alignment with inner spiritual values. A deep belief in Spirit is best gained through the immediacy of real living and not in simply embracing a code of beliefs. No one need believe in Spirit to initiate his or her own path of transformation but there should be a receptivity to the possibilities of Spirit in an open universe of alternative spiritualities. As the seeker progresses on the path, values and beliefs change and evolve, aspiration clarifies, develops, and becomes more focused and effective in initiating the appropriate changes in behavior and understanding. It is a present-centered process, a creative ongoing that works to actualize the creative occasion in real changes and transformation.

In developing spiritual maturity, aspiration becomes the central burning light that continually tests and unmasks habituated ways of thinking, acting, or believing. Specifically within one's self, and less critically in others, each person must formulate the goals specific to the full content of his or her aspirations. Love endures where criticism flounders over the boundaries between diverse perspectives; love opens the way between critical perspectives and creates a context for further development where criticism alone often divides and sterilizes possible creative relations. The acceptance of divergent goals and intentions is part of the creative process, and a more loving support of the healthy aspirations of others is better than a merely critical analysis of their insufficiencies or shortcomings. Within one's self, the ability to think critically is important and necessary but it is not the primary means by which one attains a more spiritually full life. Such attainment is accomplished through a deep loving concern, a recognition of limits, and a creative, imaginative engagement with a wide variety of persons and projects for the transformation and awakening of potential. In that process, critical thought has a role less central to processes of maturation than the more central values that further positive, creative relationships and a flexible, well-intended aspiration for a qualitative life of excellence. Spiritual knowledge can open the horizons of being and becoming in gentle, positive ways fully affirming the views of others without in any way denying the value of personal insight or accomplishment. In this opening, critical evaluations are secondary to qualitative living and genuine tolerance and inner flexibility.

We are partial, incomplete, unfinished, not fully realized, not all we might become; our goodness outlives us, our ignorance as well, but this is always true, even for the spirit-filled. (10.8)

Meditation: As partial, limited beings who have varied gifts and abilities, there is always the possibility that we can actualize yet other facets of our capacity. However old we are, whatever the degree of spiritual accomplishments, there is always potential for yet further development; and simultaneously, we can find rest in attainments accomplished and goals achieved. Spiritual accomplishments are by no means limited to the attainment of certain states or a specific qualitative being; these accomplishments may infuse all aspects of life and be reflected in the development of an extremely wide range of skills and abilities. Some may be more mystically inclined while others are less so; some may have more pronounced psychic abilities and others more pronounced analytical or philosophical skills; others may be healers, or teachers, or esoteric masters of ritual. None of these is superior to any other. As gifts, these abilities reflect the density of being in its particular manifestations and every gift as a capacity for enhancing the value of the Whole. What is common to all is a shared ability to engender loving concern and kindness in all our relations with others. "All our relations" includes life in all its various, multiple forms, particularly in its animal manifestations. And it includes loving the earth and valuing nature and the natural world as the grounding reality of our most profound concerns.

The spiritual path is never complete. It is an ongoing process of maturation that continues to and through dying and on into alternate states and conditions. In this process, there are stages of accomplishment and degrees of attainment that some may master to a higher degree than others. But that process of mastering is only an external index relative to the spiritual truths and teachings of others. In the context of a larger universe, these various degrees are secondary to an authentic value-centered way of living and relating. High degrees of mystical experience may or may not result in such a well-lived life of mature human relationships and may or may not clarify the understanding of others in a deeply intuitive and empathic way. A way of living may manifest without mystical experience or with only limited accomplishments in understanding the more esoteric features of esoteric thought and spirituality. In a well-rounded spiritual path, all aspects of our humanity are a possible means for spiritual development; according to circumstances, a variety of means should be pursued as potential pathways for creative occasions. The limits are the ones we choose or recognize as necessary to give focus and accomplishment to the pathways followed. Our capacity within a given lifetime is limited by many factors, psychically, historically, and culturally. Certain potentials are likely to evolve more easily than others in any given circumstance. These natural capacities should act as a basis for further development but should not act as impassible barriers to the mastery of other abilities. Always we can stretch out and develop, however slowly.

In living well, "our goodness outlives us" in the sense that we leave an impression and make an impact on others through positive, loving relations. The manifestation of that goodness goes on acting as a creative resonance within the collective potential, vibrant with the possibility of actualization in the lives of others. To the degree we are able to communicate the inflow of spiritual potency into our own lives, that potency can act on others to stimulate in them new currents of manifestation and continuity. These currents are shared through intentional connections in which we find inspiration and direction in the work and achievements of others. Those connections are not simply mental or emotional, but also spiritual insofar as we are able to find the currents through which Spirit is maximized in qualitative living. These spiritual currents are the interconnective medium through which species transformation is actualized in real beings whose relationships are conducive to the shared stimulus of a multitude of spiritual influences. The "web of relations" is very broad and complex and cannot be restricted to any one tradition or pathway. The "goodness" manifesting through these pathways are primary resources for the betterment of all human beings. Wherever we look, there are possibilities for enlightenment and illumination; every spiritual path has something to contribute, some nuance or development worthy of exploration and based in the lives of committed human beings who exemplify worthy spiritual goals.

But none of these paths are finished or complete in an absolute sense; each is relative to the values of other paths and each rises to the realization of relative ideals. There are real goals and ideals that can be fulfilled on any spiritual path, but those goals and ideals are also capable of development and transformation. Our "ignorance outlives us" because even in the most developed spiritual traditions, there are limits, errors, inappropriate emphases, exculsivism, marginalization, and sometimes out-and-out denial of the spiritual rights of others (both within and outside of those traditions). All ideal types are capable of embodying error or misjudgment. Like the negative pole of an archetype, there is a shadow side to every teaching that can distort or obscure something unfinished or incomplete in the more orthodox interpretations. Even the making of an orthodox perspective becomes a matter of sifting and evaluating all that might contribute to a collective view of the teaching and then rejecting what creates tension and disagreement. In such a case, much that is authentic is lost and much that is worthy and valuable is distorted or transformed into something less and less meaningful or accurate. The "ignorance" is the limit where the teaching becomes unsatisfactory or inadequate in answering genuine questions relative to real circumstances of need and aspiration. No teaching can answer all questions and it is a vain ideal to present a spiritual teaching as anything other than a relative truth. Our ignorance is far greater than either our collective wisdom or maturity, and our beliefs about the nature of reality far from accurate or complete.

The road we are traveling to collective wisdom is hundreds of thousands of years long, and includes all human creative efforts and insights in a cosmos of great complexity and subtlety. Our spiritual pathways are unfinished, our maturation is advancing only very slowly and our collective and individual understanding is limited by incomplete and partial truths that many take to be absolute and unquestionable. The overturning of these partial truths for more comprehensive insights and synthesis gives rise to an increasing pluralism and relativity that can easily fail to see the value in these older, less flexible teachings. Yet these teachings are also part of the inheritance of past individuals whose understanding often exceeded, in many ways, the shallow materialism of the present. We must learn to winnow from the past all that is good, valuable, and reflective of genuine spiritual accomplishments. Holding those values and teachings as part of an ongoing inheritance, we must then seek to add our own quantum of insight to the opening horizons of the future. These horizons are vast and complex and the cumulative teachings of past and present generations are not adequate for a full understanding of those horizons. These horizons are emergent, creative manifestations of Spirit still far from the full expressiveness of both the deepest Mysteries of Being, and even of human becoming in such a multidimensional cosmos.

Yet we may attain to illuminations in Spirit that reveal that Mystery in real contours of actuality for the benefit of others and thereby lift the veils in order to reveal yet more possible horizons awaiting exploration. In the past these veils have been lifted to reveal a multitude of spiritual pathways, all of which reflect some authentic facet of the Mystery. But always that Mystery exceeds our human understanding even while catalyzing the most profound realizations of its potential. In that process, each individual has a potential for realization that can attain to such a "knowing" that they find rest, peace, and finality in their search. Such is the nature of spiritual life to attain to some central isle, some centric point in the mandala of a spiritual awakening that acts as a pivot for all further expression and realizations. These "points of light" are found in the lives of real individuals whose attainments have maximized spiritual potential to the utmost without limiting the possible horizons of future realizations. Such points are also found in the transformative moments of real spiritual awakening and illumination that act to guide and direct individual life toward fulfillment and inner peace. Hermetic-gnostic illumination is one affirmation by which a spiritual consciousness is evolved and completed in a relative, transformative becoming. Growth and maturity remain open-ended insofar as alternative potentials can be developed in the light of those illuminations as an ongoing awakening of potential. The illuminative matrix is boundless; its application, inexhaustible; its manifestations, beyond counting. In this way, the door remains open for all future development while we can also fully affirm the real attainments of any and each individual.

Closing Meditation

The gift of life is precious, the feelings of the heart invaluable, the intuitions of the heart, unique—but Spirit lifts us, gives us wings, and carries us beyond. (88)

Meditation: In growing older, life becomes more and more precious insofar as we live it fully and fully realize the value it has for others. There is an amazing richness to life in all its possibilities and enactments, in the diversity of cultural differences, and in the celebration of life in all its dramas, rituals, and emotional dynamics. Whatever the history or biography of an individual life, there are always others stories and happenings in the lives of others that enrich our own experience. The "gift of life is precious" because each life is a unique expression of possibility, a synthesis of experience and understanding that reverberates within the collective as an inseparable part of our shared well-being. What enhances others enhances each of us and what diminishes others, diminishes each of us. However subtle the impression, or however strong, each life is an intimate aspect of the Whole. The human currents of our collective life are constantly affected by the quality and lives of others, every joy enhances us all and every sorrow and pain acts as a limitation in need of healing. Our capacity to live lives of integrity, with honesty and loving concern for others, has far-reaching effects whose ripples are a sensitizing medium within the collective. The crystallization of specific abilities and the full realization of spiritual gifts act to enhance similar possibilities in the lives of others.

Each person becomes a model of what is possible or desirable in the realms of human potential and when this is done in a loving and compassionate way, it sets a mood for the ease by which others may follow similar patterns of relations. This is by no means a matter of conformity or blind imitation but of taking a pattern and reformulating it in ways that bring out new creative occasions congruent with that pattern. No one actually becomes the Buddha or Christ, but each follower of Buddhism or Christianity may internalize the life and teaching of the founder as a means to a more personalized realization of individual potential. The model is an example or a lens through which the light of everyday understanding may be refocused. What the model becomes is unique for the individual, even while actualizing shared states of awareness confirming the reality of the teaching. The visionary worlds of diverse teachings may indeed be actualized in a shared collective sense; individuals can affirm the reality of illumination or enlightenment in ways consistent with the expectations of those who have previously attained those states. These actualizations act to establish norms and interpretations that form an elaboration of that reality known and experienced by generations of authentic practitioners. Yet these actualizations also reverberate within the larger collective as relative influences acting on the Whole, acting in various subtle ways to transform human potential.

The relative truths of these teachings, when contextualized within a particular tradition, become absolutized according to conventional interpretations, patterns of orthodoxy or in sheer repetition of fundamental ideas. Each interpretation adds its human energy and passion to the contestations of truths found at the boundaries between traditions and alternative psychic, philosophical, or scientific perspectives. And each individual embodies to various degrees a synthesis of those truths that matures over time and adds its quantum of understanding to various communities within that Whole. This is an ongoing, creative process by which human beings seek to maximize their understanding and contribute meaning to a richer, more complete life within Spirit. In each case, the individual follows that path most conducive to the affirmation of certain truths they hold as viable and self-guiding. These truths then become guiding influences in the shaping of intention and in the actualization of potential. Each realization or commitment to a spiritual path becomes a means for the propagation of patterns of actualizing potential, and the divergences within these paths represent creative alternatives whose realizations may challenge original or mainstream teachings. Such is the pattern within Spirit, to lift us beyond a known truth and into the unknown boundaries where creative emergence requires actualizing new possibilities in real lives and commitments.

The qualitative differences between these truths are many and the goals are diverse and, at times, contradictory. But those contradictions only indicate the creative boundaries where human understanding has yet to attain a full comprehension of the value and significance of these differences. Creative value is found in the ways such truths force us to reevaluate and reconsider a truth we might take to be unquestionably correct. Value is found in articulating a creative relationship between alternative perspectives or in defending a perspective against inauthentic criticism. Always Spirit presses us to move beyond the boundaries and into a more fluid and comprehensive understanding without devaluing the commitments and beliefs of others. The mature understanding of differences clearly involves respecting the views and values of others and it means holding a view that is authentic and valuable to self. But these views are not absolute; they are relative to the maturity, experience and understanding of those who hold them. As such, they are all subject to possible spiritual transformations; they are capable of being radically altered by subsequent experience and creative insights. And they are capable of being respected and held as primary examples of and a creative means for living a valuable, Spirit-guided life. Spirit may "carry us beyond" through emergent creative understanding within a tradition as well as outside of any tradition, and both are valuable and significant.

The "feelings of the heart are invaluable" because those are the feelings that relate us to others and provide a living context for the appreciation of differences. Our sense of empathy is a primary necessity in working through all the differences and divisions that tend to divide and deny others the worth of their beliefs. And opening to others, having a sense of empathy, is not static ability, it is not a mere capacity to feel what others may feel. Rather it is a willingness to feel the reality and viability of other ways of life and thought and to allow those feeling to act on us as viable resources for the reformation of our own ideas and way of life. Empathy is dynamic and not passive; it is interactive and alive with capacity for change in our own life. Thus feelings of the heart open us to possible development and ongoing creative reformulations of our present understanding.

They provide a meaningful basis for a shift in values, for a reconstitution or reframing of understanding on certain issues highly relevant to others. Those feelings provide a means for deepening communication through receptivity that fully respects the life, commitments, and feelings of others. And in that process, Spirit can act through that openness to deepen and fill out our capacities for a more enhanced and comprehensive understanding of the complexity and fullness of shared, species life.

"Intuitions of the heart are unique" because what one intuits and senses may not be at all the same as what others sense or intuit even under similar circumstances. In the real world of complex human relations, individual perceptions are paramount over collective assent even though consensus may emerge as a normative response. Consensus does not invalidate the real intuitions we each may have in a given circumstance; this is a matter of individual predilection and focus. Each person has a capacity for these intuitions that arise out of a spiritual context of principled living. By "intuitions of the heart" I mean spiritual intuitions that result from a particular value orientation and a relative degree of maturity and experience. Such spiritual intuitions can be very powerful and revealing because they often result in a predictive or probable seeing of the consequences of action or patterns of thought or belief. Such seeing is a natural ability that springs from seeing how coherently beliefs, actions, and ideas are related in clear patterns of intentional living. Where there is a high degree of coherence and integrity, certain possibilities emerge intuitively as consequences. This is also true where there is incoherence and lack of integrity, but only in a more limited, often more dramatic sense such that intuition tends to predictively synthesize incoherent tendencies into more dramatized consequences based on the inner tensions and conflicts.

The value of these unique intuitions is that they give alternative perspectives on how we relate to others and on possible future developments. They represent a creative ground for establishing new directions and for reinforcing positive tendencies and patterns. But they are relative intuitions and participate in a larger probability of concurrent influences, all of which are evolving dynamically in relationship to one another. The spiritual dynamics of maturation and collective evolution are inseparable from a variety of epistemological transformations or ways of knowing that may increasingly enhance our self-awareness and relationships to others. But such spiritual knowing is in the constant process of undergoing reevaluation and development. What is the role of imagination or reason, or intuition or empathy, or psychic impressions or dreams and visions in an evolving world of diverse epistemological alternatives? Spiritually, the spectrum of possible ways of knowing is undergoing tremendous expansion and development. In this process, intuition and empathy are fundamental abilities whose value will increasingly act to enhance awareness insofar as we are able to embrace a full-spectrum metaphysics using all our abilities as a means for understanding and knowing the world. These intuitions are relative and co-related within the larger scale processes of species maturation and for each individual, such abilities reflect particular gifts through which Spirit acts to increase our understanding.

The Mystery has no form nor boundary, but "God" is too easily bound by books and laws and traditions, yet what "God" Is cannot be bound; therefore let us not claim knowledge that lies beyond our shared becomings. (89)

Meditation: I have not used the word "God" in this work in any substantive sense and have, in fact, consciously elected to avoid the use of that word. The reason I have made this choice is because in my own thinking the word "God" remains ambiguous, unclear, and fraught with inherited meanings, prejudice, and male bias that I find to be a severe limitation in understanding the actual reality to which that word points. That such a reality exists, I have no doubt. Further, the reality exceeds any word that I can find to express it. I have the deepest reverence and love for both Spirit and Mystery and in my own life these concepts are channels for higher perception and luminous states of awareness and understanding. Always for me, Mystery is that reality that subsumes the Whole and yet transcends it in ways that are completely beyond my ability to understand or comprehend. As a limited and imperfect human being, I can only hope that my understanding of that greater reality is congruent with the deeper principles through which it manifests in the limited world of human incarnational life. Spirit is the active, creative (and for me, feminine) principle and Mystery in the ground (and Ur-ground) of all being and the primal basis of all that IS. Beyond affirming Mystery and Spirit as two inseparable concepts within a single, unitary dynamic of creative becoming and ongoing transformation, I feel that I can say little or nothing about "God."

Because I understand Mystery as boundless and beyond all form while containing all form, luminous while containing all darkness, subtle while giving birth to actual beings and intentional purposes, the word "God" seems constricted to rationalized explanations and codified beliefs in a much more reductive sense than the personal dynamic and wonder of life I experience as a practitioner of a Hermetic path. Further, my own experience has clearly shown me that it is possible and desirable to experience the Mystery directly, through visions, dreams, and states of illumination. There is no impassible gulf between humanity and the deepest of all Mysteries, no chasm whatsoever between Spirit and personal self-becoming. There is only an immediate, intimate, intensity of presence usually masked by human preoccupations and materialistic thinking. I do not wish to deny the reality of "God" as that word is defined and used in traditional religious teachings. I respect and understand that from within those traditions "God" is a viable reality and a profoundly meaningful basis for all that a tradition may hold as sacred or worthy of reverences. But in a pluralistic world of alternative spiritual possibilities, that word does not speak to me in a direct, unmediated sense. Always it is filtered through the institutions, offices, and dogmas of various faiths leaving behind an impression of contraction, competition, and overrationalization.

To those for whom the word "God" speaks well, I say peace and more peace; but for me, it is not a word that is necessary for a thoroughly spiritual explanation of human development and awakening to higher spiritual potential. Like the Dao, there is Mystery, and to put any word forth as subsuming the Whole immediately limits and falsifies the reality to which the word points. Thus Mystery remains undefined and Spirit becomes the means for a discussion of dynamic principles and processes of spiritual awakening. Yet I want to clearly and emphatically affirm that Mystery is not removed from human experience but the very basis for human experience and as such IS accessible, through individual creative occasions and profound visionary, luminous manifestations. Yet those manifestations are all relative and nonabsolute. No one of them can contain or be all that Mystery is, and "absolute experience" is an index of human capacity, not divine potential. The binding of "God" by the thoughts of men (or any spiritual teacher), to their codes and ideas and limits, is also an indication of where human capacity remains restricted and confined, perhaps out of necessity in the face of human disrespect and immorality. There is no doubt that human beings need guidance and direction for living better, more compassionate, and loving lives. Often the strictures of a faith will provide those in a rudimentary, relative sense. But these are boundaries created by human beings, for human beings, even through the means of inspired visionary experience, later interpreted through processes of social and cultural rationalization.

Inevitably, the question of revelation looms as an authenticating basis for holding a spiritual view and following a particular, creditable religious teaching. Those paths that lead to a fuller, more complete life may indeed be bound by covenant and submission to sacred writings and accepted moral patterns. But these are all relative to one another, and some will be judged to be qualitatively better than others for specific persons and in specific circumstances. There is no one hierarchy in which these truths can be organized as acceptable to the followers of all traditions. Every tradition has its own hierarchy of values and its own way of viewing the others. To say that "God" is the supreme and highest truth is to speak in a relative sense; there are other traditions for whom this observation is neither true nor accurate. Only an intolerant faith refuses to accept the viability of the faiths of others, and only one whose followers are blinded by ideology would insist on their truth as the sole basis for all human knowledge. There are many paths of knowledge and Spirit is present in all, in the creative, relative sense by which we as relative beings come to fulfill our utmost in potential. Some may follow "God" and others may not, but all engage in processes of spiritual transformation if the path they follow is a living faith.

What "God" IS cannot be bound by human laws or revelations. Those revelations are only luminous awakenings and momentary flashes of deeper truths whose contours are indistinguishable from the Unknowability of "God." Always those truths and revelations dissolve into this mysterious ground, into this all-absorbing, limitless Infinity whose depths cannot be measured and whose purposes are veiled in Spirit and in all creative becomings. But being "unknowable" is not the same as being inaccessible. The Mystery is right here, right now, in this place and every other place and time. It is there on the threshold of our higher psychic and spiritual potential, awaiting manifestation in creative occasions of revelatory being. The relative truths of individual experience confirm the reality of that presence, give it depth and meaning, and sketch out ever more fully its sacred and undefinable depths. As we grow and evolve through our species history, over and over, Spirit bursts through to confirm the ever-opening horizons of yet further possibility in the realms of human transformation and illumination. In this process, the reality of "God" slips away from its concrete and historical manifestations, in texts, individuals, events, to reveal yet further horizons through which we must pass in order to better yet comprehend the scope of our own species capacities in a fully spiritualized cosmos. Through an array of teachings the "masks of god" drop away to reveal an ever-expanding universe of vaster complexity and power than ever we first imagined or knew. And still, it expands that concept of Mystery—into the groundless ground of all cosmic becomings, dissolving into the vaster energies, luminous spaces, and timeless cycles of all planetary and cosmic manifestations.

When I write, "let us not claim knowledge that lies beyond our shared becomings" I mean that our knowledge is conditioned by the actual history and spiritual teachings that make up our collective, species identity. That knowledge, the entire collective history of human spiritual teachings, is the real basis for understanding our spiritual capacities. Such knowledge cannot be found in only one tradition, as in a religion or a science, but is a collective inheritance demonstrated through all diverse spiritual paths and disciplines. What is needed is a deep and thorough understanding of those traditions and histories as relevant to understanding what might be or might become. The receding horizons of spiritual possibility strongly suggest that all of our spiritual concepts and ideals will necessarily undergo profound changes and adaptations. In that process, it is possible to accept with credibility our incapacity for knowing absolutely the reality of "God" or Spirit or Mystery. We do not know absolutely, only relatively, the actuality of what may become through spiritual processes of creative occasioning. In those processes, there has been and will continue to be, an overturning of "God concepts" such that they become relative terms in a larger process of spiritual awakening and authentic, principled living.

There is no "death of God" because there was no original birth or beginning in which the "God" concepts originated and evolved.

Rather, these concepts evolved over millennial periods of growth and development and resulted in a vast plurality of alternative meanings and specific types of synthesis. Such is the process of creative self-becoming, the constant internalizing and creative reshaping of understanding resulting in brief periods of cultural synthesis followed by yet more change and interaction on an increasingly global scale. This process is ongoing and highly active in the present generations. The constant overturning and reprocessing of ideas and beliefs is only an index of our constant need to see more deeply into the relative structures of truth. "God" and Spirit and Mystery are constants in that process that defy final and absolute definitions. As concepts and spiritual guidelines, they change and evolve as a consequence of our species maturation and development. The real question of spiritual authenticity is not found in such definitions or in playing the definition game. Authenticity is found in living a genuine, committed, and principled life through embracing and formulating those values most helpful in actualizing higher awareness and loving concern for others. In this process, less bound definitions of the higher truths serve as a stimulus to further exploration and that exploration is the very essence of all human self-becoming. The joyful wisdom comes, step by step, and in each step it discards what is unnecessary and embraces what can never be fully put into words or concepts. In this way, the door is open and the adventure, ongoing and freely creative, inspiring and luminous.

Spirit is my mistress, my guide, my teacher, my life; I give her my body, my heart, my soul, and my being; I ask her to mercifully guide and direct me and all that love Her with me—in wisdom, joy, and peace, now and forever. Amen. (90)

Meditation: I say "Her" because, for me, Spirit is feminine, nurturing, caring, demanding, the one who seizes my soul, transforms my awareness, gives me ecstasy, transports me to far places and reveals the Mystery. The gender of Spirit as feminine is a metonym, a part-whole metaphor that strikes deep into heart of yet another metonym, "life as creation." I experience that life source, in its most spiritual dimensions, as feminine, as a life-giving, birthing, procreative primal source of emergence and creative development. As a nurturing presence, Spirit acts to engender inner development and individual capacities, "nature nurturing" as a process of constant infolding of psychic, physical, and spiritual potentials whose archetypal forms encompass all Goddess imagery related to natural procreation and fruitfulness. The Earth as Goddess is part of that archetypal form and in a slightly less earthy sense, woman as life-bearing mother and nurturing caretaker also embodies that form. In a more transformative sense, the feminine Spirit is the Divine Sophia and the Holy Shakti, all the archetypes of intuitive wisdom and purity, the Prajnaparamita, the Virgin Mary, the White and Green Taras, Kuan Yin, Sita Mahamaya, as well as the erotic, beautiful, and sexually potent forms such as Aphrodite or the Chinese Queen of Heaven or Krishna's lover, Radha. This feminine archetype embodies the nurturing, nonjudgmental qualities of mercy, compassion, loving kindness, and a luminous lucid wisdom whose joyful, sexual nature is uncontainable in strictly rational philosophies or any constricting metaphysical schemes.[72]

When I write "mercifully direct me," I ask Spirit to show me the way by which I can attain the inmost desires of the heart, a direct and luminous knowledge of the Mystery, the experiences of Presence. I ask Spirit to help me actualize the successive transformations of a lifetime of searching, questioning, and desiring. This refers to Spirit as intrinsic to a spiritual path and to all the life stages, the inward motions, aspirations, returns, retrogressions, mistaken choices or doubts, the successes and joyful accomplishments. Each of us must cultivate his or her own way to receive Spirit, Her joy, Her ecstasy, Her creative inspirations and presence. By "guide me" I mean through an intuitive presence, an illumination of the events of day-to-day life, through immediate interactions, personal encounter, and in times of solitude and inner devotions. Following the spiritual path means undertaking those actions and practices most conducive to cultivating that nurturing presence in privacy and in the midst of work or play or rest. When I call Spirit "my mistress," I mean my teacher, my dearly beloved guide, my inspiration and image of creative awakening in multiple forms and diverse appearances. There is no "one form" only a diversity of forms whose collective expressions do not equal the fullness and potency of Her inner capacity and spiritual depths. And these forms are not restricted to only female forms, for others may experience Spirit in more masculine forms or in forms devoid of gender or sexuality or as a synthesis of all male-female potentials.

The personal symbolism of such forms, the relative *Ishtha-devata* or "image of divinity" in the direct personal sense, the representative image or aspects of divinity chosen by the individual, is developed through personal inclination and the spontaneous arising of imagery consistent with spiritual intentions and aspirations. These aspects may take three forms: those of faith (selected external images for prayer and mediation); psychic manifestations that guide the individual in transformative awakenings, usually through archetypal experiences in dreams and visions; and the universal revelatory forms by which the deepest spiritual mysteries are opened to those realizing higher consciousness. In this process, forms are superseded by widening horizons of an increasingly transpersonal nature leading to states of mystical union and entry into transpersonal, imageless realms of conscious being and becoming. There is no "absolute hierarchy" of experience, and "form" and "formlessness" are equally valuable and significant in creating a mature understanding of spiritual processes. Further, specific forms are relative to various states and experiences (usually visionary in nature) and are powerful conduits of psychic and spiritual energy focalized through shared concentration and devotions. The devotional aspect is a powerful means for communal (and personal) development, and the various images used all have specific psychic qualities and capacities, and therefore should be chosen carefully.

When I write that I give "my body, heart, soul, and being" I mean giving my whole self, my full capacity to the project of a creative spiritual evolution, Spirit inspired and guided, including both a deep emotional commitment and a complete focus of mental and psychic abilities. Every spiritual path requires commitment and full sincerity and devotion to the goals of that path. In this path, the goals are a cultivation of positive human relationships, loving concern, creative development, and living a principled life while seeking to maximize the gnostic awakening and attain to increasingly higher degrees of illumination and mystical affirmation of Spirit. Imaging Spirit in relative feminine forms is simply a means toward the actualization of that pathway in a direct personal sense and does not mean that those forms are in any way ultimate or even necessary. But they have, for me, arisen spontaneously and do act as a means for channeling intentions and fostering certain positive attitudes of mind. Like the Divine Sophia, the image acts as a focal lens to bring into view ways in which Spirit acts to stimulate a spiritual transformation. There are times when the arms of Spirit enwrap me like those of a passionate lover embracing and protecting, comforting, and also conveying an intensity of presence whose feminine qualities make that intensity bearable, desirable, and an act of sacred union. And yet I know there are dimensions far beyond that image and far greater than any such sense can embody even though that embodiment is overwhelming and utterly profound and joyful.

But Spirit is not Mystery, only the activity, the "Shakti," and the expression of Mystery. All-consuming, she nourishes my thirst and feeds my hunger; modest, revealing, tempestuous, seductive and holy beyond words, she unfolds the hidden orders to awareness and the multidimensionality of diverse worlds and planes of being. She is Virgin, Lover, Mother, Companion, and Crone, the entire spectrum or Child, Maiden, Wife, and Wise Woman—the spinning, dancing Lila, the masking illusion of Maya—the Goddess and the Great Witch, the Shamaness and Mistress of Animals. She becomes all women in all time forever, but not constrained by the imagery or archetype, in process, in evolution, engaged with human becoming, inseparable from our heart-felt needs, aspirations, or the cry of the human soul in song, pain, or desire. For others, she might be male, or both, or neither. This is Spirit speaking, Spirit lifting, Spirit impoverished by words, Spirit uncontainable in the personal experiences of only one being and reduced to the limited constructs of individual language and partial communication. The Mystery is Silence, Immeasurable Depth, Infinity unbound by imagery, the Unspeakable, the Bounty beyond rapture, the formless holy unsurpassable Reality of whom little can be said. So I turn to Spirit, to the intensity of creation in the human plane and to the activities by which we as real, incarnate beings come to the realizations of potential and, then, surpass the boundaries we ourselves have constructed. And I see a dancing woman, her hair aglow, her eyes like bright embers, standing at the center, she reaches out a hand and from it pours forth a multitude of spiritual energies and potentials, all as gifts and blessings.

I write "now and forever" because following a spiritual path is an unending process, a consuming transformation bound to the creative processes of life, illumination, and spiritual awakening. There is rest, renewal, and immersion, but the waves are immeasurable, light-filled, and most deep and luminous. They immerse us constantly, washing over us and carrying us to the shores of our accomplishments and granting us peace when we reach that far attainment, when we have made actual and real the inner capacity yet awaiting expression and sharing. In this process, "wisdom, joy, and peace" are the deep and lasting guidelines by which we establish harmonic relations with others and accept the diversity and fullness of Spirit as She pours herself out for the transformation and development of all life and all beings. We are all children of Spirit. Regardless of age, culture, or genetic backgrounds, without exception every being, plant, animal, human, or more than human, is a member of that spiritual family that goes back to the earliest possible stages of human history and far beyond that into the very formation of galactic space and planetary evolution. In a unified cosmos of diverse beings engaged in innumerable creative projects and diverse interpretations of meaning and significance, Spirit is present, an abiding quiet presence filled with immense potency and potential, always encouraging openness of mind, heart, and soul. In such a life, we are asked to live in a principled way, to hold noncoercive and creative values, and to pursue those values without incriminating or denying the value of other perspectives and realization. To know Spirit, we need only live creative, peaceful, joyful lives and hold a deep reverence for all life while seeking to enhance our own awareness. In that seeking Spirit abides and is present—we need only open our hearts to know and receive Her.

Peace, Wisdom, and Well-Being to All!

! OM GURU SHAKTI !

The Ninety Aphorisms

Chapter One

The First Principle of Spirit is the gift of life; this means that the very experience of being alive, having life, is the primary manifestation of Divine Mystery. (1.1)

Whatever exists has life, both the animate and inanimate—human, animal, vegetable, or mineral; everything we see, wherever it exists, all that is visible or invisible. (1.2)

Is there such a thing as "dead matter"? No! This is an illusion perpetuated by mental necessity to separate ourselves from the overwhelming ocean of everything living. (1.3)

The abundance of Spirit is the overflowing fullness of life: this rock, this grain of sand, this minute particle of energy are all living, all participating in profound activity. (1.4)

To appreciate the immensity of Spirit, which is greater than the manifest forms of its expression, it is first necessary to appreciate being alive—this requires an attitude of reverence. (1.5)

There is no reverence without humility; we do not stand "at the pinnacle," we only represent a timely expression of creative unfolding; we must learn therefore to sense the continuity that comes before and after. (1.6)

Life is not bound by the past or present, its nets of interconnected joy and beauty are spread throughout all space and all time; yet at every level of organization there is the chaos of death and rebirth. (1.7)

Sorrow and brutality arise because we fail to recognize this most primordial truth—unless we revere life in all its forms and possibilities, we cannot hope to comprehend its sources. (1.8)

Chapter Two

The Second Principle of Spirit is that every manifestation of life has its own unique awareness, a being that constitutes its form; there is no life without such awareness. (2.1)

Even on the "subatomic" level, there is awareness; there is reaction and interaction, loss and gain, an exchange, a reconfiguration, always in motion, yet stable, enduring, and powerfully bound by the conventions of its own reality. (2.2)

On all levels, from the simplest to the most complex combinations, there is hidden power and potential; because there is motion and interaction, there is transformation—these are the qualities of life, awareness, and soulful being. (2.3)

The particles that make up the form of common clay give the energy of interaction and unity to the substance, but those particles are themselves permeated with life fields of increasingly complex potential. (2.4)

The Earth itself, as a living entity, enhances life within, upon, and about it with its own higher potential; the same potential that animates the celestial bodies, planets, asteroids, and moons. (2.5)

At every level of organization, life has awareness; in every ecological niche, it is shaped and informed by the totality of interactions, a complex net of spiritual and bio-energetic attractions and repulsions. (2.6)

To be aware, to live, is to participate in the interactions, however remote or distant or infinitesimal; when an atom ceases to exist, it affects the total configuration, it changes the quantum totality. (2.7)

If we reverence life, we must also reverence its capacity for awareness, even of a stone or grain of sand; how much more so the immense complexity of a multitude of living beings! (2.8)

Chapter Three

The Third Principle of Spirit is understanding: this means being able to sense, feel, intuit, and empathize with every living thing; analysis and reason without understanding is both dangerous and destructive. (3.1)

Strange that we should lose the primordial sense of the other, the immediate impression of life, the direct knowledge unobscured by any "values or lessons," the participation in the Whole. (3.2)

We came out of wholeness, found ourselves, walked upright, and lost our innocence; the ancient primordial sense of wonder perished with every step we took toward dominion and supremacy. (3.3)

Coexistence changed to conquest and participation to subordination; our fears and shadows gave us imagery, and every image, an artifact; every artifact, a creation, a contraction, a warning. (3.4)

How easy to deny! To turn away, to see much and understand less; to compress the world into our own isolated images, into our pride and dogmas, to contract the totality into the lessons of an hour, into the immediate, observable, and ordinary. (3.5)

Understanding is a divestment of everything unnecessary, a perception of the whole, a direct experience of totality, without qualification; it is the joy of the unmediated, the open, the expansive and vaster totality; it is the deepest truth of soul's making and unmaking. (3.6)

Understanding does not simply deny or turn the other cheek; it stands firm and is resolute before the destructive forces of approval or disapproval, self-indulgence or self-denial; it rejoices in community without clinging to fixed doctrines and authoritative dogmas. (3.7)

Understanding is unique, for every perspective of the whole is limited by the perceiver; each contributes to the multifaceted complexity of the whole, adds to the desire to create—for understanding is never "finished or complete." (3.8)

Chapter Four

The Fourth Principle of Spirit is its unknowable immensity; this is not first because only after life, awareness, and understanding is such knowledge possible, a knowledge of the hidden foundations, the Mystery. (4.1)

No doctrine, teaching, belief, or experience is equal to the Whole, yet every being participates in its primary manifestations; the depths of Wholeness are unfathomable and mysterious. (4.2)

There are no necessary pathways to the "top of the mountain," only images that dissolve into shades of darkness and light, only shadows reabsorbed into the unending transformations. (4.3)

Every circle has a center because it has a boundary; where there is no boundary, there is no one center, no particular image, no specific form, only an unbound totality of diverse formulations. (4.4)

Knowledge consists in the exploration of form, content, image, and feelings—the archaic, the immediate, or the far future, all possibilities woven into the unique, distinctive patterns of the Mystery. (4.5)

The true "eternal life" is the unending expression of Spirit through the processes of creation, manifestation, and absorption, the interwoven "jewel net" of all possible patternings. (4.6)

The human transformation is the opening of the "inner eye" that sees Mystery in the heart of life; that perceives directly the life-bestowing pulsations and rhythms of contraction, expansion, and rebirth; that knows soul and world-soul and what lies beyond. (4.7)

Giving birth, it falls back; dying, it moves forward; coming to rest, it vanishes; having been born, it thrives; in thriving, it overflows; in overflowing, it gives birth. (4.8)

Chapter Five

The Fifth Principle of Spirit is compassionate love—sensual, emotional, intellectual, aesthetic, and spiritual—it gives itself to others, it receives them without shame. (5.1)

This love entrances, it absorbs and transforms, it illuminates the darkness and fills every particle with joy; it cannot be contained or reduced to an image or a manifestation. (5.2)

Love binds us and sets us free, it compels us and gives us rest and renewal; it draws us with the glance of its passing, suggesting unity, merging, becoming—the soul's union and dissolution. (5.3)

Love is neither will nor desire, neither grasping nor letting go; it emanates through life, awareness, and empathy, it gives birth to understanding and shows the full capacities of the soul. (5.4)

Love is the healing power of Spirit, it rejuvenates and restores, it opens new horizons of intimacy, it brings balance and calm; love arises from desire, seeks expression in passion, and finds its fullness in maturity and the wisdom of the heart. (5.5)

Sexuality without love is empty, mechanical, self-serving; to enter into love means to revere, respect, and rejoice in sexuality; in a healthy, thriving love, there is no submission, no external demands or denials, only deep affirmation. (5.6)

From love comes compassion, from compassion, harmony and sharing; separation, division, and jealousy enter where love has failed, where it has not taken root in soulful being and led to transformation. (5.7)

Freedom to love means letting go, not denying the worth of others, not refusing their freedom; love is not confined to one-dimensional relationships, or to one person—love is not possession but creative and shared exploration. (5.8)

Fulfillment in love means a deep trust and openness, a complete sharing, with no positive desires unexpressed or unexplored; it means loyalty, enduring companionship, and mutual growth through creative insight and understanding. (5.9)

Without understanding and trust there is no love, only routine, habit, and false expectation; without understanding, there is censure, blame, or an unspoken hardness of heart. (5.10)

With understanding, love becomes a staging ground for wisdom and insight, establishing positive conditions for tolerance and empathy, a basis for maturity in valuing alternatives, however alien or strange. (5.11)

Spirit manifesting through love is very rare, very fine, subtle, and pervasive; it elevates without words or actions, it uplifts through presence and inspires renewal and hope, it knows no boundaries and has no limitation. (5.12)

Chapter Six

The Sixth Principle of Spirit is the manifestations of wisdom and illumination; from the illumination of the heart to the illumination of body, mind, and will. (6.1)

The illumination of the heart proceeds through love to accomplish the first opening, the irradiations of expansive joy and sharing, the unfolding of mutuality and trust. (6.2)

The second opening of the heart comes through compassion for all life, in all diversity of form, in both essence and manifestation; this is the source of peace, stability, and creative exchange. (6.3)

The third opening of the heart comes through Spirit, when the "eye of the heart" sees directly the presence and power; when penetrated to the bones, the will is transformed. (6.4)

The transformed will seeks only to actualize the impulses of Spirit, to flow into the deeper channels of life—with the current or against the current—to manifest its joy and renewal. (6.5)

To touch the heart of another is wisdom; to lift the veil, to uncover the presence, is to share the host, for the true host is Spirit in all its diversity, plurality, and perfection. (6.6)

When the "eye of the heart" has seen essences and manifestations, has actualized the flow of presence, has been both uplifted and cast down, then wisdom begins to truly give birth. (6.7)

Then mind is subdued, enters calm, and perceives the Source; when the will is enrapted it cannot differentiate; but will resolved in Spirit's nurturing, knows both its purpose and its consequence. (6.8)

From this, the body heals, irradiated from the heart; it dissolves conflicts and contradictions, releases fears, angers, or hidden anxieties and no longer cushions itself in habits or denials. (6.9)

Chapter Seven

The Seventh Principle of Spirit is ecstasy, the union of individual life with the eternal, with the ultimate source of renewal and transformation, with the unextinguished Light. (7.1)

Light within Light! Where there is neither light, nor life, nor unknowing! Where all is known as inexhaustible infinity; as sourceless Source, as Spirit's inner formless form. (7.2)

Thus the world is turned inside out, the perceived becomes perceiver and the manifestation, the essence; individuality ceases to construct and is constructed by the all-absorbing flow. (7.3)

Where silence reigns, where thought and image have no face, words no sound, gesture devoid of signs, rapture-filled; there Spirit uplifts and revels deep foundations of our ongoing visionary dreams. (7.4)

How is it possible to divide it into "steps and stages," into progressions gradual or sudden, into expansion and contraction, into higher and lower, into inner and outer? (7.5)

There is no ecstasy greater than another; no unity less than all; no enlightenment that is complete, no extinction of the soul—these are only metonyms, a part standing for the whole. (7.6)

Ecstasy is a moment of eternity, a permeation of body, mind and soul, a radical revisioning, an inward-turning outcome, a realization of endless paths and possibilities, where no joy exceeds another. (7.7)

All the paths, philosophies, dogmas, rules, and paternal hierarchic guides are only moments of engendered power seeking to direct; the footsteps of ecstasy are free to fall or rise wherever they may. (7.8)

Do not be bound by law or tradition, by consensus, comfort, family, or nation; throw off your bounds of consanguinity and language, for Spirit is not bound and ecstasy is its norm. (7.9)

Chapter Eight

The Eighth Principle of Spirit is freedom from constraint; the wild grasses of the field know nothing of the plow, their seeds are scattered by the winds, not by human hands. (8.1)

This requires courage, humility, and patience—the virtues of the untrammeled, those wandering spiritual seekers who have renounced all coercive codes of law and never injure or harm another. (8.2)

There is still life and death, still sorrow, joy, or pain, but in the reborn context of a dynamic present, not inscribed as a static "moment of creation" nor determined for all time. (8.3)

The traditions are like chains made of gold and silver strands, jeweled with the lives of "saints and martyrs"—how brilliantly they enwrap the soul, how subtly they bind and constrain the heart or mind. (8.4)

It is the work of a lifetime to be truly free, not bound by tradition, not enslaved to the past, not conditioned by futurity, not entranced by images of contracted light, present, past, or future. (8.5)

Learning to see with both eyes is difficult, as many have only learned to see with one eye, one path, one way; both eyes must open, to compare one image with another, to not surrender to sentiment and habit. (8.6)

Freedom is born of curiosity unrestrained by artifice or "moralities" of the past; the "eye of the heart" sees clearly life as it is—a gift, a challenge, a plurality—not as a constraint or a demand for conformity but as a joyful wisdom that gathers together and celebrates. (8.7)

There is no system that adequately explains the whole, no morality that recognizes every exception to the rule, no theology justified in the totality of its claims, no authority deserving respect because it wields power. (8.8)

Through freedom, let us respect the views of others, accepting alternatives and other means and ways; let us cast off our gold and silver chains to live freely together by choice, with reverence, not by demands, or by gross conformity. (8.9)

Chapter Nine

The Ninth Principle of Spirit is peace, nonviolence, and creative joy; the birth of new worlds, the opening of horizons free of fear, uncontaminated by possessive lust, lies, or confusion. (9.1)

Out of Spirit, everything flows and moves and has life, is aware and immersed in the webs and fields of others; it images and we respond, it provokes and we question, it vanishes and we doubt. (9.2)

To survive and flourish, there must be an expansive heart, an uplifting power, an inner unfolding flow; adaptive, responsive, fluid honesty and exchange. (9.3)

Such exchange requires no violence, no oppression, no anger or denial of the other; it values others, the perspectives of others, their struggles and their search. (9.4)

Inflexibility, rigidity, unmoving and falsely motivated care are the signs of illness, confusion, and contraction; the strength of peace is its power to uncontract, to restrain without force, to redirect and to channel through permissive love. (9.5)

The Spirit of nonviolence is also the source of life; it procreates through its many manifestations by forming a Whole, not by bartering a fragmented patchwork of conflicting views! (9.6)

Freedom from conflict means not espousing popular opinion or a party view, not taking the part for the whole, not being entrapped by "impartiality or objective claims." (9.7)

Such freedom comes from the heart, through a reverence for life, based on inspiration, trust, compassion and maturity; wisdom unites, then divides; it is free and then, chooses. (9.8)

Let the Spirit guide, let the life force flow into the thoughts, words, heart and actions of nonviolence, to liberate every life from its contractions, sorrows, pains, and fears. (9.9)

Chapter Ten

The Tenth Principle of Spirit is solitude, calm, and repose; everything grows old, matures, deepens and acquires the luster of age; this is natural and good—every death is a new beginning. (10.1)

Maturity is a gift of Spirit as is calm and repose; they are the fruits of compassion, love, and trust, the manifestation of depth, the immeasurable links between lives. (10.2)

Death is not to be feared, it is only transformation; if life has been fluid, so is death; if stagnant, cathected, blocked, or denied, then death is terror or confused by fear and ignorance. (10.3)

To live in Spirit requires many deaths, none less great than the body's death or denial; affirm the body, affirm death, and accept the transformation coming; then there will be calm and joy. (10.4)

Solitude is healing, renewal, rest, and relaxation; it is creative regeneration, a time of reflection, prayer, and reconsiderations; a time to redress the past through present relations. (10.5)

Share your thoughts and reflections if you desire, or choose silence and inner peace; do not be driven by the past; make peace, see your shortcomings and your gifts, give thanks for both. (10.6)

Self-knowledge sees the boundary, the horizon beyond, and knows the strength of the aspiration; it does not take comfort falsely, nor does it blame unnecessarily the weaknesses within self or others. (10.7)

We are partial, incomplete, unfinished, not fully realized, not all we might become; our goodness outlives us, our ignorance as well, but this is always true, even for the spirit-filled. (10.8)

Closing Meditation

The gift of life is precious, the feelings of the heart invaluable, the intuitions of the heart, unique—but Spirit lifts us, gives us wings, and carries us beyond. (88)

The Mystery has no form nor boundary, but "God" is too easily bound by books and laws and traditions, yet what "God" Is cannot be bound; therefore let us not claim knowledge that lies beyond our shared becomings. (89)

Spirit is my mistress, my guide, my teacher, my life; I give her my body, my heart, my soul, and my being; I ask her to mercifully guide and direct me and all that love Her with me—in wisdom, joy, and peace, now and forever. Amen. (90)

Selah, Selah, Selah.

"On the Wings of Spirit"

Appendix: The Divine Sophia

The following is a retelling of a once ancient Gnostic tale, said to have been narrated by the Valentinian Gnostics (c. 175 C.E.), modified and rewritten as a contemporary meditative analogue on spiritual transformation involving the awakening of Wisdom, the recognition of limits, the lower aspects of mind engendered through grief and loss, and the reclaiming of those diverse aspects of self that are still a necessary part of who and what we are as authentic, fully incarnate beings in a world of challenging needs, demands, and becoming. An introductory explication of this narrative may be found in my article, "The Divine Sophia: Isis, Achamoth and Ialdabaoth" (*Alexandria: Journal of Western Cosmological Traditions* (1995): 51–81).

The Narrative

They say that once there was only the Fore-Creation, invisible, without form or gender, all-pervasive, filling the depths and heights of what was, and which, desiring to manifest an inward potential, gave birth to many holy dyads—that is, pairs, the first of which were the Abyss and Forethought. Then a desire arose in Forethought and it meditated on Silence, who conceived and gave birth to twins: the first visible female form called Truth and the first visible male form called Mind, in turn they together gave birth to Life and Word. Life was the form-mother of the Pleroma and Word was the form-father of those manifest within the Pleroma. The Pleroma is the fullness of the as-yet subtle spiritual world, uninfluenced by matter, energy, or light. Many other dyads were born, called Aeons, or holy powers, the last of which was the Divine Sophia, or Holy Wisdom.

Of all the Aeons, the Divine Sophia desired most intensely to know the origins of her own creation, that is, the nature of the Fore-Creator. Though Mind told her that such knowledge was impossible, nevertheless, Sophia began to search high and low, after Mind was restrained by Silence. None of the Aeons comprehended the Fore-Creation other than Truth, whose perfect reflection was a transparent presence invisible to Sophia. She separated Herself from Her consort, the Beloved, ranged the vastness of the uncreated Immensity, and far outdistanced all the other Aeons. Sensing her separation from the other Aeons, and lacking a clear knowledge of the Fore-Creator, she felt pain and sorrow, she wept and grieved deeply, she desired with all her heart to comprehend the vast, unending totality of the Fore-Creator, also called the great Abyss. But the Abyss was vast beyond comprehending, and her sorrow increased and her passions flowed out of her in waves and she risked utter dissolution into the Abyss as she radiated forth a turbulence into the stillness of Immensity. Then, suddenly, she encountered Horos, the Limit, Boundary, and understood that the Fore-Creation was unknowable, holy and profound, beyond the comprehension of Mind, Word, or even Truth. This was the First Gnosis.

But now, the manifestations of her intentions and passions remained as viable presences in the Immensity, they overflowed the Pleroma and began to take on a more substantive appearance. Sophia beheld these manifestations, the consequences of her passions, and was again stirred with grief, fear, uncertainty, and sorrow because she understood that these were the manifestations of her own desires and uncertainties concerning the Fore-Creation. A dim, barely lightlike haze began to appear, a first visible manifestation in the Primal Void, the concatenation of passion and desire unfulfilled, slowly evolving into manifest forms—the stirrings of light, energy, and chaos. All the Aeons together were concerned about the appearance of these admixtures of Chaos and so they, with the Divine Sophia, prayed in depth and a new dyad was manifested: Christos and the Holy Spirit, his female counterpart. Together, these last Aeons calmed the first Aeons and soothed their fears, also instructing them in the unknowableness of the Fore-Creation while simultaneously revealing to them the inner unity, harmony, and illumination of the Pleroma—this was the Second Gnosis.

Yet the haze and protoforms of Chaos remained and among these emerging forms was a fractal image of Sophia, called the Lower Wisdom, for she had divided herself in the passion of her search and now the Lower Wisdom abided in the midst of Chaos. This Lower Wisdom desired to return and be united with her own Higher Self, rather than remain trapped in her passions and desires and when she felt the emanations of the Holy Spirit and the Christos, when they manifested their healing and harmony within the Pleroma, she began to seek a way to return to the primal harmony and illumination of the Second Gnosis. And when Lower Wisdom discovered that she too was bound by Limit and could not return or ascend to the Pleroma, she once again grieved and sorrowed. And from this second grief, from the waves and energy of that sorrow, the first material substances began to form, divide, and align themselves in patterns of light, dimness, and darkened matter. Then the Aeons together asked the Christos to assist the Lower Sophia and he manifested in the lower world of protomatter as Yeshu'a, and soothed her and comforted her and revealed to her all the many luminous beings that manifested in the Void as spiritual companions.

But the protomatter of the Void was now mixed with passion, desire, and sorrow, and the luminous lights of the Void were the spiritual presences inherent to the newly evolving forms of matter, inherent to each and every elemental substance, to their combinations and consequent appearances. Thus the spiritual qualities of matter are the inherent emanations of Wisdom stimulated through the manifestation of Christos and the Holy Spirit and illumined through the subtle attributes of the Aeons. And Wisdom was reunited with her own Higher Self, and perceiving the holiness of the manifestation, and seeing clearly both the psychic and material character of those manifestations, gave birth to one last entity—called "Father of the Material Realm" or the Maker and creator of the Lower Visible Realm.

This Father God created, then, seven realms, each more material than the last, until finally, slowly, this human world was formed and the beings of this world rose and walked, crawled, or flew through the skies. But the Father God was said to be vain and jealous, an angry and forbidding God, not knowing the power of the higher Aeons, nor of the Pleroma, nor even of his own Mother, the Divine Sophia. And when the Divine Sophia instructed him and opened his mind to Truth, he was amazed and refused to divulge these mysteries to those of his own creation. Being a god of the material, social, and psychic order, it was not possible for him to be a teacher of the higher mysteries, and Sophia was dismayed by his wrath, anger, and jealousy. So when he created the first human beings, she was there and secretly, without his knowing, she gave to them the gift of the Holy Spirit as a divine spark in every human heart.

And it is said that in the Garden of Eden, created by the lower Father God, that Eve was the manifestation of the Lower Wisdom and that the serpent or snake of the tree, was actually the Christos who urged Eve to eat the fruit of the Tree of Knowledge that she might attain the Third Gnosis or knowledge of her origins and realize, while incarnate in human form, the Higher Sophia in perfect illumination and bliss. But the Father God, discovering that this secret teaching was disturbing his supremacy in the lower realms, grew angry and cast them out of the garden and into the suffering of the world. Yet each and every descendent has this spark and the potential to recover the Third Gnosis.

It is also said that it was for this reason that the Christos manifests as a human being, in many unique incarnations, to bring the gift of the Holy Spirit, in all its female power and capacity, to liberate those who, cast free from the illusions of the material and psychic realms, become transformed, and ascend through visions of compassion and knowledge to the Higher Illuminations—who reunite the lower and higher self and attain visionary truth and perfect transparency. The Divine Sophia is the manifest presence of that vision, and this tale, one of her symbolic forms. And the snake, an image of Higher Wisdom, is a true teacher that reconciles the desires and passions of knowledge with higher insight, overcomes the limitations of a jealous and demanding lesser god and transmits the teachings of the Divine Sophia. In this way, it is said, the faithful attain peace and the passionate, true union, holiness, and joy. May such a Wisdom guide and enlighten us!

Notes

Opening Meditation

1. Lee Irwin, *Visionary Worlds: The Making and Unmaking of Reality* (Albany: State University of New York Press, 1994).

Chapter One

2. See Paul Davies, *The Mind of God: The Scientific Basis for a Rational World* (New York: Simon & Schuster, 1992), 87ff.

3. David Abram, *The Spell of the Sensuous* (New York: Vintage Books, 1996), 89–92, 201–4; also see Rupert Sheldrake, *The Rebirth of Nature: The Greening of Science and God* (London: Century, 1990).

4. John Briggs and David F. Peat, *Looking Glass Universe: The Emerging Science of Wholeness* (New York: Simon & Schuster, 1984), 126–31.

5. See John Briggs and F. David Peat, *Turbulent Mirror: An Illustrate Guide to Chaos Theory and the Science of Wholeness* (New York: Harper & Row, 1989); also Ralph Abraham, *Chaos, Gaia, Eros: A Chaos Pioneer*

Uncovers the Three Great Streams of History (San Francisco: HarperSan-Francisco, 1994).

Chapter Two

6. See David Bohm, *Wholeness and the Implicate Order* (London: Routledge & Kegan Paul, 1980); also Ken Wilbur (ed.), *The Holographic Paradigm and Other Paradoxes* (Boulder: New Science Library, 1982), 83–84.

7. See James Lovelock, *The Ages of Gaia: A Biography of Our Living Earth* (New York: W. W. Norton, 1988); Thomas Berry, *The Dream of Earth* (San Francisco: Sierra Club Nature and Natural Philosophical Library, 1988).

8. See Teilhard de Chardin, *The Phenomenon of Man* (New York: Harper & Row, 1965) and Peter Russell, *The Global Brain: Speculations on the Evolutionary Leap to Planetary Consciousness* (Los Angeles: Jermey Tarcher, 1983).

9. See Rupert Sheldrake, *New Science of Life* (Los Angeles: J. P. Tarcher, Inc., 1981).

10. Michael Talbot, *The Holographic Universe* (New York: HarperCollins, 1991), 139–46.

Chapter Three

11. Mark St. Pierre and Tilda Long Soldier, *Walking in a Sacred Manner: Healers, Dreamers, and Pipe Carriers—Medicine Women of the Plains Indians* (New York: Simon & Schuster, 1995), 109–25; Matthew Fox and Rupert Sheldrake, *The Physics of Angels: Exploring the Realm Where Science and Spirit Meet* (San Francisco: HarperSanFrancisco, 1996), 193–95.

12. David Abraham, *The Spell of the Sensuous*, 57–65.

13. Brian Swimme and Thomas Berry, *The Universe Story: From the Primordial Flaring Forth to the Ecozoic Era, A Celebration of the Unfolding of the Cosmos* (San Francisco: HarperSanFrancisco, 1992), 163–76.

14. Jane Marie Law (ed.), *Religious Reflections on the Human Body* (Bloomington: Indiana University Press, 1995); see also Michael Taussig, *Shamanism, Colonialism and the Wildman: A Study in Terror and Healing* (Chicago: University of Chicago Press, 1987).

15. Thomas Moore, *Care of the Soul* (New York: HarperCollins, 1992), 155–76.

16. David Spangler, *Everyday Miracles: The Inner Art of Manfestation* (New York: Bantam Books, 1996), 28–38.

17. Swami Sivananda Radha, *Realities of the Dreaming Mind* (Boston: Shambala, 1996), 9–14.

18. Antoine Faivre, *Access to Western Esotericism* (Albany: State University of New York Press, 1994), 10–15.

Chapter Four

19. Denise Lardner Carmody and John Tully Carmody, *Mysticism: Holiness East and West* (New York: Oxford University Press, 1996).

20. Holger Kalweit, *Shamans, Healers, and Medicine Men* (Boston: Shambala, 1992), 222–27.

21. Michael von Brück, "Christ and the Buddha Embracing," in Beatrice Bruteau, *The Other Half of My Soul: Bede Griffiths and the Hindu-Christian Dialogue* (Wheaton, Ill.: Quest Books, 1996), 224–42.

22. Huston Smith, *The Forgotten Truth: The Primordial Tradition* (New York: Harper & Row, 1976); also Frithjof Schuon, *The Transcendent Unity of Religions* (Wheaton, Ill.: Theosophical Publishing House, 1984); for a critique of Smith's ideas, see David Ray Griffin, *Primordial Truth and Postmodern Theology* (Albany: State University of New York Press, 1989).

23. Daniel C. Noel, *The Soul of Shamanism: Western Fantasies, Imaginal Realities* (New York: Continuum Publishing, 1997), 139–61.

24. Gerhard Staguhn, *God's Laughter: Physics, Religion, and the Cosmos* (Tokyo: Kodansha International, 1994), 106–11.

25. See the appendix for a fuller account of the Sophia mythos; also Lee Irwin, "The Divine Sophia: Isis, Achamoth and Ialdabaoth" in *Alexandria: Journal of Western Cosmological Traditions* 3 (1995): 51–81.

Chapter Five

26. Georg Feuerstein (ed.), *Enlightened Sexuality: Essays on Body-Positive Spirituality* (Freedom, Calif.: Crossing Press, 1989); Lucy Goodison, *Moving Heaven and Earth: Sexuality, Spirituality, and Social Change* (London: Women's Press, 1990).

27. Robert Sardello, *Love and the Soul: Creating a Future for Earth* (New York: HarperCollins, 1995), 171–86.

28. Ioan P. Couliano, *The Tree of Gnosis: Gnostic Mythology from Early Christianity to Modern Nihilism* (San Francisco: HarperSanFrancisco, 1992), 249ff.; and Giovanni Filorama, *A History of Gnosticism* (Cambridge, Mass.: Blackwell, 1994), xi–xix.

29. Thomas Moore, *Soul Mates: Honoring the Mysteries of Love and Relationship* (New York: HarperCollins, 1994), 45–69; and John Welwood, *Journey of the Heart: Intimate Relationship and the Path of Love* (New York: HarperCollins, 1990), 183–99.

30. Welwood, *Journey of the Heart*, 71–74.

31. Tenzin Gyatso, the XIV Dalai Lama, "Giving and Receiving: A Practical Way of Directing Love and Compassion," *The Power of Compassion: A Collection of Lectures by His Holiness the XIV Dalai Lama*, trans. Geshe Thupten Jinpa (New York: HarperCollins, 1995), 58–82.

32. *Narada's Way of Divine Love: The Narada Bhakti Sutra* (Madras: Sri Ramakrishna Math, 1986); Swami Shivanada, *Bhakti Yoga* (Perth, Australia: Divine Life Society, 1986).

Chapter Six

33. See Proverbs 1:20–33; 8:1–36; 9:1–6; Wisdom of Solomon 6.12–16; 6.21–10.21; and Ecclesiasticus (Wisdom of Sirach) 1:1–20; 24; the last two in Edgar Goodspeed (trans.), *The Apocrypha: An American Translation* (New York: Vintage Books, 1959); Pheme Perkins, "Sophia and the Mother-Father: The Gnostic Goddess," *The Book of the Goddess Past and Present*, ed. Carl Olsen (New York: Crossroad Press, 1985), 97–109; Caitlín Matthews, *Sophia Goddess of Wisdom: The Divine Feminine from Black Goddess to World-Soul* (New York: HarperCollins, 1992).

34. Andre van Lysebeth, *Tantra: The Cult of the Feminine* (York Beach, Me.: Samuel Wiser, 1995); Pushpendra Kumar, *The Principle of Shakti* (Delhi: Eastern Book Linkers, 1986); John George Woodroffe, *Mahamaya: The World as Power: Power as Consciousness* (Madras: Ganesh, 1954).

35. Pushpendra Kumar, *Tara: The Supreme Goddess* (Delhi: Bharatiya Vidya Prakashan, 1992); Marylin Rhie, *Wisdom and Compassion: The Sacred Art of Tibet* (New York: Asian Art Museum of San Francisco and Tibet House in Association with Harry N. Abrams, 1991); Edward Conze, *Buddhist Wisdom Books, Containing The Diamond Sutra, and The Heart Sutra* (London: George Allen & Unwin, 1958).

36. See appendix.

37. Dan Merkur, *Gnosis: An Esoteric Tradition of Mystical Visions and Unions* (Albany: State University of New York Press, 1993), 111–16.

38. See Irwin, *Visionary Worlds*, 181–89.

39. Antoine Faivre, *The Eternal Hermes: From the Greek God to Alchemical Magus* (Grand Rapids, Mich.: Phanes Press, 1995), 55–71; Arthur Versluis, *TheoSophia: The Hidden Dimensions of Christianity* (Hudson, N.Y.: Lindisfarne Press, 1994), 45–57.

Chapter Seven

40. Bruno Borchert, *Mysticism: Its History and Challenge* (York Beach, Me.: Samuel Wiser, Inc., 1993), 25–66; Donald Bishop, *Mysticism*

and Mystical Experience: East and West (Selingsgrove, Pa.: Susquehanna University Press, 1995); Sophy Burnham, *The Ecstatic Journey: The Transforming Power of Mystical Experience* (New York: Ballantine Books, 1997).

41. Steve Katz, *Mysticism and Language* (Oxford: Oxford University Press, 1992).

42. For more developed descriptions, see Aurobindo Ghose, *The Future Evolution of Man: The Divine Life upon Earth* (Wheaton, Ill.: Theosophical Publishing House, 1974); Gopi Krishna, *The Real Nature of Mystical Experience* (Norton Heights, N.J.: Kundalini Research Foundation, 1987).

43. Tung-pin Lu, *Secrets of the Golden Flower: The Classic Chinese Book of Life*, trans. Richard Wilhelm with commentary by Carl Jung (New York: Causeway Books, 1975).

44. Kyriacos C. Markides, *The Magus of Strovolos: The Extraordinary World of a Spiritual Healer* (New York: Penguin Books, 1985), 192–96.

45. Antoine Faivre and Jacob Needleman (eds.), *Modern Esoteric Spirituality* (New York: Crossroads Press, 1992); also see Rudolph Steiner, *The Evolution of Consciousness as Revealed through Initiatic-Knowledge*, trans. V. E. Watkin and C. Davy (London: Rudolph Steiner Press, 1991).

46. Roger Walsh and Francis Vaughan (eds.), *Paths beyond Ego: The Transpersonal Vision* (Los Angeles: J. P. Tarcher/Perigee, 1993); Charles Tart, *Transpersonal Psychologies: Perspectives on the Mind from Seven Great Spiritual Traditions* (San Francisco: HarperSanFrancisco, 1992).

47. See Faivre, *Access to Western Esotericism*, 49–110.

Chapter Eight

48. John Hick, *God Has Many Names* (Philadelphia: Westminster Press, 1980); Alfred North Whitehead, *Process and Reality*, ed. David Ray Griffin and Donald Sherbrune (New York: Free Press, 1978).

49. William C. Chittick, *Imaginal Worlds: Ibn al-'Arabi and the Problem of Religious Diversity* (Albany: State University of New York Press, 1994), 46–50.

50. Sardello, *Love and the Soul*, 108–27.

51. Edward Albert Shils, *Tradition* (Chicago: University of Chicago, 1980).

52. Claire Disbrey, *Innovation and Tradition in Religion: Towards an Institutional Theory* (Brookfield, Vt.: Avebury, 1994).

53. William Thompson, *Fire and Light: The Saints Theology, On Consulting the Saints, Mystics, and Martyrs in Theology* (New York: Paulist Press, 1987).

54. Lee Irwin, *The Dream Seekers: Native American Visionary Traditions of the Great Plains* (Norman: University of Oklahoma Press, 1994), 48–49; Howard Harrod, *Renewing the World: Plains Indian Religion & Morality* (Tucson: University of Arizona Press, 1987).

55. Thomas Dean (ed.), *Religious Pluralism and Truth: Essays on Cross-Cultural Philosophy of Religion* (Albany: State University of New York Press, 1995), 33–43.

56. Milton K. Munitz, *Cosmic Understanding: Philosophy and Science of the Universe* (Princeton: Princeton University Press, 1986), 228–35.

Chapter Nine

57. David Ray Griffin, "Creativity in Post-Modern Religion," in Michael Mitias (ed.), *Creativity in Art, Religion, and Culture* (Warzburg: Konigshausen & Neuman, distributed by Humanities Press, 1985).

58. Gergory Pritchard (ed.), *Hermeneutics, Religious Pluralism, and Truth* (Winston-Salem, N.C.: Wake Forest University Press, 1989).

59. Robert Corrington, *Ecstatic Naturalism: Signs of the World* (Bloomington: Indiana University Press, 1994), 16–26; also *Nature and Spirit: An Essay in Ecstatic Naturalism* (New York: Fordham University Press, 1992).

60. William Johnston, *The Inner Eye of Love: Mysticism and Religion* (New York: Fordham University Press, 1997).

61. Mahatma Gandhi, *Ghandi on Non-Violence: Selected Texts from Mohandas K. Gandhi's Non-Violence in Peace and War*, ed. Thomas Merton (Boston: Shambala, 1996); Leslie E. Sponsel & Thomas Gregor (eds.), *The Anthropology of Peace and Non-Violence* (Boulder, Colo.: L. Rienner, 1994).

62. Thich Nhat Han, *The Blooming of a Lotus: Guided Meditation Exercises for Healing and Transformation* (Boston: Beacon Press, 1993); Deepak Chopra, *Journey into Healing: Awakening the Wisdom within You* (New York: Harmony Books, 1994); G. Frank Lawlis, *Transpersonal Medicine: The New Approach to Healing Body-Mind-Spirit* (Boston: Shambala, 1996).

Chapter Ten

63. Lynn Kear, *Reincarnation: A Selected Annotated Bibliography* (Westport, Conn.: Greenwood Press, 1996); Joseph Head and Sylvia Cranston (eds.), *Reincarnation: The Phoenix Fire Mystery* (Pasadena, Calif.: Theosophical University Press, 1994); Rudolph Steiner, *A Western Approach to Reincarnation and Karma: Selected Lectures and Writings* (Hudson, N.Y.: Anthroposophic Press, 1997).

64. James R. Lewis, *Encyclopedia of Afterlife Beliefs and Phenomena* (Detroit: Gale Research, 1994); Harold Coward, *Life after Death in World Religions* (Maryknoll, N.Y.: Orbis Books, 1997).

65. I intend to write about this subject more fully in another work; see Vickie Mackenzie, *Reborn in the West: The Reincarnation Masters* (New York: Marlowe & Co., 1996); Antonia Mills and Richard Slobodin, *Amerindian Rebirth: Reincarnation Belief among North American Indians* (Toronto: University of Toronto Press, 1994).

66. Sogyal Rinpoche, *The Tibetan Book of Living and Dying* (San Francisco: HarperSanFrancisco, 1994), 349–55; Stanislav Grof, *Books of the Dead: Manuals for Living and Dying* (London: Thames and Hudson, 1994).

67. Stanislav Grof, *The Holotropic Mind: The Three Levels of Human Consciousness and How They Shape Our Lives* (San Francisco: HarperSanFrancisco, 1992), 83–88; Stanislav Grof (ed.), *Human Survival and Consciousness Evolution* (Albany: State University of New York Press, 1988).

68. Georges Ivanovitch Gurdjieff, *Life in Real Only Then, When "I Am"* (New York: Viking Arkana, 1991); Beryl Pogson, *The Work Life: Based on Teachings of G. I. Gurdjieff, P. D. Ouspenski, and Maurice Nicoll* (York Beach, Me.: Samuel Wiser, 1994).

69. Elisabeth Kubler-Ross, *The Cocoon & the Butterfly* (Barrytown, N.Y.: Barrytown, 1997); on Hermeticism, see Luc Benoist, *The Esoteric Path: An Introduction to the Hermetic Tradition* (New York: Sterling, 1988). Arthur Versluis, *The Hermetic Book of Nature: An American Revolution in Consciousness* (Belding, Mich.: Grail, 1997).

70. Elisabeth Kubler-Ross, *Death Is of Vital Importance: On Life, Death, and Life after Death* (Barrytown, N.Y.: Station Hill Press, 1995); Hans Holzer, *Life Beyond: Compelling Evidence for Past Lives and Existence after Death* (Chicago: Contemporary Books, 1994).

71. Francesca Fremantle and Chögyam Trungpa, *The Tibetan Book of the Dead* (Boston: Shambala, 1992).

Closing Meditation

72. Peter Russell, *The Image of Woman as a Figure of Spirit: Four Lectures Given at the Carl Jung Institute* (Arezzo, Italy: Pian Discò, 1991).

Bibliography

Abraham, Ralph. *Chaos, Gaia, Eros: A Chaos Pioneer Uncovers the Three Great Streams of History* (San Francisco: HarperSanFrancisco, 1994).

Abram, David. *The Spell of the Sensuous* (New York: Vintage Books, 1996).

Benoist, Luc. *The Esoteric Path: An Introduction to the Hermetic Tradition* (New York: Sterling, 1988).

Berry, Thomas. *The Dream of Earth* (San Francisco: Sierra Club Nature and Natural Philosophical Library, 1988).

Bishop, Donald. *Mysticism and Mystical Experience: East and West* (Selingsgrove, Pa.: Susquehanna University Press, 1995).

Bohm, David. *Wholeness and the Implicate Order* (London: Routledge & Kegan Paul, 1980).

Borchert, Bruno. *Mysticism: Its History and Challenge* (York Beach, Me.: Samuel Wiser, 1993).

Briggs, John and David F. Peat. *Looking Glass Universe: The Emerging Science of Wholeness* (New York: Simon & Schuster, 1984).

———. *Turbulent Mirror: An Illustrate Guide to Chaos Theory and the Science of Wholeness* (New York: Harper & Row, 1989).

Bruteau, Beatrice. *The Other Half of My Soul: Bede Griffiths and the Hindu-Christian Dialogue* (Wheaton, Ill.: Quest Books, 1996).

Burnham, Sophy. *The Ecstatic Journey: The Transforming Power of Mystical Experience* (New York: Ballantine Books, 1997).

Carmody, Denise Lardner and John Tully Carmody, *Mysticism: Holiness East and West* (New York: Oxford University Press, 1996).

Chittick, William C. *Imaginal Worlds: Ibn al-'Arabi and the Problem of Religious Diversity* (Albany: State University of New York Press, 1994).

Chopra, Deepak. *Journey into Healing: Awakening the Wisdom within You* (New York: Harmony Books, 1994).

Conze, Edward. *Buddhist Wisdom Books, Containing The Diamond Sutra, and The Heart Sutra* (London: George Allen & Unwin, 1958).

Couliano, Ioan P. *The Tree of Gnosis: Gnostic Mythology from Early Christianity to Modern Nihilism* (San Francisco: HarperSanFrancisco, 1992).

Corrington, Robert. *Nature and Spirit: An Essay in Ecstatic Naturalism* (New York: Fordham University Press, 1992).

———. *Ecstatic Naturalism: Signs of the World* (Bloomington: Indiana University Press, 1994).

Coward, Harold. *Life after Death in World Religions* (Maryknoll, N.Y.: Orbis Books, 1997).

Davies, Paul. *The Mind of God: The Scientific Basis for a Rational World* (New York: Simon & Schuster, 1992).

Dean, Thomas (ed.). *Religious Pluralism and Truth: Essays on Cross-Cultural Philosophy of Religion* (Albany: State University of New York Press, 1995).

Disbrey, Claire. *Innovation and Tradition in Religion: Towards an Institutional Theory* (Brookfield, Vt.: Avebury, 1994).

Faivre, Antoine. *Access to Western Esotericism* (Albany: State University of New York Press, 1994).

———. *The Eternal Hermes: From the Greek God to Alchemical Magus* (Grand Rapids, Mich.: Phanes Press, 1995).

Faivre, Antoine and Jacob Needleman (eds.). *Modern Esoteric Spirituality* (New York: Crossroads Press, 1992).

Feuerstein, Greog (ed.). *Enlightened Sexuality: Essays on Body-Positive Spirituality* (Freedom, Calif.: Crossing Press, 1989).

Filorama, Giovanni. *A History of Gnosticism* (Cambridge, Mass.: Blackwell, 1994).

Fox, Matthew and Rupert Sheldrake. *The Physics of Angels: Exploring the Realm Where Science and Spirit Meet* (San Francisco: HarperSanFrancisco, 1996).

Fremantle, Francesca and Chögyam Trungpa. *The Tibetan Book of the Dead* (Boston: Shambala Press, 1992).

Gandhi, Mahatma. *Ghandi on Non-Violence: Selected Texts from Mohandas K. Gandhi's Non-Violence in Peace and War*. Edited by Thomas Merton (Boston: Shambala, 1996).

Ghose, Aurobindo. *The Future Evolution of Man: The Divine Life upon Earth* (Wheaton, Ill.: Theosophical Publishing House, 1974).

Goodison, Lucy. *Moving Heaven and Earth: Sexuality, Spirituality, and Social Change* (London: Women's Press, 1990).

Goodspeed, Edgar (trans.). *The Apocrypha: An American Translation* (New York: Vintage Books, 1959).

Griffin, David Ray. *Primordial Truth and Postmodern Theology* (Albany: State University of New York Press, 1989).

Grof, Stanislav. *Human Survival and Consciousness Evolution* (Albany: State University of New York Press, 1988).

———. *The Holotropic Mind: The Three Levels of Human Consciousness and How They Shape Our Lives* (San Francisco: HarperSanFrancisco, 1992).

———. *Books of the Dead: Manuals for Living and Dying* (London: Thames and Hudson, 1994).

Gurdjieff, Georges Ivanovitch. *Life in Real Only Then, When "I Am"* (New York: Viking Arkana, 1991).

Gyatso, Tenzin (The XIV Dalai Lama). *The Power of Compassion: A Collection of Lectures by His Holiness the XIV Dalai Lama.* Translated by Geshe Thupten Jinpa (New York: HarperCollins, 1995).

Han, Thich Nhat. *The Blooming of a Lotus: Guided Meditation Exercises for Healing and Transformation* (Boston: Beacon Press, 1993).

Harrod, Howard. *Renewing the World: Plains Indian Religion & Morality* (Tucson: University of Arizona Press, 1987).

Head, Joseph and Sylvia Cranston (eds.). *Reincarnation: The Phoenix Fire Mystery* (Pasadena, Calif.: Theosophical University Press, 1994).

Hick, John. *God Has Many Names* (Philadelphia: Westminister Press, 1980).

Holzer, Hans. *Life Beyond: Compelling Evidence for Past Lives and Existence after Death* (Chicago: Contemporary Books, 1994).

Irwin, Lee. *The Dream Seekers: Native American Visionary Traditions of the Great Plains* (Norman: University of Oklahoma Press, 1994).

———. *Visionary Worlds: The Making and Unmaking of Reality* (New York: State University of New York Press, 1994).

———. "The Divine Sophia: Isis, Achamoth and Ialdabaoth." *Alexandria: Journal of Western Cosmological Traditions* 3 (1995): 51–81.

Johnston, William. *The Inner Eye of Love: Mysticism and Religion* (New York: Fordham University Press, 1997).

Kalweit, Holger. *Shamans, Healers, and Medicine Men* (Boston: Shambala, 1992).

Katz, Steve. *Mysticism and Language* (Oxford: Oxford University Press, 1992).

Kear, Lynn. *Reincarnation: A Selected Annotated Bibliography* (Westport, Conn.: Greenwood Press, 1996).

Krishna, Gopi. *The Real Nature of Mystical Experience* (Norton Heights, N.J.: Kundalini Research Foundation, 1987).

Kubler-Ross, Elisabeth. *Death Is of Vital Importance: On Life, Death, and Life After Death* (Barrytown, N.Y.: Station Hill Press, 1995).

————. *The Cocoon & the Butterfly* (Barrytown, N.Y.: Barrytown, Ldt., 1997).

Kumar, Pushpendra. *The Principle of Shakti* (Delhi: Eastern Book Linkers, 1986).

————. *Tara: The Supreme Goddess* (Delhi: Bharatiya Vidya Prakashan, 1992).

Law, Jane Marie (ed.). *Religious Reflections on the Human Body* (Bloomington: Indiana University Press, 1995).

Lawlis, G. Frank. *Transpersonal Medicine: The New Approach to Healing Body-Mind-Spirit* (Boston: Shambala, 1996).

Lewis, James R. *Encyclopedia of Afterlife Beliefs and Phenomena* (Detroit: Gale Research, 1994).

Lovelock, James. *The Ages of Gaia: A Biography of Our Living Earth* (New York: W. W. Norton, 1988).

Lu, Tung-pin. *Secrets of the Golden Flower: The Classic Chinese Book of Life*. Translated by Richard Wilhelm with commentary by Carl Jung (New York: Causeway Books, 1975).

Mackenzie, Vickie. *Reborn in the West: The Reincarnation Masters* (New York: Marlowe & Co., 1996).

Markides, Kyriacos C. *The Magus of Strovolos: The Extraordinary World of a Spiritual Healer* (New York: Penguin Books, 1985).

Matthews, Caitlín. *Sophia Goddess of Wisdom: The Divine Feminine from Black Goddess to World-Soul* (New York: HarperCollins, 1992).

Merkur, Dan. *Gnosis: An Esoteric Tradition of Mystical Visions and Unions* (Albany: State University of New York Press, 1993).

Mills, Antonia and Richard Slobodin. *Amerindian Rebirth: Reincarnation Belief among North American Indians* (Toronto: University of Toronto Press, 1994).

Mitias, Michael (ed.). *Creativity in Art, Religion, and Culture* (Warzburg, Germany: Konigshausen & Neuman, distributed by Humanities Press, 1985).

Moore, Thomas. *Care of the Soul* (New York: HarperCollins, 1992).

————. *Soul Mates: Honoring the Mysteries of Love and Relationship* (New York: HarperCollins, 1994).

Munitz, Milton K. *Cosmic Understanding: Philosophy and Science of the Universe* (Princeton: Princeton University Press, 1986).

Noel, Daniel C. *The Soul of Shamanism: Western Fantasies, Imaginal Realities* (New York: Continuum Publishing Co., 1997).

Olsen, Carl (ed.). *The Book of the Goddess Past and Present* (New York: Crossroad Press, 1985)

Pogson, Beryl. *The Work Life: Based on Teachings of G. I. Gurdjieff, P. D. Ouspenski, and Maurice Nicoll* (York Beach, Me.: Samuel Wiser, 1994).

Pritchard, Gregory (ed.). *Hermeneutics, Religious Pluralism, and Truth* (Winston-Salem, N.C.: Wake Forest University Press, 1989).

Radha, Swami Sivananda. *Realities of the Dreaming Mind* (Boston: Shambala, 1996).

Rhie, Marylin. *Wisdom and Compassion: The Sacred Art of Tibet* (New York: Asian Art Museum of San Francisco and Tibet House in Association with Harry N. Abrams, 1991).

Rinpoche, Sogyal. *The Tibetan Book of Living and Dying* (San Francisco: HarperSanFrancisco, 1994).

Russell, Peter. *The Global Brain: Speculations on the Evolutionary Leap to Planetary Consciousness* (Los Angeles: Jeremy Tarcher, 1983).

———. *The Image of Woman as a Figure of Spirit: Four Lectures Given at the Carl Jung Institute* (Arezzo, Italy: Pian Discò, 1991).

Sardello, Robert. *Love and the Soul: Creating a Future for Earth* (New York: HarperCollins, 1995).

Schuon, Frithjof. *The Transcendent Unity of Religions* (Wheaton, Ill.: Theosophical Publishing House, 1984).

Sheldrake, Rupert. *The Rebirth of Nature: The Greening of Science and God* (London, 1990).

———. *New Science of Life* (Los Angeles: J. P. Tarcher, Inc., 1981).

Shils, Edward Albert. *Tradition* (Chicago: University of Chicago Press, 1980).

Shivanada, Swami. *Bhakti Yoga* (Perth, Australia: Divine Life Society, 1986).

Smith, Huston. *The Forgotten Truth: The Primordial Tradition* (New York: Harper & Row, 1976).

Spangler, David. *Everyday Miracles: The Inner Art of Manifestation* (New York: Bantam Books, 1996).

Sponsel, Leslie E. & Thomas Gregor (eds.). *The Anthropology of Peace and Non-Violence* (Boulder, Colo.: L. Rienner, 1994).

Staguhn, Gerhard. *God's Laughter: Physics, Religion, and the Cosmos* (Tokyo: Kodansha International, 1994).

St. Pierre, Mark and Tilda Long Soldier. *Walking in a Sacred Manner: Healers, Dreamers, and Pipe Carriers—Medicine Women of the Plains Indians* (New York: Simon & Schuster, 1995).

Steiner, Rudolph. *The Evolution of Consciousness as Revealed through Initiatic-Knowledge.* Translated by V. E. Watkin and C. Davy (London: Rudolph Steiner Press, 1991).

———. *A Western Approach to Reincarnation and Karma: Selected Lectures and Writings* (Hudson, N.Y.: Anthroposophic Press, 1997).

Swimme, Brian and Thomas Berry. *The Universe Story: From the Primordial Flaring Forth to the Ecozoic Era, A Celebration of the Unfolding of the Cosmos* (San Francisco: HarperSanFrancisco, 1992).

Talbot, Michael. *The Holographic Universe* (New York: HarperCollins, 1991).

Tart, Charles. *Transpersonal Psychologies: Perspectives on the Mind from Seven Great Spiritual Traditions* (San Francisco: HarperSanFrancisco, 1992).

Taussig, Michael. *Shamanism, Colonialism and the Wildman: A Study in Terror and Healing* (Chicago: University of Chicago Press, 1987).

Teilhard de Chardin, Pierre. *The Phenomenon of Man* (New York: Harper & Row, 1965).

Thompson, William. *Fire and Light: The Saints Theology, On Consulting the Saints, Mystics, and Martyrs in Theology* (New York: Paulist Press, 1987).

van Lysebeth, Andre. *Tantra: The Cult of the Feminine* (York Beach, Me.: Samuel Wiser, 1995).

Versluis, Arthur. *TheoSophia: The Hidden Dimensions of Christianity* (Hudson, N.Y.: Lindisfarne Press, 1994).

———. *The Hermetic Book of Nature: An American Revolution in Consciousness* (Belding, Mich.: Grail, 1997).

Walsh, Roger and Francis Vaughan (eds.). *Paths beyond Ego: The Transpersonal Vision* (Los Angeles: J. P. Tarcher/Perigee, 1993).

Welwood, John. *Journey of the Heart: Intimate Relationship and the Path of Love* (New York: HarperCollins, 1990).

Whitehead, Alfred North. *Process and Reality*. Edited by David Ray Griffin and Donald Sherbrune (New York: Free Press, 1978).

Wilbur, Ken (ed.). *The Holographic Paradigm and Other Paradoxes* (Boulder, Colo.: New Science Library, 1982).

Woodroffe, John George. *Mahamaya: The World as Power: Power as Consciousness* (Madras: Ganesh, 1954).

INDEX

actualization
  of potential, 201, 303
  of self, 38, 45, 183
  spiritual, 93, 100, 205, 330
  see also potential
aggression, 62, 71, 73–74, 192, 237,
    258, 261, 268, 273, 286
  and competition, 278
  as dogmatism, 73
  as male stance, 71
  cycles of, 258
  defensive, 276
  in religion, 74, 317
  in love, 145
  pathological, 237
  sexual, 138
  totalitarianism, 249, 253
alchemy, 162, 312
  reduction, 166
  see also transformation; Hermeti-
    cism; symbolism
alienation, 20, 35–36, 157, 181, 274,
    276, 313
  and isolation, 142, 268
  healing of, 156
  in art, 122, 134

in love, 130
  see also love; healing
animals, 16, 29, 34, 258, 296
  rights of, 260
anthropology, 104
  of Spirit, 1–5
archetypes, 16, 53, 203, 278, 285, 298
  of journey, 109
  visionary, 313
art, 134, 135, 267, 271
asceticism, 55, 57, 81, 138, 184
autonomy, 84, 201
awakening, 105, 174, 189, 211, 215,
    243, 324
  to Spirit, 35, 69, **92**, 100
  see also spiritual; love
awareness, 39, 55, 56, 92, 174, 230
  experiential, 41, 92
  full spectrum, 130–131, 197
  higher, 47, 59, 215, 295
  horizontal, 203
  not passive, 61
  vertical, 203–204, 267

balance, 66, 134, 136, 144, 151, 167,
    219, 275, 298

and calm, 134, 299, 302
imbalance, 276, 282
being, 37
ancestral, 171
authentic, 188, 208, 223, 298, 337
currents of, 205, 206, 220
in-relation, 61, 171, 174
interdependent, 172
new horizons, 48, 173, 230
plentitude of, 206
seen, 204
soulful, 39, 243
see also spirituality
becoming, 67, 106, 107
process of, 80, 87, 95, 108
eternal, 110, 197
beauty, 52, 68, 122, 134
body, **47–48**, 70, 73, 116, 181, 191,
194, 217, 310, 312
as machine, 17, 72
as temple, 189
body-mind, 311
centers of, 117, 196
embodiment, 25, 132
energies of, 48, 138, 140, 281
non-Cartesian, 48
reflects the psyche, 47
spiritualization of, 194
transformed by love, 140
wisdom of, 163
see also perception
boundaries, 82, 246, 262, 283, 284
Buddhism, 5, 55, 74, 103, 104, 113,
162, 253, 330
Buddha, 243, 279, 285, 298,
330
emptiness, 170
enlightenment, 213
Kuan Yin, 338
mandala, 313
middle way, 190
Prajnaparamitra, 162, 338
sudden or gradual, 212, 227
suffering, 185
tantra, 293
Tara, 162, 338
Tibetan, 313

wisdom eye, 173
Zen, 219

center, 26–27, 57, 66, 68, 76, 83,
101, 108
as temenos, 263
in body, 117
merging of, 124
no boundary, 112, 126, 322
no loss of, 125
no one center, 103, 203
of love, 124
with others, 125
chaos, 29–30, 56, 87
Lords of, 30
children, 33, 81, 128, 234, 311, 341
deformation of, 193
rights of, 260
Christianity, 5, 74, 103, 104, 330
Christ, 243, 279, 285, 298, 330,
356–357
Greek Orthodox, 55
evangelical, 262
future rewards, 323
God, 334
host, 183
Holy Spirit, 357, passim
Mother Teresa, 280
monotheism, 253
proselytizing, 317
redemption, 142
resurrection, 142
saints, 163, 240, 242
transubstantiation, 273
Virgin Mary, 338
see also Divine Sophia; Judeo-
Christian; revelation
collective, 84, 99, 103, 109, 164,
291, 318, 327, 332
as tribal, 70
beliefs, 43, 114, 318
condemnation, 103
consent, 75, 226
denial, 296
majority, 279
norms, 322
opinion, 288

pathologies, 276, 301
will, 249
colonialism, 249, 294
coming-into-being, 38, 220, 290
community, 3, 70, 72, 85, 100, 114,
148, 214, 218
alternative, 250
and creativity, 84, 135, 231
of Spirit, 251, 255, 263, 266, 281,
318, 320
standards of, 235
see also spiritual
compassion, 47, 120, 124, 140, 143,
155, 169, 172, 186, 254, 292,
302, 304
see also love; values
complexity, 26, 32, 34, 46, 62, 89,
169, 244
conditioning, 35, 92, 93, 108, 212,
236, 267
and death, 300
biological and social, 231
see also socio-cultural
conformity, 85–86, 88
as a destructive force, 84
popular opinion, 288, 290
conjunctio oppositorum, 184
connectedness, 30, 47, 178, 190,
284, 305, 326
consciousness, 2, 183, 203, 282
false, 184
leap of, 32, 203, **204**, 227
multiple, 202
new, 237
of stars, 200
planes, 203
spreads out, 203, 204
see also transformation; spiritual
convergence, 103
correspondence, 62, 112, 167, 173,
174, 175, 177, 292
cosmology, 7, 80, 195, 213, 267
dark matter, 178
enfolded order, 201
fractal, 178, 179, 199, 230
heart of, 206
holo-universe, 48

incorporative, 204
macrocosmic, 42, 47, 305, 308
not bottomless, 206, 270, 272
transformative, 207
see also emergence; being
courage, 232, 233, 236
creation, 80, 239
co-creation, 133, 138, 145, 230,
231, 239, 244, 294
constant genesis, 201
cycles of, 27
eternal, 197
humanity of, 54
initial conditions, 52, 70
mythic, 37
not empty, 31
creativity, 43, 46, 92, 93, 134, 151,
169, 189, 205, 230, 286, 287
and intelligence, 102, 188
as process of knowing, 204, 230,
330
cycles of, 136
in community, 84
in relationships, 66, 67

death, 16, 30, 32, 201, 284,
299–302, 306–310, 312,
313
after-death state, 300, 307, 313
and calm, 301
and denial, 308
and dreams, 308
and liberation, 310
and rebirth, 16, 32, 99, 142, 179,
186, 212, 236, 299
art of, 307
confusion in, 307
dying, 306
embracing, 300
in life, 300
in nature, 20
intimacy of, 308
life-after-death, 299, 300, 313
like swimming a river, 307
meaninglessness and despair in,
306
preparation for, 302

survival of, 37, 300
deconstruction, 5, 35, 244, 282
development, 108, 211, 271
  selective, 267
  see also psychic; species, spiritual
dialectic, 14, 17, 220, **221–223**
  asymmetry, 221
  we-they, 224, 279
dialogue, 7, 84, 124, 209, 222, 223,
    239, 251, 261, 262, 266
  empathic, 96
  spiritual, 182
dimensionality, 31, 112, 115, 118,
    175, 186, 191
  multiple, 51–52, 116, 169, 201
discipline, 86, 172
divine milieu, 50, 250
Divine Sophia, 112, 118, 161, 162,
    256, 338, 339, **355–358**
  see also Appendix
Daoism, 103, 253, 281, 285
  Dao of, 334
dominance
  ethic of, 34, 72, 253
dreams
  and visions, 78, 106, 180, 206,
    214, 217, 231, 244, 333, 334
  in death, 308
  morbid, 78
  rejected, 18
dualism, 14, 17, 54, 220, 221, 292,
    311
  good-evil, 292, 293
  form-formlessness, 339
  inner-outer, 318
  male-female, 292
  mind-body, 311
  spirit-matter, 312
  see also values

earth, 15, 24, 47, 51, 54
  as goddess, 338
  as sacred, 54
  earth-soul, 170
  Gaia principle, 52
ecologies
  as cultural, 55

  as global, 56
ego-identity, 192, 216, 300
emergence, 49, 52, 67, 70, 78, 80,
    85, 90, 94, 117, 126, 146, 174,
    175, 230, 235, 259, 266, 273,
    290, 291
  into novelty, 222
  secret of, 87
  see also cosmology; being
emotion, 51, 189, 268, 288, 322–323
  and heath, 296
  attachment in dying, 309
  fear and anger, 191, 277, 279
  fear and ignorance, 309
  male, 268
  negative types of, 320
  see also love; empathy
empathy, 16, 96, 117, 132, 141, 142,
    295, 320, **331–333**
  lack of, 28
  loss of, 71
  over-empathic, 66
energy, 22, 231
  joyful, 126
  of transformation, 46, 138
  psychic, 141
  spectrum of, 39, 196
enlightenment, 89, 213, 214, 215,
    217
  postponed, 295
  see also gnosis
epistemology, 5, 188, 289, 332
  full spectrum, 289
  interactive, 224
  new, 222
eros
  of ideas or intellect, 121, 122
  of Spirit, 256
  lack of, 122
  see also love
eschatology
  no final endings, 75, 239
essence, 205
  and manifestation, 171, 184, 202
experience, 41, 92, 106, 201, 222,
    313
  denial of, 214

see also spiritual
evolution, **53**, 122, 201, 230, 231,
    237, 255, 271, 313, 332
  coevolution, 29, 49, 63, 286
  spiritual, 49, 267

faith, 35, 75
feminine, 161–162, 163, 292
  interaction, 223
form, 105–106, 198
  and formlessness, 202
freedom, 143, 150, 229, 244, 252,
    254, 260, 261, 279, 291, 292,
    294
friends, 128, 129
fusion of perspectives, 274, 275

Gaia principle, 52
gifts
  of Spirit 12, 13, 22, 24, 26, 35, 229
God, 333–337, 357–358
  death of, 336–337
  masks of, 336
  no absolute definition, 337
Goddess, 338, 340
gnosis, 23, 31, 41, 68, 82, **91**, 93, 96,
    97, 104, 113, 163, 173, 178, 206,
    286, 297, 334, 356, 357, 358
  as flashes, 89, 220
  higher, 118, 215, 306
  ineffable, 198
  not omniscient, 97
  enstatic, 175, 182, 198
  see also illumination; mysticism
gnostic, 112, 117, 138, 189
  narrative of, 355–358
  old attitudes, 132
Golden Flower, 202

habit, 35, 46, 192, 319
harmony, 122, 140, 143, 144, 216,
    303
  harmonic traces, 51
Hasidism, 103
healing, 40, 69, **133**, 136, 145, 156,
    187, 192, 193, 238, 261, 283,
    296–297, 298, 313

alienation, 156
  and illness, 281
  and wisdom, 181
  manifestations, 181
  not technical, 296
  of others, 295
  of the world, 237
  old wounds, 33, 157, 281, 282
  the past, 282, 316
heart
  eye of, 173, 174, 184, 186, 255,
    320
  illumination of, 118, 159, 165, 331
  openings of, 165, 166, 169, 172,
    173, 175, 176
Hermes, 112
Hermeticism, 7, 187, 189, 205, 238,
    311, 312, 334
  Caduceus, 238–239
  Great Work, 285, 294
  Hermetic circle, 19, 31, 67, 80,
    125, 126, 216, 280
  plenum, 31
  principled living, 312
  see also symbolism
hierarchy, 49, 97, 116, 117, 211, 220,
    221, 222, 223, 240, 253, 335,
    339
Hieros Gamos, 121, 137, 183, 184
Hinduism
  avatars, 102
  ishtha-devata, 339
  jnanas, 209
  karma, 280
  Krishna-Arjuna, 77
  liberation, 219
  mantra, 199
  prana, 163
  Radha, 338
  samadhi, 209
  Sat-Cit-Ananda, 41, 159
  shakti, 161, 338, 340, 341
  Sita, 338
  yogi, 163
history, 30, 188, 282
  and culture, 55, 279
  as conquest, 74

as spiritual, 103
lessons of, 73
of dominance and abuse, 71
repression, 294
past not golden, 73
reconfiguring the past, 43, 247, 281
shadows of, 74
holomovement, 48
humanity, 15, 18, 54, 219, 286
as participant-creators, 54
as thrown, 185
depersonalized, 288
male-female, 292
potential of, 330
see also body; emotion; mind; relationships; sexuality
humility, 28, 232, 233, 236, 280

illumination, 2, 31, 40, 89, **97**, 139, 161, 189, 196, 198, 206, 207, 215, 216, 259, 283, 294, 334, 338, 358
and ecstasy, 195, 196, 208, 213, 217, 220, 224, 227, 338
as radiance, 89
enstatic, 175, 176, 189, **190**, 201, 217, 218
ineffable, 198
no extinction, 216
postponed, 295, 297
of heart, 118, 159, 165, 187, 331
subtilizes, 190
supramental, 105
see also enlightenment; gnosis
images, 78, 98–99, 106
and imageless, 206
human, 171
of darkness, 99
of light, 99, 197
imagination, 42, 109, 116, 117, 122, 159, 189, 288, 333
incubation, 56, 57, 114, 135, 136
incarnation, 16, 37, 107, 108, 229, 282, 301, 311
individuation, 19, 129, 174, 193, 321

inner eye, 112, 113, 114, 173, 184
instrumentalization, 95, 118, 141, 192, 210, 212, 230, 280
integrity, 60, 68, 100, 106, 155, 259
intentionality, **49–50**, 51, 52, 56–57, 68, 92, 176, 208, 215, 314, 323 330
attractions and repulsions, 57
co-creative, 77, 134
cosmological, 201
hidden, 49
in love, 158
spiritual, 59
unified, 61
visionary, 49
interdependence, 26, 126
interpretation, 174, 221, 232
intuitions, 109, 188, 273, 294
of the heart, 329, 331, **332–333**
mystical, 217, 220
involutions
of spirit, 52, 95, 99, 111
Islam, 5, 74
see also Sufism

jewel net, 109–111, 126, 129, 305
joy, 166–167, 186, **217**, 238
Judeo-Christian
morality, 253, 254, 257, 259
theology, 3, 256, 257, 259

knowledge, 112
levels and stages, 105, 196, 209, 227, 305
of future, 107
of whole, 112
see also self

language, 2, 70, 116, 215, 224
broken vessel, 200
limits of, 198, 199, 206
poetic, 116
life
coexistent, 171
emotive-mental, 203
energetic, 199, 202, 231
fields, 12, 49, 51

gift of, **329**
matrix, 201, 202, 233
non-accidental, 24
not valuing, 33
qualitative, 227, 318
web of, 312, 326
light
  burst of, 220
  inner, 199
  nor life, 200
  not metaphorical, 200
  one light, 215
  phenomenal sign, 199
  points of, 328
  spiritual, 198–202
  within light, 199
  see also symbolism
limitations, 22, 252
love, 29, 47, 67, 69, **120**, 165, 274,
    275, 277, 296, 301, 302, 311,
    324, 325
  an adornment, 123
  and alienation, 130
  and being, 160
  and sacrifice, 150
  and trust, 149
  and will, 102, 133
  and wisdom, 154–155
  anger in, 152, 276
  as actualization, 131
  as energy, 158
  as kindness, 40
  attachment, 134
  awakening to, 123
  blame and censure in, 153
  can bind, 128,
  capacity for, 131
  compromise, 127, 246
  currents of, 134, 179
  depths of, 126
  dyads, 124, 125
  ecstasies of, 121, 126, 158, 159,
    227
  eros of, 113, 121, 127
  freedom in, 143
  fulfillment in, 146
  higher, 126

  in art, 122
  lack of, 138
  loyalty in, 149
  mutuality, 123, 124, 151, 160
  not clinging, 131
  not other worldly, 121
  not passive, 131, 132
  not selfless, 123
  not surrender, 128
  nuturance, 122
  passion, 123, 135, 219
  qualities of, 157, 158, 159
  reciprocal, 145, 149
  rhythms of, 127
  romantic, 57
  sensual, 121, 137
  sexual, 137
  soul-guided, 165
  spiritual, 124–125
  transformative, 140, 156
  transpersonal, 132
  visionary aspect, 159
  vulnerability, 129, 148, 285
  see: compassion; *Hieros Gamos*;
    relationships

manifestations
  and essence, 171, 202
  creative, 172, 212
  entangled, 175
  primary, 95, 285
  see also self; spiritual
marriage, 137, 183
  see: Hieros Gamos
martial arts
  T'ai Chi and Akido, 258
mater materia, 189
materialism, 16, 18, 50, 55, 231,
    265, 279, 296, 327
maturity, 2, 46, 50, 66, 68, 136, 140,
    233, 261, 299, **302–305**, 309,
    315
  as spiritual path, 305, 324
  stages of, 320
matter, 17, 18–19, 38
  structural levels, 48
  subatomic, 41–42, 59

meditation, 177, 189, 302
  as inner stillness, 191
metaphysics, 54, 196, 215, 231
  of transformation, 234, 267, 312
  of freedom, 235, 244, 279
  of soul, 285
  see also truth
methodology, 6
mind, 187, 189, 217
  dualistic, 292
  verticality, 197, 203, 267
  full-spectrum, 197
  wholistic, 292
monasticism, 81, 310
monomyths, 84, 273
Mundus Imaginalis, 31, 53, 54, 105,
  117, 199, 313
Mystery, 11–14, 44, 45, 111, 112,
  118, 161, **195–198, 207**, 216,
  217, 275, 306, 314, 327, 328,
  333–337
  accessible, 334
  as boundless, 334
  as hidden pearl, 207
  ineffable, 198, 207, 216
mysticism, 96–97, 189, 196, 198,
  213, 214, 215, 216, 218, 219,
  275, 325
  criticisms of, 214
  decontextualized, 214
  goals of, 196
  reports of, 215
  states, 198
  traditions of, 210
  see also spiritual; illumination;
    gnosis
myth
  in science, 18–19
  mythology, 53

nature, 116, 285, 286
  animate or inanimate, 14
  as dead matter, 18
  as living, 15–16, 20, 45
  inner structure, 203
  natural potencies, 287, 290
  nurturing, 201, 271, 272, 285

  rhythms of, 140
noetic, 117, 194, 203
  as image-ideas, 117
  magnetism, 121
nonintrusion, 62
nonviolence, 61, 73, 232, 233, 234,
  235–236, 254, 258, **265**, 277,
  278, 295, 283, 284, 286,
  see also peace; values

objectivity, 288, 289, 290
  and subjectivity, 289, 290
  see also science; values
Olam ha'Yesirah, 113
OM (or *AUM*)
  as symbol, 79–80, 234
one way
  no, 45
ontology, 80
organization
  levels of, 31

pater familias, 93
  ways of the fathers, 253
path, 210–211, 213, 237, 249
  endless, 218
  heart-centered, 294, 331
  more than adventitious, 212
  more than one, 249, 250
  not all equal, 115
  see also spiritual
patience, 232, 236
peace, 72, 169, 254, **265**, 269, 277,
  281, 286, 295, 317, 341
  peaceful warrior, 278, 283
perception, 2, 39, 56, 60, 147, 148,
  222
  neural-psychic, 199, 204, 218
  paranormal, 130
  rationalized, 72
  too narrow, 288
  wings of, 205
persecution, 71
personhood, 31, 47–48, 255
pluralism, 1, 6, 84, 169, 170, 182,
  234, 235, 250, 267, 279,
  287

pluracultures, 254, 259, 262, 265, 273
postmodern, 5–7, 265
potential
  actualization of, 201, 205, 326
  complex, 49
  hidden, 68, 70, 218, 278
  higher, 53, 96, 215, 336
  human, 330
  in love, 128
  luminous, 206
  threefold, 44–45
  unknown, 94
power, 220, 256, 260, 283
  creative, 133
  hidden, 47
  individual, 96
  institutional, 214
  primal sources, 136
prayer, 177, 199, 314
principles
  see spiritual
process
  see becoming
psyche
  at death, 300, 307
  collective stratum, 59, 78, 249, 327
  latent impressions, 58
  not energy, 58
  precognitive, 59
  receptive, 205
  subtle structure of, 310
  wholistic model, 255
  wisdom of, 315
psychic, **58**, 273, 275, 279, 314, 325
  attraction, 284
  affinity, 141
  capacities, 53, 118
  development, 272, 297, 313
  effects, 58
  energy, 141, 281
  extrasensory, 289
  influence, 51, 275
  insights, 58
  interactions, 37
  organization, 193

planes or levels, 113, **286**, 312
polarity, 289, 290
sensitivity, 47, 314
spectrum, 39, 196
transformation, 282, 301
worlds, 117, 196
psychokinesis, 58, 117

Qabbalah, 293
qualities, 46, 80, 129, 227, 318
  of love, 157, 159
quantum totality, 57, 60

rationality, 5, 17, 109, 188, 321, 333
  critical attitude, 213, 324
  dysfunctional, 289
  ideation, 188
  intellectual horizon, 188, 203, 204
  loss of empathy, 72
reality
  making and unmaking, 20, 110
  nonordinary, 78
reciprocity, 56, 67, 123, 145, 168, 178, 190, 204, 223, 235
reconfiguration, 42–43
reflexivity, 41, 222
reincarnation, 238, 240
  see also incarnation
relationships, 68–69, 89, 93, 99, 125, 128, 146, 148, 149, 151, 172, 177, 219, 224, 246, 267, **274–277**, 278, 288, 332
  affirming others, 144
  co-creative, 77, 132, 137, 160
  dependency, 281
  dialogical, 318
  floundering, 143
  great web of, 135, 170, 311, 326
  inflexibility in, 281
  life-partners, 149
  like-minded others, 226
  master-disciple, 246, 247
  mutual, 123, 146, 168
  partnership, 170
  reciprocity in, 146, 168
  resisting closure, 78
  seeing together, 133, 204

subjectivity, 288
teacher-student, 246
victimization, 281
see also being; creativity; dialogue; species; understanding;
wholeness
relativity, 50, 99
religion, 225, 240, 289, 336
and persecution, 249, 282
see also Buddhism; Christianity;
Hinduism; Sufism
revelation, **102**, 103, 104, 163, 221,
335
history of, 102
messengers of, 102
prophetic, 221, 248
reverence, 16, 29, 33, 36, 61–62,
137, 170, 201, 284
rights
human, 34

science, 188, 231, 239, 257, 264,
265, 271, 289, 336
depersonalized, 288
objectivity in, 288
Scripio
dream of, 113
semiotics, 232
self
awareness, 38, 86, 88, 96, 280,
310
definition, 144
denial, 134
destructive tendencies, 78
discipline, 85, 233
discovery, 114
dissolution, 203, 215, 216
divided, 268
doubt, 26, 35, 319, 321
honesty, 172, 276
indulgence, 85, 193
interest, 133
knowledge, 42, 68, 100, 145, 297,
321
liberation, 56
loss of, 280
manifestation, 201

not harming, 88
persona, 300, 316
realization, 44, 196, 210
surpassing, 45, 218, 231
transcending, 215
understanding, 172, 177, 255
worth, 128
see actualization; transformation
sexuality, 81, 137–140, 141, 199,
234, 311
abuse, 138
aggression, 138
creative horizon, 139
spiritual depths, 139
use of others, 139
without love, 137
see love; tantra
simplicity, 79
silence, 205, 206, 317, 318
skepticism, 35, 321, 322
socio-cultural
bias, 247, 261, 288
conditioning, 93–94, 236
context, 94, 224
contract, 93
control, 92
deformations, 192
inequalities, 234, 237
laws, 234
local and relative, 270, 287
location, 263
marginal critic, 263
norms, 147
pathology, 249, 301
virtual forms of, 231–232
withdrawal from, 317
soul
archaeology of, 243
awakening to, 143, 215, 217
capacity of, 77, 130
centered, 42
complex, 299
enhancement, 47
extinction of, 213
life of, 285
making, 50
marked by rites, 186–187

memory, 299
no extinction, 216
non-eternal, 39, 299,
related, 205
sickness of, 28
soulfulness, 39–40, 46, 53, 78, 82,
    108, 121, 126, 132, 140, 141,
    197, 243 285
sous-sol, 26, 45
sorrow, 33, 238, 295, 320
solitude, 61, 80, 136, 140, 177, 234,
    299, 302, 313, **314–317**, 318
    value of, 314
space-time
    cyclical, 108, 185, 191
    non-Cartesian, 58, 279
    past and future, 107, 244, 316
species, **53–54**, 270
    annihilation, 50
    coexistence, 63, 72
    development, 264, 267, 273
    evolution, 278
    integration, 63
    preservation of, 21, 171, 273, 291,
        294
    relationships, 53
    survival, 34
    wisdom, 191
Spirit, 11–12, 21, 25, 52, 248, 333,
    340
    actualizations of, 100, 330
    bottom up, 223
    concurrency, 76
    embodied, 3
    eros of, 256
    feminine aspect, 161–162, 248,
        267, 333, **337–338**, 340
    functions of, 59
    galactic energies, 170
    gifts of, 297, 320
    guides, 252
    healing, 60
    impulses of, 177
    in the heart, 114
    ineffable, 199
    involutions, 52, 95, 99, 111
    is not Mystery, 340
    knowledge of, 91
    nonreducible, 76
    not secondary, 110
    nurturing, 11
    omnipresent, 70
    opening to, 190
    paradoxes of, 27
    perceptions of, 34
    presence of, 13, 95, 186
    presentiments of, 317
    quickening affect, 178
    remote, 21
    sanctity, 118
    self-surpassing, 75
    source of life, 284
    still voice of, 314, 317
    unity of, 24
    see also gifts; intentions; spiri-
        tual; spirituality
spiritual
    aspirations, 323–324
    awakening, 69, 72, 92, 114, 143,
        150, 215, 219, 220, 297
    calm, **304**, 316
    commitment, 100, 280
    community, 72, 77,
    dialectic, 222
    differences, 293
    discipline, 172, 233, 304
    development, 245, 260, 262, 266,
        267, 276, 297
    ethnography, 204
    expansion and contraction, 185,
        186, 212, 275, 277
    foundations, 208, 209
    goals, 104, 109, 168, 197
    growth, 79, 85, 96, 186
    guidance, 77, 78
    history, 103
    idealism, 219
    influence, 274
    kinship, 69, **246**, 325
    knowledge, 97, 244, 324
    love, 124, 156, 160
    manifestations, 95
    marriage, 83
    messengers, 102

openness, 226, 229
paradigms, 55, 168, 171, 235,
    237, 248
path, 88, 89, **98**, 99, 100, 104,
    115, 153, 209, **210**, 211, 212,
    218, 219, 315, 316, 325
principles, 4, 6, 9–10, 11, 92, 146,
    169, 179, **209**, 237, 271, 283,
    298, 304
rapture, 208
realization, 196, 197, 210
respect for others, 262, 263
seekers, 233, 245, 251
shortcomings, 320
states, 197, 210
steps and stages, 209, 212
temperament, 251
tendencies, 210
testimony, 200
truth, 209
union, 206–207
    see also freedom; healing; knowl-
    edge; gnosis; illumination;
    spirit; spirituality
spirituality, 44, 66, 94, 189, 214,
    218, 247, 321
affirmation, 214
as experiential, 89, 91–92, 96,
    106, 116, 186, 200, 210, 213,
    323
as global process, 2–3, 76, 157,
    211, 226, 278
authentic, 88, 208, 223, 319, 327
comparative, 2
learning, 280
no complete teaching, 75
no master plan, 208
not about conformity, 214
postmodern, 7
small decisions, 60
    see also values; spirit; tradition
stereotypes, 164–165
male and female, 164, 292
sublimation, 62
suffering, 185, 238, 295, 320
and ignorance, 185, 249, 326, 327
Sufism, 103, 163

faqiir, 233, 234
hikmat al-ishraq, 161
surrender, 36, 190
symbolism, 75, 171, 172, 184, 339
of bride and groom, 183, 184, 198
of chains, 241–242, 264
of crucible, 315
of cup, 181
of dark, 198
of host, 183
of light, 197, **198**, 200
of magnetic field, 292
of pearl, 207, 218,
of veils and unveiling, 182, 183
of salt doll, 206
of spark, 11, 283, 358
of Spirit's wings, 244, 329
of veils, 25, 182
of weaving, 217, 279, 308
of winged staff, 238, 239
of web, 135, 170, 311, 312, 326
of womb, 198
    see also AUM; death; jewel–net
symbolization, 174, 183
enigmatic, 207
threefold, 174
synchronicity, 76, 109

Tantra, 139
Taoism
    see Daoism
technology, 71
theory, 257
of everything, 257
tradition, 73–74, 75, 86, 93, 94, 96,
    97, **105**, 210, 211, 224, 225,
    240–244, 249, 250, 251, 335,
    336
all are valuable, 76, 245
chains of, 240–242
dogmatism, 211
innovation, 211
esoteric, 210, 225, 325
less bound, 210
non-static, 211
secular, 225, 249, 264
transcendentalism, 104, 184

transformation, 2, 21, 29, 31, 36,
49, 67, 69, 84, 90, 92, 100, 104,
126, 163, 179, 193, 205, 211,
219, 223, 245, 272, 301, 310,
331
  alchemical, 165, 184, 187, 198
  beyond love and compassion, 173
  creative, 227
  effects of, 298
  energies of, 46, 138, 230
  global, 103, 211, 225, 249, 266
  of consciousness, 280
  of self, 280
  semiotics of, 264
  see also body; love; metaphysics;
    values; will
transhistorical, 4
transpersonal, 173, 202, 208
  horizon, 1, 2, 203–204, 212
  love, 129, 132, 139, 157
  see also love
trust, 147, 148, 149, 168, 302, 304
  see also love
truth, 32, 209, 241, 264, **268–269**,
271, 272, 331, 335
  distillations of, 279
  existential ground, 272
  local, 270
  motives, 319
  multidimensional, 271
  not intellectual property, 268, 288
  relative, 269, 270, 273, 287, 293,
    297, 327, 330, 336
  tested, 291
  see also values

unconscious, 130, 133, 190, 192, 237
  assumptions, 261
  biopsychic, 272
  tendencies, 185
understanding, 65–66, 76, 79,
82–83, 86, 88, 92, 110, 165
  and love, 132, 150
  and wisdom, 64, 83
  as synthesis, 87, 95, 234, 278
  experience, 106
  hidden depths of, 66

in love, 153–154
  interrelational, 65
  of differences, 331
  spiritual, 65, 78
  the past, 107, 316
unity, 70, 80, 103, 104, 112, 113,
138, 217
  as relative, 99
  as superessential, 97

values, 4, 6, 34, 67, 82, 88, 97, 101,
144, 150, 151, 221, 234, 252,
253, 254, 258, 260, 269, 270,
281, 381
  change, 324
  clashing, 278
  contradictory, 266
  conventional, 147, 229
  core, 223, 272
  curiosity, 254, 255
  deconstruction of, 282
  emergent, 83
  enacted, 266, 277
  family, 81–82, 281
  goodness, 326, 327
  harmonic, 302–303
  higher value life, 242, 247, 272,
    273, 274, 278, 280, 283
  individual, 148
  judgments, 213, 252, 319
  morality, 253, 254, 256, 257, 258,
    259, 283
  objectivity, 288
  popular, 291
  relative, 272, 276
  restraint, 283
  social issues, 272–273
  spiritual, 222, 227, 291, 322, 323
  tolerance, 156, 172, 254, 262, 324
  transformative, 174
  uniqueness, 63
  vegetarianism, 260
  virtues holographic, 254
  see also collective; compassion;
    dualism; nonviolence; peace;
    spiritual (principles); spiritual-
    ity, truth

veils, 25, 182
visionary, 7–8, 203–204, 273
  experience, 201
  forms, 243
  horizon, 79, 118, 179, 207
  process, 50
  seeing, 204
  synthesis, 240, 248, 278, 302
  visions relative, 243
  worlds, 31, 39, 94, 105, 183, 189,
    208, 217, 231, 313, 330

war, 28, 271
  as holy, 253
well-being, 39, 70, 101, 176, 197,
    252, 271, 287, 296
wholeness, 41, 50, **70**, 80, 91, 93,
    95, 191, 196, 214, 215, 285,
    287, 294, 296
  continuum of, 290
  part-whole relation, 41–42, 48,
    52, 59, 64, 66, 80, 99, 110, 126,
    135, **215–216**, 288, 291
  part not equal to whole, 111
will, 175–176, 187, 189, 191
  and confrontation, 177
  and love 102, 133
  enrapted, 190
  personal, 177
  transformed, 175, 176, 177
wisdom, 64, 83, **161**, 181, 292, 293
  and empathy, 162
  and knowledge, 64
  and preservation, 62
  as feminine, 161, 162, 163, 337

as illumination, 89
as mediation, 167
as synthesis, 162, 234, 278
beyond stereotypes, 164
creative, 178, 180, 212
enacted, 191, 277
gives birth, 187
higher, 358
joyful, 126, 166, 167, 168, 169,
    180, 192, 193, 235, 252, 293,
    337, 341
more than psychic, 163
not impersonal, 162
not mental construct, 162,
    187–188
not omniscient, 162, 166
of elders, 70
of the body, 163
of the heart, 136, 187
qualities of, 162, 187
requires courage, 167, 179
transpersonal, 163
unites, 163
women, 71, 73, 81
  stages of, 340
  subordination of, 73
  see also feminine; Spirit; Sophia
world-soul, 51, **54**, 59, 115, 132,
    170, 171, 305
  masks of world, 180
wonder, 70, 77

yin-yang, 137
  see also Daoism